Praise for *School, Family, and Community Partnerships, Third Edition*

"It's all here—everything you need to start, sustain, and grow an effective, research-based *Partnership Schools* program. Now, with the addition of a CD that includes electronic copies, the essential tools are even more accessible, portable, and adaptable to the challenges and opportunities facing our schools."

Joe Munnich, Family and Community Involvement Coordinator, Saint Paul Public Schools

"The link between successful partnership programs and student achievement is supported by research. This book provides the tools you need to establish and sustain partnerships, both on the district and school levels. It's an invaluable resource for anyone who wants to organize an outstanding partnership program to enhance student success."

Melissa T. McQuarrie, Director of Community Relations, Virginia Beach City Public Schools

"This *Handbook* is useful for state leaders as well as in districts and schools. It provides a research-based—yet practical—blueprint for organizing sustainable partnership programs to support student learning. We use the *Handbook* to provide training to school teams, parent leaders, school boards, superintendents and their cabinets across California. The information is useful for all!"

Jeana Preston, Director, California Parent Center, San Diego State University Research Foundation

"This practical handbook offers a wealth of resources not only for those who are starting to organize their work, but also for those who are sustaining their programs of school, family, and community partnerships. The best part is that you can make the guidelines fit your district's needs."

Lorraine Landon, Director, Parent Education Center Coordinator, Pasco School District, Washington

"*School, Family and Community Partnerships: Your Handbook for Action* is the 'bible' of parent engagement literature. It is an essential tool for any district that wants to implement, strengthen, and sustain family and community involvement. Often, parent engagement is seen as a one-time parent meeting or workshop. The *Handbook* gives step-by-step examples of strategic planning for partnership programs and practices that lead to student success."

Dave Guzman, Director, Parent Engagement, Fort Worth Independent School District

"Like the first two editions, the third edition of the *Handbook for Action* is loaded with practical tools, research-based strategies, and helpful examples for anyone wanting to implement or improve goal-linked programs of family and community involvement. A standout feature is the new CD which provides everything needed for successful workshops at your fingertips—a great time saver!"

Jean West Lewis, Family and Community Outreach Specialist, Howard County Public Schools, Maryland

School, Family, and Community Partnerships

Your Handbook for Action

THIRD EDITION

Joyce L. Epstein

Mavis G. Sanders, Steven B. Sheldon

Beth S. Simon, Karen Clark Salinas, Natalie Rodriguez Jansorn

Frances L. Van Voorhis, Cecelia S. Martin, Brenda G. Thomas

Marsha D. Greenfeld, Darcy J. Hutchins, Kenyatta J. Williams

For information:

Corwin Press
A SAGE Company
2455 Teller Road
Thousand Oaks, California 91320
www.corwinpress.com

SAGE India Pvt. Ltd.
B 1/I 1 Mohan Cooperative
Industrial Area
Mathura Road, New Delhi 110 044
India

SAGE Ltd.
1 Oliver's Yard
55 City Road
London EC1Y 1SP
United Kingdom

SAGE Asia-Pacific Pte. Ltd.
33 Pekin Street #02-01
Far East Square
Singapore 048763

Printed in the United States of America.

Library of Congress Cataloging-in-Publication Data

School, family, and community partnerships: Your handbook for action/Joyce L. Epstein [et al.] — 3rd ed.
p. cm.
Includes bibliographical references and index.
ISBN 978-1-4129-5901-8 (cloth)
ISBN 978-1-4129-5902-5 (pbk.)
1. Community and school—United States. 2. Home and school—United States.
3. School improvement programs—United States. I. Epstein, Joyce Levy. II. Title.

LC221.E68 2009
371.190973—dc22 2008027699

This book is printed on acid-free paper.

10 11 12 10 9 8 7 6 5 4 3

Acquisitions Editor: Arnis Burvikovs
Associate Editor: Desirée A. Bartlett
Production Editor: Libby Larson
Copy Editor: Cate Huisman
Typesetter: C&M Digitals (P) Ltd.
Proofreader: Wendy Jo Dymond
Indexer: Sylvia Coates
Cover Designer: Michael Dubowe

Contents

Acknowledgments

The authors are grateful to the many teachers, administrators, parents, grandparents, community partners, students, state and district leaders, and researchers who have worked with us over the years to increase knowledge on partnerships and to design and test strategies for developing excellent partnership programs. We are pleased that our research has been useful for improving policy and practice. It is equally true that policy leaders and practitioners have informed and improved our research. We have been inspired by the hard work, creative efforts, and emergence of leaders in diverse communities resulting from this unique partnership of researchers and practitioners.

Special thanks are due to Lucretia Coates, a coauthor of the first edition of this *Handbook* and retired principal of Dr. Bernard Harris Sr. Elementary School in Baltimore. Her leadership and enthusiasm for parental involvement and community connections was part and parcel of her practice. Thanks are due, too, to the Fund for Educational Excellence in Baltimore, which collaborated on early efforts to link research on family and community involvement to practice, and to the Baltimore City Public School System (BCPSS), whose district leaders and school teams of educators and parents helped us learn new ways to organize programs of school, family, and community partnerships.

This school year, more than 1100 schools, 150 districts, 21 states, and many organizations in communities across the United States and in Canada are actively participating in the National Network of Partnership Schools (NNPS) at Johns Hopkins University. Thousands more have used this *Handbook* in their work on partnerships. Some have sustained their programs and flourished; others have curtailed their efforts due to various conditions and constraints. The successes and challenges of those who partnered with us and provided data and ideas in NNPS improved our knowledge about partnerships and the contents of this book.

New partners are welcome. Schools, districts, and states that are ready to develop more effective partnership programs and practices are invited to join others in NNPS at Johns Hopkins University for ongoing assistance. See more information at www.partnershipschools.org.

We greatly appreciate the five-year grant from the National Institute for Child Health and Human Development (NICHD) to the Center on School, Family, and Community Partnerships at Johns Hopkins University. This grant supported research on scaling-up processes that enabled many districts and schools to develop and implement goal-linked partnership programs and that led to improvements in this *Handbook.* We are grateful, too, for grants from the U. S. Department of Education and numerous foundations that supported prior research and development on partnerships. Of course, the research summaries and tools in this *Handbook* were developed by the authors and do not necessarily reflect the positions of the funding agencies.

About the Authors

Joyce L. Epstein, PhD in sociology from Johns Hopkins University, is director of the Center on School, Family, and Community Partnerships and the National Network of Partnership Schools (NNPS); principal research scientist; and research professor of sociology at Johns Hopkins University. She has over 100 publications on school, family, and community connections. She is author of a text for college courses for future teachers and administrators, *School, Family, and Community Partnerships: Preparing Educators and Improving Schools* (Westview Press, 2001) and coauthor of *Family Reading Night* (Eye on Education, 2008). In 1995, she established NNPS, which continues to guide schools, districts, and state leaders to develop research-based programs of family and community involvement. Among her awards, she received the 2005 American Orthopsychiatric Association's Blanche F. Ittleson Award for scholarship and service to strengthen school and family connections. Her current research focuses on how district leaders assist schools to develop partnership programs that reach all families and increase student success. In all of her work, she is interested in the connections of research, policy, and practice.

Mavis G. Sanders, PhD in education from Stanford University, is associate professor of education in the Department of Teacher Development and Leadership in the School of Education; research scientist in the Center on School, Family, and Community Partnerships; and senior advisor to NNPS at Johns Hopkins University. She is the author of many publications on how schools and districts develop their partnership programs and on the effects of partnerships on African-American adolescents' school success. Her most recent book focuses on principals' leadership for school, family, and community partnerships (with Steven Sheldon, Corwin Press, 2009). Other books include *Building School-Community Partnerships: Collaboration for Student Success* (Corwin Press, 2005), and *Schooling Students Placed at Risk: Research, Policy, and Practice in the Education of Poor and Minority Adolescents* (Erlbaum, 2000). Dr. Sanders's interests include how schools define and develop meaningful school-community connections and how district leaders guide their schools to develop partnership programs. Dr. Sanders directs the Graduate Certificate Program in Leadership for School, Family, and Community Collaboration and teaches related leadership courses.

Steven B. Sheldon, PhD in educational psychology from Michigan State University, is research scientist with the Center on School, Family, and Community Partnerships and director of research of NNPS at Johns Hopkins University. He is the author of many publications on the implementation and effects of programs of family and community involvement. His work explores how the quality and outreach of school programs of partnerships affect parents' responses and student outcomes, such as student attendance, math achievement, student behavior, reading, and state achievement test scores. His most recent book guides principals in their leadership and work on school, family, and community partnerships (with Mavis Sanders, Corwin Press, 2009). In his current research, Dr. Sheldon is studying the influences of parents' social networks, beliefs, and school outreach on patterns of parental involvement at school and at home and on results for students.

Beth S. Simon, PhD in sociology from Johns Hopkins University, is a research manager at Blue Shield of California. She directs quantitative and qualitative research to develop marketing strategy and to improve health plan quality. Previously, Dr. Simon was a social science research analyst at the Centers for Medicare & Medicaid Services (CMS). At CMS, she led consumer research for national education and outreach campaigns and for health care quality improvement. In her prior work at Johns Hopkins, she conducted research on family and community involvement in high schools, including how school outreach and family involvement affect high school students' success. Other research focused on patterns of participation of states, districts, and schools in NNPS. Dr. Simon developed NNPS's first Web site and other tools and strategies to support partnership program development.

Karen Clark Salinas, MSW in social work from the University of North Carolina, Chapel Hill, is the disability services coordinator and a project manager at the Center for Technology in Education (CTE) in the School of Education at Johns Hopkins University. In addition to serving students with disabilities, she provides evaluation assistance to CTE school improvement initiatives. In her prior work as director of communications at NNPS, Ms. Salinas edited the network's newsletter, *Type 2*, and annual collections of *Promising Partnership Practices.* She conducted workshops and provided technical assistance to school, district, and state leaders on partnership program development. Ms. Salinas is coauthor of the inventory *Starting Points: the Measure of School, Family, and Community Partnerships*; and materials for the *Teachers Involve Parents in Schoolwork (TIPS)* process. She is also coproducer of the video *National Network of Partnership Schools: Working Together for Student Success,* which can be viewed on the NNPS Web site.

Natalie Rodriguez Jansorn, MA in education from the University of Maryland Baltimore County, is senior program manager of the Jack Kent Cooke Young Scholars Program at the Johns Hopkins University Center for Talented Youth. Through the scholarship program, Ms. Jansorn collaborates with families from low-income backgrounds to support their high-achieving teenagers in reaching their fullest academic potential. In her prior work with NNPS, she directed projects to guide district and state leaders in establishing school, family, and community partnership programs to support students' school success. She also designed materials and provided professional development to middle and high schools on partnership program development. She developed workshops, tools, and publications to increase the quality of family and community involvement at all policy levels. Ms. Jansorn was a coeditor of selected collections of *Promising Partnership Practices.*

Frances L. Van Voorhis, PhD in developmental psychology from the University of Florida, is principal investigator and consultant with the Center on School, Family, and Community Partnerships at Johns Hopkins University. She is the project director for studies of the effects of the *Teachers Involve Parents in Schoolwork* (TIPS) interactive homework process. Dr. Van Voorhis is the author of many research publications and practical materials on the homework process, teachers' design of homework, and the effects of TIPS for students and parents. Her current projects include longitudinal studies of TIPS Math in the elementary grades and TIPS Language Arts and TIPS Science in the middle grades. She also is coauthor (with Steven Sheldon) of articles on the progress in partnership program development of schools in NNPS.

Cecelia S. Martin, MEd from Towson University, is associate director of the Maryland Parental Information Resource Center (PIRC). She provides technical assistance to school systems and schools to strengthen local programs and practices of family and community involvement. In prior work with NNPS, Ms. Martin was senior program facilitator for the Military Child Initiative that assisted districts and schools to work more effectively with families in the military. She also conducted workshops and developed materials for state, district, and school leaders to build partnership programs for student success. She was coeditor of the NNPS *Promising Partnership Practices 2007.* Previously, Ms. Martin, who has a background in special education, served in the U.S. Army Reserve and National Guard, was a high school teacher in Baltimore, and was an assistant professor of English at Baltimore City Community College. She is pursuing a doctorate in organizational leadership at the University of Maryland Eastern Shore.

Brenda G. Thomas, MS in administration supervision from Morgan State University, is Maryland director of partnership program development and senior program facilitator at NNPS. She is supported by a collaborative grant of NNPS with the Maryland Parental Information Resource Center (PIRC). Ms. Thomas assists district leaders across the state of Maryland to help their schools organize, implement, and improve programs of school, family, and community partnerships. She also provides professional development workshops for other school, district, state, and PIRC leaders in NNPS. She is a coeditor of *Promising Partnership Practices*, the NNPS annual collection of members' best practices. Ms. Thomas has many years of experience as a teacher, Action Team for Partnerships leader, district level facilitator for partnerships, and coordinator of parental involvement in the Baltimore City Public School System.

Marsha D. Greenfeld is senior program facilitator with NNPS at Johns Hopkins University. She provides professional development to help leaders in districts, states, and organizations and school teams implement and sustain goal-linked programs of family and community involvement. She develops and conducts workshops and provides technical assistance on all aspects of partnership program development. She is coauthor of the book, *Family Reading Night* (Eye on Education, 2008) and a coeditor of annual collections of *Promising Partnership Practices.* Ms. Greenfeld previously was a teacher and district level facilitator for partnerships in the Baltimore City Public School System. She also worked in the Technical Assistance Branch of the Office of Federal Grants Programs in Washington D.C. Public Schools and as a partnership coordinator in the national office of Communities in Schools.

Darcy J. Hutchins, MS in education from Johns Hopkins University, is senior program facilitator with NNPS at Johns Hopkins University. She provides professional development to enable district, state, and organization leaders and school teams to establish and maintain comprehensive partnership programs that positively impact student success. Ms. Hutchins taught in the Baltimore City Public School System, where she developed and implemented family literacy workshops. She also had experience working with young children with special needs. She is coauthor of the book, *Family Reading Night* (Eye on Education, 2008), which guides educators to conduct effective literacy events. She also is a coeditor of annual collections of *Promising Partnership Practices.* She is completing her PhD in education policy at the University of Maryland-College Park.

Kenyatta J. Williams, MS in information and telecommunication systems for business from Johns Hopkins University, is an IT specialist with the Social Security Administration. He designs and develops software, defines specifications, and coordinates systems for selected programs and services at SSA. In his prior work with NNPS at Johns Hopkins University, Mr. Williams collected and coordinated data from all members and worked with the research staff on many studies. He is coauthor of annual summaries of *UPDATE* data for schools and districts in NNPS and of several research conference presentations. Mr. Williams also coordinated NNPS conferences and institutes and provided technical assistance to NNPS members across the country.

Introduction

There is no topic in education on which there is greater agreement than the need for family and community involvement.

- **Teachers and administrators** want to know how to work with parents in positive ways and how to involve the community to increase student success.
- **Parents** want to know if schools are providing high-quality education, how to help their children do their best, and how to connect and communicate with teachers and administrators.
- **Students** want to succeed in school. They know they need guidance, support, and encouragement from their parents, teachers, other family members, and others in the community.

Despite strong agreement about the importance of these goals, most schools, districts, and states still need help in developing comprehensive programs of school, family, and community partnerships.

For over 25 years, researchers at Johns Hopkins University have worked with educators, parents, students, community partners, and other researchers to learn how preschools and elementary, middle, and high schools can develop and maintain more effective programs of partnerships. We have worked with district and state education leaders to understand how they write and support policies that encourage schools to improve partnership programs. We have collaborated with organizations that assist schools, districts, and states with their work on partnerships. We have continued an active research agenda to study the nature and effects of systematic interventions that increase family and community involvement. With many partners and participants, we have learned how programs of school, family, and community partnerships can be organized to improve schools, strengthen families, and help students succeed.

With many partners, we have learned that new concepts are needed to organize effective partnership programs (Epstein & Sheldon, 2006):

1. ***School, family, and community partnerships* is a better term than *parental involvement.*** The concept of "partnership" recognizes that parents, educators, and others in the community share responsibility for students' learning and development.
2. **School, family, and community partnerships is a multidimensional concept.** A framework of six types of involvement—the result of research and exemplary practices—helps schools develop programs that involve families in many different ways.

3. **A program of school, family, and community partnerships is an essential component of school and classroom organization.** No longer off to the side, family and community involvement must be planned and evaluated just as any aspect of school improvement. In each school, an Action Team for Partnerships—a committee of educators, parents, and other partners—can work together and with colleagues to plan, implement, evaluate, and continually improve the outreach and quality of partnership programs.

4. **Programs of school, family, and community partnerships require multilevel leadership.** Although educators in a single school may organize a partnership program, district leaders play important roles in establishing a "culture of partnerships" and in assisting *all* elementary, middle, and high schools in the district to develop and sustain programs that involve students' families in productive ways. State leaders, too, may support policies and take actions that help districts and schools understand partnerships as an organizational imperative.

5. **Programs of school, family, and community partnerships must focus on increasing student learning and development.** No longer partnerships for partnerships' sake, strong programs of family and community involvement ensure that all communications among partners and all involvement activities are purposeful and productive. Practices to engage parents, community members, and others need to be linked to important goals for students in order help improve attendance, achievement, behavior, and other indicators of success in school.

6. **All programs of school, family, and community partnerships are about equity.** This *Handbook* guides schools to develop programs with practices that engage all families in all communities, not just parents who are easy to reach. Some parents have always been involved in schools and in their children's education. Now, districts and schools must conduct programs that enable all families to help their children do their best in school.

These new directions change the way partnerships are understood in schools, districts, and state departments of education. For example, when an Action Team for Partnerships is an official school committee, and its written plans are part of annual school improvement plans, more family and community involvement activities will be conducted, and more and different parents will be engaged. When activities that are implemented are evaluated, outreach to families should increase, and the quality of the partnership program should improve from year to year. These and other changes are needed to turn activities that were accidental and peripheral to school improvement into well-planned and intentional programs that are central to school improvement and that contribute to student success.

Over the past few years, our studies of partnership program development identified eight essential elements that contributed to the improvement of program quality from one year to the next. These include strong leadership, teamwork, annual written plans, well-implemented activities, adequate funding, thoughtful evaluations, strong collegial support and networking, and continuous planning for improvement. The third edition of the *Handbook* provides step-by-step strategies so that every program will take new directions and include these essential elements.

This *Handbook* translates lessons learned in research and fieldwork into practical approaches that will assist any school, district, or state with partnership program development. This includes the research-based framework and field-tested tools that help schools (a) understand the six types of family and community involvement, (b) create an Action Team for Partnerships, (c) plan and implement family and community involvement activities to reach school goals for student success, (d) mobilize community resources, (e) resolve challenges to reach all families, (f) evaluate results, and (g) continue to improve plans, practices, and programs over time. Two chapters give special attention to partnerships in middle and high schools and to interactive homework that promotes parent-teacher and parent-child communications about classwork. The *Handbook* also guides district, state, and organization leaders to strengthen their knowledge and leadership of partnerships.

Of course, each school, district, and state is different from the next. Each serves a different population of students and families, has different improvement goals, and faces unique challenges for helping all students succeed in school. We have found that all programs benefit from proven structures, but each site must tailor or customize its plans and practices to meet specific goals for student success. This mix of formal structures and flexible practices is a winning combination for involving families and community partners in ways that benefit students, families, and schools. To see how this works in diverse communities, visit www.partnershipschools.org and click on Success Stories.

What's New in the Third Edition?

The *Third Edition* of this *Handbook,* like previous editions, draws upon work conducted with thousands of educators and families over the past five years. It includes new and improved research summaries, tools, and guidelines for leaders in schools, districts, states, and organizations to increase their knowledge and skills in developing their partnership programs. These include the following:

- New article on how partnership practices help produce specific results for students (Chapter 1)
- New examples of successful partnership activities in elementary, middle, and high schools (Chapter 2)
- Improved workshop agendas and activities, with increased attention to connecting family and community involvement to goals for student success (Chapters 4 and 5)
- New inventories to guide district leaders and state leaders in developing their leadership roles and actions on partnerships (Chapter 7)
- A new chapter on how to evaluate school-based partnership programs and updated evaluation forms and guidelines (Chapter 9)
- Clearer guidelines and updated references in all chapters
- A CD (attached) with a PowerPoint presentation for team-training workshops and electronic copies of all workshop handouts, activities, planning forms, and evaluations. The CD also includes Spanish translations of selected materials for Latino parents who participate in workshops and in other audiences.

Overview of Chapters

Ten chapters offer step-by-step strategies to establish, strengthen, and sustain excellent partnership programs.

Chapter 1: A Comprehensive Framework. Three articles summarize the theory and research on which the *Handbook* is based. The first article describes the framework of six types of involvement, identifies challenges that must be met, and provides results of well-implemented programs of school, family, and community partnerships. It also discusses an action team approach for developing comprehensive partnership programs. The second article presents an overview of how connections with the community can be organized to strengthen partnership programs. The third article summarizes research on the effects of family and community involvement on student academic and behavioral outcomes. Along with excellent teachers and well-managed schools, goal-oriented family and community involvement can affect a range of important student outcomes in reading, math, science, attendance, behavior, and other important indicators of student success in school.

Chapter 2: Use the Framework to Reach School Goals—Stories From the Field. Examples from elementary, middle, and high schools illustrate how the six types of involvement and action team approach work in diverse schools and communities. The examples show how elementary, middle, and high schools are working to create a welcoming climate for partnerships and to implement partnerships that contribute to student success.

Chapter 3: Take an Action Team Approach. Twelve common questions are addressed on how to organize an effective Action Team for Partnerships. Team members—principals, teachers, parents, other school staff, and community members—play important roles and share leadership for planning, implementing, and evaluating partnership programs. Several tools and guidelines are included to help develop strong and successful teams.

Chapter 4: Conduct Workshops. Agendas are provided for district, school, and other leaders to conduct team-training workshops and end-of-year celebration workshops for schools' Action Teams for Partnerships. The chapter includes scripts, group activities, and other guidelines to help workshop leaders present key topics and to enable attendees to apply the content to their own schools. These workshops, which prepare educators, parents, and community partners to work together, are important professional development activities.

Chapter 5: Select Materials for Presentations and Workshops. Charts and diagrams are supplied for presentations, handouts, and activities for the team-training workshops described in Chapter 4 and for other presentations on partnership program development. These materials guide workshop leaders to present and discuss the framework of the six types of involvement, challenges that must be solved, results of partnerships, team structures, and how to write a One-Year Action Plan for Partnerships. These materials also are on the *Handbook* CD, along with PowerPoint slides for team-training workshops and other presentations.

Chapter 6: Strengthen Partnership Programs in Middle and High Schools. Three articles summarize research and practical approaches to family and community involvement in secondary schools. Reproducible materials are included to use in workshops attended by Action Teams for Partnerships from middle schools, junior high schools, and high schools, or in presentations to leaders who will assist middle and high schools with their partnership programs. The discussion of goal-oriented partnership programs is pertinent for elementary and secondary school teams.

Chapter 7: Develop District and State Leadership for Partnerships. District and state leadership activities are outlined and discussed to increase expertise on school, family, and community partnerships. Information is included on the costs of partnership programs and sources of funds. New inventories are provided to help district and state leaders organize their offices and activities and guide school-based partnership programs. Improved templates are included for district and state leadership plans for partnerships.

Chapter 8: Implement Teachers Involve Parents in Schoolwork (TIPS). Two research-based partnership approaches are described. *TIPS Interactive Homework* increases family involvement with students at home in positive conversations about interesting work that students learn in class. Ten purposes of homework and the components of an effective interactive homework process are discussed. *TIPS Volunteers in Social Studies and Art* increases family and community involvement at school by organizing volunteers to present prints of art masterpieces that are linked to social studies units to increase students' art appreciation and critical thinking. The chapter includes sample interactive homework assignments for the elementary, middle, and high school grades and a sample social studies and art presentation.

Chapter 9: Evaluate Your Partnership Program. An introductory article discusses basic ideas for evaluating the quality of partnership programs and results. It identifies guidelines and tools for Action Teams for Partnerships to use each year to monitor progress. An inventory, *Measure of School, Family, and Community Partnerships,* assesses how well a school is implementing activities for the six types of involvement and is meeting challenges to reach all families. The *Annual Evaluation of Activities* helps a team assess the quality of each activity for family and community involvement as it is implemented throughout the school year.

Chapter 10: Network With Others for Best Results on Partnerships. Readers of this *Handbook* are invited to join other schools, districts, states, and organizations in the National Network of Partnership Schools (NNPS) at Johns Hopkins University. NNPS provides ongoing professional development on school, family, and community partnerships and organizes opportunities for members to share ideas and progress. A Web-map is included for readers to obtain more information about NNPS, about promising practices in schools across the country, and about partnership program development.

Time for Action

Some say of partnerships: This is not hard work, but *heart* work. Not more work, but *the* work. Not harder work, but *smarter* work to mobilize all available resources that will contribute to student success. Educators and parents know *that* family and community involvement is important. This *Handbook* shows *how* to organize effective partnership programs. There are, now, research-based strategies for planning, implementing, evaluating, and improving effective programs of family and community involvement in all schools, districts, and state departments of education. It is time for action.

Reference

Epstein J. L., & Sheldon, S. B. (2006). Moving forward: Ideas for research on school, family, and community partnerships. In C. F. Conrad & R. Serlin (Eds.), *SAGE handbook for research in education: Engaging ideas and enriching inquiry* (pp. 117–137). Thousand Oaks, CA: Sage.

1

A Comprehensive Framework

This chapter includes three summaries of research and practical approaches that will help school, district, and state leaders develop and sustain excellent programs of school, family, and community partnerships.

1.1: School, Family, and Community Partnerships: Caring for the Children We Share by Joyce L. Epstein. This article summarizes the theory of ovelapping spheres of influence to explain the shared responsibilities of home, school, and community for children's learning and development. It also charts the research-based framework of six types of involvement, challenges that must be solved for each type of involvement in order to engage all families, and expected results of well-designed and well-implemented practices.

The article outlines and discusses the basic structures and processes that are needed to develop effective partnership programs. The guidelines and tools throughout the *Handbook* were designed to help implement these strategies. For example, one key structure at the school level is an Action Team for Partnerships (ATP)—a committee of the School Council or School Improvement Team. The ATP includes teachers, administrators, parents, and others who plan, implement, evaluate, and continually improve school programs of partnership. With knowledge of the underlying theory, basic structures, and useful processes, leaders in schools, districts, and states will be able to strengthen goal-oriented partnership programs that contribute to student success.

1.2: Community Involvement in School Improvement: The Little Extra That Makes a Big Difference by Mavis G. Sanders. The second article summarizes research on school and community connections in comprehensive partnership programs. Businesses, organizations, agencies, groups, and individuals in the community offer many resources and opportunities to improve schools, strengthen families, and increase student success. This article provides examples of school and community collaborations that are student-, family-, school-, and community-centered.

Sanders's research identifies four factors that support school and community partnerships: high commitment to learning, principal's support, a welcoming climate, and two-way communications and negotiated agreements between the school and community partners. The article also emphasizes the importance of reflection and evaluation for sustaining effective community partnerships.

1.3: Improving Student Outcomes With School, Family, and Community Partnerships: A Research Review by Steven B. Sheldon. The third article summarizes research on the effects of family and community involvement on student academic and behavioral outcomes. The overview presents results of family involvement for improving students' reading achievement at the preschool, elementary, and secondary levels. Results also are reported of family involvement on students' math and science skills, attendance, and behavior.

The results of many studies help educators understand why well-implemented partnership programs should be linked to school improvement goals. Along with excellent teachers and well-managed schools, goal-oriented family and community involvement can affect a range of important student outcomes.

The three articles in Chapter 1 discuss a tested theoretical model, research-based structures and processes, and evidence of results of partnerships. This information underlies and supports educators' decisions to develop and sustain programs of school, family, and community partnerships that contribute to student success.

1.1 School, Family, and Community Partnerships: Caring for the Children We Share

Joyce L. Epstein

The way schools care about children is reflected in the way schools care about the children's families. If educators view children simply as *students*, they are likely to see the family as separate from the school. That is, the family is expected to do its job and leave the education of children to the schools. If educators view students as *children*, they are likely to see both the family and the community as partners with the school in children's education and development. Partners recognize their shared interests in and responsibilities for children, and they work together to create better programs and opportunities for students.

There are many reasons for developing school, family, and community partnerships. Partnerships can improve school programs and school climate, provide family services and support, increase parents' skills and leadership, connect families with others in the school and in the community, and help teachers with their work. However, the main reason to create such partnerships is to help all youngsters succeed in school and in later life. When parents, teachers, students, and others view one another as partners in education, a caring community forms around students and begins its work.

What do successful partnership programs look like? How can practices be effectively designed and implemented? What are the results of better communications, interactions, and exchanges across these three important contexts? These questions have challenged research and practice, creating an interdisciplinary field of inquiry into school, family, and community partnerships with "caring" as a core concept.

The field has been strengthened by supporting federal, state, and local policies. Since the late 1980s, Title I of the Elementary and Secondary Education Act has included increasingly specific, research-based mandates and guidelines for programs and practices of family and community involvement. Most recently, the No Child Left Behind Act (NCLB) outlines a "nested" system of school, district, and state requirements for developing research-based programs that involve parents in ways that contribute to student achievement and success in school. These guidelines must be met to qualify for and maintain federal funding.

As important, many states and districts have developed or are preparing their own policies to guide schools in creating more systematic connections with families and with community partners. The policies reflect research results and exemplary practices that show that goals for more effective programs of family and community involvement are attainable (Epstein, 2005a).

Underlying all the policies and programs is a theory of how social organizations connect with each other; a framework of the basic components of school, family, and community partnerships for children's learning; a growing literature on positive and negative results of these connections for students, families, and schools; and an understanding of how to organize excellent programs. In this article I summarize the theory, framework, and guidelines from our research that should help elementary, middle, and high schools and education leaders take steps toward successful partnerships.

Overlapping Spheres of Influence: Understanding the Theory

Schools make choices. They may conduct only a few communications and interactions with families and communities, keeping the three spheres of influence that directly affect student learning and development relatively separate. Or, they may conduct many high-quality communications and interactions designed to bring all three spheres of influence closer together. With frequent interactions among schools, families, and communities, more students will receive common messages from various people about the importance of school, of working hard, of thinking creatively, of helping one another, and of staying in school.

The *external* model of overlapping spheres of influence recognizes that the three major contexts in which students learn and grow—the family, the school, and the community—may be drawn together or pushed apart. In this model, there are some practices that schools, families, and communities conduct separately and some that they conduct jointly to influence children's learning and development.

The *internal* model of the interaction of the three spheres of influence shows where and how complex and essential interpersonal relations and patterns of influence occur between individuals at home, at school, and in the community. These social relationships may be enacted and studied at an *institutional* level (e.g., when a school invites all families to an event or sends the same communications to all families) and at an *individual* level (e.g., when a parent and a teacher meet in conference or talk by phone). Connections between educators or parents and community groups, agencies, and services also can be represented and studied within the model (Epstein, 1987, 1992, 1994).

The model of school, family, and community partnerships locates the student at the center. The inarguable fact is that students are the main actors in their education, development, and success in school. School, family, and community partnerships cannot simply "produce" successful students. Rather, partnership activities may be designed to engage, guide, energize, and motivate students to produce their own successes. The assumption is that if children feel cared for and if they are encouraged to work hard in the role of student, they are more likely to do their best to learn to read, write, calculate, and learn other skills and talents and to remain in school.

Interestingly, studies indicate that students are crucial for the success of school, family, and community partnerships. Students are often their parents' main source of information about school. In strong partnership programs, teachers help students understand and conduct both traditional communications with families (e.g., delivering memos or report cards) and new communications (e.g., interacting with family members about homework, using e-mail to communicate with teachers, or participating in or leading parent-teacher-student conferences). As we gain more information about the role of students in partnerships, we are developing a more complete understanding of how schools, families, and communities must work with students to increase their chances for success.

How the Theory Works in Practice

In some schools, there still are educators who say, "If the family would just do its job, we could do our job." And there still are families who say, "I raised this child; now it is your job to educate her." These words embody a view of *separate* spheres of influence. Other educators say, "I cannot do my job without the help of my students' families and the support of this community." And some parents say, "I really need to know what is happening in school in order to help my child." These phrases embody the theory of *overlapping spheres of influence.*

In a partnership, teachers and administrators create more *family-like* schools. A family-like school recognizes each child's individuality and makes each child feel special and included. Family-like schools welcome all families, not just those that are easy to reach. In a partnership, parents create more *school-like* families. A school-like family recognizes that each child is also a student. Families reinforce the importance of school, homework, and activities that build student skills and feelings of success.

Communities, too, including groups of parents working together, create *school-like* opportunities, events, and programs that reinforce, recognize, and reward students for good progress, creativity, contributions, and excellence. Communities also create *family-like* settings, services, and events to enable families to better support their children. *Community-minded* families and students help their neighborhoods and other families. The concept of a community school or full-service school is gaining acceptance (Dryfoos & Maguire, 2002) This refers to a place where programs and services for students, parents, and others are offered before, during, and after the regular school day.

Schools and communities talk about programs and services that are family friendly—meaning that they take into account the needs and realities of family life, are feasible to conduct, and are equitable toward all families. When all these concepts combine, children experience *learning communities* or *caring communities* (Epstein, 1995; Henderson, Mapp, Johnson, & Davies, 2007; Lewis, Schaps, & Watson, 1995).

All of these terms are consistent with the theory of overlapping spheres of influence, but they are not abstract concepts. You will find them daily in conversations, news stories, and celebrations of many kinds. In a family-like school, a teacher might say, "I know when a student is having a bad day and how to help him along." A student might slip and call a teacher "mom" or "dad" and then laugh with a mixture of embarrassment and glee. In a school-like family, a parent might say, "I make sure my daughter knows that homework comes first." A child might raise his hand to speak at the dinner table and then joke about acting as if he were still in school. When communities reach out to students and their families, youngsters might say, "This program made my schoolwork make sense!" Parents or educators might comment, "This community really supports its schools."

Once people hear about the concepts of family-like schools and school-like families, they remember positive examples of schools, teachers, and places in the community that were "like a family" to them. They may remember how a teacher paid individual attention to them, recognized their uniqueness, or praised them for real progress, just as a parent would. They might recall things at home that were "just like school" and that supported their work as a student, or they might remember community activities that made them feel smart or good about themselves and their families. They will recall that parents, siblings, and other family members engaged in and enjoyed educational activities and took pride in the good schoolwork or homework that they did, just as a teacher would.

How Partnerships Work in Practice

These terms and examples are evidence of the *potential* for schools, families, and communities to create caring educational environments. It is possible to have a school that is excellent academically but ignores families. However, that school will build barriers between teachers, parents, and children that affect school life and learning. It is possible to have a school that is ineffective academically but involves families in many good ways. With its weak academic program, that school will shortchange students' learning. Neither of these schools exemplifies a caring, educational environment that requires academic excellence, good communication, and productive interactions involving the school, all families, and the community.

Some children succeed in school without much family involvement or despite family neglect or distress, particularly if the school has excellent academic and support programs. Teachers, relatives outside the immediate family, other families, and members of the community may provide important guidance and encouragement for these students. As support from school, home, *and* community accumulates, more students feel secure and cared for, understand and adopt the goals of education, work to achieve their full potential, build positive attitudes and school behaviors, and stay in school. The shared interests and investments of schools, families, and communities create the conditions of caring that work to "overdetermine" the likelihood of student success (Boykin, 1994).

Any practice can be designed and implemented well or poorly. Even well-implemented partnership practices may not be useful to all families. In a caring school community, participants work continually to improve the nature and effects of partnerships. Although the interactions of educators, parents, students, and community members will not always be smooth and successful, partnership programs establish a base of respect and trust on which to build. Good partnerships encourage questions and debates and withstand disagreements; provide structures and processes to solve problems; and are maintained—even strengthened—after conflicts and differences have been resolved. Without a firm base of partnerships, the problems and concerns about schools and students that are sure to arise will be harder to solve.

What Research Says

In surveys, experimental interventions, and other field studies involving teachers, parents, and students at the elementary, middle, and high school levels, some important patterns relating to partnerships have emerged.

- Partnerships tend to decline across the grades, *unless* schools and teachers work to develop and implement appropriate practices of partnership at each grade level.
- Affluent communities tend to have more positive family involvement, on average, *unless* schools and teachers in economically distressed communities work to build positive partnerships with their students' families.

- Schools in more economically depressed communities make more contacts with families about the problems and difficulties their children are having, *unless* they work at developing balanced partnership programs that also include contacts about the positive accomplishments of students.
- Single parents, parents who are employed outside the home, parents who live far from the school, and fathers are less involved, on average, at the school building, *unless* the school organizes opportunities for families to become involved and to volunteer at various times and in various places to support the school and their children. These parents may be as involved as other parents with their children at home.

Researchers from the United States and other nations have drawn the following conclusions from their studies of family and community involvement:

- Just about all families care about their children, want them to succeed, and are eager to obtain better information from schools and communities in order to remain good partners in their children's education.
- Just about all teachers and administrators would like to involve families, but many do not know how to efficiently and effectively build positive and productive programs and, consequently, are fearful about trying. This creates a "rhetoric rut" in which educators are stuck expressing support for partnerships without taking necessary actions.
- Just about all students at all levels—elementary, middle, and high school—want their families to be more knowledgeable partners about schooling and are willing to take active roles in assisting communications between home and school. However, students need much better information about how their schools view partnerships and more guidance about how they can conduct important exchanges with their families about school activities, homework, and school decisions.

The summary of results reflect findings in articles and chapters by Baker and Stevenson (1986), Bauch (1988), Becker and Epstein (1982), Booth and Dunn (1996), Burch and Palanki (1994), Clark (1983), Connors and Epstein (1994), Dauber and Epstein (1993), Davies (1991, 1993), Dornbusch and Ritter (1988), Eccles and Harold (1996), Epstein (1986, 1990, 2001, 2005c), Epstein and Connors (1994), Epstein and Dauber (1991), Epstein, Herrick, and Coates (1996), Epstein and Lee (1995), Epstein and Sanders (2000), Lareau (1989), Lee (1994), Sanders (2005), Scott-Jones (1995), Sheldon (2005, 2007a, 2007b), Sheldon and Van Voorhis (2004), Simon (2004), Van Voorhis (2003), Van Voorhis and Sheldon (2004), and others.

The research results are important because they indicate that caring communities can be built intentionally, that they include families that might not become involved on their own, and that, by their own reports, just about all families, students, and teachers believe that partnerships are important for helping students succeed across the grades.

Good programs of family and community involvement will look different at each site, as individual schools tailor their practices to meet the needs and interests, time and talents, and ages and grade levels of its students. However, our studies have identified some commonalities across successful partnership programs at all grade levels. These include attention to the overlapping spheres of influence on student development; attention to various types of involvement that promote many different opportunities for schools, families, and communities to work together; and an Action Team for Partnerships (ATP) to coordinate each school's work and progress on family and community involvement. The best school-based programs are supported by district leaders for partnerships, whose expertise grows and who help all elementary, middle, and high schools in the district to plan, implement, and evaluate their programs and share best practices (Epstein, 2007).

Six Types of Involvement—Six Types of Caring

A framework of six major types of involvement is based on the results of many studies and from many years of work by educators and families in elementary, middle, and high schools. The framework (summarized in the accompanying tables) helps educators develop more comprehensive programs of school and family partnerships. The framework also helps researchers locate their questions and results in ways that can inform and improve practice (Epstein, 1992, 1995).

The six types of involvement are *parenting, communicating, volunteering, learning at home, decision making,* and *collaborating with the community.* Each type of involvement includes many different *practices* of partnership (see Table 1.1.1). Each type presents particular *challenges* that must be met to involve all families and needed *redefinitions* of some basic principles of involvement (see Table 1.1.2). Finally, each type is likely to lead to different *results* for students, parents, teaching practices, and school climates (see Table 1.1.3). Thus, schools must select which practices will help achieve the goals they set for student success and for creating a climate of partnerships. The tables provide examples of practices for each type of involvement, challenges for successful implementation, redefinitions for up-to-date understanding, and results that have been documented and observed in diverse school settings.

Charting the Course

The entries in the tables are illustrative. The sample practices displayed in Table 1.1.1 are a few of hundreds of activities that may be selected or designed for each type of involvement. Although all schools may use the framework of six types as a guide, each school must chart its own course in choosing practices to meet the needs of its families and students.

The challenges in Table 1.1.2 are a few of many that relate to the sample practices for each type of involvement. There are challenges—that is, problems—for every activity that must be resolved in order to reach and engage all families in the best ways. Often, when one challenge has been met, a new one will emerge.

The redefinitions, also in Table 1.1.2, redirect old notions so that involvement is not viewed solely as or measured only by "bodies in the building." For example, the table calls for changes in how we define, organize, and conduct workshops, communications, volunteers, homework, decision making, and connections with community. By redefining these familiar terms, it is possible for partnership programs to reach out in new ways to many more families.

The selected results in Table 1.1.3 should help correct the widespread misperception that any practice that involves families will raise children's achievement test scores. Instead, it can be seen that certain practices are more likely than others to influence students' attitudes, attendance, and behavior in school, whereas other practices will influence skills, test scores, and other achievements over time.

Although students are the main focus of partnerships, the various types of involvement also promote various results for parents and teachers. For example, expected results for parents include not only leadership in decision making, but also confidence about parenting, productive curriculum-related interactions with children, and many interactions with other parents and the school. The expected results for teachers include not only improved parent-teacher conferences and clearer school-home communications, but also better understanding of students' families, improved ability to take new approaches to homework, and more productive connections with families and the community.

The results listed in Table 1.1.3 have been measured in at least one research study and/or observed as schools conducted their work on partnerships. The entries are listed in positive terms to indicate the results of well-designed and well-implemented practices. It should be fully understood, however, that results may be negative if poorly designed practices exclude families or create barriers to communication and exchange. More research is needed on the results of specific practices of partnership in various schools, at various grade levels, and for diverse populations of students, families, and teachers. It will be important to confirm, extend, or correct the information on results listed in Table 1.1.3 to help schools make purposeful choices among practices that foster various types of involvement.

The tables cannot show the connections that occur when one activity promotes several types of involvement simultaneously. For example, volunteers may organize and conduct a clothing swap shop (Type 3) that allows parents to obtain school uniforms or children's clothes at no cost (Type 1), and community businesses may offer discounts on school uniforms purchased at the swap shop (Type 6). The participating parents may serve as volunteers to keep the swap shop operating, thereby perpetuating activities and results for Types 1, 3, and 6.

As another example, an afterschool program may be conducted by parent and community volunteers and the community's parks and recreation department, combining Types 3 and 6. The afterschool program also serves as a Type 1 activity, because it assists families in supervising their children in a safe and purposeful place. The program also may alter the way homework is completed and how interactions about homework are conducted at home between students and parents (Type 4). Research is needed to understand the combination of types of involvement in complex activities. Practitioners should realize that various practices may activate several types of involvement.

The tables also simplify the influences that produce results over time. For example, the involvement of families with children in reading at home may make students more strongly motivated to read and to give more attention to reading instruction in school. This, in turn, may help students maintain or improve their daily reading skills in class and their reading report card grades. Over time, good classroom reading instruction and ongoing home support should increase students' skills and confidence in reading and significantly improve their reading achievement test scores. The time between a Family Reading Night or other family involvement activities in reading and the time that students increase their reading achievement test scores will vary depending on the quality and quantity of the reading-related activities in school and out.

TABLE 1.1.1 Epstein's Framework of Six Types of Involvement for Comprehensive Programs of Partnership and Sample Practices

Type 1* *Parenting	***Type 2* *Communicating***	***Type 3* *Volunteering***	***Type 4* *Learning at Home***	***Type 5* *Decision Making***	***Type 6* *Collaborating With the Community***
Help all families establish home environments to support children as students	Design effective forms of school-to-home and home-to-school communications about school programs and their children's progress	Recruit and organize parent help and support	Provide information and ideas to families about how to help students at home with homework and other curriculum-related activities, decisions, and planning	Include parents in school decisions, developing parent leaders and representatives	Identify and integrate resources and services from the community to strengthen school programs, family practices, and student learning and development
			Sample Practices		
Suggestions for home conditions that support learning at each grade level Workshops, videotapes, computerized phone messages on parenting for each age and grade level Parent education and other courses or training for parents (e.g., GED, college credit, family literacy) Family support programs to assist families with health, nutrition, and other services Home visits at transition points to preschool and to elementary, middle, and high school; neighborhood meetings to help families understand schools and to help schools understand families	Conferences with every parent at least once a year, with follow-ups as needed Language translators assist families, as needed Weekly or monthly folders of student work sent home for review and comments Parent-student pickup of report cards, with conferences on improving grades Regular schedule of useful notices, memos, phone calls, newsletters, information on the school Web site, and other communications Clear information on choosing schools or courses, programs, and activities within schools Clear information on all school policies, programs, reforms, and transitions Information for parents on Internet safety	School and classroom volunteer program to help teachers, administrators, students, and other parents Parent room or family center for volunteer work, meetings, resources for families Annual postcard survey to identify all available talents, times, and locations of volunteers Class parent, telephone tree, or other structures to provide all families with needed information Parent patrols or other activities to aid safety and operation of school programs	Information for families on knowledge and skills required for students in all subjects at each grade Information on homework policies and how to monitor and discuss schoolwork at home Information on how to assist students to improve skills on various class and school assessments Regular schedule of homework that requires students to discuss and interact with families on what they are learning in class Calendars with activities for parents and students to do at home or in the community Family math, science, and reading activities at school Summer learning packets or activities Family participation in setting student goals each year and in planning for college or work	Active PTA/PTO or other parent organizations, advisory councils, or committees (e.g., curriculum, safety, personnel) for parent leadership and participation Independent advocacy groups to lobby and work for school reform and improvements District level councils and committees for family and community involvement Information on school or local elections for school representatives Networks to link all families with parent representatives	Information for students and families on community health, cultural, recreational, social support, and other programs or services Information on community activities that link to learning skills and talents, including summer programs for students Service integration through partnerships involving school; civic, counseling, cultural, health, recreation, and other agencies and organizations; and businesses Service to the community by students, families, and schools (e.g., recycling, art, music, drama, and other activities for seniors or others) Participation of alumni in school programs for students and as mentors for planning for college and work

TABLE 1.1.2 Challenges and Redefinitions for the Successful Design and Implementation of the Six Types of Involvement

Type 1 Parenting	***Type 2 Communicating***	***Type 3 Volunteering***	***Type 4 Learning at Home***	***Type 5 Decision Making***	***Type 6 Collaborating With the Community***
			Challenges		
Provide information to all families who want it or who need it, not just to the few who can attend workshops or meetings at the school building Enable families to share information about culture, background, and children's talents and needs Make sure that all information for families is clear, usable, and linked to children's success in school	Review the readability, clarity, form, and frequency of all memos, notices, and other print and nonprint communications Consider parents who do not speak English well, do not read well, or need large type Review the quality of major communications (e.g., the schedule, content, and structure of conferences, newsletters, report cards, and others) Establish clear two-way channels for communications from home to school and from school to home	Recruit volunteers widely so that *all* families know that their time and talents are welcome Make flexible schedules for volunteers, assemblies, and events to enable employed parents to participate Organize volunteer work; provide training; match time and talent with school, teacher, and student needs; and recognize efforts so that participants are productive	Design and organize a regular schedule of interactive homework (e.g., weekly or bimonthly) that gives *students* responsibility for discussing important things they are learning and that helps families stay aware of the content of their children's classwork Coordinate family-linked homework activities, if students have several teachers Involve families with their children in all important curriculum-related decisions Provide timely information to students and families on credits required for high school graduation, credits earned, and steps for planning postsecondary education	Include parent leaders from all racial, ethnic, socioeconomic, and other groups in the school Offer training to enable leaders to serve as representatives of other families, with input from and return of information to all parents Include students (along with parents) in decision making groups	Solve turf problems of responsibilities, funds, staff, and locations for collaborative activities Inform families of community programs for students, such as mentoring, tutoring, and business partnerships Assure equity of opportunities for students and families to participate in community programs or to obtain services Match community contributions with school goals; integrate child and family services with education
			Redefinitions		
"Workshop" to mean more than a meeting about a topic held at the school building at a particular time; "workshop" also may mean making information about a topic available in a variety of forms that can be viewed, heard, or read anywhere, anytime	"Communications about school programs and student progress" to mean: two-way, three-way, and many-way channels of communication that connect schools, families, students, and the community	"Volunteer" to mean anyone who supports school programs and students' activities in any way, at any place, and at any time—not just during the school day and at the school building—and those who are audiences for student events, sports, activities, and performances	"Homework" to mean not only work done alone, but also interactive activities shared with others at home or in the community, linking schoolwork to real life "Help" at home to mean encouraging, listening, reacting, praising, guiding, monitoring, and discussing—not "teaching" school subjects	"Decision making" to mean a process of partnership, of shared views and actions toward shared goals, not a power struggle between conflicting ideas "Parent leader" to mean a real representative, with opportunities and support to hear from and communicate with other families	"Community" to mean not only the neighborhoods where students' homes and schools are located but also neighborhoods that influence student learning and development "Community" rated not only by low or high social or economic qualities but also by strengths and talents to support students, families, and schools "Community" means all who are interested in and affected by the quality of education, not just families with children in the schools

TABLE 1.1.3 Expected Results for Students, Parents, and Teachers of the Six Types of Involvement

Type 1* *Parenting	***Type 2* *Communicating***	***Type 3* *Volunteering***	***Type 4* *Learning at Home***	***Type 5* *Decision Making***	***Type 6* *Collaborating With the Community***
			Results for Students		
Awareness of family supervision; respect for parents Positive personal qualities, habits, beliefs, and values, as taught by family Balance between time spent on chores, on other activities, and on homework Good or improved attendance Awareness of importance of school	Awareness of own progress and of actions needed to maintain or improve grades Understanding of school policies on behavior, attendance, and other areas of student conduct Informed decisions about courses and programs Awareness of own role in partnerships, serving as courier and communicator	Skill in communicating with adults Increased learning of skills for which students receive tutoring or targeted attention from volunteers Awareness of many skills, talents, occupations, and contributions of parents and other volunteers	Gains in skills, abilities, and test scores linked to homework and classwork Homework completion Positive attitude toward schoolwork View of parent as more similar to teacher, and home as more similar to school Self-concept of ability as learner	Awareness of representation of families in school decisions Understanding that student rights are protected Specific benefits linked to policies enacted by parent organizations and experienced by students	Increased skills and talents through enriched curricular and extracurricular experiences Awareness of careers and options for future education and work Specific benefits linked to programs, services, resources, and opportunities that connect students with community
			Results for Parents		
Understanding of and confidence about parenting, child and adolescent development, and changes in home conditions for learning as children proceed through school Awareness of own and others' challenges in parenting Feeling of support from school and other parents	Understanding of school programs and policies Monitoring and awareness of student progress Effective responses to student problems Interactions with teachers and eased communications with school and teachers	Understanding of teacher's job, increased comfort in school, and carryover of school activities at home Self-confidence about ability to work in school and with children, or to take steps to improve own education Awareness that families are welcome and valued at school Gains in specific skills of volunteer work	Knowledge of how to support, encourage, and help student at home each year Discussions of school, classwork, and homework Understanding of instructional program each year and of what child is learning in each subject Appreciation of teaching skills Awareness of child as a learner	Input into policies that affect child's education Feeling of ownership of school Awareness of parents' voices in school decisions Shared experiences and connections with other families Awareness of school, district, and state policies	Knowledge and use of local resources by family and child to increase skills and talents or to obtain needed services Interactions with other families in community activities Awareness of school's role in the community and of community's contributions to the school
			Results for Teachers		
Understanding of families' backgrounds, cultures, concerns, goals, needs, and views of their children Respect for families' strengths and efforts Understanding of student diversity Awareness of own skills to share information on child development	Increased diversity and use of communications with families and awareness of own ability to communicate clearly Appreciation and use of parent network for communications Increased ability to elicit and understand family views on children's programs and progress	Readiness to involve families in new ways, including those who do not volunteer at school Awareness of parent talents and interests in school and children Greater individual attention to students, with help from volunteers	Better design of homework assignments Respect of family time Recognition of equal helpfulness of single parent, dual income, and less formally educated families in motivating and reinforcing student learning Satisfaction with family involvement and support	Awareness of parent perspectives as a factor in policy development and decisions View of equal status of family representatives on committees and in leadership roles	Awareness of community resources to enrich curriculum and instruction Openness to and skill in using mentors, business partners, community volunteers, and others to assist students and augment teaching practice Ability to make knowledgeable, helpful referrals of children and families to needed services

Consider one more example. Studies using longitudinal data and rigorous statistical controls on student background and prior influences found important benefits for high school students' attitudes, behaviors, and report card grades as a result of continuing several types of family involvement from middle school through high school (Lee, 1994; Simon, 2004). However, achievement test scores, stable by twelfth-grade, were not greatly affected by partnerships at the high school level. By contrast, elementary school students' math achievement test scores increased significantly when their teachers assigned interactive math homework (Epstein, 2005b; Van Voorhis, in press). Even with prior math test scores accounted for, elementary students' standardized achievement can be influenced by effective homework designs and interactions with parents. In the future, longitudinal studies of practical interventions at different grade levels will increase an understanding of the complex patterns of results that can develop from various partnership activities (Epstein, 1991; Epstein & Dauber, 1995; Epstein & Sanders, 2000; Henderson & Mapp, 2002; and see article 1.3 on results in this chapter).

The six types of involvement guide the development of a balanced, comprehensive program of partnerships, including opportunities for family involvement at school, at home, and in the community, with potentially important results for students, parents, and teachers. The results will depend on the particular activities that are implemented and the quality of the design, implementation, and outreach.

Action Teams for Partnerships

Who will work to create caring school communities that are based on concepts of partnership? How will the necessary work on all six types of involvement get done? Although a principal or a teacher may be a leader in working with some families and with some community groups, one person cannot create a lasting, comprehensive program that involves all families as their children progress through the grades.

From the hard work of many educators and families in hundreds of schools and districts, we have learned that, along with clear policies and strong support from district and state leaders and from school principals, an Action Team for Partnerships (ATP) in each school is an essential structure. The ATP—a committee of the School Council or School Improvement Team—is dedicated to improving plans and practices of family and community involvement. The ATP guides the development of a comprehensive partnership program linked to school improvement goals for student success. Using the framework of six types of involvement, the ATP integrates all family and community connections that occur in the school in a single, unified plan and program.

The trials and errors and the efforts and insights of hundreds of schools across the country have helped identify five important steps that any school can take to develop more positive school, family, and community connections.

Step 1: Create an Action Team for Partnerships

A team approach is an appropriate and effective way to build school, family, and community partnerships. The Action Team for Partnerships (ATP) is an "action arm" of a School Council or School Improvement Team, if one exists in the school. The ATP takes responsibility for assessing present family and community involvement practices, organizing options for new partnerships, implementing selected activities, delegating leadership for other activities, evaluating next steps, and continuing to improve and coordinate practices for all six types of involvement. Although the members of the ATP lead some of activities, they are assisted by other teachers, parents, students, administrators, and community members who take leadership or support roles for planned partnerships.

The ATP team should include at least two or three teachers from different grade levels, departments, or specialties; at least two or three parents from different neighborhoods or cultural groups with children in different grade levels; and at least one administrator. Teams may also include at least one member from the community at large and, at the high school level, at least two students from different grade levels. Others who are central to the school's work with families also may be included as team members, such as a school counselor, social worker, nurse, school psychologist, cafeteria worker, secretary, or custodian. Such diverse membership ensures that the team will plan activities that take into account the various needs, interests, and talents of teachers, parents, the school, and students.

The chair (or, better, co-chairs) of the action team should be members who have the respect of the other members, as well as good communication skills and an understanding of the partnership approach. At least one member of the action team should also serve on the School Council, School Improvement Team, or other advisory body.

Members of the ATP may serve as chairs or co-chairs of subcommittees organized to implement family and community involvement activities on specific school improvement goals (e.g., family and community involvement to help improve students' reading, math, and behavior, and to improve the school's climate of partnerships) or on the six types of involvement. A team with at least six members (or as many as 12 or more) ensures that responsibilities for leadership can be shared and delegated so that one person is not overburdened with all family and community involvement activities. The work of the action team also ensures that plans for partnership will continue even if members move or change schools or positions. Members may serve renewable terms of two to three years, with the replacement of members who leave in the interim. Other thoughtful variations in assignments and activities may be created by small or large schools using this process. See Chapter 3 for details on organizing effective Action Teams for Partnerships.

In the first phase of our fieldwork in 1987, projects were led by "project directors" (usually teachers) and were focused on one type of involvement at a time. Some schools succeeded in developing good partnerships over several years, but others were thwarted if the project director moved, if the principal changed, or if the project grew larger than one person could handle. Other schools were guided to try a team approach to work on many types of involvement simultaneously and to focus on activities that create a climate of partnerships and that help students reach important results in learning and behavior. These schools showed that the team approach was the best structure for strong and sustainable program. Now, a team approach guides all of our research and development projects in elementary, middle, and high schools.

Step 2: Obtain Funds and Other Support

A modest budget is needed to guide and support the activities planned by each school's Action Team for Partnerships. Funds also are needed for district leaders for partnerships who will help each school with its plans and programs of family and community involvement. Investments are needed at the state level for leadership on partnerships, as well.

Funds for schools, districts, and states may come from a number of sources. These include federal, state, and local programs that mandate, request, or support family involvement, including Title I and other "titled" funding streams. At the district level, funds are needed to support the salaries of a director and facilitators who help all schools develop their partnership programs and for program costs (e.g., staff development and training workshops on school, family, and community partnerships; parent coordinators or liaisons to serve as ATP chairs or co-chairs; activities in schools' One-Year Action Plans for Partnerships). In addition, local school-business partnerships, school discretionary funds, and fund-raising targeted to the schools' partnership programs can support the plans and activities of school-based ATPs. Recent data indicate that schools' ATPs need at least $2,500 per year to support activities in a typical, start-up Action Plan for Partnerships. See details on levels and sources of funds for partnership programs at the school, district, and state levels in Chapter 7.

The ATP also must have sufficient time and social support to do its work. This requires explicit support from the principal and from district leaders for team training, meetings to plan and evaluate activities, and time to conduct the activities in the annual plan for partnerships. Time during the summer also may be used to plan new approaches and projects for the start of the new school year.

Step 3: Identify Starting Points

Most schools have some teachers and administrators who conduct some practices of partnership with some families some of the time. How can good practices be organized and extended so that all teachers at all grade levels inform and involve all families in ways that support student learning and success in school? How can some schoolwide involvement activities build a sense of community with all students and families?

The Action Team for Partnerships (ATP) works to systematize and improve typically haphazard patterns of involvement. The ATP starts by gathering information about the school's current practices of partnership along with the views, experiences, and wishes of teachers, parents, administrators, and students. See *Starting Points* (pp. 174–177 and CD) and *Measure of School, Family, and Community Partnerships* (pp. 324–329 and CD) for two ways of assessing the nature and extent of present practices.

Starting points also may be identified in other ways, depending on available resources, time, and talents. For example, the ATP might use formal questionnaires (Epstein, Connors, & Salinas, 1993; Epstein & Salinas, 1993; Sheldon & Epstein, 2007) or telephone interviews to survey teachers, administrators, parents, and students, if funds and experts are available to process, analyze, and report survey data. Or, the ATP might organize a panel of teachers, parents, and students to speak at a PTA or PTO meeting to discuss the goals and desired activities for improving family and community involvement. Structured discussions may be conducted at a series of principal's breakfasts for representative groups of teachers, parents, students, and others; random-sample phone calls may also be used to collect suggestions and reactions; and formal focus groups may be convened to gather ideas about school, family, and community partnerships at the school.

What questions should be addressed to take stock of present practices and to plan next steps? Regardless of how information is gathered, the following areas should be part of any information gathering:

- *Present strengths.* Which practices of school, family, and community partnerships are, presently, working well for the school as a whole? For individual teachers and specific grade levels? For which types of involvement? On what school goals for student success?
- *Needed changes.* Ideally, how do we want school, family, and community partnerships to work at this school three years from now? Which present practices should continue and which should change? To reach school goals, what new practices are needed for each of the major types of involvement?
- *Expectations.* What do teachers expect of families? What do families expect of teachers and other school personnel? What do students expect their families to do to help them negotiate school life? What do students expect their teachers to do to keep their families informed and involved?
- *Sense of community.* Which families are presently involved, and which are not yet engaged with the school and with their children's education? Who are the "hard-to-reach" families? What might be done to communicate with and engage these families? Are current partnership practices coordinated to integrate all families as a school community? Or, are families whose children receive special services (e.g., Title I, special education, bilingual education) separated from other families?
- *Links to goals.* How are students doing on measures of academic achievement, including test scores and report card grades? On measures of attitudes and attendance? On other indicators of success? How might family and community connections assist the school in helping more students reach higher goals and achieve greater success? Which practices of school, family, and community partnerships could contribute to the attainment of particular goals?

Step 4: Develop a One-Year Action Plan

With the information on a school's starting points and with understanding of the goals and ideas for partnerships collected from teachers, administrators, parents, and students, the Action Team for Partnerships (ATP) will develop a detailed One-Year Action Plan for Partnerships (see Chapters 4 and 5). The annual action plan includes a set of selected goals or objectives, desired results, measures to assess results, and specific involvement activities that will be implemented, improved, or maintained each year; dates scheduled; types of involvement; actions needed to prepare the activity; people responsible for implementing the activities and those assisting; funds or resources required; and other important details.

The One-Year Action Plan for Partnerships should be shared with the School Council or School Improvement Team, parent organization, all teachers, and, in various ways, with all parents and students. Corrections and additions from the various groups contribute to a final plan for partnerships for the school year.

If the ATP takes one step forward each year to improve family and community involvement for each of the specific academic and behavioral goals in the One-Year Action Plan, it will continually improve the quality of partnerships and student success. If the ATP makes one step forward each year on each of the six types of involvement, it will take 18 steps forward over three years to improve the school climate for partnerships. Good plans and actions lead to a more comprehensive, coordinated, and goal-oriented program of school, family, and community partnerships.

In short, the ATP, with input from others, will complete an annual, detailed Action Plan for Partnerships that addresses these issues:

- *Details.* What will be done each year to implement activities that involve families in ways linked to specific goals for student success? What activities for the six types of involvement will be activated? How will these activities also create a welcoming school climate for all students and their families? What, specifically, will be accomplished over the next school year to improve family and community involvement?
- *Responsibilities.* Who will be responsible for developing and implementing the practices of partnership that are in the One-Year Action Plan for Partnerships? Will staff development or other guidance be needed to plan and implement activities? How will teachers, administrators, parents, and students be supported and recognized for their work? What role will district leaders for partnership or others play in assisting schools' ATPs with activities?
- *Costs.* What costs are associated with implementing the planned activities? What sources will provide the needed funds? Will small grants or other special budgets be needed? What funds and in-kind contributions are needed to maintain and improve the activities from year to year?
- *Evaluation.* How well are activities implemented? What are the effects of each activity on the school climate and/or on students, teachers, and families? What indicators will be used to measure the quality of implementation and the results?

Step 5: Continue Planning, Evaluating, and Improving Programs

The ATP should schedule an annual presentation and celebration of progress at the school so that all teachers, families, and students know about the work that was done each year to build partnerships. Or, a district coordinator for school, family, and community partnerships may arrange an annual midyear or end-of-year conference for all schools in the district. At a districtwide annual meeting, ATPs from all schools can display and share their accomplishments and best practices for involving families and the community in ways that improve students' attitudes, behaviors, and achievements in specific subjects. Panels of ATP members may discuss serious challenges and solutions for reaching all families, share ideas for the six types of involvement, and gather ideas for improving programs in the next school year.

In short, the ATP considers the following questions: How will the ATP increase the number of families who are partners with the school in their children's education over the next school year? What opportunities will be arranged for teachers, parents, and students to come together with individual teachers, in grade level groups, or as a whole school to support student learning and development? How will the ATP evaluate, strengthen, and sustain the school's partnership program to continue to improve results for students?

Each year, the Action Team for Partnerships develops a new and improved One-Year Action Plan for Partnerships for the next school year. The ATP shares its plans and gathers input so that educators, families, students, and the community are aware of progress, new plans, and how they can help.

Characteristics of Successful Programs

Hundreds of schools have taken these five steps over the years. Their experiences helped identify some important properties of successful partnership programs.

Incremental Progress

Progress on partnerships is incremental, including more families each year in ways that benefit more students. Like reading or math programs, assessment programs, sports programs, or other school investments, partnership programs take time to develop; they must be periodically reviewed and evaluated and continuously improved. Schools and districts in our projects have shown that some progress can be made immediately, but it tends to take at least three years to demonstrate that a partnership program is a "permanent" component of school and district organization.

The development of an excellent partnership program is a process, not a single event. All teachers, families, students, and community groups are unlikely to participate all at once. Not all activities that are implemented the first time will succeed in engaging all families. But with good planning, thoughtful implementation, well-designed activities, thoughtful evaluations, and pointed improvements, more and more families and teachers can learn to work with one another on behalf of the children they share.

Similarly, not all students instantly improve their attitudes or achievements when their families become involved in their education. After all, student learning depends mainly on good curricula, engaging and appropriate instruction, students' interests and commitment, and the work students complete. However, with a well-implemented program of partnerships, more students receive support from their families and more will be motivated to work harder in school.

Connections to Curricular and Instructional Reform

A program of school, family, and community partnerships that focuses on children's learning and development is an important component of curricular and instructional reform. For example, helping families understand, monitor, and interact with students on homework is an extension of classroom instruction. Volunteers who bolster and broaden student skills, talents, and interests extend classroom learning. Improving the content and conduct of parent-teacher-student conferences and goal-setting activities are important aspects of curricular reform; family support and family understanding of child and adolescent development and school curricula are necessary to assist students as learners. All of these activities—homework-help interventions, volunteers and tutors linked to student learning, the redesign of parent-teacher-student conferences, and similar activities are part of curricular and instructional reform and should be supported with the appropriate federal, state, and local funds for school improvement.

One important new direction for partnership programs connects family and community involvement directly to the School Improvement Plan. This is done by focusing family and community involvement on specific curricular and instructional goals for student learning and by appending the One-Year Action Plan for Partnerships to the annual School Improvement Plan. These organizational changes move partnerships from being peripheral and unplanned activities for parents to being official components of a school's program for student learning and development.

Redefining Professional Development and Shared Leadership

The action team approach to partnerships changes the definition of "professional development," because teachers, administrators, parents, and other partners are trained together, as a team, to develop, implement, evaluate, and continue to improve practices of partnership. The development of a well-functioning Action Team for Partnerships is not the result of a "dose" of inservice education but is a long-term process of developing and extending educators' and parents' talents and capacities for organizing and conducting effective partnerships. Teachers, administrators, parents, and others on the Action Team for Partnerships must be helped to become the experts on this topic for their school. With this definition, program development can be supported by various federal, state, and local funds for professional development for school improvement.

An effective program of family and community involvement also stretches the definition of "shared leadership"—an important concept in educational administration. Usually, the term means that teachers will share leadership with principals and specialists in improving school organization, curriculum, and instruction. In effective partnership programs, shared leadership means that all members on the team of teachers, administrators, parents, and community partners will take responsibility for developing, implementing, evaluating, and continually improving plans and practices of family and community involvement.

Developing excellent partnership programs in all districts and schools would be easier if educators came to their positions prepared to work productively with families and communities. Courses or classes are needed in preservice teacher education, continuing studies, and advanced degree programs that define professional work in terms of partnerships. Today, most teachers, principals, counselors, and district leaders enter their professions without an understanding of family backgrounds, concepts of caring, the framework of six types of involvement, or partnership program development. Thus, most principals and district leaders are not prepared to guide school teams in developing, evaluating, and sustaining effective partnership programs.

Schools, colleges, and departments of education that prepare future teachers, administrators, and others who work with children and families should identify where in the curriculum students are asked to study and learn the theory, research, policy, and practical ideas of partnerships, or where these topics should be added to better prepare their graduates for their professional work (Chavkin & Williams, 1988: Christenson & Conoley, 1992; Epstein, 2001; Epstein & Sheldon, 2006; Hinz, Clarke, & Nathan, 1992; Swap, 1993).

Even with improved preservice and advanced coursework, however, each school's Action Team for Partnerships and other practicing educators will need inservice education and targeted team training to tailor plans for partnerships to the needs and goals of the teachers, families, and students in the school. The framework and guidelines in this article can be used by thoughtful educators to organize high-quality, ongoing professional development on partnerships, school by school.

The Core of Caring

Years ago, a school in Baltimore named its partnership program the *I Care Program.* It developed an *I Care Parent Club* that fostered fellowship and leadership of families, an *I Care Newsletter,* and many other events and activities. Other schools also gave catchy, positive names to their programs to indicate that families, students, teachers, and community partners were developing relationships and conducting actions to assist all students toward success.

Interestingly, synonyms for "caring" match the six types of involvement:

Type 1–Parenting: supporting, nurturing, loving, and child raising

Type 2–Communicating: relating, reviewing, and overseeing

Type 3–Volunteering: supervising and fostering

Type 4–Learning at Home: managing, recognizing, and rewarding

Type 5–Decision Making: contributing, considering, and judging

Type 6–Collaborating With the Community: sharing and giving

Underlying all six types of involvement are two defining synonyms of caring: trusting and respecting. Of course, the varied meanings are interconnected, but it is striking that various elements of caring are associated with activities for the six types of involvement. If all six types of involvement are operating well in a school's program of partnerships, then all of these caring behaviors could be activated to assist children's learning and development.

Summary: Battleground or Homeland?

Despite real progress in many states, districts, and schools over the past few years, there still are too many schools where educators do not understand the families of their students. There still are too many families who do not understand their children's schools, and too many communities that do not understand or assist their schools, families, or students. There still are too many districts and states without the policies, departments, leadership, staff, and fiscal support needed to help all schools develop excellent and permanent programs of partnership.

Relatively small financial investments are needed to support district leaders for partnerships and the work of school-based Action Teams for Partnerships. Yet, those investments yield significant returns for all schools, teachers, families, and students. Educators who have led the way in constructing research-based programs with the necessary components provide evidence that any state, district, or school can create similar programs.

Schools have choices. There are two opposing approaches to involving families in schools and in their children's education. One approach emphasizes conflict and views the school as a battleground. The conditions and relationships in this kind of environment guarantee power struggles and disharmony. The other approach emphasizes partnership and views the school as a homeland. The conditions and relationships in this kind of environment invite mutual respect, shared leadership on partnerships, and attention to activities that foster student learning and development. Even when conflicts flare, however, peace must be restored, and the partners in children's education must work together.

Next Steps: Strengthening Partnerships

Collaborative work and thoughtful give-and-take among researchers, policy leaders, educators, parents, and community partners are responsible for the progress that has been made over the past two decades in understanding and developing school, family, and community partnerships. Similar collaborations will be important for future progress in this and other areas of school reform.

To promote these approaches, I established the National Network of Partnership Schools (NNPS) at Johns Hopkins University in 1996. NNPS provides school, district, state, and other education leaders with research-based tools and guidelines to help elementary, middle, and high schools plan, implement, and maintain comprehensive and goal-oriented programs of school, family, and community partnerships. With the efforts of many colleagues, many of whom are coauthors of this *Handbook,* NNPS has been able to encourage and guide educators, parents, and other community leaders to organize stronger program of family and community involvement.

Partnership schools, districts, and states have worked hard to put the recommendations of this chapter into practice in ways that are appropriate for their locations. Implementation includes applying the theory of overlapping spheres of influence, the framework of six types of involvement, and the action team approach. Systemic advances include district leaders who assist all schools to use teamwork and develop and sustain partnership programs. The researchers and staff of NNPS at Johns Hopkins University disseminate information, guidelines, and newsletters; offer e-mail and Web site assistance; hold annual conferences; and conduct workshops to help state and district coordinators and school leaders learn new strategies and share successful ideas. The members of NNPS share best practices at all policy levels in annual collections of *Promising Partnership Practices* (Maushard et al., 2007). With a strong research base, NNPS guides state and district leaders, educators, and parents to recognize their common interests in the children they share, and to work together, with care, to strengthen programs of family and community involvement that contribute to student success.

Note

The first version of this article appeared in *Phi Delta Kappan,* 1995, *76*(9), 701–712. The new version has been updated with recent research and knowledge gained by working with more than 1,000 schools, 150 districts, and many states and organizations in the National Network of Partnership Schools (NNPS) at Johns Hopkins University.

References

Baker, D. P., & Stevenson, D. L. (1986). Mothers' strategies for children's school achievement: Managing the transition to high school. *Sociology of Education, 59,* 156–166.

Bauch, P. A. (1988). Is parent involvement different in private schools? *Educational Horizons, 66,* 78–82.

Becker, H. J., & Epstein, J. L. (1982). Parent involvement: A study of teacher practices. *Elementary School Journal, 83,* 85–102.

Booth, A., & Dunn, J. F. (Eds.). (1996). *Family-school links: How do they affect educational outcomes?* Mahwah, NJ: Erlbaum.

Boykin, A. W. (1994). Harvesting culture and talent: African American children and educational reform. In R. Rossi (Ed.), *Schools and students at risk* (pp. 116–139). New York: Teachers College Press.

Burch, P., & Palanki, A. (1994). Action research on family-school-community partnerships. *Journal of Emotional and Behavioral Problems, 1*(4), 16–19.

Chavkin, N., & Williams, D. (1988). Critical issues in teacher training for parent involvement. *Educational Horizons, 66,* 87–89.

Christenson, S. L., & Conoley, J. C. (Eds.). (1992). *Home-school collaboration: Enhancing children's academic competence.* Silver Spring, MD: National Association of School Psychologists.

Clark, R. M. (1983). *Family life and school achievement: Why poor Black children succeed or fail.* Chicago: University of Chicago Press.

Connors, L. J., & Epstein. J. L. (1994). *Taking stock: The views of teachers, parents, and students on school, family, and community partnerships in high schools* (Center Report 25). Baltimore: Johns Hopkins University, Center on Families, Communities, Schools and Children's Learning.

Dauber, S. L., & Epstein, J. L. (1993). Parents' attitudes and practices of involvement in inner-city elementary and middle schools. In N. Chavkin (Ed.), *Families and schools in a pluralistic society* (pp. 53–71). Albany: State University of New York Press.

Davies, D. (1991). Schools reaching out: Family, school and community partnerships for student success. *Phi Delta Kappan, 72,* 376–382.

Davies, D. (1993). A more distant mirror: Progress report on a cross-national project to study family-school-community partnerships. *Equity and Choice, 19*(1), 41–46.

Dornbusch, S. M., & Ritter, P. L. (1988). Parents of high school students: A neglected resource. *Educational Horizons, 66,* 75–77.

Dryfoos, J., & Maguire, S. (2002). *Inside full-service community schools.* Thousand Oaks, CA: Corwin Press.

Eccles, J. S., & Harold, R. D. (1996). Family involvement in children's and adolescents' schooling. In A. Booth & J. F. Dunn (Eds.), *Family-school links: How do they affect educational outcomes?* (pp. 3–34). Mahwah, NJ: Erlbaum.

Epstein, J. L. (1986). Parents' reactions to teacher practices of parent involvement. *Elementary School Journal, 86,* 277–294.

Epstein, J. L. (1987). Toward a theory of family-school connections: Teacher practices and parent involvement. In K. Hurrelmann, F. Kaufmann, & F. Losel (Eds.), *Social intervention: Potential and constraints* (pp. 121–136). New York: DeGruyter.

Epstein, J. L. (1990). Single parents and the schools: Effects of marital status on parent and teacher interactions. In M. Hallinan (Ed.), *Change in societal institutions* (pp. 91–121). New York: Plenum.

Epstein, J. L. (1991). Effects on student achievement of teacher practices of parent involvement. In S. Silvern (Ed.), *Literacy through family, community, and school interaction* (pp. 261–276). Greenwich, CT: JAI Press.

Epstein, J. L. (1992). School and family partnerships. In M. Alkin (Ed.), *Encyclopedia of educational research* (6th ed., pp. 1139–1151). New York: MacMillan.

Epstein, J. L. (1994). Theory to practice: School and family partnerships lead to school improvement and student success. In C. L. Fagnano & B. Z. Werber (Eds.), *School, family and community interaction: A view from the firing lines* (pp. 39–52). Boulder CO: Westview Press.

Epstein, J. L. (1995). School/family/community partnerships: Caring for the children we share. *Phi Delta Kappan, 76,* 701–712.

Epstein, J. L. (2001). School, family, and community partnerships: Preparing educators and improving schools. Boulder, CO: Westview Press.

Epstein, J. L. (2005a). Attainable goals? The spirit and letter of the No Child Left Behind Act on parental involvement. *Sociology of Education, 78*(2), 179–182.

Epstein, J. L. (2005b). Results of the Partnership Schools-CSR model for student achievement over three years. *Elementary School Journal, 106,* 151–170.

Epstein, J. L. (2005c). School, family, and community partnerships in the middle grades. In T. O. Erb, (Ed.), *This we believe in action: Implementing successful middle level schools* (pp. 77–96). Westerville, OH: National Middle School Association.

Epstein, J. L. (2007). Research meets policy and practice: How are school districts addressing NCLB requirements for parental involvement? In A. R. Sadovnik, J. O' Day, G. Bohrnstedt, &

K. Borman (Eds.), *No Child Left Behind and the reduction of the achievement gap: Sociological perspectives on federal educational policy* (pp. 267–279). New York: Routledge.

Epstein, J. L., & Connors, L. J. (1994). *Trust fund: School, family, and community partnerships in high schools* (Center Report 24). Baltimore: Johns Hopkins University, Center on Families, Communities, Schools and Children's Learning.

Epstein, J. L., Connors, L J., & Salinas, K. C. (1993). *High school and family partnerships: Surveys and summaries (Questionnaires for teachers, parents, and students).* Baltimore: Johns Hopkins University, Center on School, Family, and Community Partnerships.

Epstein, J. L., & Dauber, S. L. (1991). School programs and teacher practices of parent involvement in inner-city elementary and middle schools. *Elementary School Journal, 91,* 289–303.

Epstein, J. L., & Dauber, S. L. (1995). Effects on students of an interdisciplinary program linking social studies, art, and family volunteers in the middle grades. *Journal of Early Adolescence, 15,* 237–266.

Epstein, J. L., Herrick, S. C., & Coates, L. (1996). Effects of summer home learning packets on student achievement in language arts in the middle grades. *School Effectiveness and School Improvement, 7*(3), 93–120.

Epstein, J. L., & Lee, S. (1995). National patterns of school and family connections in the middle grades. In B. A. Ryan, G. R. Adams, T. P. Gullotta, R. P. Weissberg, & R. L. Hampton (Eds.), *The family-school connection: Theory, research, and practice* (pp. 108–154). Thousand Oaks, CA: Sage.

Epstein, J. L., & Salinas, K. C. (1993). *School and family partnerships: Surveys and summaries.* Baltimore: Johns Hopkins University, Center on School, Family, and Community Partnerships.

Epstein, J. L., & Sanders, M. G. (2000). School, family, and community connections: New directions for social research. In M. Hallinan (Ed.), *Handbook of sociology of education* (pp. 285–306). New York: Plenum.

Epstein J. L., & Sheldon, S. B. (2006). Moving forward: Ideas for research on school, family, and community partnerships. In C. F. Conrad & R. Serlin (Eds.), *SAGE handbook for research in education: Engaging ideas and enriching inquiry* (pp. 117-137). Thousand Oaks, CA: Sage.

Henderson, A., & Mapp, K. L. (2002). *A new wave of evidence: The impact of school, family, and community connections on student achievement.* Austin, TX: Southwest Educational Development Laboratory.

Henderson, A. T., Mapp, K. L., Johnson, V. R., & Davies, D. (2007). *Beyond the bake sale.* New York: The New Press.

Hinz, L., Clarke, J., & Nathan, J. (1992). *A survey of parent involvement course offerings in Minnesota's undergraduate preparation programs.* Minneapolis: University of Minnesota, Humphrey Institute of Public Affairs, Center for School Change.

Lareau, A. (1989). *Home advantage: Social class and parental intervention in elementary education.* Philadelphia: Falmer.

Lee, S. (1994). *Family-school connections and students' education: Continuity and change of family involvement from the middle grades to high school.* Unpublished doctoral dissertation, Johns Hopkins University, Baltimore.

Lewis, C. C., Schaps, E., & Watson, M. (1995). Beyond the pendulum: Creating challenging and caring schools. *Phi Delta Kappan, 76,* 547–554.

Maushard, M., Martin, C. S., Hutchins, D. J., Greenfeld, M. D., Thomas, B. G. Fournier, A., et al. (2007). *Promising partnership practices 2007.* Baltimore: Johns Hopkins University, Center on School, Family, and Community Partnerships. (See additional annual collections of practices at www.partnershipschools .org in the section Success Stories.)

Sanders, M. G. (2005). *Building school-community partnerships: Collaborating for student success.* Thousand Oaks, CA: Corwin Press.

Scott-Jones, D. (1995). Activities in the home that support school learning in the middle grades. In B. Rutherford (Ed.), *Creating family/school partnerships* (pp. 161–181). Columbus, OH: National Middle School Association.

Sheldon, S. B. (2005). Testing a structural equation model of partnership program implementation and parent involvement. *Elementary School Journal, 106,* 171–187.

Sheldon, S. B. (2007a). Getting families involved with NCLB: Factors affecting schools' enactment of federal policy. In A. R. Sadovnik, J. O' Day, G. Bohrnstedt, & K. Borman (Eds.), *No Child Left Behind and reducing the achievement gap: Sociological perspectives on federal educational policy* (pp. 281–294). New York: Routledge.

Sheldon, S. B. (2007b). Improving student attendance with school, family, and community partnerships. *Journal of Educational Research, 100,* 267–275.

Sheldon, S. B., & Epstein, J. L. (2007). *Parent and student surveys on family and community involvement in the elementary and middle grades.* Baltimore: Johns Hopkins University, Center on School, Family, and Community Partnerships.

Sheldon, S. B., & Van Voorhis, V. L. (2004). Partnership programs in U.S. schools: Their development and relationship to family involvement outcomes. *School Effectiveness and School Improvement, 15,* 125–148.

Simon, B. S. (2004). High school outreach and family involvement. *Social Psychology of Education, 7,* 185–209.

Swap, S. M. (1993). *Developing home-school partnerships: From concepts to practice.* New York: Teachers College Press.

Van Voorhis, F. L. (2003). Interactive homework in middle school: Effects on family involvement and science achievement. *Journal of Educational Research, 96,* 323–338.

Van Voorhis, F. L. (in press). Longitudinal effects of family involvement with students on math homework.

Van Voorhis, F. L., & Sheldon, S. B. (2004). Principals' roles in the development of U.S. programs of school, family, and community partnerships. *International Journal of Educational Research, 41*(1), 55–70.

1.2 Community Involvement in School Improvement: The Little Extra That Makes a Big Difference

Mavis G. Sanders

Rationale for School-Community Partnerships

Families and schools traditionally have been viewed as the institutions with the greatest effects on the development of children. Communities, however, have received increasing attention for their role in socializing youth and ensuring students' success in a variety of societal domains. Epstein's (1987, 1995) theory of overlapping spheres of influence, for example, identifies schools, families, and communities as major institutions that socialize and educate children. A central principle of the theory is that certain goals, such as student academic success, are of interest to each of these institutions and are best achieved through their cooperative action and support.

Similarly, Heath and McLaughlin (1987, p. 579) argued that community involvement is important, because "the problems of educational achievement and academic success demand resources beyond the scope of the school and of most families." They identified changing family demographics, demands of the professional workplace, and growing diversity among students as some of the reasons that schools and families alone cannot provide sufficient resources to ensure that all children receive the experiences and support needed to succeed in the larger society.

When describing the importance of community involvement in educational reform, Shore (1994) focused on the mounting responsibilities placed on schools by a nation whose student population is increasingly placed "at risk." She stated, "Too many schools and school systems are failing to carry out their basic educational mission. Many of them—in urban and rural settings—are overwhelmed by the social and emotional needs of children who are growing up in poverty" (p. 2). She contended that schools need additional resources to successfully educate all students and that these resources, both human and material, are housed in students' communities.

Other authors also have emphasized the importance of schools, families, *and* communities working together to promote students' success. Toffler and Toffler (1995) asserted that school-family-community collaborations are one way to provide a caring component to today's often large, assembly line schools. Still others have suggested that school-community partnerships that focus on educational improvement and neighborhood revitalization can strengthen the social networks, resources, and capital available to children and youth (Benson, 1997; Crowson & Boyd, 1993; Decker, Decker, & Brown, 2007; Dryfoos, 1998; Warren, 2005).

School-community partnerships, then, can be defined as the connections between schools and community individuals, organizations, and businesses that are forged to directly or indirectly promote students' social, emotional, physical, and intellectual development. Community, within this definition of school-community partnerships, is not constrained by the geographic boundaries of neighborhoods, but refers more to the "social interactions that can occur within or transcend local boundaries" (Nettles, 1991b, p. 380).

Forms of School-Community Partnerships

School-community partnerships can take a variety of forms. The most common linkages are partnerships with businesses, which can differ significantly in focus, scope, and content. Other school-community linkages involve universities and educational institutions, government and military agencies, health care organizations, faith-based organizations, national service and volunteer organizations, senior citizen organizations, cultural and recreational institutions, other community-based organizations, and community volunteers that may provide resources and social support to youth and schools (see Table 1.2.1).

Partnership activities also may have multiple foci. As shown in Table 1.2.2, activities may be student, family, school, or community centered.

- Student-centered activities include those that provide direct services or goods to students. These include, for example, mentoring and tutoring programs, contextual learning, and job-shadowing opportunities, as well as the provision of awards, incentives, and scholarships to students.
- Family-centered activities are those that have parents or entire families as their primary focus. This category includes activities such as parenting workshops, GED and other adult education classes, parent and family incentives and awards, family counseling, and family fun and learning nights.
- School-centered activities are those that benefit the school as a whole, such as beautification projects or the donation of school equipment and materials, or activities that benefit the faculty, such as staff development and classroom assistance.
- Community-centered activities have as their primary focus the community and its citizens, such as charitable outreach, art and science exhibits, and community revitalization and beautification projects (Sanders, 2001, 2005).

Role of Community Involvement in School, Family, and Community Partnership Programs

Community involvement activities are an important part of a school's comprehensive partnership program. Community activities may support or strengthen all six types of involvement: (1) parenting, (2) communicating, (3) volunteering, (4) learning at home, (5) decision making, and (6) collaborating with the community (Epstein, 1995). For example, community partners can provide meeting space for parenting workshops (Type 1), interpreters for school meetings with families (Type 2), volunteer tutors (Type 3), information on books that families can read to and with their children at home (Type 4), and meals to increase parents' attendance at school meetings (Type 5).

Community collaborations can be developed to enhance schools' curricula, identify and disseminate information about community resources, and support community development efforts (Type 6). One school in the National Network of Partnership Schools (NNPS), for example, worked with its state Department of Environmental Protection to help the science faculty integrate local resources and environmental concerns into the science curriculum. Another NNPS school developed a community

TABLE 1.2.1 Examples of Community Partners

Community Partners	*Examples*
Businesses and Corporations	Local businesses, national corporations, and franchises
Universities and Educational Institutions	Colleges and universities; community colleges; vocational, trade, and technical schools; high schools; and other educational institutions
Health Care Organizations	Hospitals, health care centers, mental health facilities, health departments, health foundations, and associations
Government and Military Agencies	Fire departments, police departments, chambers of commerce, city councils, and other local and state government agencies and departments
National Service and Volunteer Organizations	Rotary Club, Lions Club, Kiwanis Club, VISTA, Concerned Black Men, Inc., Shriners, Boy Scouts, Girl Scouts, YMCA, United Way, AmeriCorps, Urban League, and other associations
Faith-Based Organizations	Churches, mosques, synagogues, and other religious organizations and charities
Senior Citizen Organizations	Nursing homes and senior volunteer and service organizations
Cultural and Recreational Institutions	Zoos, museums, libraries, and recreational centers
Media Organizations	Local newspapers, radio stations, cable networks including foreign language outlets, and other media
Sports Franchises and Associations	Major and minor league teams, NBA, NCAA, and other sports-related groups
Other Community Organizations	Fraternities, sororities, foundations, neighborhood associations, and political, alumni, and local service organizations
Community Individuals	Individual volunteers from the community surrounding the school

TABLE 1.2.2 Focuses of Partnership Activities and Examples of School-Community Partnership Activities

Student Centered	*Family Centered*	*School Centered*	*Community Centered*
Student awards, student incentives, scholarships, student trips, tutors, mentors, job shadowing, and other services and products for students	Parent workshops, family fun-nights, GED and other adult education classes, parent incentives and rewards, counseling, and other forms of assistance to parents	Equipment and materials, beautification and repair, teacher incentives and awards, funds for school events and programs, office and classroom assistance, and other school improvements	Community beautification, student exhibits and performances, charity, and other outreach

Adapted from Sanders, M. G. (2001). A study of the role of "community" in comprehensive school, family, and community partnership programs. *The Elementary School Journal, 102*(1), 19–34.

resource handbook for its families describing available services and contacts. A third NNPS school partnered with a local library to hold a community art exhibit of students' work, and another school partnered with local hospitals, dentists, nurses, and dieticians to develop a low-cost health care site to provide preventive and maintenance health care for students, families, and community members. These and other reported activities show how important community partnerships can be for students, schools, families, and communities (Sanders, 2005).

Outcomes of School-Community Partnerships

Community partnership activities can lead to measurable outcomes for students and schools (Sanders & Campbell, 2007). Mentoring programs have been found to have significant and positive effects on students' grades, school attendance, and exposure to career opportunities (McPartland & Nettles, 1991; Yonezawa, Thornton, & Stringfield, 1998). Afterschool programs have had measurable effects on students' achievement (Fashola & Cooper, 1999; Gardner et al., 2001). School-community collaborations focused on academic subjects have been shown to enhance students' attitudes toward these subjects, as well as the attitudes of teachers and parents (Beyerbach, Weber, Swift, & Gooding, 1996). Nettles (1991b) also reported positive effects of school-community collaborations with an instructional component on students' grades, attendance, and school persistence.

Documented benefits of school-linked service integration initiatives include behavioral and academic gains for students who receive intensive services (Newman, 1995; Wagner, 1995). Researchers have also reported results of improved student attendance, immunization rates, and student behavior at schools providing coordinated services (Amato, 1996). Finally, partnerships with businesses and other community organizations have provided schools with needed equipment, materials, and technical assistance and support for student instruction (Longoria, 1998; Mickelson, 1999; Sanders & Harvey, 2002). School-community partnerships, then, are an important element in schools' programs of improvement and reform and an important part of a comprehensive program of school, family, and community partnerships.

What Schools Can Do to Promote Community Involvement

Case study research identified four factors that support a school's ability to develop and maintain meaningful community partnerships (Sanders & Harvey, 2002). These factors are (a) high commitment to learning, (b) principal support for community involvement, (c) a welcoming school climate, and (d) two-way communication with potential community partners about their level and kind of involvement.

High Commitment to Learning

Interviews with community partners representing faith-based organizations, nonprofit foundations, health care organizations, businesses, educational institutions, and senior citizen organizations revealed a common desire to support students' academic achievement. Community partners wanted to be a part of an effective school that was visibly focused on students' learning and to engage in activities that had demonstrable effects on student outcomes. Community partners identified schools that were well organized, student centered, family friendly, and academically rigorous as the most desirable partners for collaboration.

Principal Support for Community Involvement

Community partners also stated that a principal's support for community involvement was critical for successful collaboration. A school principal who not only allowed but also created opportunities for community involvement was viewed as necessary, if not sufficient, for effective collaboration. Indeed, principal support largely explained the community partners' continued engagement in the case study school. One community partner stated, "I don't want to pinpoint any schools, but I've gone into some and have been totally turned off by the administration. If I'm turned off, what's the interest in helping you?"

A Welcoming School Climate

Similarly, community partners expressed the importance of a school that is receptive to and appreciative of community involvement. Community partners stated that being greeted warmly at the school by staff, faculty, and students strengthened their commitment to the partnership and increased the enjoyment of their involvement. Although most community partners in the study agreed that formal acknowledgment was not necessary, they valued the school's expressions of gratitude. Several community partners reported that they received thank-you letters and notes from students, were thanked for their assistance over the intercom system, were stopped on the street by students and their parents and thanked for their service, were acknowledged in the school newsletter, and received certificates of appreciation at the school's annual awards ceremony.

Two-Way Communication

Community partners and school administrators interviewed for the case study also emphasized the importance of honest, two-way communication between schools and potential community partners so that each party is fully aware of the intent and expectations of the other. The school principal stated that initial honest and "up-front" conversations prevented both parties from "wasting each other's time." She used a simple measure to determine if a community partnership was "right" for the school. Her measure was whether the partnership would be positive for students.

The four factors that promote community partnerships were linked to the principal's actions as school leader. She created fertile ground in which school-community partnerships flourished by maintaining a school environment where teachers and parents focus on students' academic success, modeling for faculty and staff a genuine openness to community involvement and establishing an expectation for partnerships, actively networking with individuals in the community to inform them of her school's needs and goals, and supporting others in developing leadership in the area of family and community involvement.

Factors That Improve School-Community Partnerships

In theory, then, community involvement in schools is an opportunity for a more democratic and participatory approach to school functioning that can revitalize communities, enhance students' achievement and wellbeing, assist families, and build stronger schools. In reality, however, community involvement is too often a reminder of the difficulty of implementing inclusive, collaborative strategies for school improvement. Evaluative studies of different forms of school-community collaboration underscore key challenges that, if addressed, may help to move the reality of community involvement in schools closer to theory (Sanders, 2001, 2005; Sanders & Lewis, 2005).

Professional Preparation

One issue that is highlighted in the community involvement literature is the importance of professional preparation for partnerships. Such preparation is especially important for educators at the state, district, and school levels who, arguably, should be in the forefront of educational improvement.

Ideally, professional preparation for collaboration would begin during the preservice stage of teacher and administrator training. It should include structured opportunities for future educators to develop the skills and capacity to work collaboratively with other educators and community service providers, as well as with adults in students' families and communities. Partnerships should be a theme throughout educators' professional training so that they enter schools, classrooms, offices, and departments of education with a clear understanding of the rewards and benefits of collaboration and a working knowledge of strategies for successful partnerships. Collaboration also should be an ongoing theme in the inservice professional development of educators so that the day-to-day reality of teaching and managing schools and district and state departments and offices does not cloud educators' views of themselves as partners in the development of children and youth.

Schools that have successfully built a sense of community within their walls—that is, schools that are collaborative, communicative, and inclusive—appear to have the greatest success in developing strong connections with the community outside their walls (Crowson & Boyd, 1993; Merz & Furman, 1997; Sanders & Harvey, 2002). This is no coincidence. When the capacity to collaborate becomes a part of educators' professional identity and knowledge base, community involvement becomes "business as usual" (Stroble & Luka, 1999). In complex school-community collaborations, challenges around turf, funding, roles, and responsibilities will surely arise (Crowson & Boyd, 1993; Dryfoos & Maguire, 2002; Epstein, 1995; Jehl & Kirst, 1992; Mawhinney, 1994). However, educators who have been prepared to collaborate will have the resources and skills to minimize and resolve these challenges (Epstein, 2001; Welch, 1998).

Partnership Selection

Professional development also will assist educators in selecting appropriate community partners and partnership opportunities. There are many community partners and opportunities available to schools. School districts and state departments of education also have choices of community partnership opportunities. The selection of partners should be based on shared goals and a common commitment to the basic tenets of successful collaboration—open communication, joint decision making, and respect for all stakeholders. Therefore, before a partnership begins, representatives from the partnering groups or organizations should meet to discuss the goals of the potential connection and how their work together will be organized.

When selecting community partners and partnership opportunities, educators also should consider the intensity and duration of collaborations. Community involvement in schools can range from very simple, short-term connections to very complex, long-term arrangements. For example, a school, a local health care agency, and community leaders may partner to hold a community health fair on the school grounds. This short-term partnership would require only basic collaborative skills, knowledge, and expertise. These same partners, however, may collaborate to open a school-based preventative health care clinic for students, families, and community members. This complex, long-term partnership would require more planning time to address issues related to funding, operational hours, program development and services, building security and maintenance, and other responsibilities and issues. Consequently, it also would require more sophisticated organizational processes and structures to ensure its successful implementation.

A school with little experience in community collaboration might elect to engage in some simple connections before venturing into more complex collaborations such as school-linked service integration initiatives. This purposeful, measured approach to the selection of community partners and community partnership opportunities would provide educators the necessary time to hone their collaborative skills, identify partnerships that are most important for achieving their schools' goals, and reflect on factors that influence their ability to successfully work with community partners.

Partnership Reflection and Evaluation

Finally, the literature on community involvement in schools highlights the importance of reflection and evaluation. Because school-community collaboration is a process and not an event, it is important that partners take the time to reflect on and evaluate the quality of their interactions and the implementation of their partnership activities. This exercise will assist in the refinement of collaborative efforts and the enhancement of collaborative skills. To engage in reflective action, partners need time to meet. Time is an increasingly rare commodity, especially among professional educators in schools. The challenge of finding time for professional educators to engage fully in collaborative efforts with the community is perhaps greatest in resource-poor urban schools that stand to benefit most from well-planned community partnerships.

This challenge has been successfully met in many schools (Sanders, 2005). One factor that is crucial to schools' planning and evaluation of partnerships is principal leadership. Many studies of community involvement cite the importance of effective principal leadership for successful school-community collaboration. An effective school leader is one who supports the faculty and staff in developing their professional skills as collaborators. This requires that the principal models such behavior, rewards such behavior, and provides teachers with the necessary time to plan partnerships and engage in collaborative action and evaluation (Sanders & Harvey, 2002).

Research and practice clearly show that community involvement in schools can benefit students, schools, families, and communities. The success of such involvement requires that partners have collaborative skills, common goals, structures for inclusive decision making, and time for reflection and evaluation. For all its promise, community involvement is not a panacea for the ills of many of today's schools. It cannot replace sound educational policies, adequate funding, excellent teaching, and effective partnerships with families. It can, however, enhance the effect that these elements have on schools and on students. When properly executed, community involvement in schools can be the little extra that makes the big difference.

References

Amato, C. (1996). Freedom Elementary School and its community: An approach to school-linked service integration. *Remedial and Special Education, 17*(5), 303–309.

Benson, P. (1997). *All kids are our kids: What communities must do to raise caring and responsible children and adolescents.* San Francisco: Jossey-Bass.

Beyerbach, B. A., Weber, S., Swift, J. N., & Gooding, C. T. (1996). A school/business/universitypartnership for professional development. *School Community Journal, 6*(1), 101–112.

Crowson, R. L., & Boyd, W. (1993). Coordinated services for children: Designing arks for storms and seas unknown. *American Journal of Education, 101,* 140–179.

Decker, L., Decker, V., & Brown, P. (2007). *Diverse partnerships for student success: Strategies and tools to help school leaders.* Lanham, MD: Rowman & Littlefield.

Dryfoos, J. (1998). The rise of the full-service community school. *High School Magazine, 6*(2), 38–42.

Dryfoos, J., & Maguire, S. (2002). *Inside full-service community schools.* Thousand Oaks, CA: Corwin Press.

Epstein, J. L. (1987). Toward a theory of family-school connections: Teacher practices and parent involvement. In K. Hurrelmann, F. Kaufmann, & F. Losel (Eds.), *Social intervention: Potential and constraints* (pp. 121–136). New York: DeGruyter.

Epstein, J. L. (1995). School/family/community partnerships: Caring for the children we share. *Phi Delta Kappan, 76*(9), 701–712.

Epstein, J. L. (2001). *School, family, and community partnerships: Preparing educators and improving schools.* Boulder, CO: Westview Press.

Fashola, O., & Cooper, R. (1999). Developing the academic talents of African-American students during the non-school hours: Four exemplary programs. *The Journal of Negro Education, 68*(2), 130–137.

Gardner, R. III, Cartledge, G., Seidl, B., Woolsey, M., Schley, & G., Utley, C. (2001). Mt. Olivet after-school program: Peer-mediated interventions for at-risk students. *Remedial and Special Education, 22* 22–23.

Heath, S. B., & McLaughlin, M. W. (1987, April). A child resource policy: Moving beyond dependence on school and family. *Phi Delta Kappan, 68,* 576–580.

Jehl, J., & Kirst, M. (1992). Getting ready to provide school-linked services: What schools must do. *Future of Children, 2,* 95–106.

Longoria, T., Jr. (1998). School politics in Houston: The impact of business involvement. In C. Stone (Ed.), *Changing urban education* (pp. 184–198). Lawrence: University Press of Kansas.

Mawhinney, H. B. (1994). The policy and practice of community enrichment of schools. *Proceedings of the Education and Community Conference, Department of Educational Administration.* Toronto: Ontario Institute for Studies in Educational Administration.

McPartland, J. M., & Nettles, S. M. (1991). Using community adults as advocates or mentors for at-risk middle school students: A two-year evaluation of project RAISE. *American Journal of Education, 99,* 568–586.

Merz, C., & Furman, G. (1997). *Community and schools: Promise and paradox.* New York: Teachers College Press.

Mickelson, R. (1999). International business machinations: A case study of corporate involvement in local educational reform. *Teachers College Record, 100*(3), 476–512.

Nettles, S. M. (1991a). Community contributions to school outcomes of African-American students. *Education and Urban Society, 24*(1), 132–147.

Nettles, S. M. (1991b). Community involvement and disadvantaged students: A review. *Review of Educational Research, 61*(3), 379–406.

Newman, L. (1995, April). *School-agency-community partnerships: What is the early impact on students school performance?* Paper presented at the annual meeting of the American Educational Research Association, San Francisco, CA.

Sanders, M. G. (2001). The role of "community" in comprehensive school, family, and community partnership programs. *The Elementary School Journal, 102*(1), 19–34.

Sanders, M. G. (2005). *Building school-community partnerships: Collaboration for student success.* Thousand Oaks, CA: Corwin Press.

Sanders, M., & Campbell, T. (2007). Securing the ties that bind: Community involvement and the educational success of African American children and youth. In J. Jackson (Ed.), *Strengthening the African American educational pipeline* (pp. 141–164). Albany: State University of New York Press.

Sanders, M. G., & Harvey, A. (2002). Beyond the school walls: A case study of principal leadership for school-community collaboration. *Teachers College Record, 104*(7), 1345–1368.

Sanders, M. G., & Lewis, K. (2005). Building bridges toward excellence: Community involvement in high schools. *High School Journal, 88*(3): 1–9.

Shore, R. (1994). *Moving the ladder: Toward a new community vision.* Aspen, CO: Aspen Institute.

Stroble, B., & Luka, H. (1999). It's my life, now: The impact of professional development school partnerships on university and school administrators. *Peabody Journal of Education, 74*(3–4), 123–135.

Toffler, A., & Toffler, H. (1995). Getting set for the coming millennium. *Futurist, 29*(2), 10–15.

Wagner, M. (1995). What is the evidence of effectiveness of school-linked services? [Electronic edition] *The Evaluation Exchange: Emerging Strategies in Evaluating Child and Family Services, 1*(2). Retrieved March 3, 2008 from http://www.hfrp.org/evaluation/the-evaluation-exchange/issue-archive/evaluating-school-linked-services

Warren, M. (2005). Communities and schools: A new view of urban education reform. *Harvard Educational Review, 75*(2), 133–175.

Welch, M. (1998). Collaboration: Staying on the bandwagon. *Journal of Teacher Education, 49*(1), 26–37.

Yonezawa, S., Thornton, T., & Stringfield, S. (1998). *Dunbar-Hopkins Health Partnership Phase II evaluation: Preliminary report—year one.* Baltimore: Center for Social Organization of Schools.

1.3 Improving Student Outcomes With School, Family, and Community Partnerships: A Research Review

Steven B. Sheldon

The academic success of students—often measured by student grades and achievement test performance—depends on several school factors, including exposure to high-quality teaching, a safe and well-maintained school facility, and dedicated and caring teachers. Equally important are out-of-school influences such as family involvement and the presence of home environments that support academic achievement. Because of these multiple influences, schools need to attend to school, family, and community contexts and develop programs and practices that enable parents and community partners to help students reach school goals for high achievement and school success.

High-quality and high-performing schools have strong partnerships with their students' families and communities. This is true for all schools, including "high-performing, high-poverty schools," where students are learning and achieving at high levels, despite what might be expected, given family and neighborhood economic disadvantages (Chrispeels, 1996; Hoffman, 1991; Purkey & Smith, 1983; Teddlie & Reynolds, 2000).

Research also shows that successful students have strong academic support and involvement from family members. Evidence of the powerful effect family life and environment have on academic success has existed for many decades and is continually reaffirmed in research on the influence of school, family, and community partnerships on student outcomes (Epstein & Sheldon, 2006; Fan & Chen, 2001; Henderson & Berla, 1994; Henderson & Mapp, 2002; Jeynes, 2003, 2005; Jordan, Orozco, & Averett, 2001; Wang, Haertel, & Walberg, 1993). With this evidence, it is near-universally accepted that students need family and/or community members who support and encourage their academic development in order to excel in school.

Despite the evidence of the importance of school, family, and community partnerships for students' academic success, this topic rarely receives adequate attention from school, district, and state education leaders. With budget deficits and increasing demands for accountability, educational leaders often are forced to make difficult decisions about how to spend limited resources. Understandably, educational leaders are demanding more and better research demonstrating the connections of parent involvement with student outcomes to help them decide whether and how to allocate financial resources and personnel to this component of school improvement.

This article provides an overview of research on the effects of family and community involvement on student outcomes, including achievement and other academic and nonacademic outcomes. The information should help educators understand the value of goal-oriented partnership programs and encourage the development of systematic approaches to help more students achieve and excel in school.

Effects of Parent Involvement

Helping family members strengthen their involvement in their children's education is an important and attainable goal for educators. Studies indicate that schools with strong family and community involvement programs tend to have higher levels of parent involvement (Epstein & Dauber, 1991; Sheldon, 2005; Sheldon & Van Voorhis, 2004). Many studies show that educators can foster the kinds of support and encouragement from home that students need to be more successful in school.

Until recently, studies of family involvement tended not to differentiate between the effects of particular types of involvement on distinct student outcomes. Early research conducted analyses of the connections of general measures of parent involvement with student report card grades and achievement test scores (Ho & Willms, 1996; Keith et al., 1998; Muller, 1993). These studies were important in establishing a base of research about the importance of parent involvement, overall.

More recently, researchers have begun studying how different types of involvement relate to specific student outcomes. The evolution in research on school, family, and community partnerships is important for increasing knowledge on how different types of involvement may affect children's learning and development (Jeynes, 2003; Sheldon, Epstein, & Galindo, under review; Shumow & Miller, 2001); and see Chapter 1.1 in this *Handbook.* It is becoming increasingly clear that educators need to consider which types of involvement they want to increase in order to attain specific school goals and desired student outcomes.

Academic Outcomes

Literacy

Research provides overwhelming evidence of the connections between literacy resources at home and students' literacy development. A report from the U.S. Department of Education (Donahue, Finnegan, Lutkus, Allen, & Campbell, 2001) confirms the historic finding that children from homes with more books and more reading by parents perform higher on reading achievement tests than do children from less reading-rich environments. Because so much research examines how family involvement affects children's literacy development, this section offers a brief overview, organized by children's age and grade level.[1]

Family Involvement in the Preschool Years

Family influences on literacy and reading achievement begin before children enter formal schooling, with a home "environment for literacy" from infancy on (Edwards, Pleasants, & Franklin, 1999; Leichter, 1984; Taylor, 1983; Taylor & Dorsey-Gaines, 1988). Many studies indicate that children's early literacy experiences, such as being encouraged to talk and sing, reading books with an adult, and writing

[1] For a full review of the impact of family and community involvement on students' reading and literacy skills, see Sheldon and Epstein (2005b).

alphabet letters are associated with students' skills in school and higher scores on tests in vocabulary, print knowledge, and letter-sounds.

Children between three and five years old from low-, middle-, and upper-income families are exposed to a variety of literacy experiences at home, such as being read to, seeing others reading, and having instruction in letter naming and letter writing (Heibert, 1980; Teale, 1986). Although stories, signs, and labels help children learn that words have a communicative function, other experiences provide children with different understandings of word meanings and language. Parents' emphases on print and literacy activities, therefore, may affect children's early language, reading, and writing knowledge and skills (Heath, 1983; Purcell-Gates, 1996).

Most preschools conduct reading and language experiences to help all students become "ready" for school, and most preschools try to involve families with children in literacy activities. Two experimental studies conducted with families of preschool children in Early Head Start (a federal program for infants and toddlers in families with very low income) and Project EASE (Early Access to Success in Education) in Minnesota found that parents could be guided to work with their children on literacy skills and book-related activities. Both interventions found that children in the treatment groups improved their prereading language skills compared to students in the control groups (Mathematica, 2001). The programs increased parents' reading stories to children, reading at bedtime, and other reading and language-related activities. A study of the HIPPY (Home Instruction Program of Preschool Youngsters) intervention to increase mothers' reading aloud and working with children on literacy skills came to the same conclusion (A. Baker, Piotrkowski, & Brooks-Gunn, 1998).

Storybook Reading. Parent-child storybook reading, commonly encouraged by teachers in the younger grades, is one of the most studied types of parent involvement. In their review of 30 years of research on the impact of reading to preschool students, Scarborough and Dobrich (1994) concluded that there is a modest impact of shared storybook reading on students' literacy development, due mainly to the *quality* of that interaction.

Educators often conduct training workshops to help parents improve the quality of their storybook reading with young children. In a study of the effects of parent participation in reading workshops, Jordan, Snow, and Porche (2000) compared the early literacy skills of about 250 kindergarten students whose parents received training with the skills of students whose parents did not receive such training. Parents were taught ways to increase the frequency and quality of parent-child verbal interactions and to conduct structured activities provided by the child's teacher. Students whose parents were in the training group showed significantly greater improvement on early literacy tests of vocabulary, comprehension, and story sequencing, and sound awareness.

Interventions to assist parents with low incomes and limited formal schooling have demonstrated similar results. Lonigan and Whitehurst (1998) compared the effects of a shared-reading intervention on preschool children's early literacy skills. Students were randomly assigned to four groups: (1) teachers reading to a small group of children, (2) parents reading to their children at home, (3) combined teachers and parents reading to children, and (4) a control group of children who received no special intervention. In this study, students who experienced shared reading with a parent, small-group reading with a teacher, or a combination of the two performed better on reading assessments than did students' with no shared reading experiences. In addition, participation in shared reading activities with parents (either solely or in combination with teachers' use of small-group dialogic reading) was associated with higher levels of vocabulary and oral language skills, compared to participation in reading activities only with teachers.

The results of studies of parent training workshops show that parents who are assisted to become more effectively involved in reading-related activities conduct more and better interactions about reading with their children and that the students improve their reading and literacy skills. In particular, Lonigan and Whitehurst's study provides strong evidence that parents with low incomes and less formal education, who may have weaker reading skills than more economically advantaged parents, can effectively support their children's reading and education.

Family Involvement in the Primary Grades

Children's entry to formal schooling marks an important transition in learning and development. The transition to elementary school also has important consequences for parents' roles in their children's literacy development. Purcell-Gates (1996), for example, found that in some low-income families, parent involvement in reading *increased* after their children began formal schooling. Although schools and teachers are significant influences on children's learning to read in the elementary grades, parents remain influential in children's reading and literacy development.

Storybook Reading. Storybook reading continues to be an important activity for children after they enter the primary grades. Studies suggest there are long-term, multifaceted effects of parent-child storybook reading on children's language development (Sénéchal & LeFevre, 2002; Sénéchal, LeFevre, Thomas, & Daley, 1998). In one study, first grade children whose parents read more storybooks to them in the preschool years (*informal* literacy activities) scored higher on *receptive* language skills (e.g., vocabulary and listening comprehension). First grade children whose parents more often used books to teach letters and words (*formal* literacy activities) scored higher on *emergent* literacy skills (e.g., alphabet knowledge, decoding, and invented spelling). These studies showed that, over time, emergent literacy skills predicted children's reading achievement in first grade, whereas receptive language skills predicted reading achievement in the third grade.

The complex results are consistent with other studies indicating that parental involvement with children on varied reading-related activities helps students develop a number of literacy skills that are important for later reading achievement. Moreover, the findings suggest that schools can guide parents to enjoy a variety of literacy activities with their young children, including reading aloud with children, listening to stories, and learning letters and words. These readiness activities will prepare students to learn to read in school.

Literacy activities experienced at home by children from middle- and upper-income families may more closely match the school culture than do activities experienced by students from low-income families (Cairney & Rouge, 1997; Heath, 1983). Based on research on literacy classroom practices with low-income children, McCarthey (1999) suggested that teachers establish and maintain frequent and reciprocal communications with families. She argued that by developing a better understanding of children's families and by helping them understand and use reading resources with their children, teachers will increase home-school congruence and continuity for all students.

Family and Community Connections With Students on Literacy. In addition to workshops for parents, other interventions designed to help teachers incorporate families in their classrooms and with students' reading experiences have proven effective with economically and culturally diverse families. Paratore, Hindin, Krol-Sinclair, and Duran (1999) trained low-income parents who had immigrated to the United States to observe and become involved in their elementary school children's literacy activities at home. They were shown how to construct portfolios of their children's reading-related projects at home to bring to parent-teacher conferences. In addition, the researchers trained teachers to understand family literacy, how to collaborate with families, and how to use a family literacy portfolio to communicate with their students' parents. Her analyses showed that, during conferences with their children's teachers, parents who developed literacy portfolios with their children at home talked more than parents who had not developed such portfolios and provided teachers with more information about their children's literacy activities at home.

Reading Volunteers. Elementary schools often bring parent or community volunteers in to help children improve their literacy skills. Wasik (1998) reviewed empirical research on adult volunteer programs focused on helping students learn to read and found that most of these programs used community members rather than parents as volunteer reading tutors. She identified four common characteristics of these programs: a coordinator with knowledge about reading and reading instruction; structured activities for volunteer tutors to use with students; training for volunteer tutors; and, unexpectedly, poor coordination between the tutoring activities and the classroom curriculum. Wasik concluded that few programs evaluated the effects of the volunteer tutors on students' reading achievement but that such programs had potential for helping students improve their reading skills.

Building on Wasik's review, Baker, Gersten, and Keating (2000) evaluated longitudinal effects on students of a low-cost community volunteer program. After randomly assigning first grade students to either two years of one-on-one tutoring or to a control group, the researchers compared differences in students' reading achievement at the end of the first and second grades. At the end of the second grade, students in the tutoring program had significantly higher oral reading and word comprehension skills and had improved their reading skills more than did peers who were not in the tutoring program. Similarly, Fitzgerald (2001) found that use of college students as volunteer reading tutors had the potential to improve elementary school students' reading outcomes. These studies suggest that community involvement strategies, such as the use of reading tutors, can have a positive impact on students' reading achievement.

Upper Elementary and Middle Grades

Most research on parent involvement and students' reading and literacy skills has been conducted with families of young children in preschool and the primary grades. After the third grade, parents report less involvement in their children's education (Dauber & Epstein, 1993; Eccles & Harold, 1996), and educators report fewer efforts to include parents in their children's schooling (Chen, 2001; Donahue et al. 2001; Epstein & Dauber, 1991). Studies are accumulating that indicate family and community involvement has a positive influence on student achievement and other measures of success through high school (Catsambis, 2001; Simon, 2001).The success or failure of interventions to involve families with their children in reading, language arts, and other literacy skills rests on the *design* and *quality of implementation* of the parent involvement programs, and their connections to students' classwork and assessments. Most intervention studies report increases in the nature and extent of parents' involvement, but not all studies measured effects on student achievement over time.

One study provides some information about these effects. A study of third and fifth grade students from mainly African-American families with low incomes in inner-city schools found that, controlling for prior reading achievement, students in classrooms with teachers who more frequently involved families in learning activities at home had higher gains in reading achievement from one year to the next than did students in other teachers' classrooms (Epstein, 1991). The data did not identify the specific practices teachers used to involve parents in children's reading, but follow-up interviews with teachers, parents, and administrators in the schools indicated that most involvement activities focused on reading and reading-related activities.

Other intervention studies reinforce the importance of parental involvement in reading activities to influence students' reading skills. Shaver and Walls (1998) found that workshops for parents of students from second through eighth grade promoted involvement of parents with children by using learning packets for reading at home. In addition, students increased their reading comprehension skills and total reading scores.

Also, a study of 71 Title I schools in 18 school districts found that outreach to parents on several types of involvement, including providing parents with materials on how to help students at home, improved reading achievement over time as students moved from third to fifth grade (Westat and Policy Studies Associates, 2001). Test scores were 50 percent higher in reading for students whose teachers reported high levels of parent outreach in the early grades.

Parent Involvement and Adolescents' School Achievement

Family and community involvement is largely absent from discussions about adolescent literacy and how to teach reading to middle and high school students. Older students with weak reading skills often are given remedial instruction in vocabulary, comprehension, and writing skills, but little attention is given to the roles that family and community reinforcement, interaction, and support might play in encouraging students to put forth effort to master reading competencies and to ultimate success (Greenleaf, Schoenbach, Cziko, & Mueller, 2001). It still is rare for secondary schools to have well-designed interventions to assist all families to interact with their teens on homework or coursework in specific subjects (Sanders & Epstein, 2000).

Using a nationally representative sample of students in Grades 8, 10, and 12, several researchers found that after controlling for prior levels of achievement, students scored higher on reading achievement tests and/or earned higher grades in English if their parents had discussions with them about school and about their future plans, checked their homework, and maintained high educational expectations (Desimone, 1999; Ho & Willms, 1996; Lee & Croninger, 1994; Simon, 2004). These studies confirmed that parents' interest in and support for reading (and other school subjects) continue to play an important role in adolescents' academic development through high school.

Other studies also indicate that high schools' communications with families are associated with higher levels of students' reading achievement. After statistically controlling for prior achievement, researchers found that schools that communicated more often with students' families had students who gained more on their reading achievement tests than did schools that did not maintain strong communication practices (Parcel & Dufur, 2001). The results suggested that if schools established frequent, positive, and purposeful communications, more parents would be able to provide their teens with support for learning that was more closely coordinated with teachers' goals and that would translate into improved student learning. Clear and helpful communications may be essential in secondary schools, where parents often feel less confident about their abilities to help adolescents with more advanced curricular activities.

One intervention, Teachers Involve Parents in Schoolwork (TIPS), was designed to increase family involvement with students on language arts homework in the middle grades (Epstein, Salinas, & Van Voorhis, 2001; also see Chapter 8 on TIPS). A study of TIPS–Language Arts included 683 students in Grades 6 and 8 in two central city middle schools where most students were African American and over 70 percent of the students qualified for free- or reduced-price lunch (Epstein, Simon, & Salinas, 1997). The students shared writing prompts, ideas, and drafts of stories or essays, and they conducted "family surveys" to discuss their family partners' experiences that related to their own. Analyses statistically controlled for parent education, student grade level, attendance, fall report card grades, and fall writing sample scores to identify the effects of TIPS interactive homework on students' writing skills in the winter and spring. Students who completed more TIPS homework assignments had higher language arts report card grades. When parents participated, students improved their writing scores from fall to winter and from winter to spring, regardless of their initial abilities.

Mathematics

Like reading, math is a core school subject at all grade levels. This subject presents some unique challenges associated with school, family, and community partnerships. The progressively difficult nature of mathematics curricula and many parents' fears or lack of confidence about helping with math make it especially important for schools to implement strong partnership programs and activities related to mathematics from preschool on.

There are relatively few studies of school, family, and community partnerships in math. In their review of research on the effects of different types of math interventions, Baker, Gersten, and Lee (2002) found that students having difficulties in mathematics benefited most when teachers had data on student performance, used peers as tutors, provided clear and specific feedback to students about their errors, and provided explicit instruction as they were teaching math concepts and procedures. They noted that few programs sought to connect or communicate with students' families, and when they did, the practices were "add ons" to the program. The lack of attention to family involvement in math runs counter to research findings suggesting a need for more systematic interventions designed to involve families and community members to help students improve their math skills and achievements.

Mathematics and Family Involvement

School-family partnerships are essential, because parents socialize their children in ways that affect their children's self-perceptions of ability and achievement in math.

In fact, children's self-concepts of math ability may be were more closely related to their parents' perceptions of the child's ability than to the actual grades the students earned (Frome & Eccles, 1998; Parsons, Adler, & Kaczala, 1982). These complex, psychological effects are important, because other evidence indicates that children's self-perceptions shape their later career decisions (Bleeker & Jacobs, 2004). In addition to helping teachers improve students' self-perceptions of their math abilities, schools may need to help parents increase their understanding of and expectations for students' math achievement and progress.

Other studies show that parental involvement directly influences children's math achievement. Many studies have shown that, across racial and ethnic groups and across school levels, students performed better and continued further in mathematics if they participated in parent-child discussions about school and if their parents were active volunteers at the school or members of the PTA or PTO (Desimone, 1999; Ma, 1999; Valadez, 2002). Also, higher parental expectations for their children predicted higher math achievement (Hong & Ho, 2005; Yan & Lin, 2005). Catsambis and Beveridge (2001) extend these findings by showing that, at the high school level, positive neighborhood characteristics also contribute to students' math achievement. On a variety of math outcomes, then, studies demonstrate that families and communities influence students' math achievement.

There is ample evidence indicating that many, if not most, families need help structuring their interactions with their child about math. Lerner and Shumow (1997), for example, found that parents believed in the value of progressive instructional strategies in math (e.g., having children talk about their math work and learn from mistakes) but provided help that was directive and that gave students few opportunities to discover solutions to math problems on their own. Similarly, Hyde and colleagues (Hyde, Else-Quest, Alibali, Knuth, & Romberg, 2006) found significant variation in mothers' abilities to help their children with math homework. In both cases, the researchers concluded that school-family partnerships are needed to help all families understand how to interact with their children on math homework in ways that provide children support and encouragement for learning math.

One effective strategy has been teachers' use of interactive homework that requires children to discuss work and ideas with a family partner. Studying TIPS–Math in the middle grades, Balli, Demo, and Wedman (1998) found that students receiving interactive homework reported more parent involvement in math. Also, Sheldon and Epstein (2005a) found that schools assigning interactive homework in math reported greater improvement in the percentage of students scoring at or above proficient on standardized math tests than did schools that did not assign this type of homework.

The strongest evidence to support assigning interactive homework in math in the elementary grades is reported by Van Voorhis (under review), who conducted a quasi-experimental design that compared the math achievement of students in classrooms where teachers assigned TIPS interactive math homework (treatment) to those who were in classrooms where the teacher did not incorporate this type of homework into the curriculum (control). She found that students who were assigned TIPS interactive math homework reported greater family involvement in math, had more positive attitudes about math homework, and had higher levels of achievement compared to students in the control group. This study's strong research design suggests that teachers can help all families support student learning in math without making parents think that they have to "teach" math skills. This kind of parental support and conversations about math at home may translate into positive math attitudes and higher levels of student math achievement.

Other research suggests that schools can improve their students' math achievement by developing a school climate that is welcoming and that has the support of parents, families, and the community. School climate—the organizational characteristics that capture the tone or atmosphere of a school—has been associated with principals' leadership styles, sense of community, expectations for students, an ethos of caring, and a variety of student outcomes (National Research Council, 2003).

Studies show that schools that are welcoming to parents and community partners have more positive school climates (Desimone, Finn-Stevenson, & Henrich, 2000; Griffith, 1998; Haynes, Comer, & Hamilton-Lee, 1989). Also, schools with stronger partnership climates report higher levels of achievement on standardized math tests after controlling for prior levels of math achievement and poverty (Sheldon, Epstein, & Galindo, under review).

Taken together, there is a large body of evidence demonstrating that the home environment influences students' math attitudes, abilities, and achievement. The findings suggest that schools should implement strategies to help families frame their messages and interactions with children about math. These practices should result in more family involvement and improved student attitudes and performance in math.

Science

Compared to studies of reading and mathematics, there are fewer studies of the effects of school, family, and community partnerships on science achievement. Given the current interest in student achievement on science tests, it is important to understand the results of the few studies of family and community involvement effects on students' science attitudes and skills.

One study using national data from students in Grades 4, 8, and 12 found that students from low-income families performed less well in science than their more affluent peers (Von Secker, 2004). This study showed that parent education and measures of the home environment helped compensate for low science achievement associated with lower family income and minority status. That is, low-income and minority students had higher science scores if their parents had more formal education and encouraged their education at home. Moreover, Von Secker found that without these positive family resources, the achievement gap between students from low-income and more affluent families widened from Grades 4 through 12. The study suggests that family involvement may be especially important for students who are most at risk of experiencing failure in science.

As with math, family and community involvement may affect students' attitudes about science and, in turn, students' achievement. George and Kaplan (1998) found that parents play an important role in developing children's science attitudes by engaging in science activities at home and by taking their children to libraries and museums. It is important to understand how families can help students develop positive attitudes toward science, as this may help all students—including those from low-income households—increase achievement in science and other subjects.

In one of the strongest studies of the effects of teachers' efforts to increase parent-child interactions around science, Van Voorhis (2003) used a quasi-experimental design to test the effects of TIPS interactive science homework on parent involvement in science and students' science achievement. Families whose students received weekly interactive homework in science were significantly more involved with their children on science compared to families of students in the control group. The TIPS students also had higher grades in science than the other students. The findings suggest that schools can and should encourage more science-focused family involvement at home in order to increase students' completion of science homework, boost discussions about science at home, and increase students' success in science in the middle grades.

Nonacademic Outcomes

Transitions to New Schools

Evidence is accumulating that family support and guidance can help students successfully transition from one phase of education to the next (e.g., entering school or moving from one school to a new school). Research on the effects of school and family partnerships at times of educational transitions found that, controlling for prior achievement and family background, kindergarteners in schools that implemented activities designed to promote involvement and keep families informed had higher achievement than did students whose schools did not conduct this outreach (Schulting, Malone, & Dodge, 2005).

Others also have shown that students more successfully transition into middle school and high school when they have family members who more frequently discuss and monitor their schoolwork (Falbo, Lein, & Amador, 2001; Grolnick, Kurowski, Dunlap, & Hevey, 2000; Gutman & Midgley, 2000). These studies suggest that schools can help students manage educational transitions by encouraging family members to talk with and help their children navigate the new experiences and expectations that accompany these changes in education and development.

Attendance

Improving student attendance is an important goal for schools, because children who are at school have more opportunities to learn than those who are not. Meeting this goal, however, requires a holistic approach that addresses school and classroom factors, as well as factors related to school, family, and community partnerships. Although most schools have not collaborated systematically with families to reduce student absenteeism, many recognize home-school connections as an important strategy to increase student attendance. One approach, organizing comprehensive, schoolwide programs of school, family, and community partnership–and implementing them well—has been shown to help more students attend school more often (Sheldon, 2007).

In some cases, studies have identified parental behaviors related to better student attendance. These include monitoring students' whereabouts, parent-child discussions about school, volunteering at school, and PTA/PTO membership as important predictors of lower levels of truancy among students (Astone & McLanahan, 1991; Duckworth & DeJong, 1989; McNeal, 1999).

Other studies found that several specific family and community involvement practices that schools used were associated with student attendance, including communicating with families about student attendance, providing families with information about people to contact at school, conducting workshops on attendance, and providing afterschool programs for students (Epstein & Sheldon, 2002). That study suggested that student attendance should improve if schools take a comprehensive approach, including school-based activities that support good attendance, effective home-school connections, and a sustained focus on the goal of improving and maintaining student attendance. In a follow-up study, with a larger and more diverse sample, Sheldon and Epstein (2004) found that chronic absenteeism declined when schools implemented communication strategies to inform parents of their children's attendance and when schools conducted comprehensive partnership programs with a variety of family and community involvement activities.

The association between positive and frequent school-family communications and reduced absenteeism is consistent with other studies that found phone calls to parents of absent students were associated with improved student attendance (Helm & Burkett, 1989; Licht, Gard, & Guardino, 1991). Also, providing timely information to families about attendance helped improve attendance rates in high schools (Roderick et al., 1997). Keeping parents informed of their children's attendance at school allowed parents to monitor and supervise their children more effectively.

Behavior

Children's behavior, in school and out, is related to their home environment and family dynamics. Two decades ago, in their review of the literature, Snyder and Patterson (1987) concluded that neglectful and passive parenting styles, lax disciplinary approaches, poor parental monitoring, inadequate family problem-solving strategies, and high levels of conflict in the home all are predictive of delinquency among juveniles. They also found that associations between socioeconomic characteristics and delinquency are greatly reduced or disappear when these types of family interactions are statistically accounted for. More recently, studies indicate that family communication patterns and parental support of schooling were associated with lower levels of delinquency in white and minority secondary students (Davalos, Chavez, & Guardiola, 2005).

In addition to improving student behavior at school, implementing partnership practices focused on student behavior also may help improve academic achievement. Analyzing data from a large national database, Domina (2005) concluded that parental involvement activities prevented behavioral problems. The study showed that parents' homework help and volunteering had a more favorable effect on school behavior of students from low-income families than for students from high-income families.

Other studies also found that students with more parental involvement behaved better in school and that school behavior helped predict academic achievement over time (Beyers, Bates, Pettit, & Dodge, 2003; Hill et al., 2004). These studies, using advanced statistical methods and large datasets, identified an important pathway connecting family involvement to student outcomes via parents' positive effects on their children's behavior.

The connections of student behavior with family and community contexts have been understood for a long time. Many have argued that the social and cultural organization of neighborhoods shape the socialization processes of families and schools. Adolescents' exposure to violence in the community, for example, is associated with poor school attendance, low grades, and problem behavior in school (Bowen & Bowen, 1999; Bowen, Bowen, & Ware, 2002).

The impact of communities can be positive. School-community collaborations such as mentoring, safety patrols, and business partnerships may improve school programs and impact student achievement and attitudes toward school (McPartland & Nettles, 1991; Nettles, 1991; Sanders, 2005; Sanders & Harvey, 2002). The potential positive and negative effects of communities on students' achievement make school-community partnerships an essential component in any reforms whose goals include improving student behavior.

Practices to Reduce Behavioral Problems

Although many have suggested that school, family, and community resources could help reduce students' problem behaviors and improve learning in school (Adelman & Taylor, 1998; Epstein, 1995; Noguera, 1995; Taylor & Adelman, 2000), most interventions to improve student behavior have focused on what educators need to do to ensure a safe school environment. Parents have been given modest roles in helping improve student behavior, such as being asked to reinforce programs at the schools (Gottfredson et al. 1993).

There is some evidence that families and community partners can help schools become safer and more focused on student learning. A study of elementary school students found that school social workers who helped families and schools communicate with one another improved students' behavior and academic skills (Bowen, 1999). Others have shown that higher levels of family involvement (e.g., attending workshops, volunteering at the school, helping with learning at home, and being involved with school policy reviews and revisions) is associated with better behavior of middle and high school students (Ma, 2001; Simon, 2004).

Sheldon and Epstein (2002) found that schools that improved their programs of school, family, and community partnerships from one year to the next decreased the percentages of students sent to the principal, given detentions, and given in-school suspensions. Schools with more volunteering and parenting activities reported lower levels of disciplinary actions. Taken together, the findings reaffirm the importance of developing school, family, and community partnership programs with activities that will help students improve their behavior and reduce the number of disciplinary actions with students. Research is affecting practice. Many educators understand the connections of students' family life and school behavior. As they develop and improve their partnership programs, more schools are implementing family and community involvement activities that will help students improve their behavior and succeed at higher levels in school.

Conclusion

The studies summarized in this chapter show that effective programs of school, family, and community partnerships may affect a wide range of important student outcomes. We should not, however, expect too much from family and community involvement as an influence on students' achievement across the grades. Children's reading skills, for example, are most affected by high-quality instruction from skilled teachers (Snow, Burns, & Griffin, 1998). At the same time, we should not minimize the potential of family and community involvement for its "value added" to student outcomes, over and above the effects of good teaching.

Research has accumulated indicating that school practices to involve families make a difference in *whether* and *which* families become involved in their children's education and *how* they become involved. More important, if schools conduct well-designed partnership programs and activities, small effects will accumulate over time, producing sizable total effects of family involvement on student reading and literacy, math, science, and/or nonacademic outcomes related to school success.

Key to realizing these effects, however, is the willingness of schools and districts to implement high-quality partnership programs and activities. When schools set goals to help students improve reading, math, science, attendance, or behavior, there must be plans to implement family and community involvement activities that will help students attain these goals. Educators who are mindful of the potential inherent in involving family and community members, who plan and implement effective practices, and who monitor progress and meet challenges that occur will ultimately see more students experience greater success in school.

References

Adelman, H. S., & Taylor, L. (1998). Reframing mental health in schools and expanding school reform. *Educational Psychologist, 33,* 135–152.

Astone, N., & McLanahan, S. (1991). Family structure, parental practices and high school completion. *American Sociological Review, 56*(3), 309–320.

Baker, A. J. L., Piotrkowski, C. S., & Brooks-Gunn, J. (1998). Effects of the Home Instruction Program for Preschool Youngsters (HIPPY) on children's school performance at the end of the program and one year later. *Early Childhood Research Quarterly, 13,* 571–588.

Baker, S. Gersten, R., & Keating, T. (2000). When less may be more: A 2-year longitudinal evaluation of a volunteer tutoring program requiring minimal training. *Reading Research Quarterly, 35,* 494–519.

Baker, S., Gersten, R., & Lee, D. (2002). A synthesis of empirical research on teaching mathematics to low-achieving students. *Elementary School Journal, 103,* 51–73.

Balli, S. J., Demo, D. H., & Wedman, J. F. (1998). Family involvement with children's homework: An intervention in the middle grades. *Family Relations, 47,* 149–157.

Beyers, J. M., Bates, J. E., Pettit, G. S., & Dodge, K A. (2003). Neighborhood structure, parent processes, and the development of youths' externalizing behaviors: A multilevel analysis. *American Journal of Community Psychology, 31,* 35–53.

Bleeker, M. M., & Jacobs, J. E. (2004). Achievement in math and science: Do mothers' beliefs matter 12 years later? *Journal of Educational Psychology, 96,* 97–109.

Bowen, N. K. (1999). A role for school social workers in promoting student success through school-family partnerships. *Social Work in Education, 21,* 34–47.

Bowen, N. K. & Bowen, G. L. (1999). Effects of crime and violence in neighborhoods and schools on the school behavior and performance of adolescents. *Journal of Adolescent Research, 14,* 319–342.

Bowen, N. K., Bowen, G. L., & Ware, W. B. (2002) Neighborhood social disorganization, families, and the educational behavior of adolescents. *Journal of Adolescent Research, 17,* 468–490.

Cairney, T. H., & Rouge, J. (1997). *Community literacy practices and schooling: Towards effective support for students.* Sydney, Australia: Department of Employment, Education, Training and Youth Affairs.

Catsambis, S. (2001). Expanding knowledge of parental involvement in children's secondary education: Connections with high school seniors' academic success. *Social Psychology of Education, 5,* 149–177.

Catsambis, S., & Beveridge, A. A. (2001). Does neighborhood matter? Family, neighborhood, and school influences on eighth grade mathematics achievement. *Sociological Focus, 34,* 435–457.

Chen, X. (2001). *Efforts by public K-8 schools to involve parents in children's education: Do school and parent reports agree?* (NCES 2001–076). Washington, DC: National Center for Education Statistics.

Chrispeels, J. (1996). Effective schools and home-school-community partnership roles: A framework for parent involvement. *School Effectiveness and School Improvement, 7,* 297–322.

Dauber, S. L., & Epstein, J. L. (1993). Parents' attitudes and practices of involvement in inner-city elementary and middle schools. In N. Chavkin. (Ed.), *Families and schools in a pluralistic society* (pp. 53–71). Albany: State University of New York Press.

Davalos, D. B., Chavez, E. L., & Guardiola, R. J. (2005). Effects of perceived parental school support and family communication on delinquent behaviors in Latino and White non-Latinos. *Cultural Diversity and Ethnic Minority Psychology, 11,* 57–68.

Desimone, L. (1999). Linking parent involvement with student achievement: Do race and income matter?, *The Journal of Educational Research, 93,* 11–30.

Desimone, L., Finn-Stevenson, M., & Henrich, C. (2000). Whole school reform in a low-income African American community: The effects of the CoZi model on teachers, parents, and students. *Urban Education, 35,* 269–323.

Domina, T. (2005). Leveling the home advantage: Assessing the effectiveness of parental involvement in elementary school. *Sociology of Education, 78,* 233–249.

Donahue, P. L., Finnegan, R. J., Lutkus, A. D., Allen, N. L., & Campbell, J. R. (2001). *The nation's report card: Fourth-grade reading 2002* (NCES 2001–499). Washington, DC: National Center for Education Statistics.

Duckworth, K. & DeJong, J. (1989). Inhibiting class cutting among high school students. *The High School Journal, 72,* 188–195.

Eccles, J. S., & Harold, R. D. (1996). Family involvement in children's and adolescents' schooling. In A. Bloom & J. F. Dunn (Eds.), *Family-school links: How do they affect educational outcomes?* (pp. 3–34). Mahwah, NJ: Erlbaum.

Edwards, P. A., Pleasants, H. M., & Franklin, S. H. (1999). *A path to follow: Learning to listen to parents.* Portsmouth, NH: Heinemann.

Epstein, J. L. (1991). Effects of teacher practices of parent involvement on change in student achievement in reading and math. In S. Silvern, (Ed.), *Literacy through family, community, and school interaction: Advances in reading/language research* (Vol. 5, pp. 261–276). Greenwich, CT: JAI Press.

Epstein, J. L. (1995). School/family/community partnerships: Caring for the children we share. *Phi Delta Kappan, 76,* 701–712.

Epstein, J. L., & Dauber, S. L. (1991). School programs and teacher practices of parent involvement in inner-city elementary and middle schools. *Elementary School Journal, 91,* 289–305.

Epstein, J. L., Salinas, K. C., & Van Voorhis, F. L. (2001). *Teachers Involve Parents in Schoolwork (TIPS) language arts, science/health, and math interactive homework in the elementary and middle grades* (two manuals). Baltimore: Center on School, Family, and Community Partnerships.

Epstein, J. L. & Sheldon, S. B. (2002). Present and accounted for: Improving student attendance through family and community involvement. *Journal of Educational Research, 95,* 308–318.

Epstein J. L., & Sheldon, S. B. (2006). Moving forward: Ideas for research on school, family, and community partnerships. In C. F. Conrad & R. Serlin (Eds.), *SAGE handbook for research in education: Engaging ideas and enriching inquiry* (pp. 117–137). Thousand Oaks, CA: Sage.

Epstein, J. L., Simon, B. S., & Salinas, K. C. (1997, September). *Effects of Teachers Involve Parents in Schoolwork (TIPS) language arts interactive homework in the middle grades* (Research Bulletin 18). Bloomington, IN: Phi Delta Kappa, Center on Education, Development, and Research.

Falbo, T., Lein, L., & Amador, N. A. (2001). Parental involvement during the transition to high school. *Journal of Adolescent Research, 16,* 511–529.

Fan, X., & Chen, M. (2001). Parental involvement and students' academic achievement: A meta-analysis. *Educational Psychology Review, 13,* 1–22.

Fitzgerald, J. (2001). Can minimally trained college student volunteers help young at-risk students to read better? *Reading Research Quarterly, 36,* 28–46.

Frome, P. M. & Eccles, J. S. (1998). Parents' influence on children's achievement-related perceptions. *Journal of Personality and Social Psychology, 74,* 435–452.

George, R. & Kaplan, D. (1998). A structural model of parent and teacher influences on science attitudes of eighth graders: Evidence from NELS: 88. *Science Education, 82,* 93–109.

Gottfredson, D. C., Gottfredson, G. D., & Hybl, L. G. (1993). Managing adolescent behavior: A multiyear, multischool study. *American Educational Research Journal, 30*(1), 179–215.

Greenleaf, C. L., Schoenbach, R. Cziko, C., & Mueller, F. L. (2001). Apprenticing adolescent readers to academic literacy. *Harvard Educational Review, 71,* 79–129.

Griffith, J. (1998). The relation of school structure and social environment to parent involvement in elementary schools. *Elementary School Journal, 99,* 53–80.

Grolnick, W. S., Kurowski, C. O., Dunlap, K. G., & Hevey, C. (2000). Parental resources and the transition to junior high. *Journal of Research on Adolescence, 10,* 465–488.

Gutman, L. M., & Midgley, C. (2000). The role of protective factors in supporting the academic achievement of poor African American students during the middle school transition. *Journal of Youth and Adolescence, 29,* 223–248.

Haynes, N. M., Comer, J. P., & Hamilton-Lee, M. (1989). School climate enhancement through parental involvement. *Journal of School Psychology, 27,* 87–90.

Heath, S. B. (1983). *Ways with words.* New York: Cambridge University Press.

Heibert, E. H. (1980). The relationship of logical reasoning ability, oral language comprehension, and home experiences to preschool children's print awareness. *Journal of Reading Behavior, 12,* 313–324.

Helm, C. M., & Burkett, C. W. (1989). Effects of computer-assisted telecommunications on school attendance. *Journal of Educational Research, 82,* 362–365.

Henderson, A. T., & Berla, N. (1994). *A new generation of evidence: The family is critical to student achievement.* Washington, DC: National Committee for Citizens in Education.

Henderson, A., & Mapp, K. L. (2002). *A new wave of evidence: The impact of school, family, and community connections on student achievement.* Austin, TX: Southwest Educational Development Laboratory.

Hill, N. E., Castellino, D. R., Lansford, J. E., Nowlin, P., Dodge, K. A., Bates, J. E., et al. (2004). Parent academic involvement as related to school behavior, achievement, and aspirations: Demographic variations across adolescence. *Child Development, 75,* 1491–1509.

Ho, E. S-C., & Willms, J. D. (1996). Effects of parental involvement on eighth-grade achievement, *Sociology of Education, 69,* 126–141.

Hoffman, J. V. (1991). Teacher and school effects in learning to read. In R. Barr, M. L. Kamil, P. B. Mosenthal, & P. D. Pearson (Eds.), *Handbook of reading research* (Vol. 2, pp. 911–950). New York: Longman.

Hong, S., & Ho, H. (2005). Direct and indirect longitudinal effects of parental involvement on student achievement: Second-order latent growth modeling across ethnic groups, *Journal of Educational Psychology, 97,* 32–42.

Hyde, J. S., Else-Quest, N. M., Alibali, M. W., Knuth, E., & Romberg, T. (2006). Mathematics in the home: Homework practices and mother-child interactions doing mathematics. *Journal of Mathematical Behavior, 25,* 136–152.

Jeynes, W. H. (2003). A meta-analysis: The effects of parental involvement on minority children's academic achievement. *Education and Urban Society, 35,* 202–218.

Jeynes, W. H. (2005). A meta-analysis of the relation of parental involvement to urban elementary school student academic achievement. *Urban Education, 40,* 237–269.

Jordan, C., Orozco, E., & Averett, A. (2001). *Emerging issues in school, family, and community connections.* Austin, TX: Southwest Educational Development Laboratory.

Jordan, G. E., Snow, C. E., & Porche, M. V. (2000). Project EASE: The effect of a family literacy project on kindergarten students' early literacy skills, *Reading Research Quarterly, 35,* 524–546.

Keith, T. Z., Keith, P. B., Quirk, K. J., Sperduto, J., Santillo, S., & Killings, S. (1998). Longitudinal effects of parent involvement on high school grades: Similarities and differences across gender and ethnic groups. *Journal of School Psychology, 36,* 335–363.

Lee, V. E., & Croninger, R. G. (1994). The relative importance of home and school in development of literacy skills for middle-grade students. *American Journal of Education, 102,* 286–329.

Leichter, H. J. (1984). Families as environments for literacy. In H. Goelman, A. Oberg, & F. Smith (Eds.), *Awakening to literacy* (pp. 38–50). London: Heinemann Educational Books.

Lerner, R., & Shumow, L. (1997). Aligning the construction zones of parents and teachers for mathematics reform, *Cognition and Instruction, 15,* 41–83.

Licht, B. G., Gard, T., & Guardino, C. (1991). Modifying school attendance of special education high school students. *Journal of Educational Research, 84,* 368–373.

Lonigan, C. J., & Whitehurst, G. J. (1998). Relative efficacy of parent and teacher involvement in a shared-reading intervention for preschool children from low-income backgrounds, *Early Childhood Research Quarterly, 13,* 263–290.

Ma, X. (1999). Dropping out of advanced mathematics: The effects of parental involvement. *Teachers College Record, 101,* 60–81.

Ma, X. (2001). Bullying and being bullied: To what extent are bullies also victims? *American Educational Research Journal, 38,* 351–370.

Mathematica Policy Research Inc. & Center for Children and Families at Teachers College, Columbia University. (2001). *Building their futures: How Early Head Start programs are changing the lives of infants and toddlers in low-income families.* Retrieved September 24, 2008, from http://www.mathematics-mpr.com/publications/PDFs/bildingvol1.pdf

McCarthey, S. (1999). Identifying teacher practices that connect home and school. *Education and Urban Society, 32,* 83–107.

McNeal, R. B. (1999). Parental involvement as social capital: Differential effectiveness on science achievement, truancy, and dropping out. *Social Forces, 78,* 117–144.

McPartland, J. M., & Nettles, S. M. (1991). Using community adults as advocates or mentors for at-risk middle school students: A two-year evaluation of project RAISE. *American Journal of Education, 99,* 568–586.

Muller, C. (1993). Parent involvement and academic achievement: An analysis of family resources available to the child. In B. Schneider & J. S. Coleman (Eds.), *Parents, their children, and schools* (pp. 77–114). Boulder, CO: Westview Press.

National Research Council. (2003). *Engaging schools: Fostering high school students' motivation to learn.* Washington, DC: National Academies Press.

Nettles, S. M. (1991). Community contributions to school outcomes of African-American students. *Education and Urban Society, 24,* 132–147.

Noguera, P. A. (1995). Preventing and producing violence: A critical analysis of responses to school violence. *Harvard Educational Review, 65,* 189–212.

Paratore, J. R., Hindin, A., Krol-Sinclair, B., & Duran, P. (1999). Discourse between teachers and Latino parents during conferences based on home literacy portfolios. *Education and Urban Society, 32,* 58–82.

Parcel, T. L., & Dufur, M. J. (2001). Capital at home and at school: Effects on student achievement. *Social Forces, 79,* 881–912.

Parsons, J. E., Adler, T., & Kaczala, C. M. (1982). Socialization of achievement attitudes and beliefs: Parental influences. *Child Development, 53,* 310–321.

Purcell-Gates, V. (1996). Stories, coupons, and the TV guide: Relationships between home literacy experiences and emergent literacy knowledge. *Reading Research Quarterly, 31,* 406–428.

Purkey, S. C., & Smith, M. S. (1983). Effective schools: A review. *The Elementary School Journal, 83,* 426–452.

Roderick, M., Arney, M., Axelman, M., DaCosta, K., Steiger, C., Stone, S., et al. (1997). *Habits hard to break: A new look at truancy in Chicago's public high schools.* Chicago: School of Social Service Administration, University of Chicago.

Sanders, M. G. (2005). *Building school-community partnerships: Collaborating for student success.* Thousand Oaks, CA: Corwin Press.

Sanders, M. G., & Epstein, J. L. (2000). Building school-family-community partnerships in middle and high schools. In M. G. Sanders (Ed.), *Schooling students placed at risk* (pp. 339–362). Mahwah, NJ: Erlbaum.

Sanders, M. G., & Harvey, A. (2002). Beyond the school walls: A case study principal leadership for school-community collaboration, *Teachers College Record, 104,* 1345–1368.

Scarborough, H. S., & Dobrich, W. (1994). On the efficacy of reading to preschoolers. *Developmental Review, 14,* 245–302.

Schulting, A. B., Malone, P. S., & Dodge, K. A. (2005). The effect of school-based kindergarten transition policies and practices on child academic outcomes. *Developmental Psychology, 41,* 840–871.

Sénéchal, M., & LeFevre, J. (2002). Parental involvement in the development of children's reading skill: A five-year longitudinal study, *Child Development, 73,* 455–460.

Sénéchal, M., & LeFevre, J., Thomas, E., & Daley, K. (1998). Differential effects of home literacy experiences on the development of oral and written language. *Reading Research Quarterly, 32,* 96–116.

Shaver, A. V., & Walls, R. T. (1998). Effect of Title I parent involvement on student reading and math achievement. *Journal of Research and Development in Education, 321,* 90–97.

Sheldon, S. B. (2005). Testing a structural equation model of partnership program implementation and parent involvement. *Elementary School Journal, 106,* 171–187.

Sheldon, S. B. (2007). Improving student attendance with school, family, and community partnerships. *Journal of Educational Research, 100,* 267–275.

Sheldon, S. B., & Epstein, J. L. (2002). Improving student behavior and school discipline with family and community involvement. *Education and Urban Society, 35,* 4–26.

Sheldon, S. B., & Epstein, J. L. (2004). Getting students to school: Using family and community involvement to reduce chronic absenteeism. *School Community Journal, 14,* 39–56.

Sheldon, S. B., & Epstein, J. L. (2005a). Involvement counts: Family and community partnerships and math achievement. *Journal of Educational Research, 98,* 196–206.

Sheldon, S. B. & Epstein, J. L. (2005b). School programs of family and community involvement to support children's reading and literacy development across the grades. In J. Flood & P. Anders (Eds.),

Literacy development of students in urban schools: Research and policy (pp. 107–138). Newark, DE: International Reading Association.

Sheldon, S. B., Epstein, J. L., & Galindo, C. L. (under review). Not just numbers: Creating a partnership climate to improve levels of math proficiency. Manuscript submitted for publication.

Sheldon, S. B., & Van Voorhis, V. L. (2004). Partnership programs in U.S. schools: Their development and relationship to family involvement outcomes. *School Effectiveness and School Improvement, 15,* 125–148.

Shumow, L., & Miller, J. D. (2001). Parents' at-home and at-school academic involvement with young adolescents. *Journal of Early Adolescence, 21,* 68–91.

Simon, B. S. (2001). Family involvement in high school: Predictors and effects. *NASSP Bulletin, 85,* 8–19.

Simon, B. S. (2004). High school outreach and family involvement. *Social Psychology of Education, 7,* 185–209.

Snow, C. E., Burns, S., & Griffin, P. (Eds.). (1998). *Preventing reading difficulties in young children.* Washington, DC: National Academy Press.

Snyder, J., & Patterson, G. (1987). Family interaction and delinquent behavior. In H. C. Quay (Ed.), *Handbook of juvenile delinquency* (pp. 216–243). New York: Wiley.

Taylor, D. (1983). *Family literacy: Young children learning to read and write.* Portsmouth NH: Heinemann.

Taylor, D., & Dorsey-Gaines, C. (1988). *Growing up literate: Learning from inner-city families.* Portsmouth NH: Heinemann.

Taylor, L., & Adelman, H. S. (2000). Connecting schools, families, and communities. *Professional School Counseling, 3,* 298–307.

Teale, W. H. (1986). Home background and young children's literacy development. In W. H. Teale & E. Sulzby (Eds.), *Emergent literacy: Writing and reading* (pp. 173–206). Norwood, NJ: Ablex.

Teddlie, C., & Reynolds, D. *The international handbook of school effectiveness research.* London: Falmer Press.

Valadez, J. R. (2002). The influence of social capital on mathematics course selection by Latino high school students. *Hispanic Journal of Behavioral Sciences, 24,* 319–339.

Van Voorhis, F. L. (Under review). *Longitudinal effects of family involvement with students on math homework.* Baltimore: Center on School, Family, and Community Partnerships at Johns Hopkins University.

Van Voorhis, F. L. (2003). Interactive homework in middle school: Effects on family involvement and science achievement. *Journal of Educational Research, 96,* 323–338.

Von Secker, C. (2004). Science achievement in social contexts: Analysis from National Assessment of Educational Progress. *Journal of Educational Research, 98,* 67–78.

Wang, M. C., Haertel, G. D., & Walberg, H. M. (1993). Toward a knowledge base for school learning. *Review of Educational Research, 63,* 249–294.

Wasik, B. A. (1998). Volunteer tutoring programs in reading: A review. *Reading Research Quarterly, 33,* 266–292.

Westat and Policy Studies Associates. (2001). *The longitudinal evaluation of school change and performance in Title I Schools* (Vol. 1, Executive summary). Washington DC: U.S. Department of Education.

Yan, W., & Lin, Q. (2005). Parent involvement and mathematics achievement: Contrast across racial and ethnic groups. *Journal of Educational Research, 99,* 116–127.

2

Use the Framework to Reach School Goals

Stories From the Field

This chapter describes how the framework of six types of involvement is implemented in practice to improve schools' partnership climate and to increase student success. The examples in this chapter are from leaders of Action Teams for Partnerships in schools that have worked with the National Network of Partnership Schools (NNPS) at Johns Hopkins University to strengthen their programs of family and community involvement. Their ideas and experiences document the importance of planning, evaluating, and continually improving activities to develop successful partnership programs.

The framework of six types of involvement guides schools' Action Teams for Partnerships to select and implement practices that involve families and the community in many different ways that make the school a welcoming place and to help students succeed at high levels. Goal-oriented involvement activities focus family and community involvement to help students improve reading, math, science, writing, skills in other subjects, attendance, behavior, transitions from one school to the next, postsecondary planning, multicultural understanding, and other specific goals for student success. The activities, across types of involvement, also may strengthen parents' knowledge of child and adolescent development, improve communications between families and educators, identify volunteers for the school, increase parents' discussions and interactions with their children, encourage parents' participation in school decisions, and build connections with community partners.

The framework of six types of involvement is not an end in itself. Rather, it guides schools' Action Teams for Partnerships in designing, developing, and improving comprehensive partnership programs that contribute to excellent schools and successful students.

Six Types of Involvement to Improve School Climate and Student Success

Twelve examples of activities from elementary, middle, and high schools illustrate how to use the six types of involvement to create a welcoming, family-friendly school and to help students reach important results.

Type 1–Parenting activities illustrate how schools are working to increase families' understanding of child and adolescent development. The sample activities include the following:

- Strengthen the school climate by helping elementary school parents discuss age-appropriate topics concerning school and schoolwork with their young children.
- Assist high school parents to gain confidence about guiding their teens to apply to college or community college for postsecondary education and training.

Schools must "know their families" to select Type 1 activities that meet family and student needs and interests. Each school is different from the next, but all schools can assist parents to increase knowledge and strengthen skills to meet parenting responsibilities at each age and grade level and to influence their children's growth and development.

Type 2–Communicating activities illustrate ways to increase two-way connections about school programs and students' progress. The sample activities include the following:

- Systematize communications in a weekly folder in order to encourage ongoing exchanges from school to home and from home to school. After exploring the folders, parents can send reactions, ask questions, and respond in other ways.
- Improve parent-teacher conferences by including students, who lead the discussions about their work, goals, and next steps in school.

Two-way communications increase understanding and cooperation between school and home and show students that their teachers and parents are in contact to help them succeed in school. Because information must be useful and clear to all families, schools must translate messages, provide interpreters, or offer guidelines for families who speak languages other than English at home.

Type 3–Volunteering activities mobilize parents and others who can share their time and talents to support the school, teachers, and student activities at the school or in other locations. The sample practices include the following:

- Increase the number of parent volunteers from groups who may feel excluded.
- Help parents who cannot volunteer at the school building to contribute to students' career awareness and understanding of how different jobs use school skills.

Parents and other family and community volunteers may assist individual teachers by helping students practice specific skills, or they may help the school in the library, family room, computer room, playground, cafeteria, afterschool programs, or other locations. Volunteers also include those who support the school and students by attending student performances, sports activities, assemblies, celebrations, and other events.

Type 4–Learning at Home activities provide families with information about the academic work that their children do in class, how to help their children with homework, and other curriculum-related activities and decisions. The sample activities include the following:

- Encourage parents and children to enjoy reading, and provide parents with ideas about how to help at home in ways that will improve students' reading skills and attitudes about reading.
- Increase student and parent interest in science.

Learning at Home activities also may guide parents in how to help children practice skills; discuss their work in a particular subject; complete homework; choose courses, summer programs, or other learning opportunities; and plan for postsecondary education.

Type 5–Decision Making activities enable families to participate in decisions about school programs that affect their own and other children. These include the work of parent representatives on the School Council, School Improvement Team, and various committees. It also includes the work of leaders and members of a PTA, PTO, or other parent organization. The sample activities include the following:

- Increase PTA participation by, periodically, taking PTA meetings and information to community centers in neighborhoods served by the school.
- Increase parents' voices in school processes by including parents with teachers on a special-project committee of the School Improvement Team.

All families need information about school policies and opportunities to offer ideas and reactions to improve their schools. When parent representatives do their jobs well, they gather ideas from and return information to the families they represent. Type 5 activities not only include parents as partners on school committees but also focus on the projects that are developed and sponsored to improve the school and student success.

Type 6–Collaborating With the Community activities encourage the cooperation of schools, families, community groups, organizations, agencies, and individuals. Connections go in both directions: Community resources assist the schools, students, and families; educators, students, and families can assist the community. The sample activities include the following:

- Develop mentoring and "pen pal" connections that increase students' writing and other school skills, as well as positive adult-student relationships.
- Involve families and students in field trips in the community that enrich learning in science and in other subjects.

All communities offer human, economic, material, and social resources that can help improve schools, strengthen families, and assist students to succeed in school and in life. Some schools create "community portraits" to identify programs and services for teachers, families, and students. Others connect with business and industry on special projects (e.g., conducting afterschool programs or constructing a new playground). Still others work with organizations to increase students' problem solving abilities and opportunities for community service.

The examples for the six types of involvement illustrate how all elementary, middle, and high schools can improve their programs of school, family, and community partnerships and help students reach academic and behavioral goals. The selected activities are among over 700 practices in the annual collections of *Promising Partnership Practices* at www.partnershipschools.org in the section Success Stories.

SCHOOL STORIES

TYPE 1–PARENTING

Calendar for School Success

Highland View and College Park Elementary Schools
Greendale, Wisconsin

Goal for Partnership Climate: Increase parents' confidence about discussing school and schoolwork with their children.

Level: Preschool/Kindergarten (adaptable to other grade levels)

In the Time-4-Learning kindergarten program, Highland View and College Park Elementary Schools jointly designed a calendar with parenting tips, resources, and activities to ensure early school success, as well as to advance students' social and behavioral development. The calendar helped parents of prekindergarten students get involved with their children's education from the beginning.

Various subgroups of the Action Team for Partnerships (ATP) researched and designed monthly topics in engaging formats. The school then distributed one calendar to each family. The $1,000 cost of creating and distributing this calendar was supported by a charter school implementation grant and fund-raising events.

The hanging calendar included a full page of parenting information above each month's date grid. Some pages related to activities that would take place at the school that month. For instance, September's page had a guide for preparing children for the first day of school. Parents also received tips for asking good questions. Everyone knows that "How was school today? Or "What did you do in school today?" will not yield the same answers as very specific questions. The calendar guides parents to find out about and discuss actual activities from the day's instruction and frame questions around them, such as: "Did you learn about alligators today? What was most interesting to you? Did you make a mask in school today? What did your mask look like?" Such questions allow a child to extend learning from the classroom to the home.

February's page had a guide to expressions of parental love, including ideas to support students' interests and hobbies, express love and limits at the same time, and notice when a child does something correctly, among many suggestions. Other pages had tips for discipline, a guide to preschool developmental stages, and ideas for exploring reading, writing, and math with young children. For example, one section suggested how parents may discuss math-related concepts every day by using number words in conversations, estimating time, and measuring in cooking. The calendar also provided parents with contacts at the school.

The timely resource proved helpful to parents as they guided their children through the first year of school. One parent said, "I learned some things about what to expect from my child at this age that I was not aware of before." Just by using the calendar, parents honed their parenting skills and increased participation in school to increase students' readiness and academic and developmental success.

Source: From *Promising Partnership Practices* 2006

TYPE 1–PARENTING

Financial Aid Workshop for Parents and Students

Mullins High School
Mullins, South Carolina

Goal for Student Success: Improve students' college and career planning.

Level: High School

To show parents and students how to complete the Free Application for Federal Student Aid (FAFSA) for postsecondary schooling, Mullins created a financial aid workshop. The workshop was held in February, after parents had received wage statements and before they started their tax returns.

The area surrounding Mullins has a high unemployment rate. Many parents of students at Mullins have difficulty navigating the complex financial aid form for college or training. As a result, many students cannot access the financial assistance that they qualify for and need in order to take advantage of postsecondary education opportunities.

To develop the workshop, Mullins researched how other schools helped their students and families navigate the financial aid system and borrowed several practices. The guidance office contacted local college financial aid advisors to help design and implement the workshop. These advisors planned the content and supplied the required materials. The sessions demonstrated a step-by-step process to fill out the forms and addressed the questions and concerns of students and their parents. The advisors provided each parent with a copy of the FAFSA form. By the end of the workshop, each student's financial aid application was complete.

Mullins knew its biggest challenge would be getting parents to attend. Other parent involvement initiatives had drawn only handfuls of participants. To publicize the financial aid classes, the Action Team for Partnerships (ATP) offered a bonus incentive to students who attended: a "tardy pass" that could be used once anytime until the end of the school year. Guidance counselors visited classrooms to invite juniors and seniors to attend, and the school's daily televised broadcast included announcements and reminders about the tardy pass incentive. The school encouraged students to remind their parents about the workshops. The ATP also used traditional publicity methods to reach out to the parents directly, including signage outside the school, flyers for visiting parents, the Web site, and newsletter announcements.

In the end, 56 students and 73 parents participated in the workshop. Thanks to the efforts of teachers, administrators, community members who acted as financial aid advisors, and students who helped with publicity, the event was a success. Students and parents received valuable information about financial aid, and they realized how much the school cared that they attend the workshops. Best of all, the students walked out of the meetings with filled-out financial aid applications in hand!

Source: From *Promising Partnership Practices* 2006

Explore these and other Type 1 applications in the annual collections of *Promising Partnership Practices* at www.partnershipschools.org in the section Success Stories. See, for example the activities in the following table:

Type 1 Activities	School	Goal	Summary
College and Career Guide	Naperville North High School, Naperville, IL	Provide parents and students with clear information on postsecondary education.	Create a College and Career Planning Guide for students in Grades 9–12 with information on searching for a college, applications, entrance exams, college visits, questions to ask college admissions staff, how to write essays, and financial aid, as well as checklists and other tips.
Dads, Art, and Donuts With Students	Parents Plus with John Muir Middle School, Milwaukee, WI	Help fathers and other male figures in students' lives to understand the importance of their involvement with their students.	Provide breakfast, a speaker, and information on community resources. In addition, organize an art project designing T-shirts for students to complete with their dads or other guests.
Information Fair	Lincoln Elementary School, Wausau, WI	Increase parents' knowledge and confidence about health, nutrition, safety, and other parenting topics for healthy child development.	The information fair—organized by the PTA/PTO, district, and community agencies and held on the school's well-attended parent-teacher conference days—provides parents with information to meet health and wellness goals for student growth and development.
Tiger Closet Clothes Exchange	John Tyler Elementary School, Hampton, VA	Help parents reduce clothing expenses.	Set up clothing exchange dates for coats, uniforms, or other clothing so that families need not purchase new clothes if their funds are low.

SCHOOL STORIES

TYPE 2–COMMUNICATING

Folder for Family Support

Riverview Specialty School

Brooklyn Park, Minnesota

Goal for Partnership Climate: Increase parents' awareness of school programs and students' activities.

Goal for Student Success: Improve student behavior.

Level: Elementary Grades (adaptable to other grade levels)

Everything you want or need to know as a parent can be found in the Partnership Action Team folder provided by the Riverview Partnership Action Team (RPAT). The weekly pocket folder is chock-full of information, ideas, and announcements. The initiative to distribute these folders was created in conjunction with the school's Second Step conflict resolution program.

Riverview decided that inappropriate behavior by some students was distracting from instructional time. The RPAT decided to get parents involved by supporting their parenting skills and efforts, knowing that children are more disciplined learners when they are supported as students at home. In a survey conducted by the RPAT, Riverview parents had indicated that they were interested in receiving ideas for parenting at all ages and levels of development.

RPAT instituted a weekly folder that would create a consistent medium for school-parent communications. The consistency would increase parents' attention to the information, including materials that addressed the needs that parents outlined in the survey. The program was designed to increase students' self-esteem and confidence, thus decreasing incidences of inappropriate behavior.

The first folder was sent home with a cover letter, RPAT brochure, Ideas for Parents flyer, Parenting Book Club flyer, Parent Resource Library information, and a parenting question-of-the-month. The Ideas for Parents flyer, which is distributed by the Search Institute's Healthy Communities–Healthy Youth initiative, includes activities, discussion items, and practical tips for parents. The Parenting Book Club identifies books on parenting, and the parenting question-of-the-month invited parents to communicate with each other and the school. The school also publicized school events and announcements in the folder and placed the same information on its Web page for families and the community at large.

Since the beginning of the program, RPAT has received positive feedback and suggestions for improvement. The team plans to reduce the amount of material in each weekly folder. Some parents felt overwhelmed by the number of papers they received. By simplifying the folder, RPAT hopes to make it more user friendly and accessible to all families. It is expected that as parents get used to this communication from school, they will respond and participate regularly.

The Riverview folder successfully guided many parents in supporting their children's education. More students at this magnet school were able to work and learn in an environment that was as supportive at home as it was in the classroom. Most reactions matched that of the district director of elementary curriculum, who said, "What a wonderful idea and resource to provide for families. This idea could be easily replicated by other schools in the district."

Source: From *Promising Partnership Practices* 2006

TYPE 2–COMMUNICATING

Student-Led Conferences

West Carrollton Middle School

West Carrollton, Ohio

Goal for Student Success: Improve students' knowledge about their own work. Enable students to set goals, with school and family support, for high achievement and positive attitudes and behavior.

Level: Middle Grades (adaptable to other levels)

West Carrollton Middle School gave the traditional parent-teacher conference an interesting twist. Some years ago, school administrators were concerned that a very important person was missing from these conferences—the student! With a new design, students at West Carrollton individually met with their parents and teachers at the school. They actually led their conferences, taking responsibility for their own accomplishments and progress or lack of it.

Students presented a portfolio that showcased their work and used measurement tools to chart their academic progress. Teachers were available on conference nights to meet with parents, answer questions, and help the parents and students work together to evaluate the students' progress. From the beginning of the year, students knew they would participate in at least two conferences. This encouraged them to do their best work for their conference portfolios.

Conferences were held after the first- and second-quarter report cards were sent home, so students had the opportunity to improve by the end of the academic year. Some grade level teams also opted to do a standard home conference after the third quarter.

Two weeks before the end of the quarter, teachers mailed invitations to parents with sign-up sheets. To prepare for the conferences themselves, teachers helped students evaluate their progress on check lists that used a 1-to-5 scale. These evaluation sheets also included the student's grade in the course and self-stated next-quarter goals. The children rehearsed their own presentations with a classmate.

Since the school began these student-led conferences, participation of parents grew from 30 to 78 percent. The conferences also were counted as a percentage of students' grades in the core subjects: math, social studies, English, reading, and science.

Although, initially, it was a challenge to adopt the student-led conference system, West Carrollton, with careful planning, was able to phase in the program. The administration asked each team of teachers to start with a small number of conferences. As teacher teams began to see the advantages, they shared ideas and worked out the best way to implement the new system. The teams stuck to an implementation calendar that helped ease teachers' apprehensions about the program. In the end, the school allowed each team of teachers the flexibility to adapt the program to its needs.

Thanks to student-led conferences, middle school students at West Carrollton felt more in control of their own education. The program reinforced the need for organization, decision making, goal setting, communication, and leadership skills. It also strengthened the relationship between the school and its families, creating more interest among students and parents and giving them more responsibility at school. "This has been the perfect fit for us to get our parents actively involved within our building," said the principal.

Source: From *Promising Partnership Practices* 2006

Explore these and other Type 2 applications in the annual collections of *Promising Partnership Practices* at www.partnershipschools.org in the section Success Stories. See, for example the activities in the following table:

Type 2 Activities	***School***	***Goal***	***Summary***
Neighborhood Outreach	Ethel Schoeffner Elementary School, Destrehan, LA	Improve school climate by building trust with reluctant families.	Create a neighborhood event for staff to meet families, discuss ideas, and enjoy refreshments with parents who had not been involved at school.
Rob TV—Digital Video Streaming to Communicate	Roberts Elementary School, Wayne, PA	Increase connections with grandparents and parents at a distance.	Bring school events home with a click of the mouse for parents and others to experience school programs and for students learn the power of mass media.
Standardized Test Prep	Ladysmith Elementary School, Ladysmith, WI	Increase math skills, concepts, attitudes, and scores.	Help parents understand state standards, state tests, and NCLB requirements. Provide opportunities for students to practice skills and concepts at school and at home.
Welcome Back Picnic	Longfellow Elementary School, Pasco, WA	Improve school climate at the start of the school year for all students and families.	Before school starts, invite students, families, and teachers to meet, hear about school program, have a picnic, and build a sense of community.

SCHOOL STORIES

TYPE 3–VOLUNTEERING

Increasing Volunteerism in a Multicultural School

Harmony Hills Elementary School

Silver Spring, Maryland

Goal for Partnership Climate: Increase the number of volunteers available to conduct activities that benefit students and welcome parent volunteers who do not speak English.

Level: Elementary Grades (adaptable to other grade levels)

At the start of school last year, Harmony Hills Elementary School had only one or two parent volunteers. After a well-planned and comprehensive recruitment effort, the number of volunteers increased to nearly 40. In a multilingual community with communication challenges, the magnitude of this increase was just short of miraculous.

Harmony Hills has a sizable Hispanic student population, and many parents felt insecure about offering their services to the school because English is not their first language. In order to overcome their concerns and increase volunteerism, Harmony Hills developed a multistep program.

First, the school identified a parent partnership outreach coordinator to oversee the initiative. The coordinator held volunteer orientation meetings at various times of day and provided interpreters and babysitters as needed. Each volunteer tried to bring a friend to future meetings to help grow the program. All materials about volunteer opportunities sent home to parents were translated into Spanish, and a concerted effort was made to match parents' interests and expertise with teachers' needs. To help the new corps of volunteers, Harmony Hills set up a parent-teacher resource lounge and printed ID cards for the volunteers. The coordinator also celebrated the contributions of volunteers each semester with a Volunteer Tea and certificates.

Harmony Hills took two other important steps to increase the number of parent volunteers. They embraced NNPS's redefinition of volunteering to include all instances in which parents support children's education. In addition, they made sure that all volunteers felt welcome in the school and received the support they needed.

Thanks to their new approaches, the Harmony Hills staff received assistance from a slew of new volunteers. Students benefited from the volunteers, who gave one-on-one attention. Teachers appreciated the volunteer support and found the extra classroom help useful for students' learning. The volunteers themselves felt more invested in the success of the school and, of course, had valuable experiences in helping students succeed.

Harmony Hills Elementary School's pursuit of volunteers through newsletters, invitations, phone calls, and PTA mailings not only led to an improved educational environment but also to the realization of a dream. This year, for the first time, the school intends to hold a Spring Fair—an event that could never occur without the support of many volunteers. The hard work of the increasing number of Harmony Hills volunteers will continue to improve life for students, teachers, and the community for years to come.

Source: From *Promising Partnership Practices* 2005

TYPE 3–VOLUNTEERING

BES Goes to Work

Ballentine Elementary School

Irmo, South Carolina

Goal for Student Success: Increase students' career explorations and understanding of how different jobs use school skills. Enable parents who cannot come to the school building to be volunteers by sharing information about their occupations.

Level: Elementary Grades (adaptable to other levels)

BES the bear went to work. Nearly every week she had a different job—firefighter, nurse, construction worker, office manager. BES was a busy bear, and the students at Ballentine Elementary School kept track of BES's travels and adventures.

BES is a miniature version of the school's mascot. BES Goes to Work was designed to involve hard working parents in the school and to showcase the parents' diverse careers for the student body. Ballentine Elementary encouraged parents to take turns each week bringing BES to their workplaces. Each parent photographed BES at work (e.g., donning a construction hat, standing at a lecture podium, or sitting at a television news anchor's desk) and wrote a short summary of what BES saw on the job.

"BES had fun learning about all the cool jobs in a bank," reported a parent who is the market development manager of a bank. "BES went to class and saw how college students take notes. The students were curious why BES was there," reported another parent who is a professor of criminology.

Inspired by a similar idea shared at a counselors' conference, BES Goes to Work was developed as an extension to Ballentine's career program. The guidance office sent out questionnaires about the program several times each year. Interested parents responded and the guidance office worked out BES's busy travel schedule. Families from all grades participated, but because of high demand for BES, participation was limited to only one parent from each family.

Each week that BES went to work, the participating child received a blue bag containing the bear, a T-shirt, a disposable camera, and a BES Goes to Work folder with a sheet for the parents to tell students about his or her job. The child wore the T-shirt to school so everyone knew whose family had BES for the week. When the student returned the bag, he or she had a photo taken in front of Big BES, the school's full-sized bear mascot. When the photos of BES at work were developed, they were pasted into a collage along with the parent's report. Everyone enjoyed the collages, which were displayed prominently in the school's minitheater.

Since the program began, BES has visited high schools, churches, hospitals, police stations, a local television station, and many offices. The program improved home-school connections at the small-town school; many of the students' working parents commute 30 minutes or more to work and cannot take time off to visit the school.

In addition to providing busy parents an opportunity to involve themselves in the school, BES Goes to Work taught students about various jobs and careers and gave them many reasons to take pride in what their parents do. The program was a definite community builder—increasing school spirit and enhancing Ballentine's image.

Source: From *Promising Partnership Practices* 2006

Explore these and other Type 3 applications in the annual collections of *Promising Partnership Practices* at www.partnershipschools.org in the section Success Stories. See, for example, the activities in the following table:

Type 3 Activities	*School*	*Goal*	*Summary*
All the World's a Stage	Bullard TALENT K–8 School, Fresno, CA	Involve the whole school and hundreds of volunteers in all aspects of an annual school musical.	Parent, community, and educators work with students to produce a play, give 14 performances for schools and the community, and develop many different talents in students.
Barnum Buddies	Barnum School, Taunton, MA	Improve reading readiness.	Volunteers give extra help to prekindergarten students who need reading readiness skills.
High Five Afterschool Program	Spooner Elementary School, Spooner, WI	Sharpen students' school skills, homework completion, and other talents.	Parent and community volunteers work with teachers to organize enriching clubs and activities after school.
Ruediger Achievers	Ruediger Elementary School, Tallahassee, FL	Improve students' goal setting and achievements in learning and citizenship.	Students set and attain ambitious goals and celebrate learning and citizenship at quarterly award and recognition assemblies, with parents as audience.

SCHOOL STORIES

TYPE 4–LEARNING AT HOME

Literacy Night With Dr. Seuss

Hill Field Elementary School

Clearfield, Utah

Goal for Student Success: Improve students' reading skills and attitudes; improve parents' abilities to support students' independent reading, fluency, and comprehension.

Level: Elementary Grades (adaptable to other grade levels)

Even with 95 percent of its students from military families and half of its students moving in and out each year, Hill Field Elementary was able to attract someone for its literacy night that everyone recognized—Dr. Seuss! The school's principal dressed up as the popular children's author and was accompanied by some of his favorite friends—the Cat in the Hat, the Grinch, and Thing One and Thing Two—for a celebration of literacy and Dr. Seuss's birthday.

And what a celebration it was, with more than 300 people attending. "It was a hugely successful event and exceeded my expectations," said one teacher, who is a member of the literacy council. The event ended with everyone eating cake and punch and singing "Happy Birthday" to Dr. Seuss. All of the children took home goodie bags of books and other things to read.

Because its student body is in constant flux, the Hill Field staff decided to involve parents in as many activities as possible to add some stability to the children's education. Located near Hill Field Air Force Base, the school was among the first to receive training for its involvement effort through the Military Child Initiative (MCI), an NNPS program designed to promote family involvement in schools with a large number of military families.

By holding a literacy night, Hill Field hoped to help parents learn about the components of literacy: independent reading, reading aloud, fluency, and comprehension. School tests indicated that students needed to improve in all of these skills.

Students arrived in their pajamas with their families. They visited stations where they read books, made craft items related to Dr. Seuss and other stories, and attended readers' theaters, where older students dramatically read stories out loud. Literacy Night exposed students to the fun of reading. Parents learned how to help their children at home and how to access materials to use at home to support the school curriculum.

Three of the school's reading teachers coordinated the event, working with the PTA, the Joint Staff School Committee, and the Community Council. Older students prepared the readers' theaters and decorated banners highlighting their favorite books—many by Dr. Seuss.

Title I and other school-based funds covered the $400 cost. Staff from the nearby base and the PTA worked at the event. The added help came in handy when the crowd far exceeded the number expected.

Next year, the school plans to hold events in classrooms throughout the building rather than concentrating them in the gym. This will allow people to spread out and to reduce noise levels. The school also aims to celebrate literacy throughout the month of March and to set reading goals, with incentives, for the month.

In addition to increasing literacy awareness, the night gave families who do not often get to meet one another a chance to get acquainted and to bond with the school and its staff.

Source: From *Promising Partnership Practices* 2006

TYPE 4–LEARNING AT HOME

Science "Sci-Fari" Adventure

Newtown Road Elementary School

Virginia Beach, Virginia

Goal for Student Success: Improve students' science skills and attitudes and help parents understand and support students' science learning.

Level: Elementary Grades (adaptable to other grade levels)

On a mission to raise science test scores, the Science Action Team at Newtown Road Elementary School set its sights on building interest in science. After much brainstorming, the team focused on the idea of a science discovery night. The team called it the Science Sci-Fari Adventure.

The trek led parents and students through a maze of stations in the school gymnasium, where they made discoveries and found answers to various science questions posed for the event. The goal was to answer 12 or more questions to receive a science fair button. Each teacher selected a topic months in advance and put together a discovery station with posters created by the students.

In the fifth grade area, for instance, the questions included, "Which item did mold grow on the fastest?" In the first grade area, one question was, "Did the plant that received Coke instead of water grow? How tall?"

"This was as much fun for me as for my child," said one parent. "Wow, can you believe the number of people who turned out for this?" commented a happy teacher. More than 200 students and 150 parents—over half of Newtown Road's student body—went on the Sci-Fari.

Held in the spring, the Sci-Fari Adventure culminated a year's worth of work on a redesigned curriculum that called for Newtown's teachers to teach science more actively. On the night of the Sci-Fari, families and students received two booklets, one to use during the Sci-Fari and a larger one of activities to complete at home.

In addition to setting up the school learning stations, the Science Action Team invited several local science clubs to attend. The Back Bay Amateur Astronomers and the Old Dominion Earth Science Society (ODESS) both put up displays.

The day after the fair, teachers took students through the gym, so that even those who could not attend the Sci-Fari could view the learning stations.

The increased interest generated by the event showed in higher scores on the science exams. The school's fifth graders improved by 13 percent.

The Science Action Team's success with this event has encouraged its members to begin planning for next year's Sci-Fari. They are working on ways to speed up registration and bring in more community partners to share their enthusiasm for science with Newtown's students.

Source: From *Promising Partnership Practices* 2006

Explore these and other Type 4 applications in the annual collections of *Promising Partnership Practices* at www.partnershipschools.org in the section Success Stories. See, for example, the activities in the following table:

Type 4 Activities	***School***	***Goal***	***Summary***
Chats & Chews: Partnering for Success of Students With Disabilities	Lowndes Middle School, Lowndes County, GA	Increase progress of students with disabilities on state tests.	Conduct breakfast discussions with parents to help students organize supplies and maintain notebooks, and to help parents to support student work and studying at home.
Family Math Night	Conococheage Elementary School, Washington County, MD	Increase math skills and improve attitudes toward math	Give students extra practice in math skills, and help students and families enjoy doing math together.
Fathers Reading Every Day (FRED)	Roosevelt Elementary School, Saint Paul, MN	Increase fathers' connections with the school and their involvement with students on reading at home. Improve students' reading skills and habits.	Dads, father figures, and some moms were invited to school for dinner, storytelling, guest readers, take-home books, and good fellowship. They were encouraged to read with their children at home, and they gained strategies for reading aloud and for listening to their children read.
Reading Takes You Places	Isaac Stevens Middle School, Pasco, WA	Increase reading skills and love of reading.	Create a series of "rooms" for reading; one each for multicultural poems and stories, campfire stories, reading stories aloud to younger children, playing reading games, and reading original poetry.

SCHOOL STORIES

TYPE 5–DECISION MAKING

Bringing the PTA to the Parents

William H. Farquhar Middle School
Olney, Maryland

Goal for Partnership Climate: Increase the number of parents who are comfortable with the PTA, improve the dissemination of information on middle school programs and curriculum, and strengthen parent networks.

Level: Middle Grades (adaptable to other grade levels)

Noticing poor attendance at the school's PTA meetings, Farquhar's principal asked why. One answer from some parents was that the PTA seemed to have cliques that made them feel unwelcome. As a solution, the principal worked with four parent volunteers to plan PTA meetings at three locations in the school community. The meetings enabled the school to share important curriculum and contact information and the parents to share their best practices with one another in small groups.

After a pizza dinner, the principal began the meetings with a 20-minute PowerPoint presentation about the middle school curriculum and how it connects to course choices in high school. The PTA vice president provided a handout with school contact numbers, educational Web sites, the homework hotline, and other useful information. The PTA president explained how parents can access their children's grades via the Internet.

Perhaps, the most innovative element of the meeting followed. Parent volunteers facilitated three breakout sessions based on parents' interests: (1) balancing students' schoolwork and outside activities, (2) discussing students' progress with teachers and the student, and (3) setting boundaries for middle school students. Together, the parents and facilitators assembled what they believed were the ten best practices for their topics and then shared them with the large group.

To plan the meetings, parent volunteers identified a community center or church in each area of the school community. Invitations were mailed to families living in those locations. Staff advertised the meetings in the weekly bulletin and monthly PTA newsletter and made phone calls to remind parents of the meetings. At the close of the meetings, the staff distributed evaluations to assess the usefulness of the sessions and to identify ways in which they could be improved.

As a result of the meetings, more parents knew more about the opportunities open to their children, students increased their participation in tutoring sessions, and parents and students learned more about their options in selecting rigorous courses. Parents appreciated the school's willingness to reach out into the community, and staff members better understood parents' concerns. Important discussions took place face-to-face, with thoughts shared honestly. More outreach meetings in each of the three sections of the school community are planned.

Source: From *Promising Partnership Practices* 2005

TYPE 5–DECISION MAKING

Parent Involvement With School Improvement Team

Washington Junior High School

Naperville, Illinois

Goal for Partnership Climate: Include parent representatives on the school committee focused on improving classroom tests and assessments.

Goal for Student Success: With parent input, improve students' test-taking experiences and, ultimately, test scores.

Level: Junior High (adaptable to other grade levels)

As members of the School Improvement Team at Washington Junior High School, three parents got a behind-the-scenes look at how classroom tests are developed. They learned about the philosophies and strategies that drive assessment. These parents also helped school administrators and teachers improve the school's assessment practices.

"It was exciting and interesting to be included as part of this team. It gave us an opportunity to see how teachers and administrators tackle issues like assessment and learning," said one parent. "We were treated as equal partners."

The school administration wanted to find ways for parents to help evaluate the testing practices for the school's sixth, seventh, and eighth graders. After discussing this with parents and the principal, three parents joined the School Improvement Team to work with teachers and administrators. Beginning in July 2004, the group met monthly to discuss issues surrounding classroom testing, assessment strategies, and achievement scores. The principal assigned readings from the book *Student-Involved Classroom Assessment* by Rich Stiggins, which each member came prepared to discuss at the meetings. The readings led team members to examine trends, strategies, and current practices in testing as they applied to their school.

School Improvement Team members also shared information with others in the school. Teachers were responsible for spreading the word among other teachers, and parents shared information at Home and School meetings (the school's PTO) and through the monthly school newsletter.

During the school year, teachers began to use new assessment strategies. Teachers in all grades and subjects applied the same strategies, so students experienced continuity in instruction and assessment. "Adding parents to the school improvement process has been very positive for the school," said the school's principal. "Parents' perspectives have been well received and taken back to the team for discussion."

Not surprisingly, one of the group's biggest challenges was finding enough time for discussions. Teachers' time was especially limited. Having a focus and an agenda for each meeting helped the group use its time well. Reading and studying the issues beforehand meant team members were ready to give feedback, ask questions, and participate in discussions.

Washington Junior High plans to continue this practice, which brought teachers and parents together with the common goal of improving assessment. In the future, the team hopes to create more time for its discussions and to increase communication between the parents on the team and other parents in the community, perhaps through informal meetings.

Source: From *Promising Partnership Practices* 2005

Explore these and other Type 5 applications in the annual collections of *Promising Partnership Practices,* at www.partnershipschools.org in the section Success Stories. See, for example, the activities in the following table:

Type 5 Activities	***School***	***Goal***	***Summary***
Breakfast With the Principal	Berendo Middle School, Los Angeles, CA	Increase parents' comfort with, knowledge of, and input to school policies and activities.	Monthly breakfasts with the principal, guest speakers, and time for questions and discussions help more families, including Latino families, feel welcome at the school and part of the school community.
Classroom Coordinators	Lincoln Elementary School for the Arts, Anoka, MN	Strengthen parent networks and increase the dissemination of information for all families about classroom and school events.	Identify "classroom coordinators" or room parents to connect with all parents, including those who do not speak English at home. The coordinators not only give information to families but also enable parents to share ideas, ask questions, and obtain services and help as needed.
Community Forum Series	Oltman Junior High School, Saint Paul, MN	Increase parent input into and feedback on school questions and decisions.	The ATP conducts monthly forums, including presentations by educators and community organizations, with outreach to include the families of the school's English Language Learners. Translators help families share their reactions and views on school issues.
Safe School Program	Kingsley Elementary School, Naperville, IL	Reduce bullying and build positive peer relationships.	The Partnership Team designed and implemented activities for students to learn to be more kind to, safe with, and respectful of others. The activity demonstrates how an ATP can initiate activities to involve parents in supporting students' positive behavior.

SCHOOL STORIES

TYPE 6–COLLABORATING WITH THE COMMUNITY

Partnership With the U.S.S. *San Jacinto*

Arrowhead Elementary School

Virginia Beach, Virginia

Goal for Partnership Climate: Create productive connections with a key community partner.

Goal for Student Success: Increase students' writing skills and improve their school behavior.

Level: Elementary Grades (adaptable to other grade levels)

Arrowhead Elementary School's partnership with sailors from the U.S.S. *San Jacinto* grew into a successful pen pal relationship and then a far-reaching lunch-buddy program called the San Jac Shipmate's Club. The students—many of whom have parents serving overseas in the navy or other branches of the military—liked the attention and encouragement of the adult role models. The sailors enjoyed the students' friendship and the different perspectives they offered.

In the spring of 2005, the school established a partnership with the *San Jacinto,* a navy cruiser based in nearby Norfolk that brought sailors into the school to help teachers run copies, tutor, and read to students. When the ship was deployed to Iraq, the school wanted the partnership to continue, so it collaborated with the ship's representatives to set up the pen pal program. Teachers at Arrowhead used the project as an instructional tool, leading children through the writing process, as they eagerly corresponded with the sailors. The children also learned about the sailors' daily lives and saw PowerPoint presentations of the sailors at work. The school provided the sailors with guidelines for encouraging students with test-taking tips and words of support.

Seeing how much the students liked the pen pal program with the sailors, the school continued and expanded the program when the *San Jacinto* returned to port. Working with representatives from both NNPS and the navy, the school established a lunch buddy mentorship program called the San Jac Shipmate's Club. Sailors came to school once a week to eat lunch and talk with their student buddies. Then, they read, studied, or played games. The third graders who had been pen pals teamed up with the sailors with whom they had been corresponding, while many other students at risk of failing in all grades also were paired with mentors. The school encouraged students' parents to meet with their child and his or her mentor.

The *San Jacinto* program helped 140 participating students both academically and behaviorally. The pen pal activity allowed students to practice their writing skills in a way that connected to their real lives. Students worked hard to improve their academic performance to please their mentors. Teachers noticed improvement in writing skills and test scores. Having a mentor also helped troubled students maintain self-control and strive to do their best in school.

The program cost approximately $400, most of which was paid by the *San Jacinto.* Even more critical than the money, however, was the crew's unwavering dedication to the pen pal and mentoring programs. The school's contacts aboard the ship invested time and energy to establish the pen pal program and to continue it once the sailors were ashore.

The Arrowhead students were not the only people who benefited from the program. The sailors also enjoyed the partnership. As the ship's chaplain explained it: "We live in a gray world [the ship is painted gray, inside and out]. The letters from the students and their smiling faces bring color to our world."

Source: From *Promising Partnership Practices* 2006

TYPE 6—COLLABORATING WITH THE COMMUNITY

Going to Dodge!

Roosevelt Elementary School

Saint Paul, Minnesota

Goal for Partnership Climate: Engage parents with students on a field trip to learn about an important community resource.

Goal for Student Success: Increase students' science knowledge and parent-child discussions about nature.

Level: Elementary Grades (adaptable to other grade levels)

Watching a red-tailed hawk, exploring wilderness trails, and looking closely at farm animals was an unusual way for students and parents at Roosevelt Elementary School to spend a Saturday. That was what made the beautiful fall day a hit with the 135 family members who found themselves "Going to Dodge"—the Dodge Nature Center.

The family field trip to the nearby nature preserve kicked off a partnership with the newest members of Roosevelt Elementary's Action Team for Partnerships (ATP). It also acquainted families with a community resource in their own backyards and taught science lessons under the guise of fun. The school invited all students in kindergarten through third grade and their families. Roosevelt draws students from diverse backgrounds, and many families do not have the time or resources to do daytrips. The ATP planned the trip and shared the cost with the Dodge Nature Center, which helped with transportation and provided naturalists to lead tours.

Families met at the school and boarded buses to Dodge. Once there, they took guided walks with the naturalists, who helped them explore the varieties of ecosystems at the nature center. Students received nets and had the opportunity to catch and release insects. They also visited farm animals and watched demonstrations by Dodge's trained birds of prey, including a red-tailed hawk, a barred owl, and a bald eagle.

The trip gave families an opportunity not only to learn about nature but also to take a trip without worrying about costs and transportation. One community member said, "I thoroughly enjoyed the experience. I never knew how close the center was in the neighborhood. I enjoyed learning about the classes offered, too."

The school is hoping to find funds to make this field trip an annual event. Families can return throughout the year on their own for apple orchard tours, grapevine wreath workshops, the Frosty Fun Festival, and summer camps!

Source: From *Promising Partnership Practices* 2006

Explore these and other Type 6 applications in the annual collections of *Promising Partnership Practices,* at www.partnershipschools.org in the section Success Stories. See, for example, the activities in the following table:

Type 6 Activities	***School***	***Goal***	***Summary***
Arts Extravaganza Family Night	Highwood Hills Elementary School, Saint Paul, MN	Improve school climate through artistic expression and multicultural awareness.	Organize performances and hands-on activities to feature the arts and crafts of Somali, Hmong, Hispanic, Japanese, Cambodian, African-American, and other cultures.
Health and Wellness With the Buffalo Bills	Dr. Lydia T. Wright School of Excellence, Buffalo, NY	Increase student and family attention to nutrition and exercise.	With players from the football team and other community groups, students and parents enjoyed activities at many stations, ran football drills, walked with pedometers, enjoyed healthy snacks, won prizes, and took home tips.
Motion Commotion Truck Fair	Ruth Livingston Elementary School, Pasco, WA	Increase students' career awareness with a variety of trucks and vehicles representing careers in the community.	Every other year, a vehicle carnival helps students learn about the various careers and their respective trucks. These include a dump truck, library bookmobile, police car, motor home, and almost 100 commercial and recreational vehicles. The students are engaged in related reading, writing, and discussions about career options.
Passport to Possibilities	Middle Township High School, Cape May Court House, NJ	Increase participation of community groups and agencies with the school. Increase students' and families' knowledge of resources, services, and programs in the community.	At a cultural fair, community artists, musicians, businesses, and agencies demonstrate and explain the resources and services available to students, educators, and families. In preparation, students also conduct writing and research projects linked to the curriculum.

References

Brownstein, J. I., Maushard, M., Robinson, J., Greenfeld, M. D., & Hutchins, D. J. (2006). *Promising partnership practices 2006.* Baltimore: Johns Hopkins University Center on School, Family, and Community Partnerships.

Maushard, M., Martin, C. S., Hutchins, D. J., Greenfeld, M. D., Thomas, B. G., Fournier, A., et al. (2007). *Promising partnership practices 2007.* Baltimore: Johns Hopkins University Center on School, Family, and Community Partnerships.

Salinas, K. C., Maushard, M., Brownstein, J. I., & Waxman, S. (2005). *Promising Partnership Practices 2005.* Baltimore: Johns Hopkins University Center on School, Family, and Community Partnerships.

See annual collections of *Promising Partnership Practices* at www.partnershipschools.org in the section Success Stories.

3

Take an Action Team Approach

This chapter presents information and tools to help any school's Action Team for Partnerships (ATP) organize its work and succeed as a team. In a "partnership school," teachers, parents, administrators, other family members, and community partners talk and work together to support student learning and development. Teamwork is essential for implementing an excellent program of school, family, and community partnerships.

ATP members need to understand how principals, teachers, counselors, parents, community groups, and students can work as a team, share leadership, and conduct activities that involve all families in their children's education. School leaders, district facilitators, state coordinators, and others should know the steps that schools' ATPs must take to write good plans for family and community involvement, conduct effective team meetings, organize committees, and implement activities that contribute to student learning and success in school.

In this chapter, the introductory article addresses 12 common questions about the purposes, members, committees, and responsibilities of an ATP. It also explains how an ATP differs from and enhances the work of a School Council, School Improvement Team, PTA, or PTO.

The chapter provides summaries, checklists, and guidelines to assist schools' ATPs with their work. District facilitators and other leaders who help school teams may use these tools as handouts in workshops or in team meetings to explain what an ATP does, to check progress, and to improve the quality of teamwork over time.

Ten Steps to Success in School, Family, and Community Partnerships

Review 10 basic steps for creating a successful program of school, family, and community partnerships in any elementary, middle, or high school. Success starts with an ATP. The team must set goals for partnerships, write and implement annual plans, conduct thoughtful evaluations, celebrate progress, and continue to work on partnerships from year to year. District leaders should facilitate the 10 steps in all schools.

Checklist: Are You Ready?

Use this checklist to help a school's ATP keep track of its progress in initiating a program of school, family, and community partnerships.

Who Are the Members of the Action Team for Partnerships?

Compile a directory of team members, with mail and e-mail addresses and phone numbers. Note the skills and talents that each member brings to the team. Also, list the ATP chair or co-chairs and main subcommittees and their leaders for the school year. Provide copies of this list, each year, to all team members to facilitate communication and to the district's facilitator for partnerships who assists the school.

First ATP Meeting of the School Year

Start the year with a well-planned agenda for the first meeting of the full ATP. The list of suggestions guides the chair or co-chairs of the ATP to start the year with discussions of how leadership will be shared, how committees are organized, how team members will communicate, when the team will meet, what the One-Year Action Plan for Partnerships includes, and what the full team and committees will do to implement the activities that are scheduled during the next month.

Communication Ground Rules

Decide how the members of the ATP will communicate with one another. Identify rules for interactions at meetings and at other times that will foster teamwork and team spirit.

What Do Successful Action Teams for Partnership Do?

Discuss the qualities that help ATPs succeed in leading their schools' partnership programs. Good teams help members communicate with each other and with other groups, conduct well-organized team meetings, solve problems, and improve plans for partnerships from year to year.

Annual Review of Team Processes

Assess the quality of teamwork at the end of each year by rating 18 team processes. ATP members should discuss how they can be even more effective in the future. See Chapter 9 for tools to evaluate the quality of the school's partnership program and practices.

Organizing an Effective Action Team for Partnerships:

Questions and Answers

Joyce L. Epstein

Who is responsible for developing and sustaining school, family, and community partnerships? The answer, of course, is that everyone with an interest in students' success has a role to play in conducting productive partnership activities. We have learned from many schools that one principal, one teacher, or one parent working alone cannot create a comprehensive and lasting program of partnerships. Rather, an Action Team for Partnerships (ATP) is needed to plan, implement, evaluate, and continually improve family and community involvement activities to create a welcoming school climate and to help all students succeed. Also, state and district leaders can and should inform and prepare school ATPs, facilitate their plans and activities, and help them improve their programs from year to year. (See Chapter 7 in this *Handbook*.)

This chapter addresses 12 key questions to help schools organize teamwork for partnerships and to help district leaders for partnerships learn what schools must do.

- What is an Action Team for Partnerships?
- Who are the members of the Action Team for Partnerships?
- What does an Action Team for Partnerships do?
- How should an Action Team for Partnerships organize its work?
- How do members of the Action Team for Partnerships share leadership?
- How do members become an effective team?
- How often should an Action Team for Partnerships meet?
- What planning and evaluation tools help an Action Team for Partnerships?
- What will the Action Team for Partnerships be named?
- How does an Action Team for Partnerships differ from the School Council or School Improvement Team?
- How does an Action Team for Partnerships differ from the PTA, PTO, Home-School Association, or other parent organization?
- How can the action team approach be used to organize comprehensive school reform (CSR)?

What Is an Action Team for Partnerships?

The Action Team for Partnerships (ATP) is an action arm—a committee or work group—of a School Council or School Improvement Team. If a school has no council or improvement team, the ATP is a special committee for planning and conducting partnerships, working with and advising the principal on this component of school improvement.

The ATP writes and implements plans for family and community involvement that will help produce desired results for students, families, and the school as a whole. The ATP includes teachers, administrators, parents, and students at the high school level, and it may include other family members or business and community partners. Members of the ATP work together to review school goals; select, design, implement, and evaluate partnership activities; and improve practices of family and community involvement. The work of an ATP helps create and sustain a climate of good partnerships at a school, and it involves families and the community in productive ways so that more students reach important educational goals for learning and success.

Who Are the Members of the Action Team for Partnerships?

A well-functioning ATP has 6 to 12 members. Members include at least two teachers, at least two parents, an administrator, and others who have important connections with families and students (e.g., counselor, school nurse, social worker, Title I parent liaison, a PTA/PTO officer or representative, instructional aide, secretary, custodian, grandparent who is raising a student, school psychologist, or others). The ATP also may include representatives from the community (e.g., business partners, interfaith leaders, representatives from literary, cultural, or civic organizations, and others). High school ATPs must include one or two students. The diverse members contribute many points of view, connections, talents, and resources for planning, implementing, and evaluating school, family, and community partnership activities.

Very small schools may adapt these guidelines to create smaller ATPs. Very large middle and high schools may extend membership to include one parent and educator from each major school division on an ATP. Or, large schools may create multiple ATPs for the defined schools-within-the-school, grade levels, middle school houses, high school career academies, or other large subdivisions (See Chapter 6). Other structural and procedural adaptations may be needed to accommodate the characteristics and constraints in diverse schools. The ATP is a stable structure, connected to the School Council or School Improvement Team and accountable to the principal. Because the principal is a member of the ATP, the team's focus on school improvement goals should be clear.

The ATP continues from year to year, even if some team members leave. New team members must replace those who leave. Teachers who leave the team must be replaced by teachers, parents must be replaced by parents, and so on. New team members must be oriented to the annual plans of the ATP and to their roles and responsibilities. See Who Are the Members of the Action Team (pp. 107–108 and CD) to account for the active members of the ATP each year and to provide a directory of contact information to encourage communication among team members.

What Does an Action Team for Partnerships Do?

In elementary, middle, and high schools, the ATP writes a plan, implements, delegates, and coordinates activities, monitors progress, solves problems, publicizes activities, and reports on the school's program of partnerships to the School Council or similar body and to other appropriate groups. Members of the ATP do not work alone. They recruit other teachers, students, administrators, parents, and community members, the parent association, the parent liaison, the nurse or counselors, district leaders, and others to lead and participate in family and community involvement activities.

The ATP also recognizes the family and community involvement activities conducted by individual teachers and other groups (e.g., PTA/PTO, afterschool program, and business partners). The school's partnership program includes *all* family and community involvement activities that are conducted for the school as a whole, in specific grade levels, and by individual teachers each year.

The ATP, then, should be able to describe and discuss the school's program of family and community involvement and all of its parts. This includes annual activities that can be sustained or improved from year to year, new activities developed and conducted by the ATP, delegated leaders, and individual or groups of teachers at different grade levels.

Specifically, in each elementary, middle, and high school, the ATP will do the following:

- Select a committee structure to organize its work by focusing on the six types of involvement or specific school improvement goals (see the next section).
- Select or elect the ATP chair or co-chairs and committee chairs or co-chairs. Co-chairs and/or chair-elects are recommended for all leadership positions.
- Write a detailed annual One-Year Action Plan for Partnerships to improve family and community involvement linked to school improvement plans. The plan for partnerships will include activities for all six types of involvement that involve families and the community in ways that create a welcoming climate and help students reach school goals. Make the detailed plan for partnerships an official part or appendix of the School Improvement Plan.
- Identify the budget(s) and resources that will support the activities in the One-Year Action Plan for Partnerships.
- Meet monthly as a whole team to ensure continuous progress in plans and activities and to evaluate activities that were implemented in the past month.
- Meet in smaller committees, as needed, to implement activities in the One-Year Action Plan for Partnerships.
- Conduct or delegate leadership to team members or to teachers, parents, and others not on the team to implement planned activities.
- Establish goals and guidelines for teamwork, including how team members will communicate, discuss ideas, solve problems, and make decisions.
- Report progress semiannually or more often to the School Council or School Improvement Team, faculty, and parent organization.
- Publicize the partnership plans and practices to parents, students, and teachers, and, as appropriate, the broader community. All teachers, parents, school staff, community members, and students should know how they can help select, design, conduct, enjoy, benefit from, and evaluate partnership activities.
- Recognize and celebrate excellent participation from parents, other family members, students, and others in the community who contribute to the success of planned partnership activities.
- Evaluate progress to improve the quality of implementations and the strength of results of various involvement activities. Use the Annual Evaluation of Activities (pp. 330–341 and CD) throughout the school year to review and reflect on each activity that is implemented.

- Gather ideas for new activities for the *next* One-Year Action Plan from parents, parent organization, teachers, and other partners, and discuss these ideas as a team.
- Solve problems that impede progress on partnership activities.
- Write a new One-Year Action Plan for Partnerships each year to ensure an ongoing program of partnerships in the life and work of the school. Make the new detailed plan for partnerships an official part or appendix of the School Improvement Plan.
- Replace teachers, parents, administrators, or others who leave the ATP with new members from the same positions so that a full team is always ready to conduct a planned program of partnerships at the school.

These steps must be followed each year to sustain an excellent program of school, family, and community partnerships. By conducting these activities, the ATP helps everyone know that the school has a well-defined and active partnership program. From year to year, the number and quality of activities in a school's One-Year Action Plan for Partnerships should improve, as should positive results of the activities.

How Should an Action Team for Partnerships Organize Its Work?

An ATP may organize its work by focusing on specific school improvement goals *or* on the six types of involvement. This choice determines the structure of the ATP's committees, how One-Year Action Plans for Partnerships are written, and how the program is evaluated.

Organize ATP committees to help reach school improvement goals. One way to organize ATP committees, plans, and evaluations is to focus family and community involvement on helping the school and students reach specific improvement goals. In this, the "Goals Approach," the ATP creates committees with chairs or co-chairs and members who become the school's experts on how family and community involvement can help students reach selected academic and nonacademic goals such as improving reading, math, or science skills; improving attendance or behavior; or other goals and for creating a welcoming school environment for all families and students (see p. 164 in Chapter 5).

Each committee writes one section (one page) of the One-Year Action Plan for Partnerships–Form G (Goals), obtains input from the rest of the team, and takes responsibility for implementing or delegating and evaluating the activities in that section of the action plan. For example, one or two members of the ATP may chair or co-chair a committee for involving families and the community to help students improve reading skills and attitudes. The reading-goal committee of the ATP will write one page of the One-Year Action Plan for Partnerships that outlines and schedules activities that focus on involvement in reading, drawing from the six types of involvement. The plan may outline workshops for parents, communications about state standards and tests on reading, volunteer reading buddies, and so on.

If another school goal is to improve student attendance, the attendance-goal committee of the ATP will oversee that section of the plan and engage family and community members in ways that ensure that healthy students attend school every day and that they arrive on time. The attendance committee may select activities to increase families' understanding of school policies about attendance, clarify report card statistics on attendance, train volunteers to telephone absent students' families, have families pick up and monitor homework for students who are absent, and address other ways to improve student attendance and reduce lateness.

Other members of the ATP may co-chair or serve on committees to involve families and the community to help students improve skills and attitudes in math, science, or writing; or to improve attendance or behavior; or to develop a welcoming school and sense of community. The assignments will match the pages of the One-Year Action Plan for Partnerships.

Field tests indicate that ATPs can effectively address four school improvement goals each year—two academic goals, one behavioral goal, and one goal to conduct activities that create a welcoming school climate and sense of community. Experienced teams may add goals and activities over time with additional ATP members. From year to year, the quality and results of activities addressing specific school goals should improve, along with the ATP members' expertise and teamwork.

Organize ATP committees to strengthen the six types of involvement. Another way to organize ATP committees, plans, and evaluations is to focus on the six types of involvement: *parenting, communicating, volunteering, learning at home, decision making, and collaborating with the community.* In this, the "Types Approach," the ATP creates six committees, each with a chair or co-chairs and members who become the school's experts on each type of involvement (see p. 165 in Chapter 5).

In this case, each committee writes one section (one page) of the One-Year Action Plan for Partnerships–Form T (Types), obtains input from the rest of the team, and takes responsibility for implementing, delegating, and evaluating the activities for the specific type of involvement. There will be a page of planned activities to strengthen Type 1–Parenting with workshops on child development, parent-to-parent connections, activities for families to inform the school about their children's needs or family goals, and other Type 1 activities. Similarly, a page of planned activities should be written for each of the other types of involvement, led by at least one ATP member and other team or non–team members so that the planned activities are successfully implemented and reach all families. From year to year, the quality and results of activities for all six types of involvement should improve, along with the ATP members' expertise and teamwork.

The two approaches for organizing ATP committees are not mutually exclusive. Plans for partnerships based on school improvement goals must include activities for all six types of involvement. Plans for partnerships based on types of involvement must specify how the activities will help reach important school goals. The difference in the two approaches is in how ATP members organize committees, explain their roles and responsibilities, write their One-Year Action Plans for Partnerships, and complete the Annual Evaluation of Activities. (See Chapters 5 and 9 for planning and evaluation tools, respectively, organized by goals for school improvement and for types of involvement.)

How Do Members of the Action Team for Partnerships Share Leadership?

Many people play important leadership roles on an ATP. All members of the team contribute ideas to the One-Year Action Plan for Partnerships; lead, co-lead, or assist on committees; delegate leadership and mobilize support for activities; and evaluate the results of their efforts (Epstein, 2001).

Each ATP has a chairperson or, optimally, co-chairs. Co-chairs should be educators and parents who are recognized and accepted as leaders by all team members. ATP committees also have a chair or co-chairs. The co-chair structure gives greater stability to the ATP and to its committees in case some members leave the school.

Members of the ATP and other teachers, parents, school staff, and community partners who are not on the ATP may lead various involvement activities in the One-Year Action Plan for Partnerships. If the school has a parent organization (e.g., PTA, PTO), *its* annual activities should be included in or appended to the One-Year Action Plan for Partnerships. Those activities may be organized by its leaders and committees or conducted collaboratively with others. There is plenty of work to do in a full partnership program. Therefore, many individuals, groups, and committees must share leadership so that activities will be well planned and well implemented and will involve all families.

Even as school principals, guidance counselors and specialists, teachers, paraprofessional and other staff, parents, community partners, and students work as a team to ensure a successful partnership program, some members have unique roles and responsibilities. In addition, district leaders for partnerships, too, can affect the quality of schools' teamwork, programs, and progress on partnerships.

Principals

School principals are essential members of the ATP. They support and guide the ATP's connections to the School Council or School Improvement Team. At the middle and high school levels, assistant principals and/or school-within-a-school administrators also may serve on the ATP.

Principals must be able to articulate the new directions for school-based, goal-linked programs of family and community involvement outlined in this *Handbook.* No longer is a partnership program something that a principal conducts alone; it is something that an Action Team for Partnerships does, collaboratively, to involve all students' families in useful ways (Epstein & Jansorn, 2004; Sanders & Sheldon, 2009; Van Voorhis & Sheldon, 2004).

Ideally, a principal should not be the chair of an ATP. It is best to leave the leadership role of the ATP to a teacher or counselor or to educator and parent co-chairs. Some principals do want the chair's role or want to serve as co-chairs of the ATP. Others elect to act as chair or co-chair of an ATP committee for one of the targeted school improvement goals or for one of the six types of involvement. By allowing others to serve as ATP chairs, principals build leaders at their schools while still remaining key and active members of the ATP. The principal is, ultimately, a school's leader and is responsible for program plans and final decisions, but he or she does not lose that defining role by sharing leadership with others on the ATP.

There are many ways that a principal exercises leadership on partnerships. As an active member of the ATP, a principal may take the following leadership actions:

- Use the bully pulpit of the principal's office to let teachers, staff, parents, students, and the community know that you have a "partnership school." Explain how the School Council, the Action Team for Partnerships (ATP), and all staff and parents will work together to help all students succeed to their fullest potential.

- Let *all* students know—frequently—how important their families are to the school and to the students' progress and success in school.
- At the first faculty meeting each year, talk about the ATP's mission or "charge," the importance of teamwork on partnerships, and the support that will be provided.
- Allocate funds for the school's program of school, family, and community partnerships, and include the funds as a line item for partnership program development in the annual school budget.
- Provide time and space for ATP meetings. Arrange for teachers on the ATP to meet at the same time or make sure the school will be open for meetings before or after school hours.
- Publicize scheduled involvement activities throughout the school year. Encourage all educators, parents, and others to participate to develop a strong partnership program, a welcoming school climate, and a sense of community.
- Recognize all teachers' contributions to the school's program of partnerships in the activities they conduct with their students' families. Help teachers become more effective in communicating with parents about students' homework, schoolwork, grades, and test scores and in conducting parent-teacher-student conferences.
- Evaluate each teacher's activities to involve families as part of an annual or periodic professional review.
- Guide the ATP in making periodic reports on partnership plans and accomplishments to the school council, faculty, parent organization, local media, and other key community groups.
- Work with community groups and leaders to locate resources that will enrich the curriculum and that provide important services to students and families.
- Recognize and thank ATP leaders and team members, active family volunteers, business and community partners, and other participants for their time and contributions to involvement activities each year.
- Work with school district facilitators for partnerships, district administrators, and principals from other schools to arrange professional development on partnerships, share ideas, solve challenges, and improve school, family, and community partnerships.

These and other leadership actions by principals support and strengthen schools' partnership programs, family involvement, and results for students.

Guidance Counselors and Specialists

Guidance counselors, school psychologists, school social workers, and other social service professionals may be members of an ATP and may serve as ATP chair or co-chairs. They also may be leaders of ATP committees for specific goals, activities, and types of involvement. Assistant principals and guidance counselors are particularly helpful team leaders or co-chairs in middle and high schools, because their professional agendas link directly to students, families, and communities. These school professionals have time, training, and experience to plan and conduct meetings and to guide teachers, parents, students, and community members to work effectively together.

School psychologists, school social workers, nurses, and other professionals may assist one school or may have more than one school assignment. They may be members of the ATPs of the school(s) they assist and can use their expertise in leadership roles and as partners on activities.

In districts where a district level leader for partnerships lacks sufficient staff to assist schools from the central office, the social service professionals may be prepared and mobilized as "external staff" to work with the district leader to facilitate schools' ATPs in developing, improving, and sustaining their programs of partnership.

Teachers

At least two or three *teachers* must be members of the ATP and may serve as ATP chair or co-chairs and as committee leaders. They may be master teachers, lead teachers, department chairs, or classroom teachers from different grade levels. Teachers on the ATP contribute ideas for family and community involvement activities linked to academic goals for students. They also connect and communicate with all teachers in the school about schoolwide and classroom level practices of family and community involvement. Some schools increase the number of ATP members to include one teacher from each grade level to ensure that family involvement activities are planned, implemented, and shared across the grades and with all families.

Whether on the ATP or not, all teachers conduct activities with their own students' families. They also may collaborate as grade level teams to engage students and families in units of work and special projects. The ATP should collect and collate information from all teachers in the school to record their family and community involvement activities as part of the school's overall program of partnerships. The complete list of all teachers' practices should be included in or appended to the One-Year Action Plan for Partnerships. See the form, The Complete Picture on the *Handbook* CD only with other planning forms in Chapter 5.

Teachers on the ATP communicate and work with all teachers and staff to reinforce the importance of connections with students' families. Teachers should share best practices for all six types of involvement and continually improve communications and outreach with families and the community. Teachers may help each other become more effective in communicating with parents about homework, report card grades, learning standards, state and school tests, and other topics related to student success. Communications on students' good work and notable progress are as important as connections about students' academic and behavioral problems. All teachers must be invited to participate in the whole-school partnership activities organized by the ATP that involve all families in the school. All teachers can work with the ATP and with each other to improve the timing, format, and content of parent-teacher-student conferences.

Paraprofessionals

Parent liaisons (also titled parent coordinators, parent leaders, family liaisons) are paid aides who help educators connect and communicate with parents and other family members. Parent liaisons must be members of the Action Team for Partnerships (ATP). They may serve, with educators, as co-chairs of the ATP or as leaders of ATP committees. They may be particularly appropriate as leaders of workshops or activities that directly assist families on goal-linked activities for

Type 1–Parenting or Type 6–Collaborating with the Community. They also may help train and coordinate parent volunteers (Type 3–Volunteering). Bilingual liaisons may serve as translators and interpreters for parents who speak languages other than English at home (Type 2–Communicating).

Other paraprofessionals (e.g., instructional aides, assistants in school libraries, computer labs, and other locations) and other school staff (e.g., secretarial, cafeteria, custodial, and transportation staff) also may serve as members of the Action Team for Partnerships and as participants in ATP activities.

Parent leaders should not work in the "old way" as lone leaders but in the "new way" as members of an action team focused on involving families and the community to boost student success in school (Epstein, 2007; Sanders, 2008).

Families

Parents and other family members are essential members of the ATP. They may serve as co-chairs of the ATP and of ATP committees along with teachers, administrators, and school staff. Parents on the ATP should come from different neighborhoods or groups served by the school. If the school has a PTA or PTO, one representative should be on the Action Team for Partnerships.

Parents and other family members on the ATP contribute ideas and help educators understand topics that are important for families, design ways to involve all families, conduct activities on family-friendly schedules, recruit families to lead and implement activities, and encourage all families to participate in activities. Some schools recruit a family representative from each grade level to serve on the team to ensure that activities address parents' interest and children's development at all age levels. With diverse representation, all parents in the school should see that they have a voice on the ATP and a contact with whom to share ideas and questions.

Parents and all members of an ATP experience team training together to learn about new directions for school, family, and community partnerships and to write their first One-Year Action Plan for Partnerships. The One-Day Team-Training Workshop is "professional development" for teachers *and* for parent leaders on the ATP. All members of the ATP share responsibilities for leading the activities that are scheduled in the annual plan for partnerships. This approach changes definitions of professional development and shared leadership to recognize and to ensure parents' contributions to partnership programs.

Community Partners

Business and other community partners may serve on an ATP. Some ATPs include a business partner, librarian, police officer, city council official, scientist, medical expert, or faith-based leader as team members. Community partners bring expert knowledge, useful connections, and various resources to ATP committees.

Community members may take appropriate leadership roles, such as co-chairing an ATP committee or leading an involvement activity. For example, a business partner may co-chair a committee for the goal of increasing student attendance, as the involvement activities will include several agencies and other groups to help the school, students, and families improve students' on-time, daily arrival. Or, a community partner might lead Type 6–Collaborating With the Community activities, such as establishing an afterschool program with the local parks and recreation department or identifying community groups to help improve students' reading, behavior, or school safety or student and family health.

If community partners are on the ATP, they, too, experience the One-Day Team-Training Workshop as "professional development" to build their expertise on partnerships.

Students

Students must serve on the ATP in high schools. Although they may not serve as ATP chairs or co-chairs, they may share leadership with an educator, parent, or community partner for specific activities in the One-Year Action Plan for Partnerships. Teachers, parents, and others on high school ATPs value students' ideas for and reactions to plans for partnerships. Student members communicate with other high school students in various ways to gather ideas about which school, family, and community partnerships are important and acceptable to students and their families.

At all school levels, all students are the main actors in their own education. They also play key roles family and community involvement. All students deliver messages from school to home and from home to school. Students often explain, interpret, and translate memos and information to parents. They are leaders in discussions with parents about homework, report cards, school events, and problems they may have at school. Therefore, all students at all grade levels should be well informed about the goals of the ATP and how to involve their own families in open or targeted activities. Only with student involvement and support will programs of school, family, and community partnerships succeed.

All members of the ATP are expected to be able to speak knowledgeably about the school's One-Year Action Plans for Partnerships, provide leadership for implementing some family and community involvement activities, and work with others to sustain an effective team and productive partnership program.

How Do Members Become an Effective Team?

Teachers, administrators, parents, community partners, and others on an ATP must learn to function well as a team. They meet each other, learn each other's strengths and talents, set ground rules for communicating, plan and implement activities, produce results, evaluate activities, share successes, solve problems, replace members who leave, and improve plans and processes over time to sustain their work as a team. The team, itself, is a message that educators, parents, and community partners will work together to help more students succeed in school. Only a well-functioning team, however, will produce the desired results.

Over time, groups may progress through several developmental stages to become an effective team: *forming, storming, norming, and performing* (see Hirsh & Valentine, 1998, for the derivation and descriptions of these stages based on earlier work by Tuckman, 1965). Teams need to get a good start, minimize conflict, establish rules and procedures, and take action. Some ATPs move quickly or skip through these stages to become productive and successful. Other ATPs move slowly but steadily, and still other teams get stuck and fail to function. As new team members are added, some ATPs remain strong and productive, whereas others must regroup and reestablish team qualities before they can move ahead with to work on partnerships. Here, we apply this framework to discuss how to establish and sustain well-functioning ATPs.

Get a good start. When teams are *forming,* members have high expectations for success. They also have many questions about the team's mission or charge and their own roles and responsibilities. Members must learn about each other's strengths and talents and establish basic ground rules for communicating with one another (see p. 110 and CD). Each year, new members may join the ATP, either to replace those who leave the school or to increase the size of the ATP. Thus, each year it is necessary to reintroduce the mission and purpose of the team, review goals and plans, and reassign members' roles and responsibilities.

It is important to select teachers, parents, administrators, and other members of the team who believe that families and the community can support students and the school. The team should elect effective leaders—preferably *co*-chairs, provide copies of the Action Plan for Partnerships to all members, and share contact information so that all members can communicate easily with each other. It helps if an ATP elects leaders one year ahead of time, so that the chair-elect can "shadow" the present leader throughout the school year.

When teams convene at the start of the school year, the principal, chair of the School Improvement Team, and, if appropriate, a district leader for partnerships, should discuss the team's charge, express support, and outline the resources available for the team's work. The chair or co-chairs of the ATP may conduct a team-building activity to help members get to know one another.

Minimize conflict. Some teams enter short periods when individuals or subgroups seem to be *storming* with each other. If the ATP's charge is unclear or if the One-Year Action Plan for Partnerships is not addressing important goals, members may be uncertain about why they are on the team. If meetings are irregular or poorly planned, members may become critical of the team leaders and question the value of participating.

These concerns and confusions can be minimized or eliminated if the ATP writes a One-Year Action Plan for Partnerships that focuses on important goals with innovative, productive, and enjoyable involvement activities. It is imperative for the team to meet monthly for well-planned meetings so that activities can be planned and that those conducted can be evaluated.

The One-Year Action Plan for Partnerships should be written each spring for the next school year and reviewed and refreshed when the team reassembles each fall. Team-building activities can be conducted, as needed, to draw attention to important norms, rules, and skills for good teamwork, such as listening to each other, discussing disagreements, and respecting differences in opinions.

Establish rules and procedures. The process of *norming* occurs when all team members agree how the ATP will conduct its meetings and its work. Some teams assign specific roles to ensure more effective team meetings. A *recorder* or *secretary* may take notes and distribute summaries of team meetings to those who could not attend. A *timekeeper* may help keep the meeting agenda on schedule. *Links or liaisons* to the School Improvement Team and PTA or PTO may help alert and recruit participants for activities for family and community involvement.

The ATP may set procedures and rules for how team members will listen to each other, solicit ideas, express disagreements, discuss solutions to problems, agree to compromises, and make decisions. The norms for teamwork help members build trust and respect for one another and strengthen the spirit of cooperation for work that must be done.

Take action. When members understand the team's goals, know their own and others' responsibilities and talents, and agree on the rules for interaction and cooperation, an ATP can become a *high-performing* leadership committee in any elementary, middle, or high school. High-performing teams cooperate and communicate to implement planned activities, evaluate the quality and results of activities, and celebrate successes. Each year, good teams review their meeting schedules, procedures, and responsibilities. ATPs must evaluate their plans, activities, and teamwork (see Chapter 9) and write new annual plans to continually improve their partnership programs, practices, and results.

Every Action Team for Partnerships has a responsibility to minimize conflicts, create positive processes, and take action to involve families and the community in ways that produce important results for students. By using the tools and guidelines in this *Handbook*, any ATP can become a successful team.

How Often Should an Action Team for Partnerships Meet?

An ATP should conduct just the right number of meetings—not too many and not too few—on a realistic and regular schedule. An ATP should consider the following recommendations about team meetings and reports.

Whole-Team Meetings. The full ATP should meet at least monthly for one or two hours. Each meeting should have a well-planned agenda that reinforces teamwork and that keeps the activities in the One-Year Action Plan for Partnerships moving forward. Whole team meetings may be used to orient new team members; build team spirit; write, review, and revise the One-Year Action Plan for Partnerships; monitor the progress of all ATP committees; evaluate activities that were implemented in the past month; discuss activities that are scheduled for the next month; plan publicity and other communication strategies; identify and solve problems; conduct assessments at the end of the school year; celebrate progress; plan and write a new One-Year Action Plan for Partnerships for the next school year; and conduct other ATP business.

Committee Meetings. ATP committees are subgroups of the full team who take charge of planning, conducting or delegating, and evaluating the involvement activities for different sections (or pages) of the One-Year Action Plan for Partnerships. There should be one committee for each page of the plan (Form G–Goals or Form T–Types). The ATP committees may, for example, focus on involvement activities linked to school improvement goals (e.g., to help students improve reading or improve school climate) or on each of the six types of involvement. Committees or subgroups must meet as often as needed to ensure that the activities for which they are responsible are successfully planned and implemented.

Some ATPs do all of their work as a whole team. This is not as effective as having committees or subgroups take responsibility for various activities as they are scheduled throughout the year. Some ATPs create temporary committees or ad hoc work groups for each activity that is scheduled on the various pages of the action plan. Although this may not increase the expertise of team members in particular areas (e.g., family involvement in reading), ad hoc committees can be successful. Such groups must be formed in a timely way to plan and implement or delegate and oversee each activity in the One-Year Action Plan for Partnerships.

ATPs must decide the best way to organize committees in their own locations. At committee meetings, members may discuss responsibilities, list needed resources for implementing upcoming activities (e.g., facilities, materials, publicity, or outreach or assistance from the full ATP, School Improvement Team, or others), celebrate successes, plan improvements, share their evaluations with the full ATP at a whole-team meeting, and conduct other committee responsibilities.

The co-chairs of the full ATP and the leaders of the ATP committees also must prepare agendas for their meetings, secure a room, remind members of the meeting, invite special guests, conduct the meeting, see that absent members are informed of accomplishments and assignments, and take other leadership roles.

The chair, co-chairs, or designated members of the ATP should report regularly (at least twice a year) to the School Council or School Improvement Team, the full faculty, the PTA or PTO, and other groups so that all teachers, parents, students, and members of the community know about the school's plans, activities, and progress on partnerships (see p. 111 and CD). The regular reports and discussions with school groups also are occasions to gather information and ideas for changes and improvements to plans and practices of partnerships and to recruit leaders and participants for various activities.

The chair, co-chairs, or designated members of the ATP should publicize the plans, activities, and progress on partnerships to all families, students, and the community in school or community newsletters, on Web sites, with banners or posters, in other media, and in various forums to increase understanding, participation, and support for partnerships.

What Tools Help an Action Team for Partnerships Do its Work?

To fulfill its responsibilities and to develop and strengthen a program of partnerships from year to year, an Action Team for Partnerships (ATP) should address the questions in the first column. Planning and evaluation tools in this *Handbook* described in the second column may be used to answer the questions.

QUESTIONS TO ANSWER	TOOLS TO USE
1. This school's ATP is already conducting some family involvement activities. How can we take stock of the activities that teachers are doing individually, that are being done at particular grade levels, and that are being conducted by various groups schoolwide?	1. Use *Starting Points* to inventory all present practices for the six types of involvement (see pp. 174–177 and CD).
2. This school has a School Improvement Plan that identifies key goals. Can the ATP link family and community involvement to our school's goals for improvement?	2. Select the *One-Year Action Plan for Partnerships* (Form G–Goals) to write an annual plan for family and community involvement that is directly linked to specific goals in the School Improvement Plan (see pp. 181–184 and CD for Form G).
3. There are so many parent and community involvement activities to choose from. How can our ATP organize a realistic plan for this school year?	3. Complete the *One-Year Action Plan for Partnerships* with a detailed schedule of activities and specific responsibilities for members of the Action Team for Partnerships. See pages 181–190 and CD for alternatives (Form G and Form T).
4. This school is implementing its One-Year Action Plan for Partnerships. How will our ATP know if we are making progress?	4. Complete the *Annual Evaluation of Activities*. Reflect on the quality of each activity as it is implemented throughout the year. At the end of the year, review the reports and identify needed improvements (see pp. 330–341 and CD).

Also see Chapter 9 for more on how to evaluate your partnership program.

What Will the Action Team for Partnerships Be Named?

A school may call its team the Action Team for Partnerships (ATP) or select an alternative name. Some teams have named themselves the School, Family, and Community Partnership (SFCP) or have selected more unique names, such as Parent-Educator Network (PEN), Teachers Getting Involved with Families (TGIF), Partners in Education (PIE), Partners for Student Success (PASS), Partners for Progress (PFP), Teachers and Parents for Students (TAPS), and other names that refer to the concept of partnerships.

Some names should *not* be chosen. Avoid titles that refer only to parents and not to partners (such as The Parent Team or Bringing Parents to School). These are *bad* names because they suggest that the ATP is conducting a "parent program." A program of school, family, and community partnerships is *not* about the parents. It *is* about increasing student success by mobilizing the support of families and other partners. The team needs a name that conveys the fact that educators, families, and the community will work together because they share an interest in the success of all students.

How Does an Action Team for Partnerships Differ From the School Improvement Team or School Council?

School councils, improvement teams, and other decision making or advisory groups identify school goals and write and oversee broad plans. School councils are agents for change that draw the big picture of school improvement and set goals for excellence. They focus on what teachers, administrators, and other school staff must do to improve curriculum, instruction, assessments, and management of the school. Most School Councils do not write detailed plans and schedules focused explicitly on family and community involvement activities (see p. 167 in Chapter 5.)

The Action Team for Partnerships (ATP) accounts for and takes responsibility for planning and conducting family and community involvement activities. The ATP, a committee of the School Council, reports to the council or improvement team on a regular schedule to explain how family and community connections are supporting specific school improvement goals. The ATP's reports should help the School Council see that the school is developing a welcoming, family-friendly climate and that progress is being made on partnerships each year.

For example, the School Council may identify the need for students to improve their math skills and set a goal in the School Improvement Plan to assist teachers in improving the math curriculum and instructional approaches to help students increase math skills and test scores. Families and the community also can support this goal if the ATP schedules involvement activities in the One-Year Action Plan for Partnerships that focus on math-related activities such as helping students develop positive attitudes toward math, complete math homework, and share math progress.

Can the School Council *Be* the Action Team for Partnerships?

If a School Council or School Improvement Team is very large, a designated subset of teachers, parents, and an administrator may *be* the Action Team for Partnerships. In most schools, however, the School Improvement Team or School Council is limited in size and has defined responsibilities for advising the principal about school goals and for overseeing all aspects of the school's program and progress.

Most School Councils need an ATP—an action arm—to plan and implement family and community involvement activities. The ATP (like any committee) reports to the School Council on a regular schedule about its progress on family and community involvement and obtains input and ideas from the Council for the annual One-Year Action Plan for Partnerships. One member of the School Council may also serve on the ATP as a *linking member* to ensure that the School Council is always aware and informed of the plans and activities for partnerships and how to support those activities.

When different people serve on the School Council and the ATP, individual leaders are protected from trying to do too many things and burning out. Also, an ATP ensures that more teachers, administrators, parents, and community partners develop leadership skills over time.

How Does the Action Team for Partnerships Differ From the PTA or PTO?

A school benefits by having an Action Team for Partnerships *and* a PTA, PTO, Home-School Association, or other parent organization. A PTA or PTO helps develop parent leaders and brings parents' voices to bear on school policies, decisions, and activities. Typically, however, a PTA or PTO does not direct the work of school administrators or teachers. In contrast, an ATP writes plans and conducts or delegates activities to organize and improve communications with all families on student learning, homework, report card grades, curriculum matters, tests and assessments, postsecondary planning, parent-teacher-student conferences, and other important school and classroom topics.

The ATP writes an annual One-Year Action Plan for Partnerships so that family and community involvement includes activities that teachers, administrators, counselors, community partners, or others conduct to help all parents understand their children's work and learning opportunities each year. This extends the PTA or PTO's agenda to ensure that the school's program of family and community involvement is officially linked to the School Improvement Plan and goals for student success. The ATP, which includes teachers and administrators, will improve connections with families about the curriculum, students' work, and students' academic and behavioral progress.

The PTA or PTO is a *parent-oriented* group. The ATP is a *student-oriented* group that mobilizes the energies, resources, and efforts of all who are interested in student success. The PTA or PTO may be purposely independent of the school. The ATP is a committee of the School Council or School Improvement Team, and the annual written plans for partnerships are an official part of and appended to the School Improvement Plan.

An officer or representative of the PTA/PTO should be a member of the Action Team for Partnerships to make sure that the two groups are working in concert. With an ATP, all partners—including the PTA or PTO and other business and community partners—can work together to support parents, students, and the school.

This *Handbook* guides schools to have *one* school improvement plan with *one* set of improvement goals, usually developed by or with the approval of the School Council or School Improvement Team. From that base, schools should have *one partnership program* to support and advance student success. This requires an annual Action Plan for Partnerships that identifies and recognizes *all* of the family and community involvement activities that will be conducted by educators, PTA or PTO, business partners, community groups, afterschool programs, and others. In this way, everyone's work on family and community involvement is accounted for and celebrated, and the school's partnership program will continue to grow and improve.

How Can Action Teams for Partnerships Guide Comprehensive School Reform?

Schools with ambitious goals for whole-school change may organize a Partnership School–Comprehensive School Reform (CSR) model (Epstein, 2005). In the Partnership School–CSR model, *four* or *five* action teams are organized, instead of only an Action Team for Partnerships. Each action team writes and implements annual action plans to attain a major school improvement goal. For example, a school may have an Action Team for Math (ATM), an Action Team for Reading (ATR), an Action Team for Attendance (ATA), *and* an Action Team for Partnerships (ATP).

In the CSR model, *all* teachers and staff must join *only one* team to increase expertise on a school improvement topic. There also must be parents on each action team. In this way, teachers, administrators, school staff, parents, and members of the community will learn to work together to improve all aspects of the educational program for student success.

Each team's annual action plans must include specific, scheduled activities for improving the curriculum, instructional approaches, assessments, and classroom management to attain each selected school goal. In addition, each team's action plan must include activities for the six types of family and community involvement to help the school and students reach the selected goals.

In a Partnership School–CSR model, schools may select various academic and behavioral goals for their students, but all schools must include one goal and one dedicated team to strengthen and sustain a positive climate of school, family, and community partnerships. The Action Team for Partnerships will build a strong and inclusive climate of partnerships with activities for the six types of involvement that are not addressed by the action teams for the other selected academic and behavioral goals.

The Partnership School–CSR model requires a leader or leaders who will facilitate the work of the school's several teams. Each team must also have a budget for the activities that are selected, including new curricular activities and instruction. This CSR model enriches other approaches that use a team approach by extending teamwork and shared leadership to include parent representatives and the involvement of all families on all school improvement topics.

References

Epstein, J. L. (2001). Strategies for action in practice, policy, and research. In J. L. Epstein, *School, family, and community partnerships: Preparing educators and improving schools* (pp. 563–605). Boulder, CO: Westview Press.

Epstein, J. L. (2005). Results of the Partnership Schools–CSR model for student achievement over three years. *Elementary School Journal, 106,* 151–170.

Epstein, J. L. (2007). *Parent liaisons: What IS their role in partnership programs?* Type 2, #22, p. 2. Retrieved March 14, 2008 from www.partnershipschools.org in the section Publications and Products, in Type 2.

Epstein, J. L., & Jansorn, N. R. (2004). Developing successful partnership programs: Principal leadership makes a difference. *Principal, 83*(3), 10–15.

Hirsh, S., & Valentine, J. W. (1998). *Building effective middle level teams.* Reston, VA: National Association of Secondary School Principals.

Sanders, M. G. (2008). How parent liaisons can help bridge home and school. *Journal of Education Research, 101,* 287–297.

Sanders, M. G, & Sheldon, S. B. (2009). *A principal's guide to school, family, and community partnerships.* Thousand Oaks, CA: Corwin Press.

Tuckman, B. (1965). Developmental sequence in small groups. *Psychological Bulletin, 63,* 384–399.

Van Voorhis, F. L., & Sheldon, S. B. (2004). Principals' roles in the development of U.S. programs of school, family, and community partnerships. *International Journal of Educational Research, 41*(1), 55–70.

Ten Steps to Success: School-Based Programs of School, Family, and Community Partnerships

- ✔ **Create an Action Team for Partnerships.**
- ✔ **Obtain funds and official support.**
- ✔ **Provide training to all members of the Action Team for Partnerships.**
- ✔ **Identify starting points—present strengths and weaknesses.**
- ✔ **Write a One-Year Action Plan for Partnerships.**
- ✔ **Apply the framework of six types of involvement to activities linked to school improvement goals.**
- ✔ **Enlist staff, parents, students, and the community to help conduct activities.**
- ✔ **Evaluate the quality and outreach of partnership activities and results.**
- ✔ **Conduct an annual celebration to report progress to all participants.**
- ✔ **Continue working toward a comprehensive, ongoing, goal-oriented program of partnerships.**

Checklist: Are You Ready?

GETTING STARTED WITH AN ACTION TEAM FOR PARTNERSHIPS

The chair or co-chairs of the Action Team for Partnerships (ATP) will guide these activities.

CHECK (✓) WHEN YOUR SCHOOL ATP HAS COMPLETED THE FOLLOWING:

❑ **Select the members of the ATP** including 6 to 12 members, with teachers, parents, principal, and others selected for their interest in and commitment to positive school, family, and community connections.

❑ **Identify the chair or co-chairs of the Action Team for Partnerships.**

❑ **Select a committee structure for the ATP to focus on four school improvement goals or on the six types of involvement. Identify the chair or co-chairs of each committee.**

❑ **Complete an inventory of present practices** for each of the six types of involvement. Discuss the inventory with teachers, parents, students, and others and obtain their ideas about partnership activities that should be maintained, improved, and added (see *Starting Points,* pp. 174–177 and CD).

❑ **Select goals from the School Improvement Plan that would be strengthened with activities for family and community involvement.**

❑ **Complete a One-Year Action Plan for Partnerships** specifying specific activities for each of the six types of involvement or for four school improvement goals. Include details on who is responsible for implementing the involvement activities, when the activities will be conducted, and what results are expected.

❑ **Schedule a basic, One-Day Team-Training Workshop to complete many of the actions listed above, as guided by this *Handbook* (see Chapters 4 and 5).**

❑ **Establish a schedule of monthly meetings for the full ATP,** and discuss plans for meetings of ATP committees. Select the place and time of ATP meetings, and decide how the meetings will be organized.

Decide how often and in what ways the ATP will report to the following groups:

- ❑ The School Council, School Improvement Team, or other decision making body
- ❑ All teachers and staff
- ❑ All parents
- ❑ Parent organization (e.g., PTA, PTO, or other groups)
- ❑ The community (e.g., business roundtable, local media, mayor's office)
- ❑ District leaders, school board, other district offices

❑ **Design and schedule a kickoff activity** to effectively convey the message to all educators, families, and students that the school is a partnership school. Introduce the Action Team for Partnerships, and help parents learn how they can be involved throughout the school year.

Who Are the Members of the Action Team for Partnerships?

School Year ___________

What skills, talents, and experiences do members bring to the Action Team for Partnerships? For example, who has art, music, computer, financial, writing, or teaching talents? Who makes many contacts with community groups and organizations? Who is well suited to be a chair or co-chair of the ATP or of one of the ATP committees?

List the names, addresses, and positions (e.g., teacher, parent, administrator, student) of the 6 to 12 members of the Action Team for Partnerships. Discuss and note the strengths and talents each one brings to the ATP. On the next page, identify the ATP's committee structure and leadership positions.

Name: ______________ **Position:** ____________________ **Telephone:** ______________
Address: ____ **Best Time to Call:** __________
Strengths/Talents: __________________________________ **E-mail:** ________________
____

Name: ______________ **Position:** ____________________ **Telephone:** ______________
Address: ____ **Best Time to Call:** __________
Strengths/Talents: __________________________________ **E-mail:** ________________
____

Name: ______________ **Position:** ____________________ **Telephone:** ______________
Address: ____ **Best Time to Call:** __________
Strengths/Talents: __________________________________ **E-mail:** ________________
____

Name: ______________ **Position:** ____________________ **Telephone:** ______________
Address: ____ **Best Time to Call:** __________
Strengths/Talents: __________________________________ **E-mail:** ________________
____

Name: ______________ **Position:** ____________________ **Telephone:** ______________
Address: ____ **Best Time to Call:** __________
Strengths/Talents: __________________________________ **E-mail:** ________________
____

Name: ______________ **Position:** ____________________ **Telephone:** ______________
Address: ____ **Best Time to Call:** __________
Strengths/Talents: __________________________________ **E-mail:** ________________
____

If you have more than six members on the ATP, make additional copies of this form.

ATP Committee Structure and Leaders

School Year____________

Check ☑ the committee structure that the ATP will use to organize its One-Year Action Plan for Partnerships and activities on school, family, and community partnerships. Then fill in the ATP and committee leaders. Check and fill in ONLY ONE COLUMN of this form.

❑ **This ATP will organize FOUR committees for four selected school improvement GOALS**. We will use the One-Year Action Plan (Form G) and Annual Evaluation of Activities (Form G) to plan and assess progress each year.

LEADERS THIS YEAR

Chair/Co-chairs of ATP

____

____

Chair/Co-chairs of Committees

Goal 1 (Academic):

____

____

Goal 2 (Academic):

____

____

Goal 3 (Behavioral):

____

____

Goal 4 (Climate of Partnership):

____

____

❑ **This ATP will organize SIX committees for the TYPES of involvement**. We will use the One-Year Action Plan (Form T) and Annual Evaluation of Activities (Form T) to plan and assess progress each year.

LEADERS THIS YEAR

Chair/Co-chairs of ATP

____

____

Chair/Co-chairs of Committees

Type 1–Parenting: ______________

____

____

Type 2–Communicating: ______________

____

____

Type 3–Volunteering: ______________

____

____

Type 4–Learning at Home: ______________

____

____

Type 5–Decision Making: ______________

____

____

Type 6–Collaborating With the Community:

____

____

Give a copy of this information to all ATP members and other school and district leaders. Print the list of ATP members and leaders in the school newsletter, and post it on a bulletin board and on the school Web site.

First ATP Meeting of the School Year

The Action Team for Partnerships (ATP) meets at least once a month to plan, monitor, evaluate, and improve activities. ATP committees meet as needed to prepare for specific partnership activities.

At its first meeting of the school year, the ATP must lay a strong foundation on which to build an effective partnership program. The agenda for the first meeting of the year may include the following topics, discussions, and actions.

- **Recognize the value of all team members.**
  - Express appreciation for all members' willingness to serve on the ATP.
  - Reinforce the importance of attendance at this and all meetings and events.
  - Lead an icebreaker or team-building activity to celebrate members' strengths, talents, and commitment to the work of the team.
- **Review the ATP committee structure to organize specific activities in the ATP's One-Year Action Plan for Partnerships.**
- **Select team leaders and discuss shared leadership responsibilities.**
  - Positions to be filled may include the following:
  - *Chairperson* or *co-chairs* (co-chairs are recommended) of the full ATP and of each committee
  - *Recorder* of the minutes for each meeting
  - *Liaison* or link to the School Council to report the plans and events of the ATP
  - *Liaison* or link to the PTA or PTO to include the activities of the parent organization in the ATP's One-Year Action Plan for Partnerships
  - *Promoter* or *publicist* to let teachers, other staff, families, students, and the community know of team's plans, events, and progress
  - *Other roles* as needed or desired
- **Establish a communication system.**
  - Create and distribute a phone and address list of ATP members to all members and other school leaders.
  - Set a regular schedule (dates, time, place) for meetings.
  - Establish or review the team's ground rules for communicating at meetings (see p. 110 or CD).
  - Decide how the ATP will gather input from members who are unable to attend a meeting.
  - Decide how the team will provide minutes of each meeting to absent team members.
  - Plan how the team will keep the whole school community informed of partnership plans, activities, and progress.
- **Review the One-Year Action Plan for Partnerships.**
  - Review the pages of the One-Year Action Plan for Partnerships for the school year.
  - Revise the plan as needed through the year.
- **Begin implementing the planned partnership activities.**
  - Help the appropriate ATP committees and leaders with upcoming activities:
    - Which activities are scheduled during the next month or two?
    - Which committee(s) and team members or others are in charge of these activities?
    - What needs to be done to prepare for the upcoming activities?
    - Who will help implement each activity?
    - How and when will the team evaluate the effectiveness of each activity?
- **Discuss the date, time, place, and agenda for the next ATP meeting.**

Communication Ground Rules

Communication ground rules establish norms for behavior and interactions that team members agree to use to conduct meetings, manage discussions, and share ideas with each other.

How should we make decisions as an ATP?

Example: Give everyone an opportunity to share his or her ideas.

1.

2.

3.

4.

5.

How should team members communicate with each other between meetings?

Example: E-mail the agenda to all members before each meeting.

1.

2.

3.

4.

5.

Put a * next to the two rules you think are most important for discussing ideas and for making decisions at ATP meetings.

Put a * next to the two rules you think are most important for communicating between meetings.

We will discuss the top choices and compile a final list of rules for communication that all team members agree are most important for the ATP to follow.

What Do Successful Action Teams for Partnerships Do?

Good Teams . . .

Help members communicate with each other.

- Develop respect for one another's strengths and talents.
- Establish ground rules for communicating with team members.
- Identify clear roles and responsibilities for all team members.
- Create a spirit of cooperation, encouragement, and appreciation.
- Rise above school politics to communicate with all faculty, staff, and families about partnership activities.

Plan goal-oriented partnerships.

- Write an ambitious One-Year Action Plan for Partnerships with clear goals and objectives for family and community involvement.
- Link partnership activities to school improvement plans and goals.
- Identify and obtain needed resources for planned activities.

Conduct useful meetings.

- Create an appropriate meeting schedule for the full ATP and for ATP committees.
- Follow a focused agenda at each meeting.
- Start and end meetings on time.
- Invite input from all team members.

Make decisions collegially and share leadership.

- Establish guidelines for decision making.
- Agree to disagree with ideas, not people.
- Discuss and solve problems; build consensus.
- Share leadership to implement planned activities.

Continue to improve partnerships.

- Celebrate successful partnership activities and results.
- Evaluate each activity after it is implemented.
- Identify areas for improvement.
- Write new One-Year Action Plans for Partnerships every year.
- Replace team members who leave.
- Adjust roles and responsibilities as needed.
- Actively recruit new family and community partners for fresh ideas and diverse perspectives.

ANNUAL REVIEW OF TEAM PROCESSES

School Year: ______________________

***Discuss:* How well is your ATP working as a team? How should teamwork improve?**

TEAM PROCESS	RECOMMENDATION C = Continue N = Need to Improve	COMMENTS/ SUGGESTIONS
MEMBERSHIP		
• ATP members include teachers, parents, administrators, and others.		
• ATP leaders fill useful roles (e.g., chair, co-chairs, recorder, committee chairs).		
• New members of the ATP are oriented to the team and to their responsibilities.		
SCHEDULE		
• Full ATP meets on a regular schedule.		
• Time/place for meetings works well.		
• ATP committees meet as needed.		
ORGANIZATION		
• Agendas of meetings are well planned and cover important content.		
• Minutes of meetings are provided to all members who could not attend.		
• At whole-ATP meetings, all members contribute their ideas.		
• At ATP committee meetings, all members contribute their ideas.		
• Team members work well as a team, listen to each other, and disagree respectfully.		
PROGRAM IMPLEMENTATION		
• Activities in the One-Year Action Plan for Partnerships are implemented on schedule.		
• The ATP's budget for partnerships is adequate.		
• The ATP is making progress in informing and involving more families.		
• All team members take responsibility for leading or assisting with family and community involvement activities.		
• ATP members encourage all teachers, school staff, parents, students, and others to participate in scheduled involvement activities.		
• Activities are evaluated for quality and results.		
• The ATP communicates with other groups at school to report plans and progress on partnerships (e.g., school council, faculty, parent organization, school board, local media, others).		
LOOKING AHEAD. What is one way that the ATP could become even more effective next year in leading the school's program of school, family, and community partnerships?		

4

Conduct Workshops

This chapter provides an outline and agenda for two workshops: *One-Day Team-Training Workshop* for new, school-based Action Teams for Partnerships (ATPs) and *End-of-Year Celebration Workshop* for active teams to share good ideas and to solve challenges. The workshops may be conducted by district facilitators for partnerships who prepare all schools' ATPs to plan and implement their partnership programs, by school leaders who guide their own school's ATP, or by others who provide schools with professional development on partnerships. The workshops introduce the research base for developing partnership programs, provide attendees with a common vocabulary, and help educators, parents, and other team members to learn to work together to plan, implement, and continually improve their programs of family and community involvement.

One-Day Team-Training Workshop

A *One-Day Team-Training Workshop* helps members of new ATPs understand the six types of involvement, how to meet challenges to involve all families, and how to link partnership activities to goals for student success. With this information, ATPs can plan and implement their partnership programs. By understanding that school, family, and community partnerships are an official part of the School Improvement Plan and by completing a draft One-Year Action Plan for Partnerships *at the workshop,* ATPs will be able to initiate, discuss, and garner support for family and community involvement to improve the school climate and support student learning and development at all grade levels.

District leaders for partnerships and ATP chairs or members also should provide "awareness" workshops for other administrators, teachers, parents, and community members who need to know more about the importance of school, family, and community partnerships; how to work more effectively with all families; and how to assist and support school-based Action Teams for Partnerships.

This chapter includes an agenda for a One-Day Team-Training Workshop on school, family, and community partnerships. Detailed notes are provided for facilitators to present key topics along with needed overheads, handouts, and activities.

Note: All materials for the One-Day Team-Training Workshop, including a PowerPoint presentation for the facilitator, and handouts and activities for the attendees, are in Chapter 5 and on the Handbook CD.

The morning of the workshop begins with a warm-up activity and is followed by information and related activities on (a) the six types of involvement, (b) challenges that must be met to reach all families, (c) expected results for students when partnership activities are linked to school goals, and (d) structure of an Action Team for Partnerships.

In the afternoon, ATPs learn the components of a good plan for family and community involvement. Using the information gained in the morning, each ATP writes a draft One-Year Action Plan for Partnerships for their own school. The draft plan is the "exit ticket" for leaving the workshop. District facilitators keep copies of their schools' draft plans and, in follow-up meetings, assist each ATP to complete a final version of the One-Year Action Plan for Partnerships with input from other educators and parents at their school.

The one-day workshop is the recommended structure for team training. It helps educators, parents, and community partners learn to work together in a concerted way and complete a viable plan for partnerships to discuss with others at their school. When teachers, administrators, and parents take time away from school, work, and busy schedules, they want the time to be productive. It is not too much to ask team members to spend one day learning new directions for organizing and conducting an effective partnership program that, in the long term, will improve the school and help students reach important school goals.

Flexible Scheduling

The suggested agenda, format, and timing of the one-day workshop have been tested with hundreds of school teams. Still, there is flexibility in the agenda of a One-Day Team-Training Workshop. If districts or schools cannot give one full day to this essential training, the agenda may be split into two half-days or two evening workshops, preferably on consecutive days. Under these conditions, the morning agenda is the first half of the workshop and the afternoon agenda is the second half.

In unusual situations, *two* days may be scheduled for the initial team-training workshop. The extended time gives participants more time and opportunities to share ideas and information, to take stock of their present practices and needs, and to write the One-Year Action Plans for Partnerships.

In addition, sections of the workshop may be used separately for presentations to other audiences.

A One-Day Team-Training Workshop also is needed by new members that join schools' ATPs each year to replace members who leave the school or who are added to increase the number of educators or parents on the ATP.

The workshop is the beginning, not the end, of professional development on partnerships for schools' ATPs. Educators know that one-shot workshops are not sufficient for ensuring school improvement. The initial team training establishes the

ATP as a working committee of the School Improvement Team with a detailed plan for partnerships and guidelines for team meetings. This *Handbook* also provides other tools to guide teamwork, team meetings, and evaluations of the quality of activities that are implemented.

District facilitators must provide ongoing professional development and technical assistance to motivate schools' ATPs to keep improving the quality of their partnership programs and practices every year (see Chapter 7). External professional development is available from other partners, such as the National Network of Partnership Schools (NNPS) at Johns Hopkins University, for advanced training, ongoing guidance, and opportunities for networking among schools, districts, states, and organizations nationwide (see Chapter 10). Developing an excellent program of family and community involvement is a continuous process, not a one-time event.

End-of-Year Celebration Workshop

An *End-of-Year Celebration Workshop* is conducted to recognize and share progress in improving school, family, and community partnerships. This workshop, part of the ongoing professional development for ATPs, includes presentations on best practices of family and community involvement, panel discussions on problems and solutions for increasing participation, and school exhibits of particularly effective activities by type of involvement and by goal. If time is available, ATPs may outline or draft their next One-Year Action Plan for Partnerships for the upcoming school year.

Whether scheduled as a breakfast, afternoon, evening, or all-day event, an End-of-Year Workshop is an important function to bring schools' ATPs together, recognize excellent work, share ideas and practices, identify challenges and needed solutions, motivate participation, encourage improvements, and sustain partnership programs. The celebration should include discussions of the district's expectations for family and community involvement and a deadline for schools to complete their next One-Year Action Plan for Partnerships.

In this chapter, an agenda for an End-of-Year Celebration Workshop is outlined, along with ideas for sessions and panels to help schools' ATPs share ideas, report progress, and plan ahead. The agenda, flexible in design, guides district facilitators who assist many schools throughout the year to organize a culminating activity based on the schools' work and progress. The agenda for district leaders may be adapted for a single school's ATP to display and discuss its work and progress with others at the school.

One-Day Team-Training Workshop

Sample Agenda

A One-Day Team-Training Workshop for new Action Teams for Partnerships (ATPs) provides background information and related activities on school, family, and community partnerships in the morning and guides the teams of teachers, parents, and administrators from each school to write draft One-Year Action Plans for Partnerships for their own schools in the afternoon.

In the workshop, each presentation is followed by a group activity for participants to show that they can apply each new concept to their own schools. The information and exercises extend participants' understanding of school, family, and community partnerships. The topics lead from a simple, straightforward presentation of the six types of involvement, to more complex discussions of challenges that must be met in excellent programs, results of partnerships, and how to organize a well-functioning team. These four topics prepare participants to produce a workshop product—a draft One-Year Action Plan for Partnerships.

A draft One-Year Action Plan for Partnerships is the "exit ticket" for completing the workshop. The ATPs take their drafts back to their schools for input from others (e.g., School Improvement Team, faculty, parent organization). Then, the ATPs complete a final version of the One-Year Action Plan for Partnerships. District facilitators can use copies of the draft plans to help schools' ATPs review their ideas, gather input from others, and complete final plans for the next school year. All members of the ATP, other school leaders, and district facilitators should keep copies of the final One-Year Action Plans for Partnerships to see that the planned activities are implemented and evaluated throughout the year.

Following is a sample agenda for a One-Day Team-Training Workshop. Then, "Notes for Facilitators" provides key points and content for conducting workshop segments to help ATPs use the framework of six types of involvement, meet the challenges, reach results, organize an action team for partnerships, and write an action plan. Depending on the time for training, the sample agenda may be shortened or extended.

Pages in the *Handbook* for each segment of the workshop are noted in parentheses. These pages may be copied for slides, transparencies, handouts, and activities for participants. The *Handbook* CD provides the full workshop as a PowerPoint presentation and the handouts and activities for easy printing. Selected handouts and activities on the *Handbook* CD also are translated for ATPs that include Spanish-speaking parents.

Facilitators may add other topics to the workshop agenda to address specific needs, interests, and circumstances of the participants. For example, if elementary, middle, *and* high school ATPs attend the workshop, facilitators should include examples for different grade levels on the six types of involvement, meeting challenges, and results of partnerships. This may include family and community involvement activities that help ease students' transitions from one school to the next or that focus on postsecondary planning.

The workshop ensures that, in one day, ATPs gain the basics for planning and implementing their schools' partnership programs. If a school has a School Council or School Improvement Team, facilitators should make clear that the ATP is a committee of that decision making body. The ATP is an "action arm" of the School Council, charged with developing plans and implementing activities for family and community involvement that will promote a welcoming school climate and student success in school.

One-Day Team-Training Workshop

Sample Agenda

STRENGTHENING YOUR PROGRAM OF SCHOOL, FAMILY, AND COMMUNITY PARTNERSHIPS

Date

Location

8:00–8:30	**Registration and Refreshments**
8:30–8:45	**Greetings and Introductions**
8:45–9:00	**Warm-Up Activity** (p. 171)
9:00–9:45	**Facilitator Presentation: Framework of Six Types of Involvement**
	Group Activity: Starting Points Inventory (pp. 174–177)
9:45–10:30	**Facilitator Presentation: Meet the Challenges**
	Group Activity: Jumping Hurdles (p. 178)
10:30–10:45	**BREAK**
10:45–11:30	**Facilitator Presentation: Reach Results for Student Success**
	Group Activity: Reach a Goal for Student Success Using the Six Types of Involvement (p. 179)
11:30–12:00	**Facilitator Presentation: Organize Your Action Team for Partnerships** **Group Activity: How to Organize Your Action Team for Partnerships** (p. 180)
12:00–12:45	**LUNCH**
12:45–1:30	**Facilitator Presentation: Write a One-Year Action Plan for Partnerships**
	Group Activity: Good Plan/Bad Plan! Help This Plan! (CD only)
1:30–3:30	**Team Activity and Work Period: Write a Draft of Your School's One-Year Action Plan for Partnerships for the Next School Year** (pp. 181–184 or pp. 185–190)
3:30–4:00	**Questions, Answers, and Next Steps: Information on the National Network of Partnership Schools (NNPS)** (See Chapter 10)
	Workshop Evaluation (p. 191 or p. 192)

Note for Facilitators: Handbook pages are shown in parentheses. These materials also are on the *Handbook* CD. Remove these notations on the agenda for your workshop.

One-Day Team-Training Workshop

SCHOOL, FAMILY, AND COMMUNITY CONNECTIONS: STRENGTHENING YOUR PROGRAM OF PARTNERSHIPS

Overview: In a One-Day Team-Training workshop, information is presented, several applications and discussions are conducted, and a draft One-Year Action Plan is written for later discussion and completion at participants' schools. The One-Day Team-Training Workshop aims to help attendees

- Understand the framework of the six types of involvement.
- Recognize the starting points of present practices at their schools.
- Understand that they must meet specific challenges to conduct a high-quality program of productive partnerships with all families.
- Know that practices of partnership can be linked to specific school goals for improving the school climate and for helping students reach academic and behavioral results.
- Understand the structure and members of an Action Team for Partnerships.
- Write a draft of a One-Year Action Plan for Partnerships for the next school year.

This chapter guides facilitators to balance each presentation of new information with opportunities for attendees to think and talk about the information and apply the ideas and concepts to their own schools.

Time: A One-Day Team-Training Workshop requires six to eight hours in all, including time for registration, breaks, and lunch.

Materials: Laptop and projector for PowerPoint presentations or projector for overheads, screen, microphone(s), tables, chairs, nametags

Meal(s) or snacks

Handouts:
- Agenda
- Paper copies of PowerPoint slides or transparencies
- Activity pages and planning forms
- Workshop evaluation
- Folder for handouts, pens, note paper (as needed)

ATPs should bring a list of their schools' goals for student success or their School Improvement Plans to the workshop.

Other Services: Door prizes or table centerpieces may be awarded at the end of the day. Stipends to schools, planning grants, continuing education credits, and other incentives or recognitions may be awarded.

Transportation and child care for parents on the ATP may be needed.

COMPONENTS OF A ONE-DAY TEAM-TRAINING WORKSHOP

NOTES FOR FACILITATORS

Greetings and Introductions (15 minutes)

I. WARM-UP ACTIVITY (15 minutes)

GOAL: Begin the day with a short activity that focuses attendees on the concept and benefits of teamwork and partnerships. The following describes a quick warm-up activity. Suggested words for facilitators are in **bold** type.

One example of a quick, warm-up activity emphasizing teamwork is *Are Two Heads Better Than One?* (See p. 171 and CD.) Here's what to do:

1. Distribute copies of the warm-up activity. Ask participants to work alone on this puzzle for two minutes. Call "Time." Then, ask the participants to work with others at their tables for two minutes to complete the activity. Call "Time" again. Ask participants to call out their answers for item 1, 2, and so on to 20.
2. Ask: How did working together compare with working alone on this activity? Possible replies:
   - Working with a partner made the task easier.
   - We used each other's ideas, skills, and talents.
   - I didn't feel totally responsible for completing the task.
   - It was more fun.
   - And many more.
3. Explain: The same results occur when teachers, parents, students, and others work together to develop an excellent program of school, family, and community partnerships for their school. Today's workshop will help you see how to conduct an ongoing, positive program of partnerships. We will discuss ways to organize your work as an Action Team for Partnerships (ATP) in order to implement activities, monitor progress, and increase the number of families that are involved in their children's education. By working together, your team will benefit from everyone's ideas and efforts, and your school will have a program of partnerships that keeps improving year after year.

Note to facilitators: The above activity is appropriate for ATPs with English-speaking parents. It does not translate well to other languages. If your schools' ATPs include parents who do not speak English well, use the next warm-up activity.

ALTERNATIVE WARM-UP ACTIVITY (15 minutes)

A quick warm up that emphasizes good partnerships is *Discussion Dice.* This activity requires one set of dice for each table. (If dice are not available, put the numbers 1 through 12 on paper squares for attendees to pull from an envelope.) (See p. 173 and CD.) Here's what to do:

1. Place one set of dice on each table along with copies of the activity page for all participants.
2. Ask all participants to introduce themselves to the others at their table. Give clear directions: **This is a quick activity that focuses on good partnerships. Each person at your table will take a turn rolling the dice. Match the sum of the dice with a sentence on the activity page. When it is your turn, take one to two minutes to summarize a partnership experience that completes the sentence.**
3. After 10 minutes, explain: **All of you come with a wealth of experiences and understanding about different types of involvement. Your examples show that there are positive—even inspiring—partnership activities our schools and communities. We know that it is possible for educators, families, and the community to work well together. Today, we will keep these good examples in mind as we learn more about how to *organize* effective programs that involve all families and the community in ways that support student success in school.**

Here is still another quick partnership warm-up: Ask people at each table to introduce themselves and tell the others about one of their talents that would strengthen the work of an Action Team for Partnerships and contribute to their school's partnership program. For example, one person may have art skills, or computer skills . . . and so on. Summarize by noting the importance of every person on the ATP for developing and sustaining an excellent partnership program at their schools.

II. FRAMEWORK OF SIX TYPES OF INVOLVEMENT

GOAL: Present an overview of the framework of six types of involvement to help all Action Teams for Partnerships gain a common vocabulary and perspective about school, family, and community partnerships.

HANDBOOK: Refer to the following resources to prepare your presentation:

- Review Chapters 1 and 2.
- Review pages 120–123 in this chapter.
- Use the PowerPoint on the *Handbook* CD or the materials in Chapter 5, pages 149–152 for your presentation.

GROUP ACTIVITY HANDOUT: ***Starting Points.*** Make copies of pages 174–177 for all attendees, or print *Starting Points* from the CD.

INFORMATION TO PRESENT (20 minutes)

What Research Says

Start with a quick review of results from research conducted in the United States and other nations (p. 149). Present the information quickly. Ask participants to think of whether these findings pertain to their school(s) and their experiences. Point out that their school(s) will be developing a *research-based program* to involve families and the community in ways that support student learning and development.

If workshop time is short, summarize the research results in your opening comments: **Many research studies conducted in the U.S. and other countries show that educators, parents, and students want more and better family and community involvement. The studies indicate that *programs* of partnership must be developed to reach all families, with activities linked to school goals for student success. Of course, partnership programs must be customized to meet the goals and needs of each school. This means that each school's activities will be different from the next. Research shows that all schools can use a common framework and a team approach. We want to be able to organize and plan our programs of partnerships, share best practices, evaluate our work, and continually improve our programs from one year to the next.**

Overlapping Spheres of Influence

Present the theoretical model of *Overlapping Spheres of Influence* to show that children learn and grow at home, at school, and in the community. The external structure of the model shows three spheres of influence that support children's learning and development. The three contexts may be pushed apart or pulled together by the philosophies and activities of schools, families, and communities (see p. 150 and CD).

If there is time, go deeper into the model, and show the internal connections and communications that may occur among educators, families, and students. The internal structure of the theoretical model diagrams the interactions of teachers, parents, and children that will be activated by partnership practices to increase communications among all partners and boost student success (see p. 151 and CD).

If workshop time is short, summarize the theory of *Overlapping Spheres of Influence* without the slides. Or, use the "popularized picture" of the theoretical model on the *Handbook* CD to explain: **The theoretical model that guides work on partnerships states that students learn and grow at home, at school, and in the community and that students develop best when people in these three contexts work together, as partners. The theory has been supported in countless studies.**

Keys to Successful Partnerships

Explain: **Research shows that six types of involvement are important for helping educators, parents, other family members, and the community work as partners in children's education. The six types or "keys" to involvement create a comprehensive program of school, family, and community partnerships** (see p. 152 and CD.) **Activities for the six types of involvement—*parenting, communicating, volunteering, learning at home, decision making, and collaborating with the***

***community*—are conducted within the overlapping areas of the spheres of influence model. They show how home, school, and the community share responsibilities for students' success.**

Types 1, 2, 3, 4, 5, and 6

Present each type of involvement, in turn, to introduce the major ways that schools connect with families and communities to help students succeed (see these slides on the CD). Include examples of activities for each type of involvement. Tailor the examples of partnership practices to meet the special needs and interests of those attending the workshop. That is, if elementary, middle, and high school ATPs are attending the workshop, include examples of activities and challenges that arise at different grade levels. (See examples of activities for each type on the CD.)

As you present this information, ask the workshop attendees to think of the activities that are presently conducted for each type of involvement in their own schools or in schools they supervise. After you have presented Type 3 and Type 6, ask for one example of a successful activity that is conducted at their schools for each type of involvement.

GROUP ACTIVITY (25 minutes)

Give copies of *Starting Points: An Inventory of Present Practices* to all attendees. Tell the participants that you know they are already conducting some activities to involve families and community groups in school programs. The inventory helps identify their starting points on partnerships, as of today.

Assign each table or small group of participants a different type of involvement to begin their explorations, so that all six types are addressed throughout the room. Assign Table 1—Type 1, Table 2—Type 2, and so on, repeating assignments as needed. For the assigned section of *Starting Points,* each ATP should check the activities that their school *presently* conducts and, if known, the grade levels that participate in the activities.

Explain that the inventory is *not a test.* No school is expected to conduct all of the activities listed for each type of involvement. And the participants may add other activities for each type of involvement on the blank lines provided.

Explain that only one person from each ATP needs to write on the activity, but all participants should have copies of *Starting Points* to discuss their ideas. Groups that finish their assigned sections may explore other sections of *Starting Points* as time permits.

After 15 minutes, ask two or three "reporters" to share one idea or reflection that came to mind as their tables completed their assigned sections of *Starting Points.* The reporters should give their names and affiliations and indicate which type of involvement they were assigned. Typical reflections include the following:

- We conduct some activities in some grade levels but not others.
- We include some families, but we don't reach every one.
- Some of our activities are well implemented, and others are weak.
- We need to work on Type 4 activities that involve parents with children at home.
- Many other reactions.

The ATPs may complete the full *Starting Points* at their schools at a team meeting.

Note: Facilitators may send the ATPs copies of *Starting Points* before the workshop for the teams to complete. If this is done, the group activity at the workshop must change. Ask ATPs at each table to discuss how the six types of involvement are presently covered and conducted at their schools. Then, two or three volunteers may share their views with the full group.

Summary: Ask for any questions about the framework of the six types of involvement. Summarize some of the main conclusions that were discussed in the reflections on *Starting Points* or that identify next steps. Examples of possible conclusions include the following:

- Some partnership practices are useful at all grade levels; other activities need to change as students move from grade to grade.
- Students must be part of the partnership. They must know that they play important roles in connecting their teachers and families.
- Progress is incremental. Improvements and additions are based on each school's starting point.

Reinforce: To close this section of the workshop, reinforce the fact that the attendees have shown they are familiar with all six types of involvement and that many of their schools already conduct some very good family and community involvement activities. The framework of six types of involvement helps organize ideas about present practices and about needed improvements.

Note: If the attendees talked with and listened to one another about *Starting Points*, let them know that they did a good job in beginning to work together on school, family, and community partnerships. The next section of the workshop focuses on meeting key challenges for reaching all families with excellent practices of the six types of involvement.

III. MEET THE CHALLENGES

GOAL: Present an overview of some important challenges for each type of involvement that *must be met* to inform and engage all families and to have an excellent program of partnerships. By meeting key challenges, schools will involve more families (indeed, all families) in their children's education, not just those who are easiest to reach or who become involved on their own.

HANDBOOK: Refer to the following resources to prepare your presentation:

- Review Chapter 1, page 17.
- Review pages 123–125 in this chapter.
- Use the PowerPoint on the *Handbook* CD or use the materials in Chapter 5, pages 153–158, for your presentation.

GROUP ACTIVITY HANDOUT: *Jumping Hurdles.* Make copies of page 178 for all attendees, or print *Jumping Hurdles* from the CD.

INFORMATION TO PRESENT (20 minutes)

Challenges to Types 1, 2, 3, 4, 5, and 6

Explain that many schools presently conduct some activities for the six types of involvement, but most schools do not reach all families, at all grade levels, in ways that are family friendly and that produce important results. Use each slide to point out one or two key challenges for each type of involvement and to discuss the kinds of actions and activities that must be taken to solve the challenge and to involve all families at school and at home in their children's education.

The challenges include important *redefinitions* that are needed to understand school, family, and community partnerships in the twenty-first century. The redefinitions help educators and parents look at some common involvement activities in new ways.

Note: In a short workshop or in presentations on basic concepts, the information on the challenges can be incorporated *with* the overview of the six types of involvement.

GROUP ACTIVITY (25 minutes): Jumping Hurdles

Give a copy of *Jumping Hurdles* to all attendees. Ask partners or small groups to identify *one* very successful family or community involvement activity at their school (or at a school they supervise or know well), a challenge that arose, how the challenge was solved, and how they would improve the activity if it were conducted again.

One person should record ideas. After 10 to 12 minutes of discussion, ask two or three volunteers to share the activity, challenge, solution, and next steps with the full group. Select reporters who have completed *all* sections of the activity so that they will cover the topic quickly and well. Do not select reporters to speak "off the cuff," as they tend to go off topic and take more time than allotted for this section of the workshop.

Summary: Ask for questions about meeting the challenges to excellent partnerships. Summarize the main point that it is not enough to know the six types of involvement or to conduct activities that involve only a few parents. It is important to meet key challenges in each school to make sure that ATPs:

- Get information to families who cannot come to meetings at the school building.
- Reach families in their own languages and at appropriate reading levels.
- Enable volunteers to contribute at the school and in other locations.
- Work with teachers to improve the design of homework and parent-child interactions on assignments.

- Ensure that parent representatives on school committees come from all neighborhoods.
- Identify useful resources and connections in the community.

Reinforce: Schools must work to meet challenges and reach all families in order to have a successful partnership program.

Note to Facilitators

Alternative Activity on Challenges to Excellent Partnerships

The *Handbook* CD includes an alternative activity that may be used instead of *Jumping Hurdles* to call attention to the challenges that need to be solved at each school to involve all families and develop an excellent partnership program.

Challenge-Go-Round (Handbook CD only)

For this activity, each person (or partner-team) writes a challenge that must be met to involve all families at their school (or a school they supervise). At each of three signals, they pass the page to the next person (or partner teams) at the table to record possible solutions to the stated challenge. The suggestions are returned to the "starter," who identifies one suggestion that may best solve the challenge. Two or three volunteers share the challenge and selected solution with the whole group and provide a reason why the solution might work. For more interaction, full ATPs may record a challenge on charts posted around the room and then move three times to write potential solutions on other ATPs' charts in a round-robin team activity.

Jumping Hurdles identifies a challenge that arose and was solved at a school. *Challenge-Go-Round* identifies a challenge at the school that needs to be solved. Both activities make the point that challenges to involve more families can be solved with well-implemented involvement activities. Use only *one* group activity for this section of the workshop.

BREAK (15 minutes)

The next section of the workshop addresses an even more difficult question: Why should schools conduct and improve programs of family and community involvement? The answer? To help promote important RESULTS for students, families, and schools. We will see how to connect involvement activities with specific school improvement goals.

Let workshop participants know that they have worked hard and earned a 15-minute break.

Give workshop participants information on restrooms in the facility. Announce *when* they should return for the next segment of the workshop and start on time.

IV. REACH RESULTS FOR STUDENT SUCCESS

GOAL: Present information on how school, family, and community partnerships help produce a welcoming school climate and desired results for student success. By focusing on results, family and community involvement can contribute to the attainment of school improvement goals.

HANDBOOK: Refer to the following resources to prepare your presentation:

- Review Chapter 1, page 18.
- Review pages 126–129 this chapter.
- Use the PowerPoint on the *Handbook* CD or use the materials in Chapter 5, pages 159–163, for your presentation.

GROUP ACTIVITY HANDOUT: ***Reach a Goal for Student Success Using the Six Types of Involvement.*** Make copies of page 179 for all attendees, or print *Reach a Goal for Student Success* from the CD.

INFORMATION TO PRESENT (20 minutes)

Explain that research has identified two main ways to connect the six types of involvement with desired results for improving school climate and for increasing student success. Facilitators should summarize the following information, according to the time available and the interests of the workshop attendees.

1. Each of the six types of involvement produces *different* results.

Show the slide, Reaching Different Results With Types of Involvement, which outlines how the six types of involvement affect different actions and behaviors (p. 176 and CD). (Also see Table 1.1.3 on p. 18 in Chapter 1.)

For example,

- Type 1–Parenting activities that help parents understand their children as students and their roles in helping students get to school every day and on time. This links to the school's attendance policies and the need for students to be in class to learn new lessons. When parents are provided this information clearly about attendance, studies show that school attendance rates improve.
- Type 2–Communicating activities that explain and exchange information on students' progress (such as a parent-teacher-student conference and report cards) increase students' awareness of their work and families' awareness of how to help and guide their children toward learning goals.
- Type 3–Volunteering activities may increase the skills of students in the subjects that are tutored.
- Type 4–Learning at Home activities that guide parents' interactions with students on homework result in more students completing homework and better attitudes about homework.
- Type 5–Decision Making activities that bring parents' voices to bear on school decisions help families increase their attachment to the school and help students see that their families are important partners.

- Type 6–Collaborating With the Community activities help families locate needed family services and increase students' contacts and skills with community partners.

Not every type of involvement and not every involvement activity directly affect student achievement. It is important to know *which kinds of results* may be expected from activities for the six types of involvement.

2. All six types of involvement may contribute to a *particular, desired result.*

Activities for all six types of involvement can be designed to focus on specific, desired results. By targeting all six types on a specific goal, family involvement can help students improve academic skills and nonacademic behaviors. Pages 160–163 in the *Handbook* show how activities for all six types of family and community involvement may all be applied to help students improve reading, math, attendance, and the school climate of partnerships.

For example, if an elementary school has a goal to help students improve reading skills and attitudes, the ATP can select activities for all six types of involvement that focus on reading and schedule these activities in the One-Year Action Plan for Partnerships. Similarly, action plans may include activities for all six types to help students improve skills and attitudes in math, writing, science, or other subjects; attendance; behavior; or other school goals. In this way, students receive *multiple sources of support*—from their teachers, parents, and other adults—to attain goals that are important for success in school.

Explain: **Here are a few examples of how schools are applying the six types of involvement to help students reach important results.** Show slides on the following:

- Reading in the elementary grades
- Math in the elementary grades
- Attendance in the middle grades
- Postsecondary planning in high schools

Note: If the workshop includes ATPs from elementary schools only, show the examples for the younger grades. If the workshop includes ATPs from middle and high schools, include examples of how the six types of involvement focus on goals for students in the older grades (see pp. 226–232 and CD).

Explain: **I want to emphasize how important it is to link the six types of involvement to specific, desired results. Now, you can check your understanding of this in the next group activity. This will help you this afternoon when you draft a One-Year Action Plan for Partnerships for your school.**

GROUP ACTIVITY (25 minutes)

Give a copy of *Reach a Goal for Student Success Using the Six Types of Involvement* to each attendee. The activity asks workshop attendees to think pictorially and cre-atea "map" that links the types of involvement with a specific student out come. If participants complete this activity thought ully, they will have a head start in writing one of the pages of their One-Year Action Plan for Partnerships in the afternoon.

One person should record the group's ideas for the activity. Ask each group to:

1. Identify *one* important academic or behavior goal *for students* at their school(s). This should be a specific and clear goal that is in the School Improvement Plan and that is important for student success. Write this goal for students in the oval at the center of the map.

   Watchwords: Make sure the ATPs select an academic or behavioral goal for *student success* (not parent involvement).

   Ask ATPs to write a detailed goal for student success in the oval. For example, "Improve students' reading scores at least 8 percent on the next state test in all grades tested" is better than "Increase student achievement." The former lends itself to planning and measuring; the latter is too broad.

   Advise ATPs to select activities for four to six types of involvement for the selected goal for students. Not every goal can be easily addressed by all types of involvement in the first plan.

   Advise ATPs to select feasible activities to involve families and the community.

2. Discuss and record how the school will measure progress toward the selected goal. Note which indicator(s) (e.g., test scores, report card grades, attendance rates, disciplinary referrals) will be used to document progress from one year to the next.

   Watchwords: Ask the ATPs to list how results will be measured (e.g., on tests in percentages of scores, by report card grade improvements, average daily attendance, behavioral referrals, etc.).

3. Discuss and record feasible, useful, and creative family and community partnership activities that might be implemented at their school to help students reach the selected goal.

   Watchwords: Advise the ATPs to describe the activities in detail. For example, "Newsletter with a column by selected grade levels each month showing parents a new math skill" is a better description than "Newsletter." The more details they give on this activity, the easier their work will be in writing a plan in the afternoon.

   Remind the ATPs that the activities they select must be tightly linked to the stated goal. For example, if the goal is to improve students' reading skills, an involvement activity cannot stop at "donuts for dads" but must be tied directly to reading and literacy (e.g., a literacy breakfast—with donuts—and students reading their stories or poems to dads or to any parent or family member).

After about 15 minutes of discussion, ask two or three volunteers to share their "results maps" with the full group. Select volunteers whose ATPs selected different academic or behavioral goals and filled in at least four activities for the different types of involvement. Attendees should listen for whether the practices of partnership are directly linked to the stated goal.

Summary: Ask for questions on how family and community involvement activities may help students reach specific school improvement goals. Check that the participants understand that:

(1) Not every involvement activity will lead to the same results (e.g., not every activity will increase student achievement test scores).

(2) If they are well-designed and well-implemented, activities for all six types of involvement may be targeted to produce important results for student learning and behavior and for improving the school climate of partnerships.

Reinforce: Family and community involvement activities must be *tightly linked* to the desired goals. For example, involvement activities about *attendance* are likely to increase *attendance,* involvement activities about *writing* are likely to help students improve *writing,* and so on.

Note: Let ATPs know that they need to help everyone at their schools understand the importance of conducting *goal-oriented* practices of school, family, and community partnerships. Then, family and community involvement will be known as a resource for helping students reach school improvement goals, not as a *separate* plan or *extra* program.

Note to Facilitators

Alternative Activities on Results of Partnerships

The *Handbook* CD includes two alternative activities that may be used instead of the pictorial map to link the six types of involvement with a goal for student success.

School Goals and Results of Partnerships (on CD only)

This activity asks ATPs at the workshop to discuss the measure(s) that will be used to monitor progress on the selected goal for student success.

Get Ready for Action (on CD only)

This activity is most useful if schools have already implemented many goal-linked involvement activities and the ATPs need to sort existing and new practices to increase partnerships on a selected goal for student success.

Use only *one* group activity with this section of the workshop.

V. ACTION TEAM STRUCTURE

GOAL: Present information on how an Action Team for Partnerships (ATP) is linked to the School Council or School Improvement Team and how the ATP can organize committees to conduct its work on school, family, and community partnerships.

HANDBOOK: Refer to the following pages in this *Handbook* to prepare your presentation:

- Review Chapter 1, pages 19–23, and Chapter 3.
- Review pages 130–133 in this chapter.
- Use the PowerPoint slides on the *Handbook* CD, or use the materials in Chapter 5, pages 164–167, for your presentation.

GROUP ACTIVITY HANDOUT: ***Organize Your Action Team for Partnerships.*** Make copies of page 180 for all attendees, or print this handout from the CD.

INFORMATION TO PRESENT (15 minutes)

Basic Structure: The ATP Is a Committee of the School Improvement Team

Topic 1: Who are the members of the Action Team for Partnerships?

Show the outline of ATP members and explain the required and optional members.

Describe options for the terms of office and leadership roles.

Explain that other teachers, administrators, parents, students, and members of the community work *with* the ATP committees on various activities. Designated leaders of some activities may not be on the ATP but may have talents associated with particular involvement activities.

Some activities will be led by individual teachers or other groups at the school (e.g., PTA/PTO, afterschool program, school psychologist) as part of the school's overall partnership program. These leaders may not be on the ATP but collaborate with the ATP to record their activities in the complete One-Year Action Plan for Partnerships. See *The Complete Picture* form (on the *Handbook* CD *only*) to gather information on all activities for family and community involvement conducted at the school.

The core team of at least six people—teachers, parents, administrator (and, at the high school level, students) should be the participants at the One-Day Team-Training Workshop. They may increase ATP membership, over time, by adding others to the ATP who are dedicated to improving the program of family and community involvement. The ATP or the district facilitator for partnerships must provide team training to the new members who are added to the ATP.

Topic 2: How will the ATP structure its committees, plans, and evaluations?

Explain that the ATP is a committee (or work group) of the School Council or School Improvement Team. The ATP must be organized to do its work. The ATP's

One-Year Action Plan for Partnerships and annual evaluations of activities that are implemented are based on the team's structure.

There are two main ways to organize an ATP to conduct a school's program of partnerships.

1. The ATP may organize committees for four school goals—two academic, one behavioral, and one goal for good partnerships. If this structure is selected, the ATP will use the One-Year Action Plan for Partnerships (Form G–Goals) (pp. 181–184) and the Annual Evaluation of Activities (Form G–Goals) (pp. 330–334).
2. The ATP may organize committees for the six types of involvement. If this structure is selected, the ATP will use the One-Year Action Plan for Partnerships (Form T–Types) (pp. 185–190) and the Annual Evaluation of Activities (Form T–Types) (pp. 335–341).

Note to Facilitators

If a district facilitator for partnerships is assisting many schools, this person should decide *before* the One-Day Team-Training Workshop how the schools' ATPs will be organized. If all schools use the same, district-selected team structure, this section of the workshop will be clearer and easier to conduct. It also will make it easier for schools' ATPs to share ideas as they proceed with their work on partnerships. At the workshop, show only the selected ATP structure.

If a school is working on its own, the principal or ATP chair or co-chairs may decide before the workshop which committee structure will work best at the school. Show only the selected structure at the One-Day Team-Training Workshop.

If a team structure is not selected before the workshop, show both diagrams, and each ATP will decide its own structure. The team structure determines which form of the One-Year Action Plan for Partnerships is used in the afternoon.

Structure of the Action Team for Partnerships

Show the diagram of the ATP structure that was selected ahead of time or review the two diagrams of the alternative ATP structures, with committees for G–Goals or T–Types.

Explain: **The top box on the chart recognizes that the School Council or School Improvement Team is an important advisory and decision making group for the school. The next box shows that the ATP is an action arm (or committee) of the School Council focused specifically on family and community involvement.**

- The ATP will link its plans and its work to the School Improvement Plan and to specific goals for student success.
- The ATP will report to the School Council on a regular schedule, just as all school committees do.
- One member of the ATP may also be a member of the School Council.

(See Chapter 3 for details on the composition and responsibilities of the ATP.)

For the selected ATP structure, complete these explanations:

ACTION TEAM FOR PARTNERSHIPS: STRUCTURE G (GOALS)

- Serves as the action arm (a committee) of the School Council or School Improvement Team
- Has subcommittees for four improvement goals:
  - Two academic or curricular goals
  - One nonacademic goal (e.g., attendance, behavior, safety)
  - One goal for creating a welcoming climate for partnerships
- Plans, implements, documents, and evaluates activities to achieve each goal using the six types of involvement to balance the types and locations of family and community involvement
- Elects or selects an ATP chair or co-chairs and selects leaders for its subcommittees who are members of the ATP
- Delegates leadership to others to conduct specific activities and engages many teachers, parents, administrators, community partners, and students in the planned activities

ACTION TEAM FOR PARTNERSHIPS: STRUCTURE T (TYPES)

- Serves as the action arm (a committee) of the School Council or School Improvement Team
- Has subcommittees for each of the six types of involvement
- Plans, implements, documents, and evaluates activities for each type of involvement linked to desired results to improve the school climate and increase student success
- Elects or selects an ATP chair or co-chairs, and selects leaders for its subcommittees who are members of the ATP
- Delegates leadership to others to conduct specific activities and engages many teachers, parents, administrators, community partners, and students in the planned activities

Note to Facilitators

1. If there is no School Council or School Improvement Team or similar advisory group, remove the top box from these charts. In that case, the discussion of team structure focuses only on the ATP and its committees.

2. Large secondary schools (i.e., those with over 1,500 students) may include one educator and one parent representative from each major school division on the ATP. Or, each division (grade level, academy, house, or other school-within-a-school) may prefer to have its own, separate ATP. In such cases, each ATP would follow the same guidelines for membership, planning, and evaluating practices. Each ATP will report to the School Council. A coordinator on the Council will gather ATP plans and progress reports to define the

school's unified, overarching partnership program (see Chapter 6 on high schools).

GROUP ACTIVITY (15 minutes)

Give a copy of *How to Organize Your Action Team for Partnerships* (p. 180 and CD) to each attendee. One person should record ideas.

Ask partners or tables to discuss the three questions about ATP members, time to meet, and reports on partnerships to other groups. Advise teams to take two to three minutes to discuss each question. Ask for one or two volunteers to share their group's ideas for each question. Make sure these questions are discussed:

Do any ATPs at the workshop need to add members to complete their teams? (If so, each ATP will bring the additional members up to date with information from the workshop.)

When can ATP meetings be conducted? Obtain two or three different ideas about possible meeting times.

Which other groups at school and in the community need to hear from the ATP about plans, activities, and progress on partnerships? Obtain two or three different ideas.

Summary: Ask for questions about how to organize an Action Team for Partnerships.

Reinforce: All teams should complete the activity *How to Organize Your Action Team for Partnerships* and make final decisions about members, time to meet, and how plans and progress will be shared with other groups at school.

Advise the attendees to continue their discussions of team structures, leaders, meetings, committees, or other workshop topics during lunch.

Q AND A FOR THE MORNING

Before breaking for lunch, ask for questions on all topics discussed in the morning workshop: using the framework of six types of involvement, meeting challenges to involve all families, reaching results with partnership activities, and organizing an Action Team for Partnerships.

Commend the attendees for successfully completing the basic topics for organizing a school-based partnership program. They are ready to write a draft One-Year Action Plan for Partnerships after lunch.

LUNCH

Provide information about how lunch will be served or where to go for lunch.

Announce *when* the afternoon session will start. Let attendees know that the afternoon session will start on time.

VI. WRITE A ONE-YEAR ACTION PLAN FOR PARTNERSHIPS

GOAL: The afternoon of a One-Day Team-Training Workshop is devoted to helping schools' ATPs write draft One-Year Action Plans for Partnerships for the next school year. The ATPs will take the drafts back to their schools for input from others. Then, the ATPs will complete the final versions of their One-Year Action Plans for Partnerships within a set time period.

In this part of the training, ATPs are introduced to the sections of a good Action Plan for Partnerships.

HANDBOOK: Refer to the following pages in this *Handbook* to prepare your presentation and to guide schools' ATPs to write their One-Year Action Plans for Partnerships:

- Review Chapter 1, pages 22–23, and Chapter 3.
- Review pages 134–138 in this chapter.
- Use the PowerPoint on the *Handbook* CD for your presentation.

GROUP ACTIVITY HANDOUTS:

a. ***Good Plan/Bad Plan! Help This Plan!*** Make copies of this page from the *Handbook* CD for all attendees.
b. ***One-Year Action Plan for Partnerships (Form G–Goals* or *Form T–Types)*** (pp. 181–190 or *Handbook* CD

INFORMATION TO PRESENT (15 minutes)

Explain that you will outline the sections and content of a good action plan for partnerships, and that you will give a pop quiz on the information.

What does a good plan look like? How can you write a good plan? (Use the PowerPoint slide of the components of a good plan on the CD. Also ask participants to examine the handout (pp. 181–184 or pp. 185–190) to see the pages of a One-Year Action Plan for Partnerships.

A GOOD One-Year Action Plan for Partnerships includes

- *Goal:* Goals 1–3 should be *student centered* and linked to a clear academic or nonacademic outcome, written on one page each. Goal 4, on page 4 of the plan, must focus on strengthening a climate of good partnerships at the school.
- *Desired results:* Should be specific, quantitative, and measurable to monitor desired changes (e.g., increase the percentage of students at or above proficiency in math from 60 percent to 68 percent on the required math achievement test).
- *Assessments:* Must identify the instrument(s) or indicator(s) that will be used to measure the desired results. These may include formal measures, such as state standardized test scores, report card grades, attendance data, and behavior records, or informal measures, such as homework completion, survey results, and participation lists.

- *Partnership activities:* Must be activities that involve parents, other family members, or the community in ways that contribute to the four goals on the planning pages.
- *Types of involvement:* Should include activities that address all six types of involvement, if not on every page, then across all pages of the plan. Some activities will represent more than one type of involvement.
- *Dates of activity:* Should complement other activities going on in the school. Dates should be as specific as possible. Words like "all year" are not specific. It is necessary that the team and others know when an activity will occur.
- *Grade level(s):* Should match each activity with appropriate target audiences. Not every activity need be targeted for the whole school. Some may be designed to involve families of students in specific grade levels.
- *What needs to be done and when:* Should outline tasks to prepare for, implement, and follow up the planned activities.
- *Who is in charge and who is helping:* Should list the members of the action team or others as designated leaders or helpers. The same person should not be listed over and over again. Educators, parents, and community partners may take leadership roles, singly or together.

Ask for any questions about the components of a good plan. Then, give the participants the pop quiz using the Group Activity *Good Plan/Bad Plan! Help This Plan!*

Note: This activity is on the *Handbook* CD *only*. Print the activity from the CD.

GROUP ACTIVITY (20 minutes)

Ask each ATP member to work with a partner. Examine the activity *Good Plan/Bad Plan! Help This Plan!* Explain: **This hypothetical page of a plan needs help. Consider the components of a good plan. Circle the places on this activity that you think need to be improved and tell why.**

After the ATPs have worked for ten minutes, take five minutes for volunteers to identify problems that were found. Start at the top of the planning page, and ask if anyone circled a problem with the goal that was listed. Continue down the page with the sections on desired results, assessment, and so on throughout the sections of the plan.

Explain: **It is easy to find problems on a draft plan. We need to avoid those problems. Now, it is your turn to write a GOOD draft One-Year Action Plan for Partnerships for your school.**

FINAL ACTIVITY: DRAFT PLAN

One-Year Action Plans for Partnerships: Workshop leaders should preselect the form of the One-Year Action Plan for Partnerships that the ATPs will use.

- The One-Year Action Plan for Partnerships (Form G–Goals), pages 181–184 and CD, is used by teams that will organize four committees and work on family and community involvement to meet four school improvement goals: two academic goals, one nonacademic goal, and one goal of creating a welcoming climate of partnership.

- The One-Year Action Plan for Partnerships (Form T–Types), pages 185–190 and CD, is used for teams that will organize six committees and work on family and community involvement to strengthen the six types of involvement.

INFORMATION TO PRESENT (10 minutes)

Guidelines for Writing One-Year Action Plans

Show and discuss the template of the selected One-Year Action Plan for Partnerships. Show the PowerPoint slide of the planning form. Help the teams see that they will complete all sections. Note these sections:

- What goal is set? How will success be determined? What measure(s) will be used?
- Which family and community involvement activities will be conducted?
- When will each activity be conducted?
- What preparation is needed?
- Which types of involvement are tapped?
- Who is responsible for conducting the activity, and who will help?

Make sure that all ATPs understand that they will write a *detailed draft* One-Year Action Plan for their own school for the next school year.

IF FORM G is selected, teams will complete the four pages of Form G—one for each goal (two academic goals, one nonacademic goal, and one goal for creating a welcoming climate of partnership).

- *Pages 1, 2, 3:* Teams may use their School Improvement Plans or knowledge of their schools' goals to select the academic and nonacademic goals for the One-Year Action Plan for Partnerships. They may refer to the morning results map they created using the *Reach a Goal for Student Success* activity for ideas for one of the goals.
- *Page 4:* The fourth page of Form G–Goals focuses on strengthening a welcoming climate of partnership. Teams may refer to the *Starting Points* inventory and to the workshop notes to identify ongoing and new activities that will be conducted to create a partnership school.
- Before the ATPs start their work, ask for a few examples of goals for student success that they are considering for their One-Year Action Plans for Partnerships. Goals may focus on improving reading, math, writing, science, or other skills and test scores; improving behavior; reducing suspensions; increasing safety; improving health, planning postsecondary education; or on some other goal important to a particular school. A reading goal may state, for example: *Increase scores on the state reading assessment by 8 percent a year at each grade level. Also, increase students' positive attitudes about reading 10 percent on the end-of-year attitude survey for Grades 4 and 5.*
- Make sure that ATPs understand that pages 1, 2, and 3 refer to goals for students and that page 4 addresses the general goal of improving the school's partnership climate.
- Remind the ATPs to include activities for all six types of involvement across the four pages of Form G. Not every goal will have activities for all six types.

IF FORM T is selected, teams will complete the six pages of Form T–Types, one for each type of involvement. Teams may integrate activities from the morning activities on *Reach a Goal for Student Success*, the *Starting Points* inventory, and other workshop notes to identify family and community involvement activities that will be conducted for the six types of involvement to engage more families in ways that reach important results for students.

Note to Facilitators

- If the One-Day Team-Training Workshop is conducted in the *spring* of the school year, guide the ATPs to write their draft plans for the *next* full school year.
- If the workshop is conducted in the *fall* of the school year, guide the ATPs to draft 18-month plans (or plans for another appropriate time period) for the remainder of the current school year and the next full school year.

GROUP ACTIVITY (2 hours)

Each ATP will complete a draft One-Year Action Plan for Partnerships (Form G *or* Form T) for their own school.

ATPs are encouraged to bring a laptop computer to the workshop for this task. The One-Year Action Plan for Partnerships forms can be provided electronically before the workshop (or at the workshop via a flash drive) so that the ATPs can complete their draft plans on a computer. This also makes it easy for the workshop facilitator to collect copies of ATPs' draft plans.

During this work period, the facilitator may consult with each team to answer questions, review draft pages, and make suggestions that will help each ATP complete its plan.

After one hour, ask two or three volunteers to share one of the activities they outlined in detail in their draft plans. The volunteers should state the goal, desired results, activity, and details for the entry. As activities are shared, respond to any general questions that have been raised that will help all ATPs complete their plans.

Summary: Check all draft plans as they are completed and before teams leave the workshop. If possible, make copies of the ATPs' draft plans electronically (or make or collect paper copies at or after the workshop).

Announce the deadline for all ATPs to complete and submit a final version of the One-Year Action Plan for Partnerships.

Reinforce: Each ATP will:

- Discuss the draft plan with the School Council or School Improvement Team, faculty, parent organization, and other interested partners.
- Inform all parents about the plan in a school newsletter, and accept suggestions from all parents.
- Gather input and ideas to consider as a team for the final version of the One-Year Action Plan for Partnerships.

The final plan for partnerships should be appended to the School Improvement Plan (as appropriate), summarized for all parents and all teachers in the school newsletter, and posted on the school and/or district Web site(s).

The district facilitator for partnerships may visit each school to help the ATP complete the final version of the One-Year Action Plan for Partnerships for the next school year.

Note: Make sure that all members of the Action Team for Partnerships and other school leaders have copies of the final version of the One-Year Action Plan for Partnerships for easy reference.

The district facilitator for partnerships also should have copies of all schools' final plans in order to assist and encourage the ATPs with their work on partnerships throughout the school year.

VII. QUESTIONS, ANSWERS, AND NEXT STEPS (30 minutes)

GOAL: Help the workshop attendees see how much they accomplished in one day to increase their knowledge, skills, and plans for school, family, and community partnerships.

Note: Workshop facilitators may conduct this summary session at the midpoint of the teams' writing period, so that ATPs may leave the workshop as they complete their One-Year Action Plans. Some teams finish writing their draft plans before others.

Summary: List of the topics that were covered during the day:

- Theoretical model of overlapping spheres of influence
- Framework of the six types of involvement
- Challenges to meet to reach all families
- How to link school, family, and community partnerships to important results
- How to organize the Action Team for Partnerships
- Components of a good plan for partnerships
- Completion of a draft One-Year Action Plan for Partnerships linking family and community involvement to important school goals for student success

Ask for questions concerning any of the topics of the day.

Ask participants to share some of the next steps they will take when they return to their schools.

Facilitators should outline how they will help the ATPs with their work. Announce a deadline for completing a final version of the One-Year Action Plan for Partnerships and how plans from all ATPs will be collected. Tell the ATPs how they can contact the facilitator for additional information or assistance.

Facilitators may provide information on how schools can join the National Network of Partnership Schools (NNPS) at Johns Hopkins University (see Chapter 10). Outline the benefits of membership and the materials that NNPS provides to support and help evaluate partnership programs. Provide the Web site of NNPS for more information and online resources on school, family, and community partnerships (www.partnershipschools.org).

Facilitators should collect evaluations of the workshop from the participants (pp. 191–192 and CD).

End-of-Year Celebration Workshop

Sample Agenda

An End-of-Year Celebration Workshop is a good way to recognize the progress that Action Teams for Partnerships (ATPs) make each year and to help ATPs plan ahead to improve their partnership programs in the next school year.

The following pages present a sample agenda for a One-Day End-of-Year Celebration Workshop and notes to help facilitators plan and conduct these workshops. This professional development day enables ATPs to share their schools' best practices, discuss problems and solutions, and gather ideas for their next One-Year Action Plan for Partnerships.

At an End-of-Year Celebration Workshop, each school shares information on one successful practice that was implemented during the year to promote school, family, and community partnerships. The schools' exhibits (much like science fair boards) may be set up on easels or tables and may include posters, charts, photographs, slides, video- or audiotapes, handouts, or other communications. ATPs label their activities to show the goals that were addressed and the types of involvement that were activated by the activity. The displays should help ATPs learn about activities that they may use or adapt to strengthen their own schools' partnership programs. In addition, the workshop should include selected presentations, panels, and time to talk about plans for the next school year. The sample agenda for a full day may be shortened to a few hours, depending on the time available and the number of schools involved.

Districts and schools conduct End-of-Year Celebrations in many different ways as full-day, half-day, breakfast, and dinner events. Some state departments of education conduct annual conferences on partnerships, where experienced schools and districts display and discuss their best practices to assist new ATPs with their initial plans. Some districts conduct celebration and planning workshops in the middle of the year *before* the time that schools write their School Improvement Plans. These variations may alter the name of this workshop, but not its purpose.

As they plan the workshop, facilitators need to arrange microphones for presenters; easels, tables, and other audiovisual equipment for exhibits; nametags; folders for information and notes; and other materials.

Facilitators may use End-of-Year Celebration Workshops as an occasion to give guidance on and announce deadlines for schools' ATPs to complete program evaluations and to write new One-Year Action Plans for Partnerships for the next school year.

End-of-Year Celebration Workshop

Sample Agenda and Notes for Facilitators

8:30–9:00	**Registration and Refreshments**
9:00–9:30	**Greetings and Introductions** Overview and goals for the day
9:30–11:15	**Share Best Practices: Presentations by Action Teams for Partnerships** See guidelines for advance planning for this time segment (pp. 142–143).
9:30–10:00	**Selected ATPs Present Best Practices I** Topic: Involvement activities to address *one* school improvement goal (e.g., improving students' reading attitudes and skills) with different types of involvement
10:00–10:30	**Selected ATPs Present Best Practices II** Topic: Involvement activities to address *a different* school improvement goal (e.g., improving student attendance) with different types of involvement
10:30–10:45	**BREAK**
10:45–11:15	**Panel 1: Meet Challenges to Reach All Families**
11:15–12:00	**Gather Ideas—Visit the School Exhibits** See guidelines on advance planning for this time segment (pp. 143–144).
12:00–1:00	**LUNCH (provided or on own)**
1:00–1:30	**Panel 2: Meet Challenges to Reach All Families**

1:30–2:30 **Next Plans: Prepare for the Next School Year: Write the Next One-Year Action Plans for Partnerships**

School ATPs consider the various best practices, exhibits, and challenges that were presented at the workshop. Using their present One-Year Action Plans for Partnerships, their Annual Evaluation of Activities (pp. 330–334 or pp. 335–341), and the goals in their School Improvement Plans, ATPs will draft a One-Year Action Plan for Partnerships for the next school year.

2:30–3:00 **Wrap Up/Report Out/Announcements**

Action Team Updates: One reporter from each ATP will present one or two ideas from the discussion period to indicate the new directions and next steps that the ATP will take in the next school year.

Announcements:

- Awards, appreciations, and door prizes
- Deadlines for Annual Evaluation of Activities and the next final
- One-Year Action Plans for Partnerships
- Contact information for assistance from facilitator
- Other important information

Notes for Facilitators:

- Prepare a one-page agenda for your End-of-Year Celebration.
- For a half-day or part-day celebration: Schedule *one* presentation on best practices, *one* panel on meeting challenges, and the all-school exhibits.
- For an extended day to 4:00 p.m.: Include a two-hour period for the ATPs to write their next One-Year Action Plans for Partnerships and ready them for input at their schools for a final plan.

Advance Planning for an End-of-Year Celebration Workshop

Guidelines for Facilitators

District facilitators must do some *advance planning* with the ATPs that will participate in two segments of an End-of-Year Celebration Workshop: (a) presentations of best practices and (b) presentations by panelists on solving challenges for successful programs of partnership.

ADVANCE PLANNING FOR PRESENTATIONS OF BEST PRACTICES

In planning an End-of-Year Celebration Workshop, the facilitator may select a few participants to share successful family and community involvement activities that they implemented at their schools during the school year. The number of presenters depends on the time available and the number of outstanding activities for (a) involving more families, (b) improving the school climate, and (c) reaching results for students. ATPs who are not asked to make presentations at the workshop will share one of their best practices in the exhibit area that all attendees visit.

Presenters should be notified ahead of time, informed of strict time limits for their presentations, and guided in good presentation skills. Presenters may use PowerPoint slides, overheads, charts, handouts, or other technologies. All print and pictures must be large enough for the audience to see. Presentations also may include choral speakers, poems, songs, dances, and skits to demonstrate particularly effective family and community involvement activities.

Some facilitators select themes for End-of-Year Celebration Workshops and guide participants to present information relating to the theme (e.g., partnerships to improve students' reading or math skills, or partnerships with families with diverse cultural and linguistic backgrounds).

The time from 9:30 to 11:15 a.m. may be planned in 15-minute segments for presentations on best practices that show how family and community involvement are focused on specific goals for student success or for improving the school climate, using all or some of the six types of involvement. The agenda includes a 15-minute break during this time period.

For example, two presenters from different schools may share the time from 9:30 to 10:00 a.m. to describe their schools' outstanding activities to involve families with children in reading and language arts using Types 2 and 4. Between 10:00 and 10:30, each presenter has 10 minutes to speak, and 10 minutes remain for questions from the audience and for a transition to the next speaker(s).

Alternatively, four presenters from different schools could each have 5 minutes to describe their activities, leaving 10 minutes for questions and transition. Facilitators must decide how to use the time and guide presenters accordingly.

It is the facilitator's responsibility at the workshop to keep presenters *on time.* This can best be accomplished by guiding the presenters *prior to the workshop.* It also helps to signal presenters when they have one minute left to conclude their presentations. A successful workshop stays on time; an unsuccessful workshop lets presenters go on and on.

ADVANCE PLANNING FOR MEETING THE CHALLENGES PANEL PRESENTATIONS

Facilitators should identify one or two important topics that have posed challenges to the schools' ATPs throughout the year as they worked to improve partnerships and reach all families. Usually, schools struggle with similar problems, but some schools solve them sooner than others, and the solutions vary. Facilitators should make clear that the selected topics highlight a few of many challenges that the schools are trying to solve. For example, the facilitator may select panelists from ATPs at schools that solved one or two of the following challenges:

- How the ATP gets information to parents who cannot attend meetings at the school building
- How principals and Action Team chairs or co-chairs work well together
- How the ATP, School Improvement Team, and PTA communicate and connect
- How principals support their ATPs
- How the ATP evaluates the results of specific partnership practices
- How parents from diverse neighborhoods contribute to the partnership program
- Other topics relevant to schools in particular locations

Panelists may include teachers, parents, students, principals, district leaders, community partners, or others to give varied views of the challenge and solutions. The panelists should be informed of strict time limits for their presentations and guided in effective presentation skills.

Two panels may be scheduled in one hour, with three or four participants on each panel sharing their experiences and observations. There should be time for questions from the audience. If there were two panels on key topics with four participants each, speakers would have about five minutes each for their summaries, leaving 10 minutes for questions from the audience. Facilitators must decide how to use the hour and select panels accordingly.

At one workshop in this time period, for example, one panel discussed four questions to help other schools that were struggling to create an effective team structure:

- Who is on your Action Team for Partnerships?
- When do you find time to meet?
- How do you report to the School Improvement Team, faculty, and families about the ATP's work on partnerships?
- What budget and fund-raising is needed to support the work of your Action Team for Partnerships?

A second panel discussed how their ATPs measured results of particular practices of partnership that they implemented at their schools.

Thus, in one hour, two panels addressed topics that were of interest to just about all schools attending the workshop.

Other topics to consider for panel presentations. In addition to the topics described above, the following may be addressed by panels of educators, parents, students, or other partners:

- How students view school, family, and community partnerships and the help they need to succeed in school (e.g., four students from different grade levels could make up the panel).
- How to identify and connect with hard-to-reach families (e.g., a working parent, immigrant parent, parent of a child with special needs, parent who lives far from school)
- How to identify and obtain funds for programs of school, family, and community partnership activities
- Other challenges to partnerships at elementary, middle, and high schools in the district

5

Select Materials for Presentations and Workshops

This chapter includes two sections: (1) Presentations and Handouts and (2) Group Activities for Workshops. The first section provides charts, diagrams, and summaries for the One-Day Team-Training Workshop outlined in Chapter 4. These materials also are provided on the *Handbook* CD, along with a PowerPoint presentation for workshops and other professional development sessions. The research, results, and fieldwork that led to the development of these materials are noted throughout the *Handbook.*

The second section of the chapter provides the small group activities for the One-Day Team-Training Workshop to ensure that attendees understand the content of each topic and can apply the information to their own school(s).

Presentations and Handouts

Short Summary of Research on Partnerships

The summary lists a few key research results on school, family, and community partnerships and program development from studies conducted in 20 nations, including the United States (p. 149 and CD).

Theoretical Model of Overlapping Spheres of Influence

External Structure. The diagram shows the three main contexts that influence children's learning and development. The areas of overlap indicate that the family, school, and community share responsibility for children's success in school. Various practices, philosophies, histories, and other forces create more or less overlap—more or fewer connections between individuals in the three contexts. The practices and extent of overlap change over time with age-appropriate activities and with increasing participation of students in communications and decisions about their education (p. 150 and CD).

Internal Structure. The diagram also shows the interactions that occur when people in schools, families, and communities communicate and work together. The child is the central focus in these interactions and main actor in education. Connections of home, school, and community may be at an institutional level—involving all families, children, educators, and the community—or at an individual level—involving one teacher, parent, child, community partner, or a small group (p. 151 and CD).

Keys to Successful Partnerships

One chart summarizes the six types of involvement (p. 152 and CD).

Summaries of the Six Types of Involvement, Challenges, and Results

Summary Charts. Six charts summarize the types of involvement, challenges, redefinitions, and selected results of the six types of involvement. These summaries, derived from the tables in Chapter 1 and from extensive fieldwork, are useful handouts for workshops (pp. 153–158 and CD).

Note:

- For *presentations* on the six types of involvement, use the separate charts on types and challenges (described below) that are on the *Handbook* CD *only* in large type.
- See Chapter 4 for instructions on how and when to use the separate charts in workshop presentations.

Separate Charts on the Six Types of Involvement on the Handbook CD only

The following charts are included on the *Handbook* CD *only* for handouts and in PowerPoint presentations. These materials provide detailed information on the types, challenges, redefinitions, and results on the summary charts.

Six Types of Involvement. Six slides define each type of involvement. On CD *only.*

Sample Practices for Each Type. Six slides provide examples of common activities for each type of involvement that have been effectively implemented in many elementary, middle, and high schools. When schools are extending and strengthening their partnership programs, they may consider these "basic" activities. On CD *only.*

Sample Challenges and Redefinitions for Each Type of Involvement. Six slides outline important examples of challenges that must be solved to have a truly successful program of partnerships. The redefinitions summarize new ways to think about involvement activities in order to improve programs and increase outreach to more families. On CD *only.*

Sample Results from Each Type for Students, Parents, and Teachers. Six slides offer a few examples of results and benefits that have been measured or observed for each type of involvement. The lists alert participants to the fact that different results are linked to each type of involvement. On CD *only.*

Reach Results

Two kinds of information are provided in this chapter and on the *Handbook* CD to use in connection with the workshop section on Reach Results. One slide summarizes how each of the six types of involvement links to different results. Four slides illustrate how the six types of involvement may be targeted to contribute to the same goals to help improve the school climate and produce specific results for student success in the elementary grades. The activities involve families and community partners in ways that help students improve reading, math, and behavior and that improve the school's climate of good partnerships. Many of the ideas can be adapted for any grade level. See Chapter 6 for involvement activities for the six types of involvement to help reach school improvement goals in the middle grades and in high schools.

These examples, from schools across the country, are a few of hundreds of activities that have been implemented to engage families and community partners with students and teachers on important school goals. See details for conducting these and other activities in the annual collections of *Promising Partnership Practices* on the Web site, www.partnershipschools.org in the section of Success Stories.

Action Team Structures

Two diagrams show how to organize the work of an Action Team for Partnerships (ATP) by focusing on school goals or on the types of involvement. The charts assume that there is a School Council or School Improvement Team—an advisory group that sets goals and priorities for the school and that monitors progress in reaching important results. The ATP is a committee or work group that gives full attention to developing and improving a comprehensive, goal-linked program of family and community involvement.

The ATP may create subcommittees to divide and delegate responsibilities among the team members to oversee the work of family and community involvement on selected goals or on the six types of involvement to match the structure of the One-Year Action Plan for Partnerships.

The ATP reports, periodically, to the School Council or Improvement Team, just as all school committees do. If there is no council, a school may start with an ATP to establish its partnership program.

Members of the ATP

This chart shows who should serve on an ATP, including parents, teachers, administrators, support staff, community partners, students (at the high school level), and others. The number of team members, leadership roles, and terms of office are flexible, depending on conditions and constraints in each school. Each ATP must address the composition and workings of the team to ensure full membership, regular meetings, and productive work to engage all families and the community in helping students succeed at high levels.

How Does an ATP Differ From the School Improvement Team or School Council?

This slide shows how the responsibilities of the ATP differ from those of the School Improvement Team or School Council. The ATP is a committee or "action arm" of the School Council (or School Improvement Team), and the annual plan for school, family, and community partnerships should be part of or appended to the School Improvement Plan.

Levels of Commitment to Partnerships on the **Handbook** *CD* **only**

This page, which is on the *Handbook* CD *only,* outlines a hierarchy of levels of commitment to partnerships. The six types of involvement are not "levels." That is, Type 6 is not "higher" than Type 1. Each type of involvement is important for engaging families and the community in different ways. There are, however, *levels* of commitment to partnerships that increase from caring to civility, clarity, cooperation, and collaboration. A comprehensive program of partnerships will include all six types of involvement and will work toward the highest level of commitment—true collaboration.

WHAT DO WE KNOW
from U.S. and international studies of family and community involvement?

- Parents vary in how much they presently are involved.
- Parents are very concerned about their children's success in school.
- Students need multiple sources of support to succeed in school and in life.
- Schools must reach out in order to involve all families.
- Some teachers and administrators are initially resistant to increasing family involvement.
- Teachers and administrators in schools and districts need preservice and inservice education to strengthen and sustain goal-linked programs of family and community involvement.
- Subject-specific practices involve families in ways that directly assist students' learning and success.
- Partnership programs are most effective if they are research based, customized for each community, evaluated, and continually improved.

See recent research summaries supporting these points at www.partnershipschools.org.

Theoretical Model
OVERLAPPING SPHERES OF INFLUENCE OF FAMILY, SCHOOL, AND COMMUNITY ON CHILDREN'S LEARNING

External Structure

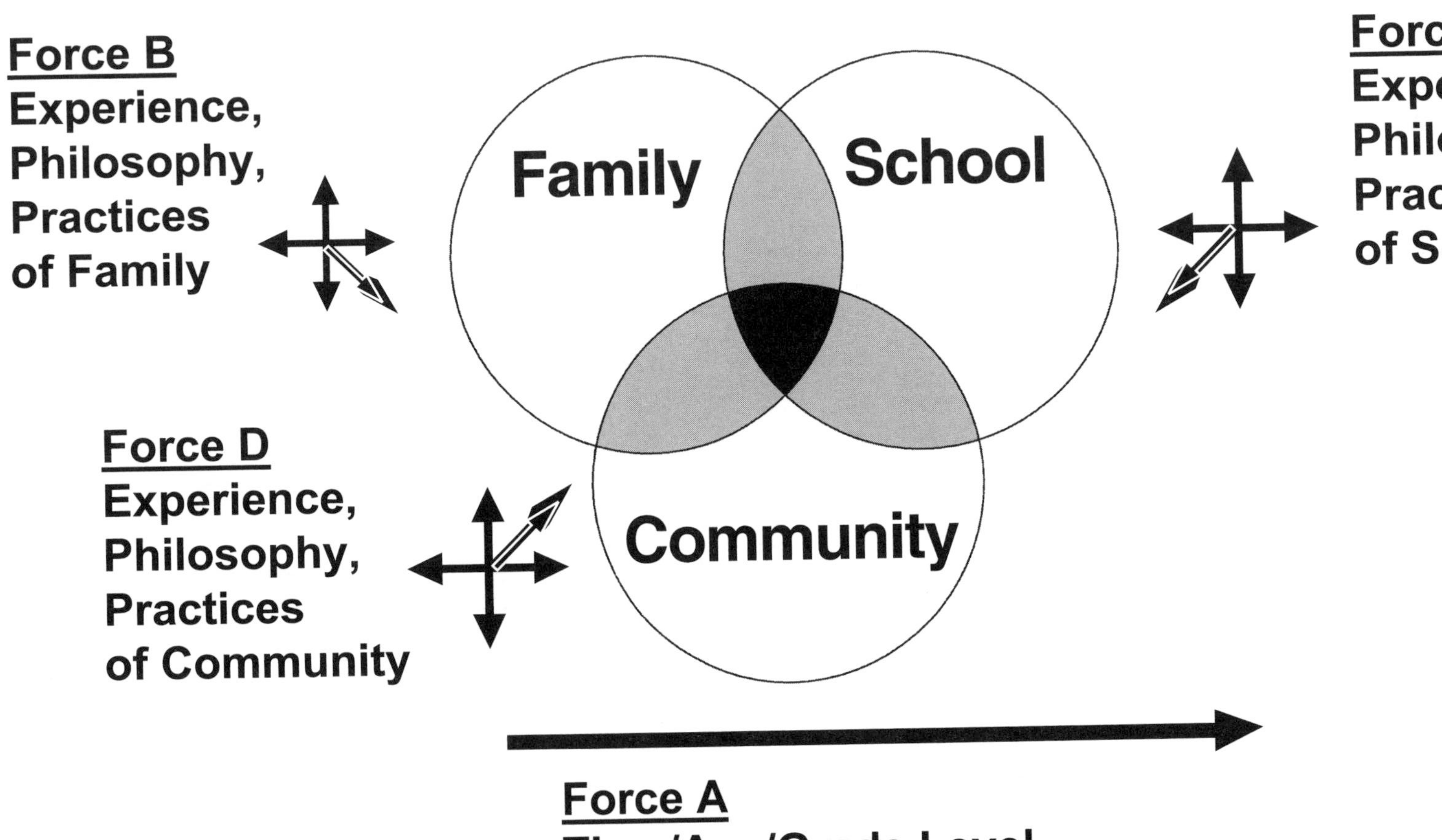

Theoretical Model
OVERLAPPING SPHERES OF INFLUENCE*
Internal Structure

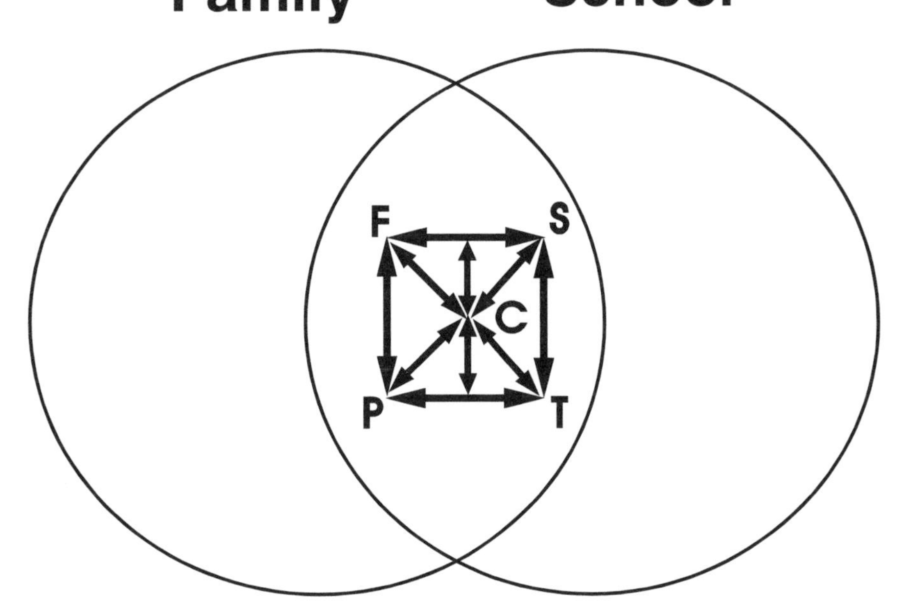

Key ***Inter*-institutional interactions (in overlapping area)**

F = Family C = Child S = School P = Parent T = Teacher

Interactions include those at the institutional level (e.g., all families, children, educators, and entire community) and at the individual level (e.g., one parent, child, teacher, community partner).

Note: In the full model, the internal structure is extended to include the community (Co) and individual business and community agents (A), and interactions in the nonoverlapping areas.

THE KEYS TO SUCCESSFUL SCHOOL, FAMILY, AND COMMUNITY PARTNERSHIPS

Epstein's Six Types of Involvement

Parenting:
Assist families in understanding child and adolescent development and in setting home conditions that support children as students at each grade level. Assist schools in understanding families.

Communicating:
Communicate with families about school programs and student progress through effective school-to-home and home-to-school communications.

Volunteering:
Improve recruitment, training, and schedules to involve families as volunteers and audiences at the school and in other locations to support students and school programs.

Learning at Home:
Involve families with their children in learning at home, including homework, other curriculum-related activities, and individual course and program decisions.

Decision Making:
Include families as participants in school decisions, governance, and advocacy through the PTA/PTO, school councils, committees, action teams, and other parent organizations.

Collaborating With the Community:
Coordinate community resources and services for students, families, and the school with businesses, agencies, and other groups, and provide services to the community.

SUMMARY
TYPE 1–PARENTING

Information and activities that assist families with responsibilities for

- Housing, health, nutrition, clothing, safety.
- Understanding child and adolescent development.
- Home conditions that support children as students at all grade levels.

And assist schools in

- Understanding family backgrounds, cultures, and goals for their children.

CHALLENGES

Provide information to all families who want it and need it, not just to the few who attend workshops or meetings at the school building.

Enable families to share information with schools about their backgrounds, cultures, children's talents, goals, and needs.

REDEFINITIONS

"Workshops" are not only meetings on topics held at the school building but also the content of the meetings to be viewed, heard, or read at convenient times and varied locations by those who could not attend.

RESULTS FOR STUDENTS

- Balanced time spent on chores, homework, and other activities
- Regular attendance
- Awareness of family supervision and importance of school

RESULTS FOR PARENTS

- Self-confidence about parenting as children proceed through school
- Knowledge of child and adolescent development

RESULTS FOR TEACHERS AND ADMINISTRATORS

- Understanding of families' goals and concerns for children
- Respect for families' strengths and efforts

For presentations, see the *Handbook* CD for usable slides on the types, challenges, redefinitions, and results for Type 1.

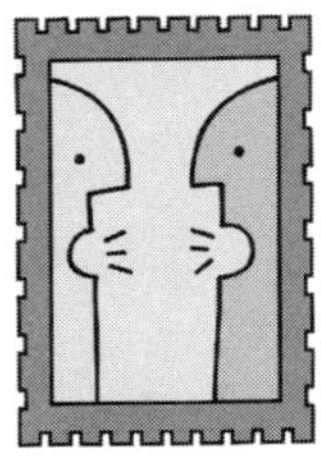

SUMMARY
TYPE 2–COMMUNICATING

SCHOOL-TO-HOME COMMUNICATIONS

- Memos, notices, report cards, conferences, newsletters, phone calls, e-mails, Web sites
- Information on school programs, state tests, report cards, and children's progress
- Information about choosing or changing schools, courses, programs, or activities

HOME-TO-SCHOOL COMMUNICATIONS

- Two-way channels of communication for questions, suggestions, and interactions

CHALLENGES

Make all memos and other print and nonprint communications clear and understandable for ALL families.

Obtain ideas from families to improve the design and content of communications, such as newsletters, report cards, and conference schedules.

REDEFINITIONS

Communications about school programs and student progress go not only from school to home but also from home to school and within the community.

RESULTS FOR STUDENTS

- Awareness of own progress in subjects and skills
- Knowledge of actions needed to maintain or improve grades
- Awareness of own role as courier and communicator in partnerships

RESULTS FOR PARENTS

- Understanding of school programs and policies
- Support for child's progress and responses to solve problems
- Ease of interactions and communications with school and teachers
- High rating of school quality

RESULTS FOR TEACHERS AND ADMINISTRATORS

- Ability to communicate clearly
- Use of parents' networks to communicate with all families

For presentations, see the *Handbook* CD for usable slides on the types, challenges, redefinitions, and results for Type 2.

SUMMARY
TYPE 3–VOLUNTEERING

INVOLVEMENT AT AND FOR THE SCHOOL

- IN schools or classrooms: Assist administrators, teachers, and students as aides, tutors, coaches, lecturers, chaperones, boosters, and mentors, and assist in other ways.
- FOR schools or classrooms: Assist school programs and student activities from any location at any time.
- AS AUDIENCES: Attend assemblies, performances, sports events, recognition and award ceremonies, celebrations, and other student activities.

CHALLENGES

Recruit widely, provide training, and create flexible schedules for volunteers so that all families know that their time and talents are welcomed and valued.

REDEFINITIONS

"Volunteer" not only means someone who comes to school during the school day but also anyone who supports school goals and children's learning and development in any way, at any place, and at any time.

RESULTS FOR STUDENTS

- Skills that are tutored or taught by volunteers
- Skills in communicating with adults

RESULTS FOR PARENTS

- Understanding of the teacher's job
- Self confidence about ability to work in school and with children
- Enrollment in programs to improve own education

RESULTS FOR TEACHERS AND ADMINISTRATORS

- Readiness to involve all families in new ways, not only as volunteers
- More individual attention to students because of help from volunteers

For presentations, see the *Handbook* CD for usable slides on the types, challenges, redefinitions, and results for Type 3.

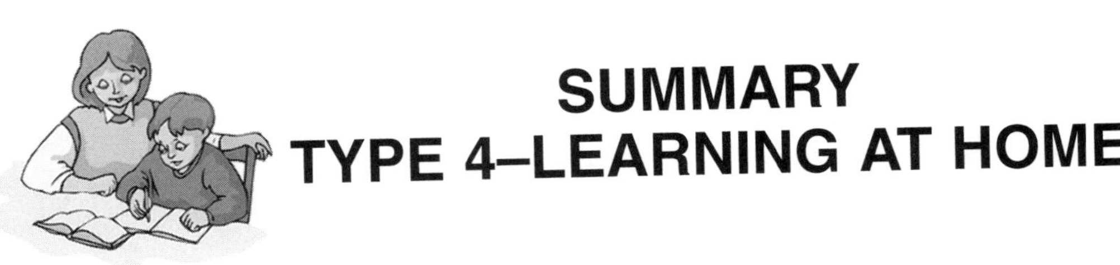

SUMMARY
TYPE 4–LEARNING AT HOME

INVOLVEMENT IN ACADEMIC ACTIVITIES

- Ways to help at home with homework
- Required skills to pass each subject
- Curriculum-related decisions by and for the student
- Development of student's other skills and talents

CHALLENGES

Design and implement interactive homework on a regular schedule that guides students to demonstrate skills and discuss ideas with their families.

Involve families with their children in important curriculum-related decisions in a timely way.

REDEFINITIONS

"Homework" not only means work that students do alone but also interactive activities that students share and discuss with others at home and in the community to link schoolwork to real-life experiences.

"Help" at home means how families encourage, listen, praise, guide, monitor, and discuss schoolwork with their children, not whether or how they "teach" school subjects.

RESULTS FOR STUDENTS

- Skills, abilities, and test scores linked to classwork
- Homework completion
- View of parent as more similar to teacher and home as similar to school
- Self-confidence in ability as learner and positive attitude about school

RESULTS FOR PARENTS

- Discussions with child about school, classwork, homework, and future plans
- Understanding of curriculum, what child is learning, and how to help each year
- Appreciation of teacher's work and skills

RESULTS FOR TEACHERS AND ADMINISTRATORS

- Respect for family time
- Satisfaction with family involvement and support
- Recognition that single-parent, dual-income, and low-income families and families of all racial and ethnic backgrounds can motivate their children and reinforce student learning.

For presentations, see the *Handbook* CD for usable slides on the types, challenges, redefinitions, and results for Type 4.

SUMMARY
TYPE 5–DECISION MAKING

PARENT PARTICIPATION AND SHARED LEADERSHIP ON

- School Council or School Improvement Team
- Action Team for Partnerships (ATP), a committee of the School Council
- PTA/PTO membership, participation, leadership, representation
- Title I advisory and other committees
- Independent advisory and advocacy groups

CHALLENGES

Include parent leaders from all racial, ethnic, socioeconomic, and other groups on advisory councils, teams, and committees.

Offer training for parent leaders to develop leadership skills and to represent other parents.

Include student representatives in high schools along with parents on committees.

REDEFINITIONS

"Decision making" in schools means a process of partnership-sharing views, solving problems, and taking action toward shared goals for excellent education and student success—not a power struggle of conflicting ideas.

"Parent leader" means a representative who shares information with and obtains ideas from other families, not just a parent who attends school meetings.

RESULTS FOR STUDENTS

- Awareness that families' views are represented in school decisions
- Specific benefits linked to policies enacted by parent organizations and committees

RESULTS FOR PARENTS

- Awareness of and input to policies that affect children's education
- Development of participation and leadership skills in responsibilities for activities and in representation of other parents.

RESULTS FOR TEACHERS AND ADMINISTRATORS

- Awareness of families' perspectives in policies and school decisions
- Recognition of equality of family representatives on school committees

For presentations, see the *Handbook* CD for usable slides on the types, challenges, redefinitions, and results for Type 5.

SUMMARY
TYPE 6–COLLABORATING WITH THE COMMUNITY

- COMMUNITY CONTRIBUTES TO SCHOOLS, STUDENTS, AND FAMILIES
  Business partners, cultural organizations, health services, recreation centers, senior citizens, faith-based programs, governmental agencies, and other groups

- SCHOOLS, STUDENTS, AND FAMILIES CONTRIBUTE TO COMMUNITY
  Service learning and special projects to share talents and solve local problems

CHALLENGES

Prevent or solve problems among partners of turf, goals, responsibilities, and funds.

Inform all families and students about community programs and services, and ensure equal opportunities for participation and for services.

REDEFINITIONS

Community includes not only families with children in the schools but also others who are interested in and affected by the quality of students' education.

Communities are rated not only on economic qualities but also on the strengths and talents of people and organizations who may support students, families, and schools.

RESULTS FOR STUDENTS

- Knowledge, skills, and talents from enriched curricular and extracurricular experiences and explorations of careers
- Self-confidence and feeling valued by and belonging to the community

RESULTS FOR PARENTS

- Knowledge and use of local resources to increase skills and to obtain needed family services
- Participation with others to strengthen the community and to build a sense of community

RESULTS FOR TEACHERS AND ADMINISTRATORS

- Knowledge and use of community resources to enrich the curriculum, instruction, and students' experiences
- Knowledge of referral processes for families and children with needs for special services

For presentations, see the *Handbook* CD for usable slides on the types, challenges, redefinitions, and results for Type 6.

Reaching Results for Students

Studies show that each type of involvement promotes *different* results.

Type 1–Parenting	⟶	**Students improve attendance when families are informed of policies and involved in meeting attendance goals.**
Type 2–Communicating	⟶	**Students increase awareness of own progress in subjects and skills with good two-way communications on classwork.**
Type 3–Volunteering	⟶	**Students gain academic skills that are tutored or taught by volunteers.**
Type 4–Learning at Home	⟶	**Students complete more homework in specific subjects.**
Type 5–Decision Making	⟶	**Students benefit from policies and projects conducted and supported by parent organizations.**
Type 6–Collaborating With the Community	⟶	**Students gain skills and talents in curricular and extracurricular projects with community partners.**

ELEMENTARY SCHOOL EXAMPLES for a One-Year Action Plan IMPROVE READING

TYPE 1 Workshops for parents on various ways to read aloud with young children.

TYPE 2 Parent-teacher-student conferences on reading goals at the start of the school year and on reading progress at midyear.

TYPE 3 Reading-partner volunteers, guest readers of favorite stories, and other read-with-me activities.

TYPE 4 Family Reading Night to demonstrate reading strategies for parents and activities to conduct with students at home.

TYPE 5 PTA/PTO support for a family room or parent center to provide information on children's reading. Conduct book swaps, make book bags for read-at-home programs, create family books, and sponsor other reading activities.

TYPE 6 Donations from business partners of books for classrooms, to school library, or for children to take home.

. . . AND MANY OTHER IDEAS FOR EACH TYPE OF INVOLVEMENT

ELEMENTARY SCHOOL EXAMPLES for a One-Year Action Plan IMPROVE MATH SKILLS

TYPE 1	**Workshops for parents to explain math standards and tests and to demonstrate and discuss how math skills are taught to students.**
TYPE 2	**Articles for parents in school or class newsletters or posted on the school Web site by students and math teachers on interesting math topics and skills.**
TYPE 3	**Volunteer math tutors to assist students who need one-on-one tutoring and extra help with specific math skills.**
TYPE 4	**Weekly interactive homework assignments for students to demonstrate mastery of a math skill for family partners and to discuss how each skill is used in everyday situations.**
TYPE 5	**PTA/PTO-sponsored Family Math Night for fun and learning.**
TYPE 6	**Afterschool programs funded by business and community partners to provide students with extra help and enrichment activities in math.**

. . . AND MANY OTHER IDEAS FOR EACH TYPE OF INVOLVEMENT

ELEMENTARY SCHOOL EXAMPLES
for a One-Year Action Plan
IMPROVE STUDENT BEHAVIOR

TYPE 1 Parent-to-parent group meetings on student behavior, age-appropriate discipline, and related topics.

TYPE 2 Student-of-the-month assembly, bulletin board, and luncheon with family partners to recognize students for good or improved behavior, character, and citizenship.

TYPE 3 Volunteers for school patrols in hallways, cafeteria, on the playground, or in other locations to increase or maintain students' good behavior.

TYPE 4 Monthly interactive homework assignments for students to talk with parents or other family partners about selected character traits, values, and behaviors.

TYPE 5 PTA/PTO-sponsored speaker series for parents on student development, with mental health, medical, and other specialists.

TYPE 6 Community connections with students on problem solving and conflict resolution skills to reduce bullying and other problem behaviors.

. . . AND MANY OTHER IDEAS FOR EACH TYPE OF INVOLVEMENT

ELEMENTARY SCHOOL EXAMPLES
for a One-Year Action Plan
CREATE A CLIMATE OF PARTNERSHIP

TYPE 1 Low-cost immunization shots and health examinations for students to assist parents with these school requirements.

TYPE 2 Student-led parent-teacher conferences to communicate with all parents about student progress.

TYPE 3 Resource directory to identify the available time and talents of parents and other volunteers to assist teachers and school staff throughout the year.

TYPE 4 Information for and exchanges with parents on homework policies, how to help at home, and whom to call with questions.

TYPE 5 PTA/PTO potluck dinners combined with School Improvement Team meetings to encourage more parents to participate in decision making.

TYPE 6 "Salute the Arts" fair for students and families where community artists demonstrate drawing and painting, music, dance, and crafts and offer information on community-based art programs and museums.

. . . AND MANY OTHER IDEAS FOR EACH TYPE OF INVOLVEMENT

Action Team for Partnerships Structure G (Focus on Goals)

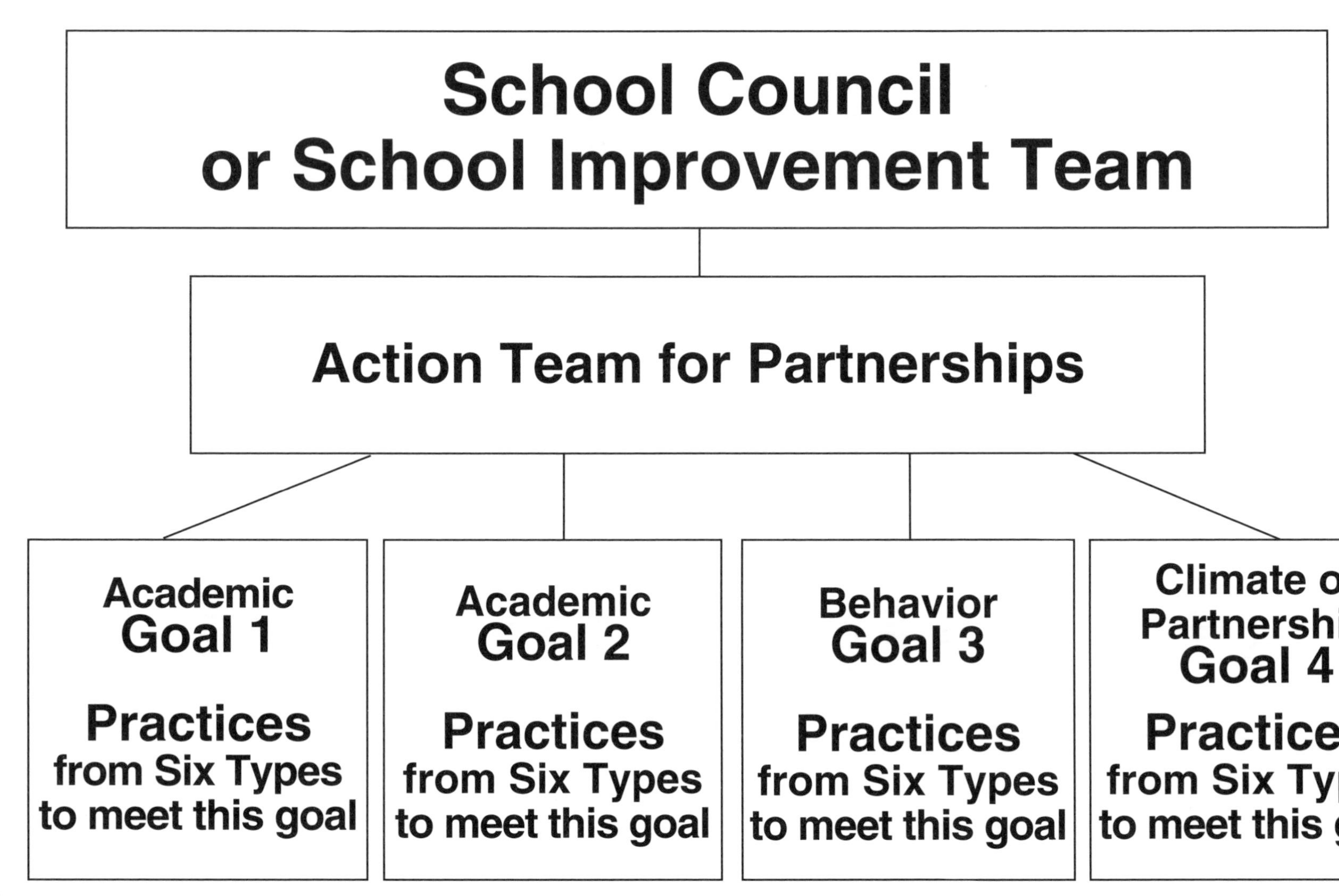

Action Team for Partnerships Structure T (Focus on Types)

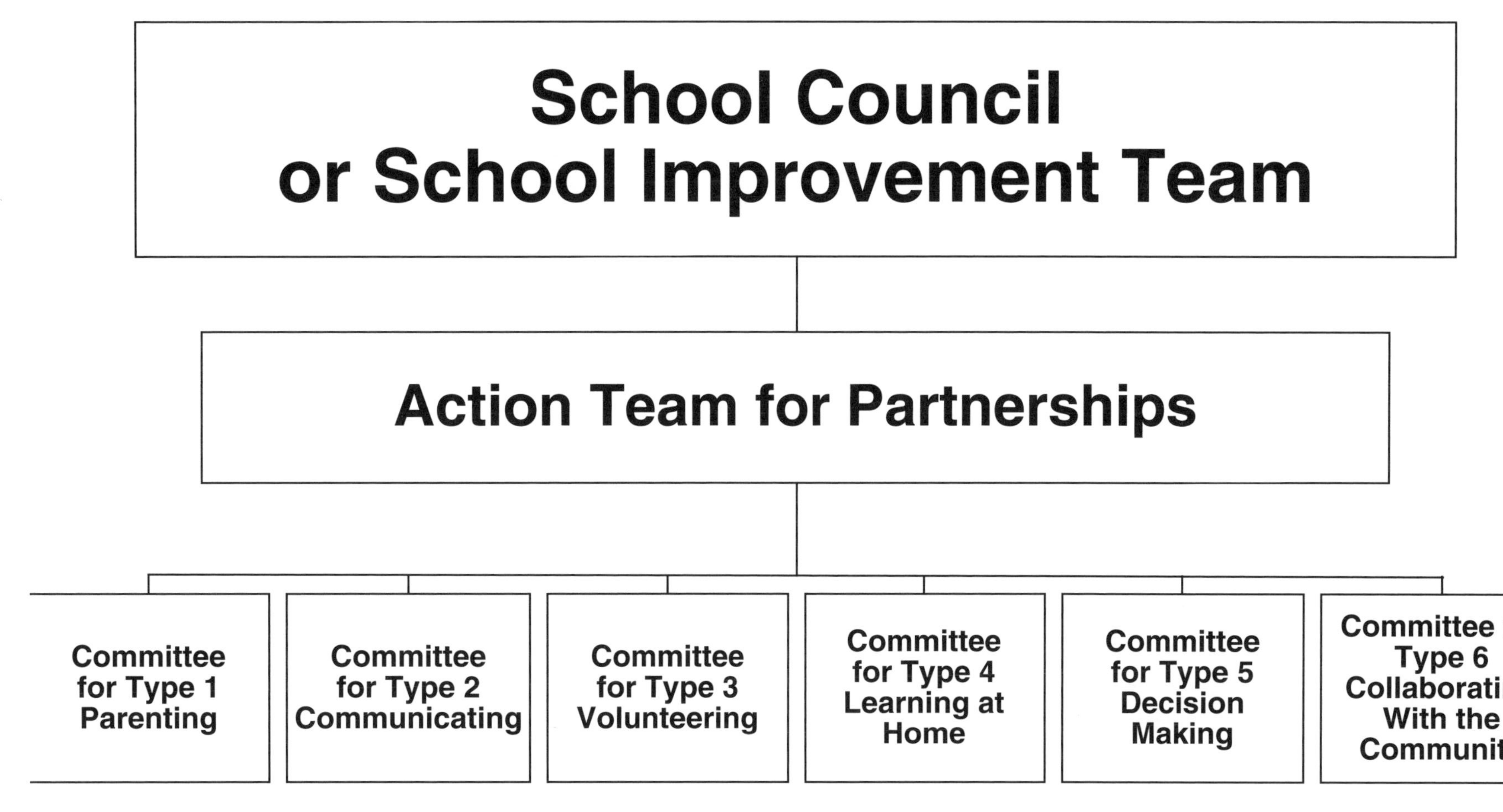

Members of the Action Team for Partnerships

How Many? 6-12 members

Who?
- 2-3 teachers or more
- 2-3 parents/family members or more
- Representatives include parent liaison, PTA/PTO officer, parents with children in different grades, families from various neighborhoods
- Principal
- 1-2 students (in high school)
- 1-2 other members or more (e.g., nurse, counselor, school psychologist, community members)

Terms?
- 2-3 years (renewable)
- Replacements made as members leave
- At least one "linking" member also serves on the School Improvement Team or School Council

Leaders?
- Chair or co-chairs communicate well with educators *and* families
- Others are chairs or co-chairs of ATP committees for specific goals, types of involvement, or planned activities
- Non-team members can be designated leaders for specific activities

All features are flexible to fit school conditions and needs.

How Does the ATP Differ From the SCHOOL COUNCIL?

COUNCIL 	ATP 
School Council or School Improvement Team contributes to the school's ENTIRE School Improvement Plan (SIP).	Action Team for Partnerships (ATP) oversees the goal for FAMILY and COMMUNITY INVOLVEMENT by writing an annual Action Plan for Partnerships.
School Council meets monthly to discuss all programs, assess progress, and plan next steps to attain goals in the SIP.	ATP meets monthly to discuss the schedule of activities for family and community involvement, assess progress, and improve plans.
SCHOOL COUNCIL hears committee reports and assists all committees in helpful ways.	ATP is one of the school's committees and reports plans and progress to the SCHOOL COUNCIL for advice and support.

Small-Group Activities for Workshops

Group activities are provided for use in workshops on school, family, and community partnerships as noted on the sample agenda.

- If a school is working alone to develop its program, the activities will be completed by the Action Team for Partnerships at its own school-based training workshop. The chair or co-chairs of the ATP will guide the workshop at their school.
- If a district leader is conducting a One-Day Team-Training Workshop for many schools' Action Teams for Partnerships, the activities will be completed by all teams throughout the day.

The activities help workshop leaders learn whether the ATPs understood the presentation and can think about how each topic (i.e., types of involvement, challenges, results, team structure, writing a good plan) applies to their own schools.

Directions for the small-group activities in this chapter also are on the *Handbook* CD for the workshop leader to reproduce and distribute to participants. There also are a few alternatives on the CD, as noted. See Chapter 4 for detailed directions on how to use the group activities.

Workshop Warm-Ups

Two examples are included.

- *Two Heads Are Better Than One* is a word puzzle that helps participants see that working together with teachers, parents, administrators, and other partners is more beneficial and more fun than working alone. It is appropriate only for teams with English-speaking parents.
- *Discussion Dice* is an activity that helps participants recall positive and enjoyable partnership activities. The activity page is on the CD in English and Spanish, and it may be translated as needed for ATPs that include parents who speak languages other than English.

Starting Points

This inventory is a group activity that is conducted after the presentation of the six types of involvement. It shows each ATP that its school already is conducting many activities for the six types of involvement and that the framework helps organize their work on partnerships.

Jumping Hurdles

This group activity is conducted after the workshop presentation on the need to meet key challenges to excellent partnerships. It shows ATPs that they have faced and solved challenges to reach more families. An alternative activity, *Challenge-Go-Round,* is provided on the *Handbook* CD *only.*

Reach a Goal for Student Success Using the Six Types of Involvement

This pictorial "map" helps ATPs show that they can activate the six types of involvement to address one academic or behavioral goal for student success.

Two alternative activities to focus on results are provided on the *Handbook* CD *only:*

- *School Goals and Results of Partnerships* is an alternative to the pictorial "map" to show how the six types of involvement can contribute to the attainment of a selected goal for student success. It includes details on how results will be measured. This activity is on the *Handbook* CD *only.*
- *Get Ready for Action* is another alternative to the pictorial "map." It asks ATPs to list all four goals that they will include in their One-Year Action Plan for Partnerships and to show how activities for the six types of involvement contribute to *one* of the four goals. This activity is on the *Handbook* CD *only.*

How to Organize Your Action Team for Partnerships

This group activity is conducted after the presentation on how Action Teams for Partnerships are structured. ATPs are asked to discuss how they will meet and work as a team at their own schools, whether more team members are needed, when the team will meet, and which other groups at the school need reports from the ATP on partnerships.

Good Plan/Bad Plan! Help This Plan!

This activity is on the *Handbook* CD *only.* After learning the components of a good One-Year Action Plan for Partnerships, the ATP will examine one page of a hypothetical plan and identify items that should be improved. One slide of answers for this activity (for the workshop leader only) also is on the CD *only.*

One-Year Action Plan for Partnerships (Form G–Goals or Form T–Types)

The final workshop activity requires each ATP to write a draft One-Year Action Plan for Partnerships for their own school. The workshop facilitator should select which form of the plan (G or T) will be used by all schools' ATPs. This makes it easier to give directions at the workshop. It also makes it easier for ATPs to share their ideas across schools in the long term. See details in Chapter 4 for guidelines on how to select which form to use.

The *One-Year Action Plan for Partnerships* asks for details and schedules on goals for partnerships, assessments used to measure results, specific activities, dates, targeted participants, actions needed, and persons responsible for conducting the activities.

Use the *One-Year Action Plan for Partnerships–Form T (Types)* if the ATP will focus its work on the six types of involvement. Form T (six pages) asks the following: *For each type of involvement, which activities will your school continue or add this year?*

Use the *One-Year Action Plan for Partnerships–Form G (Goals)* if the ATP will focus its work to involve families and community partners to help students reach academic, behavior, and climate goals. Form G (four pages) asks the following: *Which practices of the six types of involvement will you choose to help reach major goals your school has set for students and for school climate this year?*

Notes

- Even if a school writes a School Improvement Plan, the ATP must complete a One-Year Action Plan for Partnerships each year to show the details for conducting each involvement activity.
- The One-Year Action Plan for Partnerships should be appended to the School Improvement Plan each year.
- The organization of the ATP determines which form of the One-Year Action Plan for Partnerships to use. If ATP committees and subgroups focus on and monitor results for school improvement goals, then Form G–Goals should be used. If ATP committees and subgroups focus on and monitor results for the six types of involvement, then Form T–Types should be used. The selected planning form also must match the *Annual Evaluation of Activities* (G or T), which is used to assess the quality of each activity that is implemented (see Chapter 9).

The Complete Picture: Family and Community Involvement at THIS School

This activity is on the *Handbook* CD *only.* An ATP can supplement the One-Year Action Plan for Partnerships with information from individual teachers, grade level teams, the PTA/PTO, and other school organizations on the family and community involvement activities that they conduct. Use this form to collect and collate lists from all teachers and groups to give a complete picture of school, family, and community partnerships at the school.

Workshop Warm-Up

ARE TWO HEADS BETTER THAN ONE?

1.	wire just	11.	often not often not often
2.	ANKLE	12.	MIGRAINE
3.	night fly	13.	you just me
4.	WAY ________ PASS	14.	Once upon a time . . . N E S
5.	END N D	15.	GOLDEN GATE H_2O
6.	SS SS SS SS SS NE1?	16.	RASINGINGIN
7.	VAD ERS	17.	1 3 5 7 9 ________ WHELMING
8.	esroh riding	18.	ALL world
9.	DO 12" OR	19.	a chance n
10.	GIVE GET GIVE GET GIVE GET GIVE GET	20.	APPLAUSE

Answers

Are Two Heads Better Than One?

**Note: The answers to the puzzles are for facilitators only.
Do *not* duplicate as a workshop handout!**

1. Just under the wire
2. Twisted ankle, turned ankle
3. Fly by night
4. Highway overpass
5. Making ends meet, split ends
6. Tennis, anyone?
7. Space invaders
8. Horseback riding
9. Foot in the door
10. Forgive and forget, give as much as you get
11. More often than not
12. A splitting headache
13. Just between you and me
14. *West Side Story*
15. Water under the bridge
16. Singing in the rain
17. The odds are overwhelming, overwhelming odds
18. It's a small world after all
19. An outside chance
20. A round of applause

Workshop Warm-Up

DISCUSSION DICE
Share a positive partnership experience!

1. **Introduce yourself to the others at your table.** Give your name, name and location of your school or district, and position or role (parent, teacher, administrator, etc.).

2. **Roll the dice. Match the sum of the dice to a topic below.** In one or two minutes, share an experience that completes the sentence. It may be an activity you conducted, experienced, or heard about.

ROLL of . . .	**Share a positive experience!** **What good practices of family and community involvement have you conducted, experienced, or heard about?**
2	**A most inspiring family involvement activity was . . .**
3	**A successful collaboration with a community partner was . . .**
4	**An activity that made all families feel welcome at school was . . .**
5	**A great family involvement activity linked to children's reading was . . .**
6	**An excellent way that volunteers helped a school was . . .**
7	**One example of how teamwork produced a successful family involvement activity was . . .**
8	**An enjoyable family math or science activity was . . .**
9	**An example of how a principal's leadership improved school, family, and community partnerships was . . .**
10	**A great strategy to increase communication between home and school was . . .**
11	**One example of how a school district helped improve family and community involvement was . . .**
12	**One activity that kept parents involved in middle or high school was . . .**

STARTING POINTS:

An Inventory of Present Practices of School, Family, and Community Partnerships

Karen Clark Salinas, Joyce L. Epstein, and Mavis G. Sanders
National Network of Partnership Schools, Johns Hopkins University

This inventory will help you identify your school's present practices for each of the six types of involvement that create a comprehensive program of school, family, and community partnerships. At this time, your school may conduct all, some, or none of the activities listed. Not every activity is appropriate for every school or grade level.

The Action Team for Partnerships (ATP) should complete this inventory with input from teachers, parents, the School Improvement Team, and others, as appropriate. These groups have different knowledge about all of the present practices of partnership in your school.

After you complete the inventory, you will be ready to write a One-Year Action Plan for Partnerships. Activities from the six types of involvement will help your school reach goals to improve the school climate, involve all families, and increase student success.

Directions: Check the activities that your school conducts and circle all of the grade levels presently involved. On the blank lines, you may write in other activities for each type of involvement that your school conducts.

To note how well each activity is implemented, add these symbols next to the checkbox:

* **Very well implemented** with all families
+ **Good start** with many families
• **Needs improvement**

TYPE 1–PARENTING: Assist families in understanding child and adolescent development and in setting home conditions that support children as students. Assist schools in understanding family backgrounds, cultures, and goals.

	In Which Grades?
❑ We sponsor parent education workshops and other courses or training for parents.	K 1 2 3 4 5 6 7 8 9 10 11 12
❑ We provide families with information on child or adolescent development.	K 1 2 3 4 5 6 7 8 9 10 11 12
❑ We conduct family support programs with parent-to-parent discussion groups.	K 1 2 3 4 5 6 7 8 9 10 11 12
❑ We provide families with information on developing home conditions that support learning.	K 1 2 3 4 5 6 7 8 9 10 11 12
❑ We lend families books, audiotapes, and videotapes/DVDs on parenting or parent workshops.	K 1 2 3 4 5 6 7 8 9 10 11 12
❑ We ask families for information about children's goals, strengths, and talents.	K 1 2 3 4 5 6 7 8 9 10 11 12
❑ We sponsor home visiting programs or neighborhood meetings to help families understand schools and to help schools understand families.	K 1 2 3 4 5 6 7 8 9 10 11 12
❑ ______________________	K 1 2 3 4 5 6 7 8 9 10 11 12
❑ ______________________	K 1 2 3 4 5 6 7 8 9 10 11 12
❑ ______________________	K 1 2 3 4 5 6 7 8 9 10 11 12

TYPE 2–COMMUNICATING: Communicate effectively from school to home and from home to school about school programs and children's progress.

	In Which Grades?
❑ We have formal conferences with every parent at least once a year.	K 1 2 3 4 5 6 7 8 9 10 11 12
❑ We provide language translators/interpreters to assist families as needed.	K 1 2 3 4 5 6 7 8 9 10 11 12
❑ We provide clear information about report cards and how grades are earned.	K 1 2 3 4 5 6 7 8 9 10 11 12
❑ We provide clear information about state tests and student and school results.	K 1 2 3 4 5 6 7 8 9 10 11 12
Our school newsletter includes:	
❑ A calendar of school events.	K 1 2 3 4 5 6 7 8 9 10 11 12
❑ Student activity information.	K 1 2 3 4 5 6 7 8 9 10 11 12
❑ Curriculum and program information.	K 1 2 3 4 5 6 7 8 9 10 11 12
❑ School volunteer information.	K 1 2 3 4 5 6 7 8 9 10 11 12
❑ School policy information.	K 1 2 3 4 5 6 7 8 9 10 11 12
❑ Samples of student writing and artwork.	K 1 2 3 4 5 6 7 8 9 10 11 12
❑ A column to address parents' questions.	K 1 2 3 4 5 6 7 8 9 10 11 12
❑ Recognition of students, families, and community members.	K 1 2 3 4 5 6 7 8 9 10 11 12
❑ A column on activities for family and community involvement.	K 1 2 3 4 5 6 7 8 9 10 11 12
❑ We provide clear information about selecting courses, programs, and/or activities in this school.	K 1 2 3 4 5 6 7 8 9 10 11 12
❑ We send home folders of student work weekly or monthly for parent review and comments.	K 1 2 3 4 5 6 7 8 9 10 11 12
❑ Staff members send home positive messages about students on a regular basis.	K 1 2 3 4 5 6 7 8 9 10 11 12
❑ We notify families about student awards and recognition.	K 1 2 3 4 5 6 7 8 9 10 11 12
❑ We contact families of students having academic or behavior problems.	K 1 2 3 4 5 6 7 8 9 10 11 12
❑ Teachers have easy access to telephones to communicate with parents during or after school.	K 1 2 3 4 5 6 7 8 9 10 11 12
❑ Teachers and administrators have e-mail and/or a school Web site to communicate with parents.	K 1 2 3 4 5 6 7 8 9 10 11 12
❑ We provide parents with information on Internet safety.	K 1 2 3 4 5 6 7 8 9 10 11 12
❑ Parents have the telephone numbers and/or e-mail addresses of the school, principal, teachers, and counselors.	K 1 2 3 4 5 6 7 8 9 10 11 12
❑ We have an automated phone system to deliver messages to families.	K 1 2 3 4 5 6 7 8 9 10 11 12
❑ We have a homework hotline for students and families to hear daily assignments and messages.	K 1 2 3 4 5 6 7 8 9 10 11 12
❑ We conduct an annual survey for families to provide reactions to school programs and share information and concerns about students.	K 1 2 3 4 5 6 7 8 9 10 11 12
❑ ____________________	K 1 2 3 4 5 6 7 8 9 10 11 12
❑ ____________________	K 1 2 3 4 5 6 7 8 9 10 11 12
❑ ____________________	K 1 2 3 4 5 6 7 8 9 10 11 12
❑ ____________________	K 1 2 3 4 5 6 7 8 9 10 11 12

TYPE 3–VOLUNTEERING: INVOLVEMENT AT AND FOR THE SCHOOL

Organize volunteers and audiences to support the school and students.	**In Which Grades?**
❑ We conduct annual surveys to identify interests, talents, and availability of volunteers and the needs of teachers and administrators for volunteers.	K 1 2 3 4 5 6 7 8 9 10 11 12
❑ We provide initial and ongoing training and guidance to our volunteers.	K 1 2 3 4 5 6 7 8 9 10 11 12
❑ We have a parent room or family center for volunteer work, meetings, and resources for families.	K 1 2 3 4 5 6 7 8 9 10 11 12
We encourage families and the community to be involved at school by:	
❑ Assisting in classrooms (tutoring, grading papers, etc.).	K 1 2 3 4 5 6 7 8 9 10 11 12
❑ Helping on trips or at parties.	K 1 2 3 4 5 6 7 8 9 10 11 12
❑ Giving talks (careers, cultures, hobbies, etc.).	K 1 2 3 4 5 6 7 8 9 10 11 12
❑ Checking attendance.	K 1 2 3 4 5 6 7 8 9 10 11 12
❑ Monitoring halls or working in the library, cafeteria, or other areas.	K 1 2 3 4 5 6 7 8 9 10 11 12
❑ Leading clubs or activities.	K 1 2 3 4 5 6 7 8 9 10 11 12
❑ Serving as audiences at student assemblies, events, sports, etc.	K 1 2 3 4 5 6 7 8 9 10 11 12
❑ We provide ways for families to be involved at home or in the community if they cannot volunteer at school.	K 1 2 3 4 5 6 7 8 9 10 11 12
❑ We have a program to recognize and thank our volunteers.	K 1 2 3 4 5 6 7 8 9 10 11 12
❑ We organize class parents or neighborhood volunteers to link with all parents.	K 1 2 3 4 5 6 7 8 9 10 11 12
❑ We schedule plays, concerts, games, and other events at different times of the day or evening so that all parents can attend some activities.	K 1 2 3 4 5 6 7 8 9 10 11 12
❑ ______________________________	K 1 2 3 4 5 6 7 8 9 10 11 12
❑ ______________________________	K 1 2 3 4 5 6 7 8 9 10 11 12
❑ ______________________________	K 1 2 3 4 5 6 7 8 9 10 11 12

TYPE 4–LEARNING AT HOME: INVOLVEMENT IN ACADEMIC ACTIVITIES

Involve families with their children in homework, other curriculum-related activities, course and program choices, and plans for the future.	**In Which Grades?**
❑ We provide information to families on required skills in all subjects.	K 1 2 3 4 5 6 7 8 9 10 11 12
❑ We provide information to families on how to monitor and discuss schoolwork at home.	K 1 2 3 4 5 6 7 8 9 10 11 12
❑ We conduct family nights or other workshops to help parents understand school subjects and learn ways to help their children at home.	K 1 2 3 4 5 6 7 8 9 10 11 12
❑ We have a regular schedule of interactive homework that requires students to show and discuss what they are learning with a family member.	K 1 2 3 4 5 6 7 8 9 10 11 12
❑ We ask parents to listen to their child read or to read aloud with their child.	K 1 2 3 4 5 6 7 8 9 10 11 12
❑ We provide calendars with daily or weekly activities linked to grade level requirements for families to select and conduct at home.	K 1 2 3 4 5 6 7 8 9 10 11 12
❑ We provide summer learning packets to help students sustain school skills.	K 1 2 3 4 5 6 7 8 9 10 11 12
❑ We help families help students set academic goals, select courses and programs, and plan for college and careers.	K 1 2 3 4 5 6 7 8 9 10 11 12
❑ We provide information on Web sites with learning resources for students.	K 1 2 3 4 5 6 7 8 9 10 11 12
❑ ______________________________	K 1 2 3 4 5 6 7 8 9 10 11 12
❑ ______________________________	K 1 2 3 4 5 6 7 8 9 10 11 12

TYPE 5–DECISION MAKING: PARTICIPATION AND LEADERSHIP
Include families as participants in school decisions, and develop parent leaders and representatives.

	In Which Grades?
❑ We have an active PTA, PTO, or other parent organization.	K 1 2 3 4 5 6 7 8 9 10 11 12
❑ Parent representatives are on the School Council, School Improvement Team, or other school committees.	K 1 2 3 4 5 6 7 8 9 10 11 12
❑ We have an Action Team for Partnerships to develop a goal-oriented program with practices for all six types of involvement.	K 1 2 3 4 5 6 7 8 9 10 11 12
❑ Parent representatives are on a district level advisory council or committee.	K 1 2 3 4 5 6 7 8 9 10 11 12
❑ We develop formal networks to link all families with their parent representatives for decision making.	K 1 2 3 4 5 6 7 8 9 10 11 12
❑ We use e-mail and quick surveys to obtain parents' input and ideas on school policies.	K 1 2 3 4 5 6 7 8 9 10 11 12
❑ We involve parents in selecting school staff.	K 1 2 3 4 5 6 7 8 9 10 11 12
❑ We include parent representatives in professional development workshops for members of the School Council, ATP, and PTA or PTO.	K 1 2 3 4 5 6 7 8 9 10 11 12
❑ ______________________________	K 1 2 3 4 5 6 7 8 9 10 11 12
❑ ______________________________	K 1 2 3 4 5 6 7 8 9 10 11 12
❑ ______________________________	K 1 2 3 4 5 6 7 8 9 10 11 12
❑ ______________________________	K 1 2 3 4 5 6 7 8 9 10 11 12

TYPE 6–COLLABORATING WITH THE COMMUNITY Coordinate resources and services *from* the community for families, students, and the school, and provide services *to* the community.

	In Which Grades?
❑ We provide a resource directory for parents and students with information on community agencies, programs, and services.	K 1 2 3 4 5 6 7 8 9 10 11 12
❑ We provide information on community activities that link to learning skills and talents, including summer programs for students.	K 1 2 3 4 5 6 7 8 9 10 11 12
❑ We work with local businesses, industries, and faith-based or other community organizations on programs to enhance student skills.	K 1 2 3 4 5 6 7 8 9 10 11 12
❑ We offer afterschool programs for students with support from community businesses, agencies, or volunteers.	K 1 2 3 4 5 6 7 8 9 10 11 12
❑ We sponsor intergenerational programs with local senior citizen groups.	K 1 2 3 4 5 6 7 8 9 10 11 12
❑ We include alumni in school programs for students.	K 1 2 3 4 5 6 7 8 9 10 11 12
❑ We provide one-stop shopping for family services through partnerships of school, counseling, health, recreation, job training, and other agencies.	K 1 2 3 4 5 6 7 8 9 10 11 12
❑ We organize service *to* the community by students, families, and schools.	K 1 2 3 4 5 6 7 8 9 10 11 12
❑ Our school building is open for use by the community after school hours.	K 1 2 3 4 5 6 7 8 9 10 11 12
❑ ______________________________	K 1 2 3 4 5 6 7 8 9 10 11 12
❑ ______________________________	K 1 2 3 4 5 6 7 8 9 10 11 12
❑ ______________________________	K 1 2 3 4 5 6 7 8 9 10 11 12
❑ ______________________________	K 1 2 3 4 5 6 7 8 9 10 11 12

JUMPING HURDLES

All Action Teams for Partnerships (ATPs) face challenges in developing programs of school, family, and community partnerships. ATPs work to solve challenges and improve activities to reach more families, strengthen community ties, and boost students' success.

- List **ONE EXCELLENT ACTIVITY** that your school presently conducts to **involve families or the community** in students' education at home, at school, or in the community.
- Identify **ONE CHALLENGE** or obstacle that your school faced in implementing this involvement activity.
- Briefly describe how your school **SOLVED** that challenge.
- Note one **NEXT STEP** that your school could take to make the activity **even more successful.**

ONE SUCCESSFUL FAMILY or COMMUNITY INVOLVEMENT ACTIVITY

____

____

____

____

CHALLENGE

____

____

____

SOLUTION TO THE CHALLENGE

____

____

____

NEXT STEP to IMPROVE the activity EVEN MORE

____

____

____

REACH A GOAL FOR STUDENT SUCCESS USING THE SIX TYPES OF INVOLVEMENT

Choose one Goal for Student Learning or Behavior that is important in your school.

How will results be measured? ______________________________

With a partner, identify specific family and community involvement activities that support this goal.

Your ATP may use these ideas in your school's One-Year Action Plan for Partnerships.

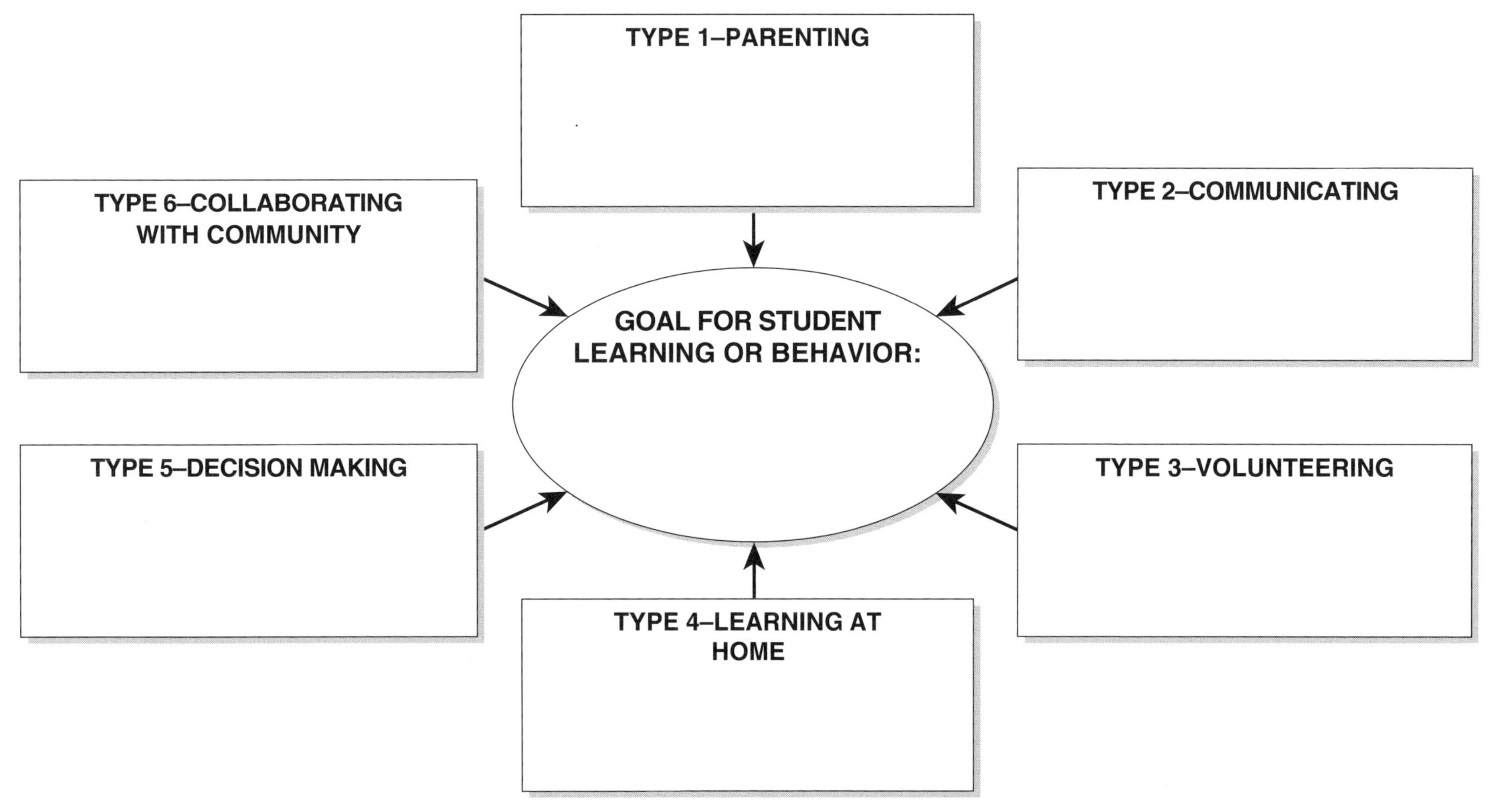

WHOLE GROUP DISCUSSION

HOW CAN YOUR SCHOOL ORGANIZE AN ACTION TEAM FOR PARTNERSHIPS (ATP)?

Discuss the following decisions to organize your school's ATP.

1. Who will be the members and leaders of your school's ATP?
REMEMBER: There should be 6-12 members of the ATP, including 2-3 teachers, 2-3 parents, the principal, and others from the community or from the school. A counselor may be one of the educators on the team.

- If there is a PTA or PTO at the school, it must have a representative on the ATP.
- If there is a parent liaison at the school, this person must be on the ATP.
- If there is an afterschool program at the school, it may have a representative on the ATP.

____________	____________	____________
____________	____________	____________
____________	____________	____________
____________	____________	____________

Are there others at your school(s) who MUST be on the ATP?

____

2. When will the whole Action Team for Partnerships (ATP) meet?

Remember: The ATP must meet at least **monthly**.
Committees of the ATP will meet **as needed** to plan and conduct activities.

How often? ______________________
What day? ______________________
What place? ______________________
What time? ______________________

How will the ATP get information from the meeting to those who could not attend?

____

3. Which groups should hear from the ATP about its plans and progress?
BE REALISTIC about how frequently reports should be made.

Which Groups?	How Often?	What Form of Report?
☐ School Council	____________	____________
☐ PTA/PTO	____________	____________
☐ ALL Parents	____________	____________
☐ ALL Faculty	____________	____________
☐ Local Media	____________	____________
☐ ____________	____________	____________

WHAT OTHER QUESTIONS DO YOU HAVE ABOUT THE ATP?

____

ONE-YEAR ACTION PLAN FOR PARTNERSHIPS
(SCHOOL LEVEL, FORM G–GOALS)

SCHEDULE OF SCHOOL, FAMILY, AND COMMUNITY PARTNERSHIPS TO REACH SCHOOL GOALS

On this 4-page plan, select 2 academic goals, 1 behavioral goal, and 1 goal for sustaining a partnership climate. For each goal, outline the desired results, how results will be measured, what family and community involvement activities will be implemented, dates, responsibilities, and needed resources.

School:

School Year:

GOAL 1–ACADEMIC: (Select **ONE curricular goal** for students from the School Improvement Plan, such as improving reading, math, writing, science, or other skills.)

Goal 1 chair or co-chairs: ______________________________

Desired result(s) for THIS goal:

How will the school measure the result(s)?

Organize and schedule family and community involvement activities to support THIS goal.

ACTIVITIES (2 or more, continuing or new)	TYPE (1–6)	DATE OF ACTIVITY	GRADE LEVEL(S)	WHAT NEEDS TO BE DONE FOR EACH ACTIVITY & WHEN	PERSONS IN CHARGE AND HELPING

Note if funds, supplies, or resources are needed for these activities.

Add pages to outline more activities that support THIS goal.

ONE-YEAR ACTION PLAN FOR PARTNERSHIPS
(SCHOOL LEVEL, FORM G–GOALS)

SCHEDULE OF SCHOOL, FAMILY, AND COMMUNITY PARTNERSHIPS TO REACH SCHOOL GOALS

GOAL 2–ACADEMIC: (Select ANOTHER curricular goal for students from the School Improvement Plan, such as improving reading, math, writing, science, or other skills.)

Goal 2 chair or co-chairs: ______________________________

Desired result(s) for THIS goal:	**How will the school measure the result(s)?**

Organize and schedule family and community involvement activities to support THIS goal.

ACTIVITIES (2 or more, continuing or new)	TYPE (1–6)	DATE OF ACTIVITY	GRADE LEVEL(S)	WHAT NEEDS TO BE DONE FOR EACH ACTIVITY & WHEN?	PERSONS IN CHARGE AND HELPING

Note if funds, supplies, or resources are needed for these activities.

Add pages to outline more activities that support THIS goal.

ONE-YEAR ACTION PLAN FOR PARTNERSHIPS

(SCHOOL LEVEL, FORM G–GOALS)

SCHEDULE OF SCHOOL, FAMILY, AND COMMUNITY PARTNERSHIPS TO REACH SCHOOL GOALS

GOAL 3–BEHAVIORAL: (Select ONE goal for improving student behavior, attendance, respect for others, safety, or other student outcome for the next school year.)

Goal 3 chair or co-chairs: ______________________________

Desired result(s) for THIS goal:	**How will the school measure the result(s)?**

Organize and schedule family and community involvement activities to support THIS goal.

ACTIVITIES (2 or more, continuing or new)	TYPE (1–6)	DATE OF ACTIVITY	GRADE LEVEL(S)	WHAT NEEDS TO BE DONE FOR EACH ACTIVITY & WHEN?	PERSONS IN CHARGE AND HELPING

Note if funds, supplies, or resources are needed for these activities.

Add pages to outline more activities that support THIS goal.

ONE-YEAR ACTION PLAN FOR PARTNERSHIPS

(SCHOOL LEVEL, FORM G–GOALS)

SCHEDULE OF SCHOOL, FAMILY, AND COMMUNITY PARTNERSHIPS TO REACH SCHOOL GOALS

GOAL 4–CLIMATE OF PARTNERSHIP (Required goal): Identify ALL OTHER family and community partnership activities for the six types of involvement that will create a welcoming school environment, not covered in GOALS 1, 2, and 3. Check Starting Points for activities to strengthen and sustain a climate of partnership.

Goal 4 chair or co-chairs: ____________________

Desired result(s) for THIS goal:	**How will the school measure the result(s)?**

Organize and schedule family and community involvement activities to support THIS goal.

ACTIVITIES (2 or more, continuing or new)	TYPE (1–6)	DATE OF ACTIVITY	GRADE LEVEL(S)	WHAT NEEDS TO BE DONE FOR EACH ACTIVITY & WHEN	PERSONS IN CHARGE AND HELPING

Note if funds, supplies, or resources are needed for these activities.

Add pages to outline more activities that support THIS goal.

ONE-YEAR ACTION PLAN FOR PARTNERSHIPS

(SCHOOL LEVEL, FORM T–TYPES)

SCHEDULE OF ACTIVITIES FOR THE SIX TYPES OF INVOLVEMENT

The One-Year Action Plan for Partnerships includes activities that are *presently* conducted at the school and *new activities* that will be implemented this year to strengthen the six types of involvement. For each type, outline the activities, dates, responsibilities, expected results and measures, and needed resources.

TYPE 1–PARENTING: Assist families in understanding child and adolescent development and in setting home conditions that support children as students. Also, assist schools in understanding family backgrounds, cultures, and goals.

Type 1 chair or co-chairs: ______________________________

Which school improvement goals will be addressed by strengthening Type 1–Parenting activities?

TYPE 1 Activities (2 or more, continuing or new)	DATE OF ACTIVITY	GRADE LEVEL(S)	WHAT NEEDS TO BE DONE FOR EACH ACTIVITY & WHEN?	PERSONS IN CHARGE AND HELPING	EXPECTED RESULTS? How will results be measured?

Note if funds, supplies, or resources are needed for these activities.

Add pages to outline more activities that support THIS goal.

ONE-YEAR ACTION PLAN FOR PARTNERSHIPS

(SCHOOL LEVEL, FORM T–TYPES)

SCHEDULE OF ACTIVITIES FOR THE SIX TYPES OF INVOLVEMENT

TYPE 2–COMMUNICATING: Communicate with families about school programs and student progress using school-to-home and home-to-school communications. Create two-way channels so that families can easily contact teachers and administrators.

Type 2 chair or co-chairs: ______________________________

Which major school goals will be addressed by improving Type 2–Communicating activities?

TYPE 2 Activities (2 or more, continuing or new)	DATE OF ACTIVITY	GRADE LEVEL(S)	WHAT NEEDS TO BE DONE FOR EACH ACTIVITY & WHEN?	PERSONS IN CHARGE AND HELPING	EXPECTED RESULTS? How will results be measured?

Note if funds, supplies, or resources are needed for these activities.

Add pages to outline more activities that support THIS goal.

ONE-YEAR ACTION PLAN FOR PARTNERSHIPS

(SCHOOL LEVEL, FORM T–TYPES)

SCHEDULE OF ACTIVITIES FOR THE SIX TYPES OF INVOLVEMENT

TYPE 3–VOLUNTEERING: Improve recruitment, training, activities, and schedules to involve families as volunteers and audiences at the school or in other locations to support students and the school's programs.

Type 3 chair or co-chairs: ______________________________

Which major school goals will be addressed by improving Type 3– Volunteering activities?

TYPE 3 Activities (2 or more, continuing or new)	DATE OF ACTIVITY	GRADE LEVEL(S)	WHAT NEEDS TO BE DONE FOR EACH ACTIVITY & WHEN?	PERSONS IN CHARGE AND HELPING	EXPECTED RESULTS? How will results be measured?

Note if funds, supplies, or resources are needed for these activities.

Add pages to outline more activities that support THIS goal.

ONE-YEAR ACTION PLAN FOR PARTNERSHIPS
(SCHOOL LEVEL, FORM T–TYPES)
SCHEDULE OF ACTIVITIES FOR THE SIX TYPES OF INVOLVEMENT

TYPE 4–LEARNING AT HOME: Involve families with their children in academic learning activities at home, including homework, goal setting, course and program choices, postsecondary education plans, and other curriculum-related activities and decisions.

Type 4 chair or co-chairs: ______________________

Which major school goals will be addressed by improving Type 4–Learning at Home activities?

TYPE 4 Activities (2 or more, continuing or new)	DATE OF ACTIVITY	GRADE LEVEL(S)	WHAT NEEDS TO BE DONE FOR EACH ACTIVITY & WHEN?	PERSONS IN CHARGE AND HELPING	EXPECTED RESULTS? How will results be measured?

Note if funds, supplies, or resources are needed for these activities.

Add pages to outline more activities that support THIS goal.

ONE-YEAR ACTION PLAN FOR PARTNERSHIPS

(SCHOOL LEVEL, FORM T–TYPES)

SCHEDULE OF ACTIVITIES FOR THE SIX TYPES OF INVOLVEMENT

TYPE 5–DECISION MAKING: Include families as participants in school decisions and advocacy activities through PTA/PTO, committees, councils, and other parent organizations. Assist family representatives to obtain information from and give information to those they represent.

Type 5 chair or co-chairs: ____________________

Which major school goals will be addressed by improving Type 5–Decision Making activities?

TYPE 5 Activities (2 or more, continuing or new)	DATE OF ACTIVITY	GRADE LEVEL(S)	WHAT NEEDS TO BE DONE FOR EACH ACTIVITY & WHEN?	PERSONS IN CHARGE AND HELPING	EXPECTED RESULTS? How will results be measured?

Note if funds, supplies, or resources are needed for these activities.

Add pages to outline more activities that support THIS goal.

ONE-YEAR ACTION PLAN FOR PARTNERSHIPS
(SCHOOL LEVEL, FORM T–TYPES)
SCHEDULE OF ACTIVITIES FOR THE SIX TYPES OF INVOLVEMENT

TYPE 6–COLLABORATING WITH THE COMMUNITY: Coordinate the resources of community businesses, agencies, and cultural, civic, and other organizations to strengthen school programs, family practices, and student learning and development. Enable students, staff, and families to contribute service and projects to the community.

Type 6 chair or co-chairs: ______________________

Which major school goals will be addressed by improving Type 6–Collaborating With the Community activities?

TYPE 6 Activities (2 or more, continuing or new)	DATE OF ACTIVITY	GRADE LEVEL(S)	WHAT NEEDS TO BE DONE FOR EACH ACTIVITY & WHEN?	PERSONS IN CHARGE AND HELPING	EXPECTED RESULTS? How will results be measured?

Note if funds, supplies, or resources are needed for these activities.

Add pages to outline more activities that support THIS goal.

Sample A

General Evaluation of Team-Training Workshop or End-of-Year Celebration Workshop

EVALUATION
WORKSHOP ON SCHOOL, FAMILY, AND COMMUNITY PARTNERSHIPS

Date ______________________________

Location ______________________________

Please circle how much you agree or disagree with each statement.

	Strongly Disagree	Disagree	Agree	Strongly Agree
Structure				
The goals of this workshop were clear.	SD	D	A	SA
The goals of this workshop were met.	SD	D	A	SA
Time was used well.	SD	D	A	SA
Content				
I gained many ideas that will help my school improve school, family, and community partnerships.	SD	D	A	SA
There were opportunities to share ideas with others.	SD	D	A	SA
Overall, this workshop was worthwhile.	SD	D	A	SA
Facilities				
The room was suitable.	SD	D	A	SA
Refreshments were satisfactory.	SD	D	A	SA

Which part of this workshop was most useful to you?

____

____

____

What assistance or follow-up would you like?

____

____

____

Thank you for your reactions!

Sample B

Reactions to Topics in a One-Day Team-Training Workshop

EVALUATION
WORKSHOP ON SCHOOL, FAMILY, AND COMMUNITY PARTNERSHIPS

Date ______________________________

Location ______________________________

How helpful were these workshop topics? Check (✓) how helpful these were to you.

	Very Helpful	Helpful	Not Helpful
Background			
1. Understanding the **six types of involvement** and examples of practice	_____	_____	_____
2. Understanding the **challenges that must be met for excellent partnerships**	_____	_____	_____
3. Linking the six types of involvement to **school goals and results** for students	_____	_____	_____
Team Discussions			
1. Taking stock of your **present partnership practices**	_____	_____	_____
2. **Gathering ideas** for your school's One-Year Action Plan for Partnerships	_____	_____	_____
3. **Writing a draft** of your school's One-Year Action Plan for Partnerships	_____	_____	_____

Other comments or ideas on the workshop:

____

____

____

What assistance or follow-up information would you like?

____

____

____

Thank you for your reactions!

6

Strengthen Partnership Programs in Middle and High Schools

Middle and high schools face unique challenges in developing and maintaining comprehensive programs of school, family, and community partnerships. Typically, middle and high school teachers have more students than do teachers in the elementary grades and, therefore, must connect with more families. Families tend to live farther away from middle and high schools and cannot come often to the school building. Most families are unsure of how to relate to several teachers that students have for different subjects, and they need more information about the middle and high school curriculum, policies, and requirements for students. Students in secondary schools are trying to balance their need for guidance with their need for greater independence. Despite these complex realities, research shows that connections of home, school, and community remain important for student success in middle and high schools.

Three short articles in this chapter explore school, family, and community partnerships in middle and high schools. The first article identifies examples of activities for the six types of involvement that have been useful in secondary schools for creating a welcoming climate of partnerships and for guiding teens toward success in school. It also discusses the challenges that must be solved and the expected results of well-implemented, age-appropriate partnerships in middle and high schools. Many activities in other chapters of this *Handbook* can be adapted for middle and high schools, and many examples in this chapter can be reframed for elementary schools.

The second article summarizes a study of over 11,000 parents of high school students. The results show that family involvement is important for student success through the twelfth grade. High schools that conducted involvement activities had more parents who were involved in their teens' education. The data indicate that, by implementing strong partnership programs, high schools can help families remain influential in their teens' lives in important ways.

The third article guides secondary schools, step by step, to take a goal-oriented approach in planning their partnership programs. Examples from middle and high schools show that Action Teams for Partnerships (ATPs) can write plans for family and community involvement to help schools reach specific improvement goals. The steps for developing a goal-oriented program are useful in elementary schools, too, and reflect the guidelines for all schools' ATPs provided throughout this *Handbook.*

The following tools and materials are included in this chapter.

Reach Middle and High School Goals Through Partnerships

Use the six types of involvement to target specific goals for secondary schools, students, and families. Activities are listed for all six types that illustrate how to help students make successful transitions into middle school; improve attendance, increase reading achievement, improve math skills, improve student health, plan for postsecondary education, and create a welcoming school environment. These pages (also on the *Handbook* CD) are useful slides and handouts for workshops or presentations on how to implement family and community involvement to reach specific results in middle and high schools. The examples for middle and high schools supplement the examples for elementary schools on pages 160–163 and on the CD.

Why Partnerships Are Important in Middle and High Schools

This summary reviews eight findings from research that explain why programs of school, family, and community partnerships are important in secondary schools.

Special Considerations for Middle and High Schools

This summary reflects on several common challenges in middle and high schools that must be addressed to help ATPs establish and sustain successful programs and partnership practices. The list presents six lessons learned from middle and high schools that are developing their partnership programs.

Transitions: Involve Families When Students Move to New Schools

Plan to involve students and families in activities that will ease students' transitions and adjustments to new schools. Schools' One-Year Action Plans for Partnerships should include activities to welcome new students and their families to the school and to prepare students and families to move successfully to the next school level (i.e., from elementary to middle and from middle to high school). This activity is on the *Handbook* CD only.

Improving School, Family, and Community Partnerships in Middle and High Schools

Joyce L. Epstein

The goal of positive and productive family and community involvement is on every school improvement list, but few secondary schools have implemented comprehensive programs of partnership. Research suggests that the goal is important, because families and communities contribute to children's learning, development, and school success at every grade level. Presently, however, most families need more information about adolescent development, middle and high school organization, and community programs and services for teens.

Just about all parents want their adolescents to succeed in school, graduate from high school, and attend college or career education. Most, however, need better information and guidance to support their teens' success through high school. Some parents are discouraged from remaining involved when faced by the multifaceted needs and problems of adolescents; the complexities of school curricula, assessments, and organization; and growing constraints on family time.

Studies are accumulating that show that well-designed programs of partnership can help all families support their children's education in middle and high school (Balli, Demo, & Wedman, 1998; Catsambis, 2001; Catsambis & Beveridge, 2001; Dauber & Epstein, 1993; Eccles & Harold, 1996; Epstein, 2001; Epstein & Lee, 1995; Henderson & Mapp, 2002; Hill et al., 2004; Kreider, Caspe, Kennedy, & Weiss, 2007; Lee, 1994; Sanders 1998, 1999; Sanders & Epstein, 2000; Sanders & Lewis, 2005; Sanders & Simon, 2002; Sheldon & Epstein, 2005b; Simon, 2001, 2004; Van Voorhis, 2001, 2003). Results indicate that when secondary schools plan and implement comprehensive programs of partnership, many more families respond, including those who would not become involved on their own.

Middle and high school teachers and administrators agree that family involvement and community connections are important, but their beliefs are not always supported by action. Three questions need to be answered to help middle and high school educators conduct more effective programs of partnership:

1. What is a comprehensive, goal-oriented program of school, family, and community partnerships in middle and high schools?
2. How do family and community partnerships link to other aspects of successful middle and high schools?
3. How can any middle or high school develop and sustain a productive program of partnerships?

What Is a Comprehensive Program of Partnerships?

A comprehensive program of school, family, and community partnerships is a planned, goal-oriented, and ongoing schedule of activities that inform and involve all families and the community in ways that promote student success. At all school levels, family and community involvement activities should be selected and implemented to address specific goals, meet key challenges, and produce results for students, families, and schools.

The framework of six types of family and community involvement guides schools in establishing full and productive programs of partnerships (Epstein, 1995). This section summarizes the six types of involvement with a few examples of practices that are being conducted in middle and high schools across the country.[1] Also noted are some of the challenges that secondary schools must solve to achieve successful partnerships and examples of results that can be expected from each type of involvement for secondary school students, families, and educators.

Comprehensive programs of partnerships include activities for all six types of involvement. Importantly, there are many choices of activities, so middle and high schools can select different ways to involve families and the community to help reach specific school goals.

Type 1–Parenting

Type 1–Parenting activities are conducted to help families strengthen parenting skills, understand adolescent development, and set home conditions to support learning at every grade level. Type 1 activities also enable families to provide information to middle and high schools so that educators better understand families' backgrounds, cultures, and goals for their teens.

Sample Practices. Many families have questions about how to relate to and support their children through adolescence. Middle and high schools can plan and implement activities and provide services that assist families to better understand adolescent development. Among Type 1 activities, middle and high schools may conduct workshops for parents on teen development; provide short, clear summaries of important information on parenting through the teen years; and organize support groups, panels, and other opportunities for parents to exchange ideas with other parents, educators, and community experts on topics of adolescent development.

Topics of interest to parents of adolescents include health, nutrition, discipline, peer pressure, preventing drug and alcohol abuse, teens' sexual development, and planning for the future. Type 1 activities also provide families with information on students' transitions to middle school and to high school and on family roles and responsibilities in student attendance, college planning, career preparation, and other topics that are important for adolescents' success in school.

Secondary schools may offer parents GED programs, family support sessions, family computer classes, and other learning and social opportunities for parents and for students. To ensure that families provide valuable information to the schools, teachers may ask parents at the start of each school year to share insights about their teen's strengths, talents, interests, needs, and goals.

Challenges. Even if workshops are well planned, not all interested parents are able to attend. As of 2006, according to the U.S. Department of Labor, more than 70 percent of mothers worked full- or part-time during the school day. They cannot often attend workshops conducted at the school building. Yet, most parents can benefit from *the content* of well-planned workshops. One major challenge that must be met for successful Type 1 activities is to get information from workshops to parents who cannot come to meetings and workshops at the school building. This may be done with videos, tape recordings, summaries, newsletters, cable broadcasts, phone calls, computerized messages, school Web sites, and other print and nonprint communications. Another Type 1 challenge is to design procedures that enable all families to share information easily and as needed about their teens with teachers, counselors, and others.

Results. If useful information flows to and from families throughout adolescent development, parents will increase their confidence about parenting, students will be more aware of and benefit from parents' continuing guidance, and teachers will better understand their students' families. If teachers, parents, and others help families find needed services, then students will benefit from medical, dental, tutoring, and other services that they need. Studies indicate, too, that if practices are designed to help families send their children to school every day on time, then student attendance improves and lateness decreases (Epstein & Sheldon, 2002; Sheldon, 2007; Sheldon & Epstein, 2004). If families are part of their children's transitions from elementary to middle school and from middle to high school, then more students will adjust well to their new schools, and more parents will remain involved across the grades (Seidman, Lambert, Allen, & Aber, 2003).

Type 2–Communicating

Type 2–Communicating activities increase school-to-home and home-to-school exchanges about school programs and student progress through notices, memos, conferences, report cards, newsletters, phone, e-mail and computerized messages, the Internet, open houses, and other traditional and innovative communications. Although middle and high schools send information home, they often lack two-way channels of communication for families to contact school administrators, teachers, and counselors with information, questions, and suggestions.

Sample Practices. Families rely on communications with teachers, administrators, and counselors to follow their children's progress and problems. Middle and high schools are, increasingly, adding new technologies to traditional communication to relay information to and from families. Among many Type 2 activities, middle and high schools may provide parents and students with clear information on each teacher's criteria for report card grades and how to interpret interim progress reports. Type 2 activities include conferences for parents with teams of teachers and, more commonly, parent-student-teacher conferences to ensure that students take personal responsibility for learning. Class parents, block parents, and telephone trees set up communication systems that may include all families in a school. School and student newsletters may be improved to include student work, a feature column for parents' questions, calendars of important events, and parent response forms. Many schools now use e-mail, voice mail, and school Web sites to encourage two-way communication between families and teachers, counselors, and administrators.

Challenges. Not all communications between middle and high school educators and families are successful. One major challenge that must be met for successful Type 2 activities is to make communications clear and understandable for all families, including parents who have less formal education or who do not speak or read English well. This may require obtaining or arranging translators and interpreters for families and encouraging middle and high school students to serve in these roles with pride. Other Type 2 challenges are to know which families are and are not receiving and understanding the communications in order to design ways to reach all families, develop effective two-way channels of communication so that all families can easily contact and respond to educators, and make sure that students in middle and high schools understand the important roles they play as couriers, interpreters, and main actors in their own learning and in facilitating school and family connections. It is still important, however, to supplement electronic and Internet communications with traditional, "low-tech" communications for families who do not have easy access to new technologies.

Results. If communications are clear and useful, and if two-way channels are easily accessed, then school-to-home and home-to-school interactions will increase; more families will understand middle and high school programs, follow their teens' progress, guide students to maintain or improve their grades, and attend parent-teacher conferences. If, for example, computerized phone messages are used to communicate information about daily homework, more families will know more about their children's daily assignments. If middle and high schools' newsletters include respond-and-reply forms, more families will offer ideas, questions, and comments about school programs and activities. Studies indicate that good communications with families at all school levels help decrease disciplinary actions (Sheldon & Epstein, 2002) and increase math achievement at the school level (Sheldon & Epstein, 2005a).

Type 3–Volunteering

Type 3–Volunteering activities are designed to improve recruitment, training, and schedules to involve parents and others as volunteers and as audiences at the school or in other locations to support students and school programs.

Sample Practices. Parents of students in middle and high school often wonder if they should continue to serve as volunteers at school. Middle and high schools can enrich, extend, and support their curricular and extracurricular programs by organizing volunteers in new ways. Among many Type 3 activities, middle and high schools may collect information on family members' talents, occupations, interests, and availability to serve as volunteers. Parents, family members, and other volunteers may help enrich students' subject classes; improve career explorations; serve as language translators; monitor attendance and call parents of absent students; conduct parent patrols and be morning greeters to increase school safety; serve as "boosters" or supporters of extracurricular clubs; and organize and improve activities such as clothing and uniform exchanges, school stores, fairs, and many other activities.

Schools may organize volunteers to serve as homeroom parents, neighborhood representatives, or sports and club contacts and establish telephone trees to help parents communicate with each other about school programs and events. Schools may establish a corps of volunteers to offer a "welcome wagon" of information about the school to students and families who enroll during the school year. Secondary schools also may create opportunities for mentors, coaches, tutors, and leaders of afterschool programs to ensure that middle and high school students have experiences that build and expand their skills and talents and that keep them safe and supervised after school. Some Type 3 activities may be conducted in a parent room or family center at the school where parents obtain information, conduct volunteer work, and meet with other parents.

Challenges. Volunteers must be well prepared to conduct specific tasks in middle and high schools, and they must feel that their efforts are appreciated. Challenges for successful Type 3 activities are to recruit volunteers widely, make hours flexible for parents and other volunteers who work during the school day, provide needed training for complex tasks, and enable volunteers to contribute productively to the school, classroom, extracurricular, and afterschool programs. Volunteer coordinators, working with the Action Team for Partnerships, must match volunteers' times and skills with the needs of teachers, administrators, and students. Another Type 3 challenge is to change the definition of "volunteer" to mean anyone who supports school goals or students' learning at any time and in any place. This includes parents and family members who voluntarily come to school as audiences for students' sports events, assemblies, musical or drama presentations, and other events that support students' work. It also includes volunteers who work for the school at home, through their businesses, or in the community. Related challenges are to help adolescents understand how volunteers help their school, encourage students to interact with volunteers who can assist them with their work and activities, and enable students to *be* volunteers for their school and in the community.

Results. If tasks are well designed and if schedules and locations for volunteers are varied, more parents, family members, and others in the community will assist middle and high schools and support students as members of audiences. If the ATP identifies a director of volunteers (whether a team member or not), more teachers and other school staff will call upon volunteers to improve school programs and activities. If parents know that their attendance at student performances and events is "counted" as volunteering, they will feel more connected to the school and more aware that they are contributing to school programs. For example, if volunteers serve effectively as attendance monitors, more families will assist teens to improve attendance. If volunteers conduct a hall patrol or are active in other locations, school safety should increase and student behavior problems should decrease due to a better adult-student ratio. If volunteers are well trained as tutors in particular subjects, student tutees will improve their skills in those subjects, and if volunteers discuss careers, students will be more aware of their options for the future. One study found that when parent volunteers shared famous art work in social studies classes, students gained knowledge of art work linked to their units of study (Epstein & Dauber, 1995, and see Chapter 8). These examples reinforce the importance of organizing volunteers to conduct activities that help the school and students reach specific goals.

Type 4–Learning at Home

Type 4–Learning at Home activities involve families with their children in academic learning activities at home that are coordinated with students' classwork and that contribute to student success in school. These include monitoring homework, discussing interactive homework, goal setting for academic subjects, and other curricular-linked activities and decisions about courses, academic programs, and postsecondary paths.

Sample Practices. Of all the types of involvement, most families want to know more about how to help their teens at home so that they will do better in school. Middle and high school teachers and counselors can work together to enable more families to connect with their teenagers about schoolwork and homework. Among many Type 4 activities, middle and high schools should provide information to students and to parents about the skills needed to pass each course and about each teacher's homework policies. Educators may implement activities that help families encourage, praise, guide, and monitor their children's work by using interactive homework strategies, student-teacher-family contracts for long-term projects, summer home-learning packets, student-led conferences with parents at home on portfolios of students' writing or work in other subjects, goal-setting activities for improving or maintaining good report card grades in all subjects, specific ways to help students improve grades or behavior, and other approaches that keep students and families talking about schoolwork at home.

Family nights in the middle grades can be a starting point to help parents and students focus on curricular-related topics and family interactions. A systematic approach to increasing parent-teen conversations about academic subjects is found in the Teachers Involve Parents in Schoolwork (TIPS) interactive homework for the middle grades (Epstein, Salinas, & Van Voorhis, 2001; Van Voorhis & Epstein, 2002). For information on how to use interactive homework in middle and high schools, see Chapter 8.

Challenges. Involving parents with teens on homework is difficult, because parents must not feel that they are expected to "teach" middle and high school subjects. Parents must not *do* students' homework at any grade level. The students, themselves, are key to the success of family involvement in learning activities at home. One major challenge that can lead to successful Type 4 activities is to design and implement a regular schedule of interactive homework that requires students to take responsibility for discussing important things they are learning in school, interviewing family members, recording reactions, and sharing their work and ideas at home. Another Type 4 challenge is to involve families with students on a regular schedule (e.g., each marking period) in setting goals for attendance, achievement, behavior, talent development, and plans for college or careers. Still another challenge connects two types of involvement. If schools provide information on course choices and learning opportunities (Type 2), then parents can discuss the options and make decisions with their teens in a timely way (Type 4).

Results. If Type 4 activities are well designed and implemented, then students should improve their homework completion, report card grades, and test scores in specific subjects, and more families will know what their children are learning in class and how to monitor, support, and discuss homework. If involvement focuses on students' curricular choices, more students should complete required course credits for high school graduation, select advanced courses, take college entrance tests, and graduate on time. For example, one high school conducted activities to help parents understand math standards, proficiency tests, sample problems, math homework requirements, and talking about homework with teens. These activities helped increase the number of students who passed major math tests.

Students and teachers will be more aware of family interest in students' work. There should be more positive conversations between students and family members about their schoolwork and academic ideas. Studies show that interactive homework in the middle grades increases parental involvement with students about their work in math (Balli et al., 1998) and improves homework completion and report card grades in language arts (Epstein, Simon, & Salinas, 1997; Van Voorhis, 2008) and in science (Van Voorhis, 2003).

Type 5–Decision Making

Type 5–Decision Making activities include families in developing, reviewing, and improving school policies and mission statements that affect their children and families. Family members are active participants on School Improvement Teams or School Councils, committees, the PTA/PTO or other parent organizations, Title I and other advisory committees, and advocacy groups.

Sample Practices. Parents may have different perspectives from teachers about many school issues. Middle and high school educators can identify and understand issues that are important to students and families and make better decisions about programs and procedures by including parent representatives on various school committees. Among Type 5 activities, middle and high schools should organize and maintain an active parent association and include family representatives on all committees for school improvement (e.g., curriculum, safety, supplies and equipment, partnerships, fund-raising, and postsecondary college planning and career development committees). At the high school level, student leaders should also be represented on all committees. Some high schools call the organization "PTSA" for the Parent, Teacher, and Student Association. Increasingly, middle and high schools are using e-mail and Web sites to keep all parents informed about school programs and to provide opportunities for them to have input to decisions that affect their children, even if they cannot attend meetings at the school.

In particular, along with teachers, administrators, and others from the community, parents are members of the school-based Action Team for Partnerships (ATP), which plans and conducts family and community involvement activities linked to school improvement goals. At the high school level, students also are on this action-oriented group to improve partnerships. Schools may offer parents and teachers training in leadership, decision making, advocacy, and collaboration. Type 5 activities help to identify and provide information desired by families about school policies, course offerings, student placements and groups, special services, tests and assessments, annual test results for students, and evaluations of school programs.

Challenges. It is important for parents to have their voices, ideas, and interests represented on school committees. One challenge that must be met for successful Type 5 activities in middle and high schools is to ensure that leadership roles are filled by parent representatives from all the major race and ethnic groups, socioeconomic groups, and neighborhoods that are present in the school. A related challenge is to help parent leaders serve as effective representatives by obtaining information from and providing information to all parents about school issues and decisions. Another Type 5 challenge is to include middle and high school student representatives along with parents in decision making groups and leadership positions.

As noted in Chapter 4, large high schools may have one ATP with multiple representatives from school divisions, or multiple ATPs—one for each major division of the school (grade levels, academies, houses, or other schools-within-a-school). If there are several ATPs, parents and students must serve on each one. With one ATP, the chair or co-chair must connect with representatives from the major school divisions. With multiple ATPs, a coordinator on the School Improvement Team must integrate plans and results of several teams so that the school has *one* partnership program.

Teachers and administrators must learn to work with parent leaders as equal partners on committees, recognizing their shared interest in student success. An ongoing challenge is to help parents, teachers, and students who serve on an Action Team for Partnerships or other committees learn to trust, respect, and listen to each other as they collaborate to reach common goals for school improvement.

Results. If Type 5 activities are well implemented in middle and high schools, more families will have input to decisions that affect the quality of their children's education; students will be more aware that families and students have a say in school policies; and teachers will increase their understanding of family perspectives on policies and programs for improving the school.

Type 6–Collaborating With the Community

Type 6–Collaborating With the Community activities draw upon and coordinate the work and resources of community businesses; cultural, civic, and religious organizations; senior citizen groups; colleges and universities; governmental agencies; and other associations in order to strengthen school programs, family practices, and student learning and development. Other Type 6 activities enable students, staff, and families to contribute their services to the community.

Sample Practices. Students' needs and interests become more diverse in adolescence than in earlier years, and their activities in the community become more numerous and noticeable. Middle and high schools need to identify and activate the resources, services, and opportunities in the community to fully serve teens and their families. Among many Type 6 activities, some middle and high schools create useful directories of community programs and resources to help families and students identify afterschool recreation, tutorial programs, enrichment in the arts, health services, cultural events, service opportunities, summer programs, and part-time jobs. The information includes how to gain access to the resources and programs.

Other middle and high schools work with local businesses to organize "gold card" discounts as incentives for students to improve attendance and report card grades. Collaborations with community businesses, groups, and agencies also strengthen the other five types of involvement. Examples include enhancing Type 1 activities by conducting parent education or family literacy workshops at community or business locations or by having businesses provide refreshments or incentives to increase the success of school-based workshops for parents; increasing Type 2 activities by communicating information about school events on the local radio and TV stations (including foreign language stations), at churches, clinics, supermarkets, laundromats, and other neighborhood locations; soliciting volunteers from businesses and the community to strengthen Type 3 activities; enriching Type 4 by offering students learning opportunities with artists, scientists, writers, mathematicians, and others whose careers link to the school curriculum; and including community members on Type 5 decision making councils and committees.

Challenges. It is not always easy for educators to collaborate with partners outside the school, and problems must be solved. For example, some school and community partners must address turf problems to clarify which organization and leaders are responsible for funding, leading, and supervising cooperative activities. The initial enthusiasm and decisions to conduct school-community partnerships must be followed by actions that sustain productive collaborations over the long term. Another Type 6 challenge is to recognize and link students' valuable learning experiences in the community to the school curriculum, including lessons that build on students' nonschool skills and talents, club and volunteer work, and part-time jobs. A major challenge is to inform families about and involve them in community-related activities that students conduct or to expand some community activities to involve families with students. Related challenges are to help adolescents understand how community partners help their school and to engage students, themselves, in service learning and volunteer activities in their own schools, other schools, and the community. These activities provide adolescents with evidence of their contributions to and value in their communities.

Results. If Type 6 activities are well implemented, families, students, and schools will increase their knowledge of community resources and programs that will help students reach important goals for learning and development. By ensuring equal access to community programs, more and different students and families should participate and benefit from various programs. If community services are better coordinated, adolescents and their families may prevent health, social, and educational problems or solve them before they become serious. Type 6 activities also can support and enrich school curricula and extracurricular programs (Sanders, 2001, 2005). For example, activities such as tutoring and mentoring can directly affect student learning, achievement, and postsecondary plans and pathways.

Summary

The six types of involvement create a comprehensive program of partnerships in middle and high schools, but the implementation challenges for each type of involvement must be solved in order for programs to be effective. The expected results are directly affected by the quality of the design, implementation, and content of the involvement activities. Not every practice to involve families will result in higher student achievement test scores. Rather, practices for each type of involvement can be selected to help students, families, and teachers reach specific goals such as improving attendance, increasing homework completion, helping plan postsecondary education and training, and achieving other results (Epstein, 1995, 2001). The examples above include only a few of hundreds of suggestions that can help middle and high schools develop strong programs of partnerships. For more examples of effective activities, see collections entitled *Promising Partnership Practices* at www.partnershipschools.org in the section Success Stories, and search by school level for middle and high school activities in schools across the country.

How Do School, Family, and Community Partnerships Link to Other Aspects of Successful Middle and High Schools?

Good schools have qualified and talented teachers and administrators, high expectations that all students will succeed, rigorous curricula, engaging instruction, responsive and useful tests and assessments, strong guidance for every student, *and* effective school, family, and community partnerships. In good schools, these elements combine to promote student learning and to create a school climate that is welcoming, safe, caring, stimulating, and joyful for all students, educators, and families.

All of the elements of successful schools are interconnected. It is particularly important for middle and high school educators to understand that family and community involvement is not extra, separate, or different from the "real work" of a school but is integral to and essential for improving the quality of a school's program and student success. As one middle school principal noted, "I think that family and community involvement and school improvement should be joint efforts . . . they support each other" (Sanders, 1999, p. 35).

The following two examples show how family involvement is linked to the success of middle and high schools' academic and guidance programs.

Family and community partnerships contribute to the quality of schools' academic programs and student learning. National and local surveys indicate that secondary school students and their families have very high aspirations for success in school and in life. Fully 98 percent of a national sample of eighth grade students said that they plan to graduate from high school, and 82 percent planned at least some postsecondary schooling, with over 70 percent aiming to complete college (Epstein & Lee, 1995). Tenth grade students have similarly high ambitions, with about 90 percent saying they sometimes or often talk with a parent about college (Simon, 2001).

In order to help students reach their high aspirations, middle and high school educators and students' families must work together to guide students to take the courses they need to earn required credits, complete high school, and attend college or other training programs. Schools, with families' support, also must provide some students with extra help and more time to learn in coaching classes, extra-help courses, summer school, tutoring, mentoring, and other responsive programs.

Families need clear information about middle and high school programs and course choices, curricular requirements, teachers' instructional approaches, and state tests or other major assessments in order to be able to discuss important academic topics with their teens at home. Others in the community (e.g., students' part-time employers) also need to know about attendance and course requirements and to support students in fulfilling their roles. Families also need to understand how their children are progressing in each subject, how to help students set and meet achievement and behavioral goals, and how to work with students to solve major problems that threaten course or grade level failure. Some middle and high schools create individual student educational and occupational plans with all students and parents (Lloyd, 1996), and some states require all students to develop postsecondary education plans for graduation.

High school students are aware that family involvement spurs their academic efforts. Explained one tenth grade student in a high school working to improve its partnership program,

> Parent involvement is important, because if you don't have a parent to encourage you and support you—ask you about your grades, and how you're doing—then, you'd think they didn't care. . . . You wouldn't have that motivation to go out there and try to get a 100 percent or 90 percent [on a test]—you'll take whatever you get, because no one else is interested. (Sanders, 1998, p. 41)

Middle and high schools use varied teaching strategies that are unfamiliar to most families. These include group activities, problem solving processes, pre-writing techniques, student-as-historian methods, interactive homework, and other innovative approaches to promote learning. Families and others in the community also need to know about major tests and their consequences for students' graduation from high school, report card criteria, and other state and local standards that schools use to determine students' progress through middle and high school. Some schools' Action Teams for Partnerships implement activities for parents to learn about and try items on state tests that may determine students' status.

With clear information about academic programs and students' progress, more families will be able to guide students in selecting courses, completing homework, studying for tests, and preparing for college or work (Anguiano, 2003). Moreover, if teachers, students, and parents communicate clearly and frequently through high school, more students will succeed at high levels and fulfill their own and their families' high expectations.

Family and community involvement contributes to the quality of middle and high schools' guidance programs and students' attitudes and behavior. School guidance and support services are likely to be stronger and serve students better if educators, students, and families are well connected. Students need to know that their guidance counselors and teachers understand and appreciate their families' cultures, hopes, and dreams. Many adolescents are trying to balance their love for their family, need for guidance, need for peer acceptance and friendship, *and* need for greater independence. By their actions, middle and high school educators and parents can help students see that these seemingly contradictory pressures can coexist.

Guidance counselors, school social workers, and school psychologists should meet with students' families and serve as key contacts for parents to call if questions arise about students' academic progress, attendance, behavior, peer relations, or interactions with teachers. In some middle and high schools, guidance counselors are members of interdisciplinary teams of teachers who meet with parents and students on a regular schedule. Some guidance counselors remain with the same students for all years that the students are in the school. In well-organized programs, guidance counselors contact parents *before* students are at serious risk of failing courses due to absence, attitudes, behavior, classwork, or homework in order to devise collaborative approaches to help students succeed in school.

Programs of school, family, and community partnerships support this agenda. Parent volunteers in a high school explained their contributions to improving student attendance in this way:

> We do a lot of things as attendance monitors. We make home visits, and we call parents to find out why the child is not in school. . . . We encourage [parents] to come in and volunteer time, find out why the child does not want to attend school, find out what the problem is. (Sanders, 1998, p. 36)

In this study, Sanders reported that parents contributed to a safe and orderly high school climate and better student behavior. A parent liaison, member of the Action Team for Partnerships, and organizer of 25 volunteers for the school's parent patrol stated,

> When I first got here, I envisioned a program where parents would come in and patrol the halls, because we had kids who would not stay in classes and would not listen to the staff. So, I felt if parents were here at the school, they would work at keeping their kids in class, plus they'd help with the other kids. . . . When the kids found out . . . there was a big turnaround. And, it wasn't just fear. Some of the students were proud that their parents were part of the school. (Sanders, 1998, p. 38)

Families need to know about the formal and informal guidance programs in middle and high schools. This includes knowing the names, phone or voice-mail numbers, and e-mail addresses of the teachers, counselors, advocates, and administrators in order to reach them with questions about their teens' progress or problems. This is particularly important at times of transition, when students move from elementary to middle school and from middle to high school. With good information, parents and other family partners can assist students to adjust successfully to their new schools.

When students, guidance counselors, teachers, and parents communicate well about students' academic, social, and emotional development and special needs through the teen years, more students are likely to succeed and stay in school.

How Can Any Middle or High School Develop and Sustain a Productive Program of Partnerships?

Many middle and high schools are demonstrating that they can use the research-based approaches outlined in this *Handbook* to design, implement, and sustain strong programs of school, family, and community partnerships (Maushard et al., 2007). Educators and parents are using the framework of the six types of involvement to ensure that families are informed about and engaged in their teens' education at school and at home. They are connecting with their communities in many ways to support the school and assist families and students. They are supported and assisted by school principals, district administrators and key staff, state leaders, and others.

In well-designed partnership programs, each middle and high school forms an Action Team for Partnerships (ATP) consisting of teachers, parents, administrators, and community partners, with students at the high school level. Each team writes an annual action plan for partnerships, implements and oversees activities, maintains an adequate budget, evaluates the quality of partnerships, and improves plans and activities from year to year.

Each ATP tailors its plans for partnerships with activities for the six types of involvement to meet specific school improvement goals, such as improving student achievement in reading, writing, math, science or other subjects, attitudes, behavior, homework completion, credits earned, postsecondary planning, and other indicators of success in middle and high schools. A well-developed program of partnerships also creates a welcoming environment for students, families, and the community.

The One-Year Action Plan for partnerships is appended to the School Improvement Plan so that educators, parents, and community partners can see that everyone has a role to play in helping students reach important goals for success in school. Even in complex middle and high schools, a program of school, family, and community partnerships is not an extra program but is part of every School Improvement Plan and an integral part of an excellent school.

The standard structures and processes outlined above and in other chapters of this *Handbook* guide all schools—preschool, elementary, middle, and high. However, very large middle and high schools face extra challenges—due to size—in organizing their programs of family and community involvement. Schools with more than 1,500 students may decide whether to organize *one ATP* for the whole school or *more than one ATP* for each major school division.

One ATP With Subcommittees. Very large middle and high schools may organize one ATP with representatives from the major school divisions. The representatives may come from grade levels, programs, "houses," career academies, or other school-within-the-school groups. The single ATP in a very large school still serves as a committee of the School Council or School Improvement Team, but it may have subcommittees headed by the division representatives for each major school division to ensure that involvement activities respond to the needs of the students and families in the identifiable sections of the school.

Multiple ATPs. Some very large middle and high schools may find it easier to have one ATP for each major division. If grade levels define the school, each grade may have an ATP. If middle school houses or high school career academies define the school, each major unit may have an ATP to plan and implement family and community involvement linked to its program. If there are multiple ATPs, a representative from each one will report to the School Council or School Improvement Team or to a coordinator for the council.

Summary

This *Handbook* provides the research base, tools, and guidelines to help all middle and high schools develop and sustain strong and productive programs of school, family, and community partnerships. Action Teams for Partnerships can use the tools and examples to plan and evaluate family and community involvement activities to help reach middle and high school goals. Moreover, middle and high schools, districts, and states can join the National Network of Partnership Schools at Johns Hopkins University to obtain ongoing professional development for school, family, and community partnerships (see Chapter 10 and www.partnershipschools.org).

Note

1. This article integrates summaries on middle and high schools, including the following:

Epstein, J. L. (2002). Family, school, and community connections. In J. W. Guthrie (Ed.), *Encyclopedia of education* (2nd ed., pp. 821–828). New York: Macmillan.

Epstein, J. L. (2005). School, family, and community partnerships in the middle grades. In T. O. Erb (Ed.), *This we believe in action: Implementing successful middle level schools* (pp. 77–96). Westerville, OH: National Middle School Association.

Epstein, J. L. (2007). Connections count: Improving family and community involvement in secondary schools. *Principal Leadership, 8*(2), 16–21.

Epstein, J. L. (2007). Family and community involvement. In K. Borman, S. Cahill, & B. Cotner (Eds.), *The Praeger handbook of American high schools* (pp. 165–173). Westport, CT: Praeger.

References

Anguiano, R. (2003). Families and schools: The effect of parental involvement on high school completion. *Journal of Family Issues, 25,* 61–85.

Balli, S. J., Demo, D. H., & Wedman, J. F. (1998). Family involvement with children's homework: An intervention in the middle grades. *Family Relations, 47,* 149–157.

Catsambis, S. (2001). Expanding knowledge of parental involvement in children's secondary education: Connections with high school seniors' academic success. *Social Psychology of Education, 5,* 149–177.

Catsambis, S., & Beveridge, A. A. (2001). Does neighborhood matter? Family, neighborhood, and school influences on eighth grade mathematics achievement. *Sociological Focus, 34,* 435–457.

Dauber, S. L., & Epstein, J. L. (1993). Parents' attitudes and practices of involvement in inner-city elementary and middle schools. In N. Chavkin (Ed.), *Families and schools in a pluralistic society* (pp. 53–71). Albany: State University of New York Press.

Eccles, J. S., & Harold, R. D. (1996). Family involvement in children's and adolescents' schooling. In A. Booth and J. Dunn (Eds.), *Family-school links: How do they affect educational outcomes* (pp. 3–34). Hillside, NJ: Erlbaum.

Epstein, J. L. (1995). School/family/community partnerships: Caring for the children we share. *Phi Delta Kappan, 76,* 701–712.

Epstein, J. L. (2001). *School, family, and community partnerships: Preparing educators and improving schools.* Boulder, CO: Westview.

Epstein, J. L., & Dauber, S. L. (1995). Effects on students of an interdisciplinary program linking social studies, art, and family volunteers in the middle grades. *Journal of Early Adolescence, 15,*114–144.

Epstein, J. L., & Lee, S. (1995). National patterns of school and family connections in the middle grades. In B. Ryan, G. Adams, T. Gullotta, R. Weissberg, & R. Hampton (Eds.), *The family-school connection: Theory, research and practice* (pp. 108–154). Thousand Oaks, CA: Sage.

Epstein, J. L., Salinas, K. C., & Van Voorhis, F. L. (2001). *Teachers Involve Parents in Schoolwork (TIPS) manuals and prototype activities for the elementary and middle grades.* Baltimore: Johns Hopkins University, Center on School, Family, and Community Partnerships.

Epstein, J. L., & Sheldon, S. B. (2002). Present and accounted for: Improving student attendance through family and community involvement. *Journal of Educational Research, 95,* 308–318.

Epstein, J. L., Simon, B. S., & Salinas, K. C. (1997, September). *Effects of Teachers Involve Parents in Schoolwork (TIPS) language arts interactive homework in the middle grades* (Research Bulletin 18). Bloomington, IN: Phi Delta Kappa, Center on Evaluation, Development, and Research.

Henderson, A. T., & Mapp, K. L. (2002). *A new wave of evidence: The impact of school, family, and community connections on student achievement.* Austin, TX: Southwest Educational Development Laboratory.

Hill, N. E., Castellino, D. R., Lansford, J. E., Nowlin, P., Dodge, K. A., Bates, J. E., et al. (2004). Parent academic involvement as related to school behavior, achievement, and aspirations: Demographic variations across adolescence. *Child Development, 75,* 1491–1509.

Kreider, H., Caspe, M., Kennedy, S., & Weiss, H. (2007). *Family involvement in middle and high school students' education* (Research Brief 3). Cambridge, MA: Harvard Family Research Project.

Lee, S. (1994). *Family-school connections and students' education: Continuity and change of family involvement from the middle grades to high school.* Unpublished doctoral dissertation, Johns Hopkins University, Baltimore.

Lloyd, G. M. (1996). Research and practical applications for school, family, and community partnerships. In A. Booth & J. F. Dunn (Eds.), *Family-school links: How do they affect educational outcomes?* (pp. 255–264). Mahwah, NJ: Erlbaum.

Maushard, M., Martin, C. S., Hutchins, D. J., Greenfeld, M. D., Thomas, B. G., Fournier, A., et al. (Eds.) (2007). *Promising partnership practices 2007.* Baltimore: Johns Hopkins University, Center on School, Family, and Community Partnerships.

Sanders, M. G. (1998). School-family-community partnerships: An action team approach. *High School Magazine, 5*(3), 38–49.

Sanders, M. G. (1999). Improving school, family and community partnerships in urban middle schools. *Middle School Journal, 31*(2), 35–41.

Sanders, M. G. (2001). Schools, families, and communities partnering for middle level students' success. *NASSP Bulletin, 85*(627), 53–61.

Sanders, M. G. (2005). *Building school-community partnerships: Collaboration for student success.* Thousand Oaks, CA: Corwin Press.

Sanders, M. G., & Epstein, J. L. (2000). Building school-family and community partnerships in middle and high schools. In M. Sanders (Ed.), *Schooling students placed at risk* (pp. 339–362). Mahwah, NJ: Erlbaum.

Sanders, M. G., & Lewis, K. (2005) Building bridges toward excellence: Community involvement in high schools. *High School Journal, 88*(3), 1–9.

Sanders, M. G., & Simon, B. S. (2002). A comparison of program development at elementary, middle, and high schools in the National Network of Partnership Schools. *The School Community Journal, 12,* 7–27.

Seidman, E., Lambert, L. E., Allen, L., & Aber, J. L. (2003). Urban adolescents' transition to junior high school and protective family transactions. *Journal of Early Adolescence, 23,* 166–193.

Sheldon, S. B. (2007). Improving student attendance with school, family, and community partnerships. *Journal of Educational Research, 100,* 267–275.

Sheldon, S. B., & Epstein, J. L. (2002). Improving student behavior and school discipline with family and community involvement. *Education and Urban Society, 35*, 4–26.

Sheldon, S. B., & Epstein, J. L. (2004). Getting students to school: Using family and community involvement to reduce chronic absenteeism. *School Community Journal, 14*, 39–56.

Sheldon, S. B & Epstein, J. L. (2005a). Involvement counts: Family and community partnerships and math achievement. *Journal of Educational Research, 98*, 196–206.

Sheldon, S. B., & Epstein, J. L. (2005b). School programs of family and community involvement to support children's reading and literacy development across the grades. In J. Flood & P. Anders (Eds.), *Literacy development of students in urban schools: Research and policy* (pp. 107–138). Newark, DE: International Reading Association (IRA).

Simon, B. S. (2001). Family involvement in high school: Predictors and effects. *NASSP Bulletin, 85*(627), 8–19.

Simon, B. S. (2004). High school outreach and family involvement. *Social Psychology of Education, 7*, 185–209.

Van Voorhis, F. L. (2001). Interactive science homework: An experiment in home and school connections. *NASSP Bulletin, 85*(627), 20–32.

Van Voorhis, F. L. (2003). Interactive homework in middle school: Effects on family involvement and students' science achievement. *Journal of Educational Research, 96*, 323–339.

Van Voorhis, F. L. (2008, April). *War or peace? A longitudinal study of family involvement in language arts homework in the middle grades.* Paper presented at the annual meeting of the American Educational Research Association, New York.

Van Voorhis, F. L., & Epstein, J. L. (2002). *Teachers Involve Parents in Schoolwork (TIPS): Interactive homework CD for the elementary and middle grades.* Baltimore: Johns Hopkins University, Center on School, Family, and Community Partnerships.

Predictors and Effects of Family Involvement in High Schools

Beth S. Simon[1]

Reports from more than 11,000 parents of high school seniors and 1,000 high school principals were analyzed to learn about high school, family, and community partnerships. Analyses revealed that regardless of students' background and prior achievement, various parenting, volunteering, and learning at home activities positively influenced student grades, course credits completed, attendance, behavior, and school preparedness. When educators guided parents and solicited their participation, parents responded with increased involvement to support student success.

A substantial body of research has explored family involvement in the elementary and middle grades. Fewer studies have focused on school and family connections in high schools. The early work revealed that family involvement tends to decrease as student move from elementary, to middle, to high school. An important and growing body of research suggests, however, that partnerships between families and schools are still important for high school students' success (Anguiano, 2003; Catsambis, 2001; Catsambis & Beveridge, 2001; Hill et al., 2004; Kreider, Caspe, Kennedy, & Weiss, 2007; Lee, 1994; Sanders & Lewis, 2005; Sheldon & Epstein, 2005; Simon, 2004).

Method

Important questions remain about the nature and intensity of high school, family, and community partnerships; the influence of partnerships on student success; and predictors of family and community involvement. To fill gaps in research and support educators' work in strengthening partnerships in high school, this study addressed three main questions:

1. What do school, family, and community partnerships look like in high school?
2. How do school–family connections influence high school students' success?
3. When high schools reach out to families, how do families respond?

Analyses were based on reports from the parents of over 11,000 high school students and from more than 1,000 high school principals in the National Education Longitudinal Study of 1988 (NELS:88). NELS:88 followed a cohort of students as they moved from the middle grades to high school and into postsecondary schooling or careers (Ingels, Thalji, Pulliam, Bartot, & Frankel, 1994). In 1988, a nationally representative sample of 24,599 eighth grade students from 1,052 schools was surveyed.

These students were followed over time and surveyed again in their sophomore and senior years of high school. School principals and students' parents were also surveyed over time, and information was gathered on a range of topics, including characteristics and practices of school, family, and community connections. Following are summaries of key research findings on the nature of high school, family, and community partnerships; on the effects of partnerships on student success; and on the relationship between school outreach and family involvement (Simon, 2001, 2004).

Results

What Do High School, Family, and Community Partnerships Look Like?

There are many reports that family involvement declines by the time teenagers are in high school. Compared to partnerships in the earlier grades, high school, family, and community connections appear weak (Clark, 1983; Dornbusch & Ritter, 1988; George, 1995). This conclusion, though, is based on research that takes a narrow view of involvement and does not consider the wide range of partnership activities that are conducted at home, at school, and in the community.

This study conceptualized partnerships broadly using Epstein's (1995) framework of six types of family and community involvement, which recognizes a wide range of partnership activities. Reports from parents of high school seniors and from high school principals were analyzed to learn about the nature and extent of involvement in various types of activities, including parenting, communicating, volunteering, learning at home, decision making, and collaborating with the community. Following are selected results of analyses of the NELS:88 data that illustrate how schools, families, and communities connected during the high school years.

Type 1–Parenting. Workshops were a popular parenting activity in many high schools. More than half of the high school principals reported that their schools offered workshops to parents on drug and alcohol abuse prevention, an important issue for many teens and their parents. About one-third of twelfth graders' parents reported that they attended a college planning workshop to learn about postsecondary educational opportunities and financial planning.

Type 2–Communicating. On average, activities involving school-to-home and home-to-school communication were intermittent or infrequent. Parents and high school teachers rarely communicated about teenagers' academic performance (except for report cards), attendance, and behavior. For example, about two-thirds of parents were never contacted by the school about their child's attendance, and about three-fourths of parents never contacted the school about their child's attendance. Although parent-teacher conferences are common activities in the elementary and middle grades, about one-third of high school principals reported that their schools did *not* conduct parent-teacher conferences to communicate about students' progress, challenges, concerns, and future plans.

Type 3–Volunteering. Most parents volunteered their time by attending school activities with their teenagers. About two-thirds of parents attended at least one school activity as an audience member, and one-third of those parents attended more than a few times. Fewer parents participated as more traditional volunteers (e.g., as teachers' aides, cafeteria monitors, or field trip chaperones). High school parents may question how helpful they can be in the classroom; teachers may not want to be monitored by parents in the classroom; and teenagers may not want their parents at the school, keeping tabs on them during the school day. These and other reasons may explain why, even though one-third of high schools reportedly had a formal program to recruit and train volunteers, only about one in eight parents volunteered.

Type 4–Learning at Home. Parents may find it daunting to help high school students study for a trigonometry or chemistry test or to review their essays on literary classics. They received little help on this from the schools. Approximately three-fourths of parents indicated that the school staff never contacted them about how to guide and assist teenagers with homework. Still, two-thirds of parents reported that they tried to help teenagers with homework or school projects sometimes or frequently. Many parents would benefit from guidance from teachers on how to work with their children on homework or school projects. According to principals, few parents solicited information from teachers about helping teenagers with homework or specific skills. In most high schools, less than one-fourth of all parents asked for information to assist teenagers with homework. Although many parents feel unprepared to help their children with homework, most talked with their teenagers about school, and almost all were aware of teenagers' academic progress.

Type 5–Decision Making. Many schools use a PTA or PTO as a forum for parents to give input to the high schools their teenagers attend. Nevertheless, about one-third of high school principals reported that their school did not have such an organization. The absence of a PTA or PTO may restrict parents' influence on school policy decisions and contribute to the growing distance parents feel from their children's high schools.

Type 6–Collaborating With the Community. Principals reported that community partners supported high schools in various collaborative activities. For example, most principals reported that employers asked the school to post job listings and to recommend students for part-time jobs. Half of the principals reported that local business organizations were involved in efforts to promote safe and drug-free school environments. In terms of giving back to the community, fewer than half of the principals reported having a community service program at their high schools. Most of these principals reported that students spent two hours a week—or fewer—volunteering at community sites.

As they develop from childhood through adolescence, youth move from a family-centered world to a wider world that includes peers and other adults in the community. Adolescents increasingly rely on social networks beyond their families, yet the data revealed that many families supported teenagers' development through the last years of high school in several ways:

- Parents continued to monitor teenagers' potentially risky behavior.
- Parents and teenagers spent some free time together.
- Parents and teenagers discussed postsecondary educational plans and current school activities.
- Parents were aware of teenagers' progress in school.

Most parents attended some school activities, and many attended postsecondary planning workshops if they were offered by the high school.

Of course, families and communities may be involved in many other activities that support adolescent learning and development. Still, the range of indicators in the NELS:88 data revealed that families participated in various partnership activities that, as the next set of analyses shows, positively influenced a range of student outcomes, including report card grades, course credits completed, attendance, behavior, and school preparedness.

How Does Family Involvement Influence High School Success?

Families, schools, and communities all may benefit from carefully planned, well-implemented partnership activities, but the bottom line in education reform is student achievement and success. Educators want to know: How do partnerships affect student learning? Will students earn better grades? Will they attend school more regularly and come to class more prepared to learn? Understanding how partnerships influence student success is an important step in refining partnership program planning and research. By clarifying links between family and community involvement and student success, partnership program planners can make the most effective and efficient use of resources within the home, school, and community, and researchers can strengthen studies with more theoretically sound measures of partnerships and results.

Some studies have addressed the influence of partnerships on student success, but many had limited partnership indicators (Astone & McLanahan, 1991; Lee, 1993; Stevenson & Baker, 1987), a limited range of student outcome measures, and analyses of partnership activities and student outcomes that were tenuously linked (Desimone, 1999; Ho & Willms, 1996; Pong, 1998; Singh, Bickley, Trivette, Keith, & Keith, 1995). In contrast to prior research that considered only a few partnership indicators, this study analyzed how 17 partnership practices—including various parenting, communicating, volunteering, learning at home, and decision making activities—influenced student success. Building on research that assessed effects of partnerships on a few indicators of student success, this study tested how particular partnership activities influenced the following student outcomes: English and math grades, standardized test scores, course credits completed in English and math, attendance, behavior, and school preparedness (e.g., students completed homework and brought books and a pen or pencil to class).

Results showed that, after controlling for race and ethnicity, family structure, gender, and the powerful influence of students' prior achievement and socioeconomic status, when parents were involved in various ways, teenagers earned higher grades in English and math, completed more course credits in English and math, had better attendance and behavior, and came to class more prepared to learn. This article highlights patterns of relationships between particular family involvement activities and substantively linked student outcomes. Analyses also revealed some significant relationships between family involvement and less well-connected measures of student success.

Grades and Course Credits Completed. Regardless of teenagers' prior grades in English and math or their family background, when parents attended college planning workshops and when parents and teenagers talked about college planning, teenagers earned better grades in English and math and completed more course credits in English and math. Parents' attendance at college planning workshops and discussions with teenagers about college planning may have positively influenced students' grades and the number of course credits they completed for various reasons. First, teenagers may have gotten the message that their parents valued their college plans and supported their efforts to get good grades and take classes required for college admission. Second, when parents attended college planning workshops, they may have learned the importance of grade point averages and course credits for college admission and, subsequently, encouraged or monitored their children's efforts to improve grades and take necessary courses to get into college.

Standardized Test Scores. Students' prior standardized test scores strongly predicted their next and future test scores. The strong influence of students' prior test scores typically leaves little room for additional factors to significantly boost or lower future test scores. This study found, however, that even after accounting for the powerful influence of prior achievement, parents and teenagers talking about college and parents attending college planning workshops had small, but significant, positive effects on test scores in the twelfth grade.

Attendance. Beyond the influence of teenagers' prior attendance or family background, when parents participated in various school activities with teenagers, teenagers attended school more regularly. In general, when parents attend school functions, they have opportunities to meet other teenagers' parents and develop a parent network. As in close-knit neighborhoods where teenagers are held accountable by the community's adults—not just their own parents—parent networks may prevent teenagers from skipping school, because they know that other parents may be keeping tabs on them. Or, they know that other students' parents—just like theirs—stress the importance of school attendance. In addition, parents may have the opportunity to chat with teachers or high school administrators who attend school events. These informal conversations reinforce the link between home and school and may remind students that what they do at school could be reported to their parents.

Behavior and School Preparedness. Various involvement activities positively influenced students' good behavior and school preparedness. For example, when students reported talking with a parent about school and college planning, they also reported better behavior and were more likely to come to class prepared. When parents talk with their teens, they may communicate the importance that they place on education and may motivate their children's school performance. Similarly, the more time that parents and teenagers spent together, the better behaved students were and the more prepared they arrived at class. Parents may reinforce norms and rules for students' behavior through leisure activities. Teenagers also may feel motivated by their extracurricular activities and how these activities matter to their parents.

Negative Relationships Between Family Involvement and Student Success. Some communications—parents contacting the school about teenagers' attendance and behavior—were negatively associated with student success. In other words, the more often parents reported contacting the schools about teenagers' attendance and behavior, the less likely it was that students were successful in school. These findings do *not* mean that home-to-school contacts caused teenagers to do poorly. Instead, analysis showed that parents contacted the school because teenagers were struggling. Compared with parents of teenagers who were doing well in school in Grade 10, parents of teenagers who had poor attendance, lower math and English grades, and lower standardized test scores in Grade 10 were more likely to contact the school about teenagers' behavior and attendance in Grade 12. The longitudinal data revealed that parents' contacts with the school occurred in the context of teenagers' continued school struggles.

In summary, analyses revealed positive relationships between Parenting, Volunteering, and Learning at Home activities and various measures of Grade 12 student success, including teenagers' report card grades; the number of course credits students completed; and teenagers' attendance, behavior, and school preparedness. The NELS:88 data, however, did not permit thorough analysis of the effects on student success of other aspects of partnerships, such as family involvement in school Decision Making and Collaborating With the Community. As with the Parenting, Volunteering, and Learning at Home activities tested, it is expected that family involvement in school Decision Making and Collaborating With the Community, when well planned and linked to specific outcome measures, may also improve specific indicators of student success.

By the senior year of high school, teenagers have some entrenched study habits, attitudes, and behavior patterns related to school. Nevertheless, this study shows that even in the last year of high school, and regardless of teenagers' background or prior achievement, families' involvement in education influences teenagers' school success. When parents support teenagers as learners in various ways, teenagers are more likely to succeed in school.

How Do High Schools Influence Family Involvement?

School and family partnerships tend to decline over the school years for many reasons. For example, the complex organization of high schools, the complicated curriculum, and the tensions of adolescence discourage some families from remaining involved in their teens' education. In this study, we considered the factors that might counter this trend and increase school and family connections over the years.

To understand the variation in levels of family involvement in high school, researchers have investigated the effects on involvement of students' background—including race and ethnicity, family structure, and socioeconomic status (Astone & McLanahan, 1991; Catsambis, 2001; Clark, 1983; Desimone, 1999; Goyette & Xie, 1999; Lee, 1994; Phelan, Davidson, & Yu, 1998; Pong, 1998; Singh et al., 1995). These studies reveal that students' backgrounds explain some of the variation in family involvement at the high school level.

Although socioeconomic status (SES) is significantly and positively related to some family involvement practices, SES is not related to other partnership activities (Epstein, 2001; Simon, 2000). Other background indicators, including students' race and ethnicity, family structure, gender, and prior achievement do not always predict whether or how families support teenagers' learning. Although frequently analyzed, family and student background variables are not the only possible predictors of family involvement. Instead, a range of conditions may influence whether and how teenagers' families are involved in their education. By examining high school outreach activities as predictors of family involvement in teenagers' learning and development, this study builds on previous research that accounted only for students' background.

This study examined how 14 high school outreach activities predicted family involvement. Some analyses focused on whether relationships between high school practices and family involvement activities were substantively linked (e.g., school contacts parents about helping teenagers with homework, and parents work with teenagers on homework). The results show that when high schools conducted specific activities, families were more likely to be involved in those ways. Regardless of teenagers' achievement, socioeconomic status, family structure, gender, and race and ethnicity, high schools' outreach activities positively predicted family involvement. In fact, in several cases, high school practices influenced family involvement more strongly than family background or teen's achievement.

Following are a few examples of how high school programs and practices to involve families positively related to family support of teenagers as learners. These analyses focused on whether there were connections between particular school practices and parents' responses. Parents of high school students reported the following:

- When high school staff contacted parents about teenagers' postsecondary plans, parents were more likely to attend postsecondary planning workshops and talked more frequently with teenagers about college and employment.
- When high school staff contacted parents about volunteering, parents were more likely to volunteer as audience members at school activities.
- When high school staff informed parents about how to help teenagers study, parents worked more often with their teenagers on homework.
- When high school staff contacted parents about a range of school-related issues, including their teen's academic program, course selection, and plans after high school, parents talked with teenagers more often about school.

Principals' reports confirmed the parents' reports. High school programs and practices influenced family involvement, above and beyond the influence of school sector (public vs. private), location (urban, suburban, rural), or the percentage of teenagers receiving free or reduced-price lunch or living in single-parent homes. Specifically, high school principals reported that when high schools had a formal program to recruit and train parents as volunteers, more parents were likely to volunteer for the school. They also reported that when high schools encouraged parent-school associations, more parents joined the PTA/PTO and attended PTA/PTO meetings.

Summary

All parents want their children to succeed in school; however, not all parents know how best to support their children as learners. This study shows that high schools can reach out and increase family involvement in partnership activities. Families' involvement habits are not fixed by teenagers' senior year of high school. Instead, high schools' practices—among other potential influences—can increase family involvement levels. Following is a summary of key findings in this research:

- Schools, families, and communities continue to partner in a range of ways through teenagers' last year of high school.
- Regardless of teenagers' achievement or background, high school and family partnerships positively influence teenagers' grades, course credits completed, attendance, behavior, and school preparedness.
- Regardless of family background or school context, when high schools reach out to involve families with age-appropriate and important activities, families respond with increased involvement (see Table 6.1).

TABLE 6.1 The Influence of High School Outreach on Family Involvement

When high schools . . .		*Parents were more likely to . . .*
Contacted parents about teens' plans after high school	→	Attend college and career planning workshops and talk with teens about college and careers
Contacted parents about volunteering	→	Volunteer as an audience member at school activities
Gave parents information about how to help teens study	→	Work with their teens on homework
Contacted parents about school-related issues	→	Talk with teens about school-related issues
Formally recruited and trained parent volunteers	→	Volunteer for the school
Encouraged parent-school associations	→	Join the PTA/PTO and attend PTA/PTO meetings

Families participate in various ways to support student learning through teens' last year of high school. High schools not only have a particular responsibility to organize partnership programs that reach out to involve all families at all grade levels, they also have the *capacity* to change the way that families support teenagers' school success.

Note

1. An earlier version of this article was published as Simon, B. S. (2001). Family involvement in high school: Predictors and effects. *NASSP Bulletin, 85*(627), 8–19. Copyright © 2001 National Association of School Principal. Published by Sage Publications, Inc. This article summarizes the results of a larger study of high school, family, and community partnerships. For the full report, including analyses of student-reported indicators, see Simon (2000). References were updated for this edition of the *Handbook.*

References

Anguiano, R. (2003). Families and schools: The effect of parental involvement on high school completion. *Journal of Family Issues, 25,* 61–85.

Astone, N. M., & McLanahan, S. S. (1991). Family structure, parental practices and high school completion. *American Sociological Review, 56,* 309–320.

Catsambis, S. (2001). Expanding knowledge of parental involvement in children's secondary education: Connections with high school seniors' academic success. *Social Psychology of Education, 5,* 149–177.

Catsambis, S., & Beveridge, A. A. (2001). Does neighborhood matter? Family, neighborhood, and school influences on eighth grade mathematics achievement. *Sociological Focus, 34,* 435–457.

Clark, R. M. (1983). *Family life and school achievement: Why poor black children succeed or fail.* Chicago: University of Chicago Press.

Desimone, L. (1999). Linking parental involvement with student achievement: Do race and income matter? *Journal of Educational Research, 93,* 11–30.

Dornbusch, S. M., & Ritter, P. L. (1988). Parents of high school students: A neglected resource. *Educational Horizons, 66,* 75–77.

Epstein, J. L. (1995). School/family/community partnerships: Caring for the children we share. *Phi Delta Kappan, 76*(9), 701–712.

Epstein, J. L. (2001). *School, family, and community partnerships: Preparing educators and improving schools.* Boulder, CO: Westview Press.

George, P. (1995). Search Institute looks at home and school: Why aren't parents getting involved? *High School Magazine, 3*(5), 9–11.

Goyette, K., & Xie, Y. (1999). Educational expectations of Asian American youths: Determinants and ethnic differences. *Sociology of Education, 72,* 22–36.

Hill, N. E., Castellino, D. R., Lansford, J. E., Nowlin, K., Dodge, K. A., Bates, J. E., & Pettit, G. S. (2004). Parent academic involvement as related to school behavior, achievement, and aspirations: Demographic variations across adolescence. *Child Development, 75,* 1491–1509.

Ho, E. S-C., & Willms, D. J. (1996). Effects of parental involvement on eighth-grade achievement. *Sociology of Education, 69,* 126–141.

Ingels, S. J., Thalji, L., Pulliam, P., Bartot, V. H., & Frankel, M. R. (1994). *National educational longitudinal study of 1988. Second follow-up: Parent component data file user's manual.* Washington, DC: Office of Educational Research and Improvement, U.S. Department of Education.

Kreider, H., Caspe, M., Kennedy, S., & Weiss, H. (2007). *Family involvement in middle and high school students' education* (Research Brief 3). Cambridge, MA: Harvard Family Research Project.

Lee, S. (1994). *Family-school connections and students' education: Continuity and change of family involvement from the middle grades to high school.* Unpublished doctoral dissertation, Johns Hopkins University, Baltimore.

Lee, S.-A. (1993). Family structure effects on student outcomes. In B. Schneider & J. S. Coleman (Eds.), *Parents, their children, and schools* (pp. 43–76). Boulder, CO: Westview Press.

Phelan, P., Davidson, A. L., & Yu, H. C. (1998). *Adolescents' worlds: Negotiating family, peers, and school.* New York: Teachers College Press.

Pong, S.-L. (1998). The school compositional effects of single parenthood on 10th grade reading achievement. *Sociology of Education, 71,* 23–42.

Sanders, M. G., & Lewis, K. (2005). Building bridges toward excellence: Community involvement in high schools. *High School Journal, 88*(3), 1–9.

Sheldon, S. B., & Epstein, J. L. (2005). School programs of family and community involvement to support children's reading and literacy development across the grades. In J. Flood & P. Anders (Eds.), *Literacy development of students in urban schools: Research and policy* (pp. 107–138). Newark, DE: International Reading Association.

Simon, B. S. (2000). *Predictors of high school and family partnerships and the influence of partnerships on student success.* Unpublished doctoral dissertation, Johns Hopkins University, Baltimore.

Simon, B. S. (2001). Family involvement in high school: Predictors and effects. *NASSP Bulletin, 85*(627), 8–19.

Simon, B. S. (2004). High school outreach and family involvement. *Social Psychology of Education, 7,* 185–209.

Singh, K., Bickley, P. G., Trivette, P., Keith, T. Z., & Keith, P. B. (1995). The effects of four components of parental involvement on eighth-grade student achievement: Structural analysis of NELS-88 data. *School Psychology Review, 24,* 299–317.

Stevenson, D. L., & Baker, D. P. (1987). The family-school relation and the child's school performance. *Child Development, 58,* 1348–1357.

A Goal-Oriented Approach to Partnership Programs in Middle and High Schools

Natalie Rodriguez Jansorn

Increase science knowledge. Strengthen writing abilities. Improve attendance. Advance math skills. These are goals that most middle and high schools set for students. Along with an effective curriculum and excellent instruction, programs of school, family, and community partnerships can support students in reaching these and other school improvement goals. A goal-oriented partnership program links directly to a school's improvement plan to enhance students' opportunities for success in school.

The following pages discuss the elements of a goal-oriented approach to partnerships and provide school, district, and state leaders with examples of partnership activities for six types of involvement (i.e., Parenting, Communicating, Volunteering, Learning at Home, Decision Making, and Collaborating With the Community) that can be selected to reach specific goals. The sample pages following this article (see pp. 226–232 and CD) may be used as slides, overheads, and handouts in workshops to help middle and high schools write goal-oriented plans for school, family, and community partnerships.

What Is a Goal-Oriented Approach to Partnerships?

An Action Team for Partnerships (ATP) using a goal-oriented approach begins with the question: What goals did this school set for students this year? The ATP reviews the school improvement plan and selects a few major goals that would benefit from family and community involvement. Goals in middle and high schools may include the following:

- Increasing academic achievement in reading, writing, science, math, social studies, or other subjects
- Improving attendance
- Promoting positive student behavior in school
- Ensuring successful transitions and adjustments to new schools
- Providing grade-appropriate counseling for college and careers
- Advancing students' health, nutrition, safety
- Attaining other important academic or nonacademic goals on the school's agenda for the year

The ATP, then, writes a One-Year Action Plan for Partnerships with family and community involvement activities that specifically link to and support the school's selected goals for improving students' academic and nonacademic progress.

A comprehensive plan will include activities for all six types of involvement to engage families and community partners in productive and age-appropriate ways. See the One-Year Action Plan Form G–Goals on pages 181–184 and CD.

Why Use a Goal-Oriented Approach?

Research shows that by middle and high school, family involvement tends to decrease. Parents continue to want to be involved, but they may not know exactly what to do at each grade level. Teachers continue to believe parent involvement is important, but they may not know specific strategies to help connect parents with their teens to address the challenging curriculum in secondary schools or the decisions high school students must make about the courses they will take.

A goal-oriented approach to partnerships enables educators and families to reach out to each other and assist students with specific results in mind. For example, an ATP at one high school developed writing-related partnership activities to engage families in helping students improve their writing skills and to meet a school goal for writing achievement. In this school, activities were developed that enabled teachers, administrators, and counselors to reach out to families with information about the writing curriculum and standards in writing achievement. Parents were guided to listen to students' read drafts of essays, stories, and poems. The ATP also designed approaches that welcomed families to communicate with teachers about their teens' work and progress in writing.

A goal-oriented partnership program makes clear to all stakeholders that school, family, and community partnerships can be designed and implemented to benefit students in the middle grades and high school. It concentrates efforts more effectively, making the most of time and resources to address critical areas for student progress.

Who Chooses the Goals for the Partnership Program?

Most often, the ATP chooses the goals for each year's Action Plan for Partnerships from the School Improvement Plan. After selecting the goals, the ATP may recruit additional members or targeted leaders whose work or interests relate to particular goals. For example, one urban middle school focused on the goal of increasing school and student safety. The ATP added the community's police captain to the team. He offered unique insights and resources to increase school safety through family and community involvement activities.

A well-functioning school improvement team, PTA, school faculty, and parents also may give the ATP input on the goals for the One-Year Action Plan for Partnerships.

How Many Goals Does an ATP Choose?

For one full school year, ATPs should select four goals that will be addressed with family and community involvement activities: two academic goals, one nonacademic goal, and one overall goal for creating and sustaining a school climate of partnership. The number of goals may vary, depending on individual school's needs, interests, and resources.

How Does an ATP Develop a Goal-Oriented Partnership Program?

First, the ATP reviews the School Improvement Plan to identify four goals that will be the basis of the One-Year Action Plan for Partnerships. For example, the goals may be to increase students' reading, writing, math, or science skills and test scores, improve student attendance, and sustain and strengthen other family and community involvement activities (e.g., positive communications with families and the community). Middle and high schools may set goals to help incoming students and their families make successful transitions in the first year at their new schools or to guide all students toward effective postsecondary education and career plans.

These and other goals for middle and high school students will more likely be met when family and community involvement activities are clearly targeted and well implemented to support and extend the efforts of teachers and administrators.

Next, the ATP develops the full One-Year Action Plan for Partnerships. A goal-oriented approach will use Form G–Goals (pp. 181–184 and CD). To write the plan, the ATP should form small committees for each goal to ensure that all team members contribute to selecting, developing, and scheduling targeted family and community involvement activities. Each goal will correspond to one page of the written plan.

Each small committee should identify at least three specific family and community involvement activities to support its goal and provide the necessary details for implementing activities on that page of the action plan. The activities may be onetime-only events, ongoing communications, a series of meetings or workshops, or other innovative strategies. The selections may be newly developed, modified, or existing activities to engage all families with their students and schools.

After each small group completes its page of plan, the full ATP will meet to share ideas, offer feedback, and make revisions to the entire One-Year Action Plan for Partnerships. For example, the ATP will check that all six types of involvement are represented among the activities in the four pages of the plan, that activities are scheduled throughout the school year (not all at once), and that leadership for the planned activities is shared among ATP members and others at the school. See other sections of this *Handbook* on developing effective teams (Chapter 3) and good plans (Chapter 4).

Importance of Evaluation

The success of any program depends greatly on its evaluation plan. The ATP must consider how the results for each goal in the One-Year Action Plan for Partnerships will be documented, measured, and monitored over time. ATPs may choose more than one way to evaluate (a) the quality of the partnership activities, (b) the responses of targeted participants, and (c) whether and how well each goal is attained.

Evaluation strategies range from simply recording the number of participants at an activity or documenting the number of families who received information to administering surveys and questionnaires or conducting complex longitudinal studies to assess the effects of family involvement activities on students' standardized test scores, grades, and attendance rates. ATPs should conduct thoughtful discussions about each activity that is implemented using the Annual Evaluation of Activities that matches the format of the entries in the One-Year Action Plan for Partnerships (pp. 330–334 and CD). These reflections will help the ATP improve the design, outreach, and quality of activities from year to year. By improving actions, outreach, parents' responses, and student outcomes, the ATP will be able to increase school and district colleagues' support for partnerships and secure funds and resources for ATP activities. See Chapter 9 for an extended discussion of evaluating partnership programs.

Annual evaluations are conducted by the National Network of Partnership Schools (NNPS) at Johns Hopkins University to help schools and districts monitor the quality and progress of partnership programs. All members of NNPS use *UPDATE*, an annual progress report, to rate the quality of key components of partnership programs and to think about needed improvements in family and community involvement for the next One-Year Action Plan for Partnerships.

After writing the One-Year Action Plan for Partnerships and identifying evaluation strategies, the ATP is ready to implement its goal-oriented partnership program with the help of many others at the school.

How Does a Goal-Oriented Partnership Program Look in Action?

A Middle School's Partnership Program. A 10-member Action Team for Partnerships at one urban middle school in a southern state included family, school staff, administrative, community, and student members to represent all of the schools' partners in learning. After reviewing the school's improvement plan, the ATP developed a One-Year Action Plan for Partnerships focused on four goals:

- Improve reading and language arts achievement.
- Improve mathematics achievement.
- Increase attendance.
- Sustain activities for a welcoming climate, and add a new, productive partnership with a community organization.

Using the framework of six types of involvement, the ATP selected a few activities to help reach each goal. For example, to help students reach the math goal, the ATP hosted a Family Math Night at which parents and students enjoyed math activities together. The school also collaborated with its community to conduct an afterschool math tutoring program and a "math-a-thon." In each school newsletter for parents, the ATP included updates on the math curriculum, examples of what students were learning in math class, and information about how parents could talk with students about math and help with homework. Newsletters also recognized students' math achievements. By keeping families informed about the math curriculum, providing guidance about interacting with their children about math, and connecting with the community for further support, the middle schools activated school, family, and community partnerships that supported teachers' efforts to increase student success in math. The ATP implemented similarly well-targeted activities for the other three goals in the action plan, thus creating a comprehensive goal-oriented partnership program.

A High School's Partnership Program. An urban high school in a mid-Atlantic state started its partnership program midyear and focused on two goals in its first year:

- Increase writing achievement.
- Improve attendance.

The large high school had an 18-member ATP. To write its One-Year Action Plan for Partnerships, the team divided into two groups, each with representatives of the school, families, community, and students. At one meeting, the two groups spent about 40 minutes brainstorming ideas on new and current partnership activities that would support the selected goals. The brainstorming session allowed the ATP members to be creative—with the sky as the limit—and consider many possible partnership activities without worrying about details. Then, the whole ATP came together to share ideas and to give feedback to each group on the potential partnership activities.

Next, the two groups met to make final decisions about the partnership activities that would be included in the One-Year Action Plan for Partnerships (for one half year). Each group selected two to four involvement activities to support its goal. For example, the writing achievement group planned an open-mike poetry night for students to share their creativity with families invited as audience members. They also planned to invite family volunteers to be assistant coaches and judges for the student debate club. As a third activity, they planned to develop a writing achievement page in the PTA newsletter with information on the curriculum, recognition of student achievement, and suggestions for parents to help their teens with homework.

After the two groups wrote their final goal-oriented action plans on writing and attendance, the full team came back together. They checked to see that the activities for all six types of involvement were included in the final plan. The full ATP made a few adjustments to the comprehensive plan to strengthen activities and to schedule them evenly throughout the school year. The ATP then assigned at least one member to oversee or coordinate each activity and identified other faculty, staff, parents, students, and community partners who would assist them in implementing the activities.

In developing their goal-oriented partnership program, the members of this high school's ATP collaborated and shared responsibilities to design a One-Year Action Plan for Partnerships for the remaining half year of school. With this experience, the ATP would write a full, four-page plan in the spring for the next school year.

What Are Some Examples of Partnership Activities for Different Goals?

The following pages provide a few examples of important goals for middle and high school students and sample activities for the six types of involvement that support each goal. Action Teams for Partnerships may select, adapt, or design activities for family and community involvement that are appropriate for their schools' goals for students and for ensuring a welcoming school climate. The activities illustrate a few of many activities that have been implemented by middle and high schools across the country. For more examples, see the annual collections of *Promising Partnership Practices* from successful teams at all school levels at www.partnershipschools.org in the section Success Stories. Use the search function to call for activities from middle and high schools.

MIDDLE SCHOOL EXAMPLES for a One-Year Action Plan to Reach Results for TRANSITIONS

TYPE 1 New students' scavenger hunt around the school for information about the school, teachers and staff, programs, curriculum, and resources, with parents invited for a tour

TYPE 2 Panel discussions at feeder elementary schools for fifth grade students and their parents to hear about middle school from sixth graders, middle school teachers, counselors, administrators, and parents of sixth graders

TYPE 3 Survey of parents on how to volunteer to share their time, specific talents, or resources at school or for the school

TYPE 4 Videos starring current middle school students, parents, and educators to inform fifth graders and their families about ways to help students succeed in middle school

TYPE 5 An Action Team for Partnerships committee focused on ensuring successful transitions of students and families

TYPE 6 Collaborating with feeder schools and hosting joint events

. . . AND MANY OTHER IDEAS FOR EACH TYPE OF INVOLVEMENT

MIDDLE SCHOOL EXAMPLES for a One-Year Action Plan to Reach Results for ATTENDANCE

TYPE 1	**"Attendance Summit" for parents featuring speakers on the importance of student attendance. Speakers may include school administrators, counselors, legal experts, teachers, health service providers, students, and family members.**
TYPE 2	**Recognition postcards for good or improved attendance**
TYPE 3	**Family volunteers as attendance monitors**
TYPE 4	**Interactive homework for students and family partners to create a poster on why good attendance is important**
TYPE 5	**PTA/PTO communications, translated as needed, for all families on school goals and requirements for student attendance and on-time arrival, and guidelines on steps to take when students return to school after illness**
TYPE 6	**Agreement with local businesses to post signs that students are welcome only during nonschool hours**

. . . AND MANY OTHER IDEAS FOR EACH TYPE OF INVOLVEMENT

MIDDLE SCHOOL EXAMPLES for a One-Year Action Plan to Reach Results for READING

TYPE 1	**Parent workshops on how to guide and encourage students in reading for pleasure at home**
TYPE 2	**A page of the school newsletter with information on the school's reading and language arts standards, suggestions for encouraging students to read aloud and for pleasure at home, and questions to discuss with students about things they read**
TYPE 3	**Family members as volunteer literacy tutors, reading buddies, or library aides during the school day or in afterschool programs**
TYPE 4	**Interactive homework in reading and writing for students to share their ideas with a family partner**
TYPE 5	**PTA/PTO-supported fund-raiser for books, magazines, and other reading materials for the school media center**
TYPE 6	**Donations from local businesses to be used as incentives for a campaign to encourage students to read many books**

. . . AND MANY OTHER IDEAS FOR EACH TYPE OF INVOLVEMENT

HIGH SCHOOL EXAMPLES for a One-Year Action Plan to Reach Results for MATH

TYPE 1 Continuing education classes for family members (e.g., GED/ABE classes), or for families and students together (e.g., computer classes)

TYPE 2 Student recognition page in the school newsletter highlighting students who improve and excel in math

TYPE 3 Parents as audience members for "math bowl" or other math competitions

TYPE 4 Information for parents on students' math requirements to prepare for entry to postsecondary education

TYPE 5 PTA/PTO support for math with the purchase of calculators, computers, and other materials

TYPE 6 Afterschool program with local college students as math tutors

. . . AND MANY OTHER IDEAS FOR EACH TYPE OF INVOLVEMENT

HIGH SCHOOL EXAMPLES for a One-Year Action Plan to Reach Results for POSTSECONDARY PLANNING

TYPE 1 Workshops for parents and students on course credits and requirements for high school graduation, college financial aid, college entry tests, and career planning

TYPE 2 Series of videos for families to borrow to learn about high school requirements and postsecondary planning

TYPE 3 Field trips for students and parents to local colleges and universities

TYPE 4 Interactive homework that requires students to discuss their academic goals and career plans with a family partner and to outline strategies for reaching these goals

TYPE 5 A postsecondary planning committee of parents, teachers, and students to implement a series of activities on college awareness and career options from ninth to twelfth grade

TYPE 6 "College Club" or "Postsecondary Planners" for linking students and families with alumni from the high school to increase knowledge and guide actions on postsecondary education and training

. . . AND MANY OTHER IDEAS FOR EACH TYPE OF INVOLVEMENT

MIDDLE AND HIGH SCHOOL EXAMPLES for a One-Year Action Plan to CREATE A CLIMATE OF PARTNERSHIP

TYPE 1 Parent support groups to discuss parenting approaches and school issues with other families

TYPE 2 "Good news" postcards, phone calls, and other two-way communications (e.g., e-mail, voice mail, Web sites) to connect teachers and families about student progress and success

TYPE 3 Volunteers for safe schools to greet, assist, or deter visitors

TYPE 4 Quarterly interactive homework assignments for students to review report card grades with family partners and to discuss academic and behavior goals for the next grading period

TYPE 5 PTA/PTO-sponsored "Showcase the School Day" with booths and displays on school programs, student clubs, academic departments, the parent association, and partnership activities

TYPE 6 Periodic community forums for educators, students, parents, and citizens to discuss school improvement topics, family and community support for education, and other important issues

. . . AND MANY OTHER IDEAS FOR EACH TYPE OF INVOLVEMENT

MIDDLE AND HIGH SCHOOL EXAMPLES
for a One-Year Action Plan to Reach Results for STUDENT HEALTH

TYPE 1 — **Parent support groups and forums to discuss parents' questions and best practices for adolescent health, nutrition, and safety**

TYPE 2 — **Articles on the school Web site or in school newsletter on school and district health and safety requirements, health tips, and topics of importance in adolescence**

TYPE 3 — **Volunteers, audiences, and participants for all-school walk-a-thons, team sports, and other active events**

TYPE 4 — **Periodic interactive homework in science, health, or physical education classes for students to discuss disease prevention, health, and wellness with a family partner**

TYPE 5 — **PTA/PTO sponsored health fair for students and families featuring community resources, services, free screenings, and discussions of careers in the health field**

TYPE 6 — **Sessions for students by community specialists in karate, yoga, dance, aerobics, and other activities before or after school or on weekends**

. . . AND MANY OTHER IDEAS FOR EACH TYPE OF INVOLVEMENT

WHY PARTNERSHIPS ARE IMPORTANT IN MIDDLE AND HIGH SCHOOLS

Research shows that

- **Students tend to do better on achievement tests, report card grades, attendance, behavior, and postsecondary plans if their parents are involved in their education.**
- **Adolescents are more likely to avoid risky or negative behaviors (e.g., alcohol or drug abuse, violence) if they feel connected to their families.**
- **Partnership activities can help create safer schools.**
- **Curriculum-related family involvement, such as interactive homework, can help students improve academic skills in specific subjects.**
- **High-performing middle and high schools inform and involve parents and community partners as a planned part of their programs.**
- **Parents want to be involved and influential in their teens' education.**
- **Students in middle and high schools want their parents involved in meaningful ways.**
- **When schools reach out to involve families, more parents become involved.**

SPECIAL CONSIDERATIONS FOR MIDDLE AND HIGH SCHOOLS

All schools that develop comprehensive partnership programs use the framework of six types of involvement, establish an Action Team for Partnerships (ATP), and write a One-Year Action Plan for Partnerships linked to school improvement goals. Middle and high schools also should consider the following guidelines.

Link Partnerships to School Improvement Goals

Partnership programs in middle and high schools must be goal oriented. There are many age-appropriate and context-specific goals to choose from, including improving students' writing, enhancing science skills, increasing attendance, reducing bullying, improving health, planning for postsecondary education, and developing a welcoming school environment. Use Form G–Goals to write the One-Year Action Plan for Partnerships and to evaluate progress.

Focus on Transition Years

Schools that emphasize family involvement for incoming students and their families are more likely to sustain school-family-community partnerships across the middle and high school years. For example, a high school that is just beginning its work on partnerships may want to focus on new activities for involving ninth graders' families and add activities for another grade level each year.

Promote Early Postsecondary Planning

Early and consistent emphases on postsecondary planning will ensure that more students set and reach goals to attend college or prepare for training or work after high school. Middle and high schools' ATPs should create a sequence of information and activities from Grade 6 to 12 to help students and families set long-term education goals, identify academic and financial requirements, and take action to attain the goals. Partnership activities may include workshops, informative flyers, articles in newsletters, interactive homework on setting goals for education and careers, field trips, panel discussions with alumni, and other targeted activities.

Actively Involve Students

Students are the main actors in their own education. Students need to be involved in school, family, and community partnership activities by delivering and interpreting information to and from their families and by providing ideas and reactions for improving involvement activities. In high schools, one or two students must be members of the ATP. Adolescents need to know that their schools and families are working together to help students succeed in school. Ironically, studies indicate that adolescents develop greater independence when their parents are knowledgeable partners in their education.

Reach Out to Families

Just about all parents of middle and high school students want to know how to help their children at home and how to help them succeed at school. Studies confirm that adolescents' families need and want more and better information and guidance from middle and high schools. Studies also show that when schools implement well-planned practices of partnership, more families become involved in those activities.

Expand Teachers' Roles Gradually

Because many middle and high school teachers were trained as academic specialists, they may not be aware of how family and community involvement helps adolescents succeed. ATPs may start by implementing partnership activities that produce important and visible results for students and the school. ATPs may encourage teachers who already conduct partnership activities to share their success stories and recruit colleagues to implement similar activities.

7

Develop District and State Leadership for Partnerships

District and state leaders play important roles in determining whether and how well schools develop and maintain successful programs of family and community involvement. This chapter describes actions that district and state leaders should take to increase their own knowledge, skills, and activities on partnerships and to facilitate the work of schools' Action Teams for Partnerships (ATPs) to strengthen their programs of family and community involvement.

Organizations also may assist schools, districts, and states to develop leadership on partnerships and to implement partnership programs. Some organizations conduct activities similar to those of state departments of education (e.g., parent information resource centers [PIRCS] or regional professional development service centers). These organizations work with many districts statewide or in large regions. Other organizations work like school districts by assisting many schools in developing programs of partnerships. Leaders in organizations may use the information and tools in this chapter for districts or for states, as appropriate.

In this chapter, an introductory article discusses the importance of clear and comprehensive district and state policies on partnerships. It also is important that district and state leaders support their written policies with "facilitative actions." Informed leadership activities are needed to "enact" written policies. The article includes information on costs and sources of funds for partnerships, based on the work of many schools, districts, and states across the country.

Several tools are provided to help district and state leaders understand their roles and responsibilities for promoting and guiding school, family, and community partnerships. The outlines, summaries, checklists, and templates should help district and state leaders sort and select activities for their annual Leadership Action Plans for

Partnerships. District and state leaders may also use these materials to make presentations to help colleagues understand district and state leadership on partnerships.

Tools for District Leaders

Lead and Succeed: An Inventory of District Leadership and Facilitation Strategies

This inventory, based on the work of many district leaders, assists district facilitators to identify strategies and activities to improve district level and school-based programs of family and community involvement. There are six main strategies for leadership on partnerships: *create awareness, align program and policy, guide learning and program development, share knowledge, celebrate milestones,* and *document progress and evaluate outcomes.* The inventory outlines 50 activities that may be selected for the six strategies, including actions to improve district level leadership and to facilitate schools' partnership programs.

District Leadership Roles

Use this handout to inform colleagues of the ways that district leaders can coordinate interdepartmental programs and activities on school, family, and community partnerships. Focus clearly on the importance of *facilitating all schools* to establish Action Teams for Partnerships and to develop school-based, goal-oriented partnership programs that involve all families.

District Leadership Checklist

Take steps to increase district leadership on school, family, and community partnerships and to support schools with their partnership programs. Check the boxes when the actions are completed.

Sample District Leadership Action Plan for Partnerships

See an example of a district plan that focuses on a few clear goals and a limited number of activities to attain each goal. The goals and activities reflect the major strategies for district leadership in the Lead and Succeed Inventory, including a balance between actions at the district level and direct facilitation of schools' Action Teams for Partnerships (ATPs). District leaders may use the template at the end of the chapter to write an annual, detailed Leadership Action Plan for Partnerships. There should be one page of the template for each goal, detailing the strategies, specific activities, people, time, resources, and evaluations needed to succeed.

What Do Facilitators Do?

Use this list to guide and assist schools' Action Teams for Partnerships. Review and adapt the list periodically to meet local requirements and expectations.

Facilitators' Tasks at the Start of the School Year

District leaders can get off to a good start in the first month of the school year by helping each school's Action Team for Partnerships organize its work.

Also, begin the school year by working effectively with colleagues in the district office.

Summary of School Visits

Keep a record of formal contacts and meetings with schools' Action Teams for Partnerships, principals, and other groups, and plan follow-up activities to assist each school. In addition to visiting schools, the form may be used for other contacts by phone, email, and quarterly cluster meetings with the chairs or co-chairs of groups of schools' ATPs. (Note: This form is on the *Handbook* CD *only.*)

Tools for State Leaders

States Lead and Succeed: An Inventory for Leadership on Partnerships

This inventory, with input from many state leaders, assists leaders for partnerships to identify strategies and activities to improve statewide approaches to school, family, and community partnerships. There are six leadership strategies: *create awareness, align program and policy, guide learning and program development, share knowledge, celebrate milestones,* and *document progress and evaluate outcomes.* The inventory outlines over 40 activities that state leaders may conduct for the six strategies to promote the improvement of partnership programs throughout the state.

State Leadership Roles

Use this handout to inform colleagues of the ways that state leaders can coordinate interdepartmental programs and activities on school, family, and community partnerships. Discuss the importance of informing and guiding districts and schools to develop comprehensive, goal-oriented partnership programs to involve all families.

State Leadership Checklist

Take steps to increase state leadership on school, family, and community partnerships and to support districts and schools. Check the boxes when the actions are completed.

Sample State Leadership Action Plan for Partnerships

See one example of a state plan that focuses on three goals for leadership on partnerships. Use the template at the end of the chapter to write an annual, detailed Leadership Action Plan for Partnerships. There should be one page of the template for each goal, detailing the objective(s), specific activities or strategies, people, time, resources, and evaluations needed to succeed.

Other state plans, activities, and ideas for improving partnership programs over time are found at www.partnershipschools.org in Success Stories. Click on examples of *Promising Partnership Practices* from districts and states and summaries of award-winning programs.

Tools for District and State Leaders

Template for Districts and States: Leadership Action Plan for Partnerships

This form, developed with input from district and state leaders working to improve their partnership programs, may be tailored to include information required in particular districts, state departments of education, and organizations. Final plans must not only include goals to improve work in leaders' offices at the state, district, or organization levels, but also goals for guiding and assisting elementary, middle, and high schools to organize and improve effective programs of family and community involvement.

Leadership and Facilitation Strategies for District and State Leaders of Partnerships

This slide shows six broad strategies that guide district and state leaders in selecting activities for developing their partnership programs. The six strategies, identified in the "Lead and Succeed" inventories, are represented by different activities that will help district and state leaders customize their programs to fit their own policy contexts.

Sample Pledges, Compacts, or Contracts

Establish agreements with parents, teachers, students, and administrators to work together for student success. The pledges, parallel in form for all partners, list a few basic responsibilities that identify common goals, shared responsibilities, and personal commitments. Some districts and states ask schools to collect pledges as the "school-parent compact" required in Title I legislation. However, the legislative language specifies that a school-parent compact is a detailed plan and schedule of activities to ensure a partnership program. This is better represented by the *One-Year Action Plan for Partnerships* (Chapters 4 and 5). Nevertheless, signed pledges or agreements can be included as a Type 2–Communicating activity within a full partnership plan.

The One-Year Action Plan for Partnerships (not a simple pledge) ensures that a school has an organized program and a detailed schedule of activities that will involve families in ways that support student achievement and success in school. By organizing and implementing a comprehensive, goal-oriented partnership program, as guided by this *Handbook,* schools, districts, and states will meet the requirements in Title I, Section 1118 for family and community involvement.

Standards for Excellent Partnership Programs

Another way to ensure high-quality partnership programs is to include eight "essential elements." Research shows that these components improve school, district, and state programs of school, family, and community partnerships from one year to the next. This *Handbook* guides school, district, and state leaders to meet all of these standards. See how these standards are being met in states, districts, and schools at www.partnershipschools.org in the section of Success Stories. See promising practices and award-winning programs at the school, district, and state levels.

District and State Leadership for School, Family, and Community Partnerships

Joyce L. Epstein

Policies at the district and state levels increasingly include goals for school, family, and community partnerships. District and state laws and guidelines are beginning to go beyond general statements of the importance of parent involvement to include explicit commitments for leadership and activities to assist all schools in developing comprehensive partnership programs that benefit students.

Districts

Most districts have policies, goals, and guidelines on school, family, and community partnerships. Some, particularly large school districts, have established offices with directors and facilitators who help all elementary, middle, and high schools plan and implement programs of partnership. Studies and fieldwork indicate that one full-time-equivalent district level facilitator can assist up to 30 schools' Action Teams for Partnerships in implementing goal-linked programs of family and community involvement.

Studies and fieldwork with several hundred school districts across the country that vary greatly in size and demographics have identified six major strategies that help organize district leaders' work on partnerships: *create awareness, align program and policy, guide learning and program development, share knowledge, celebrate milestones,* and *document progress and evaluate outcomes.* To fulfill these strategies, district leaders can select a mix of activities for district level leadership and for helping each school build its capacity to work with its students' families.

For example, to align program and policy, district leaders for partnerships will base their plans for partnerships on the language of the parent involvement policy passed by the school board. If there is no formal policy on partnerships, the district leader, colleagues, and parents will need to work together to develop one that supports research-based approaches to partnership program development. Other typical district leadership activities focus on guiding school teams to strengthen their plans and practices by conducting initial and advanced team-training workshops for schools' Action Teams for Partnerships, making school visits with principals, awarding grants to schools for initiating or improving partnership projects, and enabling schools to share best practices and celebrate successes. The inventory, *Districts Lead and Succeed: An Inventory of Leadership and Facilitation Strategies for Partnerships* (pp. 248–251 and CD) helps district leaders identify activities that will improve the district's work on partnerships.

States

Many states are increasing their leadership and improving programs that guide and support districts and schools in their work on partnerships. Some have established permanent bureaus, offices, or departments of school, family, and community partnerships with directors, coordinators, and facilitators as experts on involvement. These state leaders for partnerships are responsible for helping districts, schools, business leaders, and others increase knowledge, obtain resources, and improve their programs of family and community involvement.

State leadership takes many forms, but can be classified by the leadership headings noted above for districts. State leaders, too, must *create awareness, align program and policy, guide learning and program development, share knowledge, celebrate milestones,* and *document progress and evaluate outcomes* on partnerships. With knowledge of these strategies, state leaders for partnerships can select a mix of activities to inform and encourage all districts in the state to take new directions in guiding schools to develop goal-linked programs of family and community involvement.

For example, state leaders for partnerships must match their plans, presentations, and programs to the state policy on parent and community involvement and on state priorities for student success. State leaders also may conduct conferences or workshops to guide and support district leaders in developing their expertise and programs of family and community involvement. Some state offices make grants to districts and schools to establish or improve their partnership programs, practices, and evaluations. The inventory, *States Lead and Succeed: An Inventory for Leadership on Partnerships.* (pp. 257–260 and CD) guides state leaders to select which activities to conduct to advance this agenda. (Also see the other state outlines and tools in this chapter.)

Basic Leadership Activities on Partnerships in Districts and States

Every state is different in its history on partnerships, policy development, and number and size of school districts. For example, Maryland has a total of 24 school systems, whereas California has over 1,000, and other states fall between. The number and organization of school districts, regions, professional development service centers, and other factors affect state plans to inform and guide all districts in developing their partnership programs.

Nevertheless, states with few or many districts are taking steps to inform and assist districts and their schools to work better with students' families and communities. This is in response to state policies, federal requirements, and the recognition of the need for research-based approaches to all school improvement efforts.

Similarly, large and small districts with many and few schools are organizing leadership and actions on partnerships. Ultimately, *every school* must take responsibility for planning, implementing, budgeting, and continually improving its own partnership program. Schools must continually improve their work with families to help more students reach their full potential. District and state leadership and support make a difference in whether and how well schools design and maintain programs of family and community involvement (Epstein, 2007; Epstein, Galindo, Sheldon, & Williams, 2007; Sanders, 2005).

Basic Actions

Education leaders in districts and states across the country are taking some or all of the following actions to advance leadership skills and to guide schools with their work on school, family, and community partnerships. The following leadership activities are among many in the district and state inventories for leadership on partnerships, but they are "basic" for organizing effective partnership programs in districts and in state departments of education.

Write a policy that outlines and discusses district or state expectations and commitments for comprehensive programs of school, family, and community partnerships. The policy should define school, family, and community partnerships, including the six types of involvement. It should include language to recognize the importance of teamwork for conducting partnership programs and to explain the requirements and standards for excellent programs. The policy should include "enactments" that specify the services that the district or state will provide to enact the policy.

District and state policies concerning school, family, and community partnerships must be clear and comprehensive but also flexible and responsive. Good policies recognize that all districts and all schools have different starting points in their practices of partnerships and serve diverse populations of parents and students. The policies should guide schools in establishing teams of teachers, parents, administrators, and others to focus, exclusively, on family and community involvement plans and practices that will help students reach specific school goals for success.

Written policies are necessary, but not sufficient, for helping all schools create strong partnership programs (Epstein, 2007). District and state leaders for partnerships must have ambitious and attainable action plans to assist schools in developing, evaluating, and continually improving their partnership programs. District leaders, in particular, may help schools enact the district's policy on partnerships by providing training, funds, encouragement, recognition, and other assistance. Policies that are unfunded and unsupported by leaders will be unwelcome and ineffective (see Epstein, 2001, for examples of district and state plans for partnerships or www.partnershipschools.org in NNPS Models for districts and states).

Establish an office or department with an expert leader and adequate staff to facilitate the development and continuous improvement of programs of school, family, and community partnerships. Every state and large district should have a director of school, family, and community partnerships.

Small districts may identify part-time leaders to guide schools with their work on partnerships, and very small districts must find other ways to guide schools' ATPs on partnership program development. For example, in some small districts, each principal takes leadership for and builds expertise on one school improvement goal—including family and community involvement. Other small districts work with external service providers (e.g., regional service centers) to guide school improvements—including family and community involvement. Still others create a core team of chairs of ATPs from each school to work with a designated district leader as an internal leadership group. There are many ways to build expertise on partnerships.

State leaders for partnerships must connect with their counterparts in school districts. District leaders must guide all schools' Action Teams for Partnerships in developing their programs of family and community involvement. The leaders provide information, training, and technical assistance and conduct other activities to increase understanding, skills, and actions that will result in high-quality partnership programs at all policy levels.

Write an annual Leadership Action Plan for Partnerships. To be effective, district and state leaders must write an annual Leadership Action Plan for Partnerships that lists and schedules the actions they will take to promote and support school, family, and community partnerships. District and state leadership plans should include activities that

- Increase district or state leaders' competencies on partnerships.
- Develop interdepartmental connections to strengthen leadership on partnerships.
- Strengthen skills and increase knowledge about partnerships throughout their districts or states.
- Facilitate the efforts of all schools to develop and maintain their site-based, goal-oriented partnership programs.

Identify funds for school, family, and community partnerships to cover staff and program costs. District and state leaders must specify their budgets to support staff salaries, training programs, small grants for partnership projects, end-of-year celebrations or conferences to share best practices each year, evaluation studies, and other leadership activities on partnerships. Line items for partnership program budgets are needed to provide stable support for these activities.

State, district, and school leaders reported initial levels and sources of funds that support their partnership programs (National Network of Partnership Schools, 2007). Investments differed, because states, districts, and schools vary greatly in size and in the number of students and families served. To account for large and small states, districts, and schools, costs for partnerships were estimated as *per pupil expenditures* or as *lump sum* investments, as shown in Table 7.1. The table presents estimated ranges of allocations for partnership programs at the state, district, and school levels. Of course, funding always can be increased to expand and improve programs.

The following examples illustrate minimum funds needed to support initial programs of partnerships.

- *Schools* should plan to invest $12 to $20 (or more) per pupil per year to use *at the school level* to support the family and community involvement activities planned by the school's Action Team for Partnerships (ATP) and by individual and grade level teachers. Each school's One-Year Action Plan for Partnerships should include activities for the six types of involvement tailored to meet school goals and involve all families. Funds must support the activities listed in the plan for the school's full partnership program. This may include support for a part-time, site-based coordinator or liaison who serves on the ATP, printed materials, refreshments, incentives, workshop presenters, Web site development, and other actions and materials needed for the involvement activities in the annual action plan.
- *Districts* should plan to invest from $5 to $10 (or more) per pupil per year to use *at the district level* to fund the salaries of a district coordinator and facilitators in large districts and to fund district leadership activities and services. Funds may support training for schools' Action Teams for Partnerships, other inservice education, grants to schools, celebrations and dissemination of effective practices, and other district leadership functions that assist *all* schools and families and that facilitate *each* school's efforts in developing its plans and programs of family and community partnerships. The funds must adequately support all entries in the district leaders' annual Leadership Action Plan for Partnerships.

- *States* should plan to invest from $0.15 to $1 (or more) per pupil/per year to use *at the state level* to fund the salaries of a state director of partnerships, required staff, and state leadership activities and services. Funds may be used to support initial and advanced inservice education and training, grants for districts and schools to initiate or improve partnership programs, statewide or regional conferences, and other state leadership functions that will inform and assist all districts in the state in developing their leadership and expertise on partnerships. The funds must adequately support all entries in the state leaders' annual Leadership Action Plan for Partnerships.

The per-pupil expenditures may be translated into lump-sum investments for states, districts, and schools, taking into account the number of students served and the special needs of students, families, schools, and communities.

- *School examples.* A school of about 500 students needs a budget of $6,000 to $10,000 per year to cover the typical costs of activities in a One-Year Action Plan for Partnerships. This will enable the ATP to conduct goal-linked activities for the six types of involvement that will engage all families in their children's education. A school of 1,500 students, by contrast, would need a budget of $18,000 to $30,000 for activities in an initial program that will involve all families in productive ways.
- *District examples.* A small district serving 5,000 students (or about 10 schools) should invest from $25,000 to $50,000 or more per year for the salary and benefits of a part-time district level leader for partnerships and the services provided to all schools. By contrast, a large district serving 100,000 students (or about 200 schools) would require an annual budget of $500,000 to $1 million or more for a full-time director and six to nine facilitators to assist clusters of up to 30 schools' Action Teams for Partnerships to develop their partnership programs in order to engage all families in their children's education in all elementary, middle, and high school.
- *State examples.* A state serving 300,000 students could set an annual budget of from $45,000 to $300,000 or more to cover the costs of a part-time to full-time leader for partnerships and activities to help districts in the state begin their work on partnerships. By contrast, a state serving 800,000 students needs an annual budget of from $120,000 to $800,000 or more to conduct state level leadership development programs on partnerships. It is recommended that every state, large or small, have one full-time director of partnerships. Variation in funds in small and large states affect program costs (e.g., conferences, workshops) to guide more or fewer districts and more or fewer families. The level of funds will affect the nature and extent of services that states provide to districts and schools on partnerships (Epstein, 2001).

These estimates, based on reports from developing programs, indicate that all states, districts, and schools can easily afford to organize research-based programs of school, family, and community partnerships. The suggested investments are a fraction of annual per-pupil expenditures for education and are a thrifty way to engage all families in their children's education every year. With these decisions about funding, programs of school, family, and community partnerships will become a standard part of the organization of education for all children at the school, district, and state levels.

Table 7.1 also reports some of major sources of funds that states, districts, and school are using to support their programs of school, family, and community partnerships. This includes federal funds from Title I, which specifies funds and required practices for school, district, and state partnership programs; other federal funding streams, including Titles II, III, and IV, which encourage family involvement practices linked to professional development for teachers and principals, bilingual education and English language learning, afterschool programs, and other areas of school improvement; special education funding; PTA or PTO support; local foundations; and other sources. The information shows clearly that with minimal changes to budgeting processes, all states, districts, and schools could find ample funds to organize, implement, and sustain effective partnership programs, as guided in this *Handbook.*

Conduct ongoing inservice education on partnerships. District and state leaders should provide or support inservice education on beginning and advanced topics for developing programs of school, family, and community partnerships. Inservice education includes professional development for schools' Action Teams for Partnerships to initiate their partnership programs and advanced training to help teams continually improve the quality of their programs. (See Chapter 4 in this *Handbook* for guidelines on conducting training workshops.)

Evaluate teachers and administrators for their work on partnerships. State boards of education and district school boards should include school, family, and community partnerships in the annual or periodic evaluations of professional and paraprofessional staff. Guidelines should be provided to teachers, principals, instructional aides, superintendents, and other leaders on how to conduct high-quality programs and practices of partnerships in classrooms and for the whole school. Professionals and paraprofessionals should know how their work on partnerships will be judged along with other competencies on their evaluations.

Support state, district, and school career ladders to build expertise and leadership on partnerships. States and districts should invest in developing leaders for school, family, and community partnerships, just as professionals build expertise in academic subjects, athletic coaching, and student services. Leadership positions include district and state directors and coordinators of partnerships; district facilitators who assist schools on partnerships; and school level teachers and administrators who serve as chairs and co-chairs of the Action Team for Partnerships and ATP committees. By taking these leadership roles, educators and parents build valuable skills in organizing programs that increase a sense of community and in conducting activities that assist families and increase student success.

Develop partnership tools or products. Leaders for partnerships in states and districts not only may use the tools and guidelines in this *Handbook* but also may develop and customize tools to meet the needs and goals of schools, families, and students in their locations. Leaders may create brochures, calendars, newsletters, fax and e-mail communiqués, translations of information and materials for families with limited English skills, Web sites, summaries of survey results, and other publications and products. Site-specific materials and approaches may be needed to involve fathers, very young parents, new arrivals to the school, and other hard-to-reach families or to explain school attendance policies, district and state standards for student learning, new tests and assessments, and other innovations that parents and the community need to understand in order to help students succeed in school.

Encourage business, industry, and other community connections to strengthen school, family, and community partnerships. Some businesses have policies that permit and

TABLE 7.1 Levels of Sources of Funds for Programs of Family and Community Involvement in Schools, Districts, and States

What does it cost to support research-based partnership programs in NNPS?

Data reported by schools, districts, and states show the range of investments that support leadership and costs of initial partnership programs. Because these locations vary greatly in size, estimates of per-pupil expenditures are useful gauges for any school, district, or state department of education.

	Schools (N = 356)[1]	***Districts (N = 83)***[1]	***States (N = 12)***[1]
Levels of Funding	**Range: $100 to $88,000** Median: $2,000 Average: $5,722 **Suggested per-pupil expenditure range: $12 to $20**	**Range: $800 to $2.78 million** Median: $65,000 Average: $213,958 **Suggested per-pupil expenditure range: $5 to $10**	**Range: $2,000 to $600,000** Median: $175,000 Average: $211,088 **Suggested per-pupil expenditure range: $0.15 to $1.00**
Sources of Funds for Family and Community Involvement Programs	Bilingual education Community partners District budget Drug prevention General funds Principals' discretionary funds PTA School fund raisers Special education funds State funds Title I Titles III, IV 21st Century Schools grants Other federal, state, district, and local funds	Bilingual education Community partners District budget Drug prevention District fund-raisers General funds Local foundations PIRC support PTA Special Education State funds Title I Titles II, III, IV United Way 21st Century Schools grants Other federal, state, and district funds	IDEA–Special education funding PIRC support State professional development funds State department of education general funds Title I 21st Century Schools grants Other federal and state funds

The figures suggest that in most places, the total cost for all three policy levels—school, district, and state—may be about $30 per pupil per year. This minimal investment should support the leaders and expenses for basic programs of family and community involvement, including the following:

- Practices in schools' One-Year Action Plans for Partnerships to involve all families as partners in their children's education.
- Salaries, benefits, and program costs for district leader(s) for partnerships at a ratio of one facilitator for up to 30 schools.
- Salaries, benefits, and program costs for state leader(s) for partnerships.

[1] Source: *UPDATE* surveys of schools, districts, and states in the National Network of Partnership Schools (NNPS) at Johns Hopkins University. School data are from 1998 and are corrected for inflation to reflect 2007 dollars. District and state data are from 2007 *UPDATEs*.

encourage employees who are parents to become involved in their children's education and attend parent-teacher conferences. Some have policies for all employees, with or without school-aged children, to volunteer time to assist local schools. District and state leaders may work with legislators, business leaders, and community groups to draft legislation or offer various tax incentives, credits, preferred status, or other support and recognition for businesses that encourage parent and community involvement in schools.

District and state leaders also may encourage business, industry, university, and community agency leaders to establish media centers or resource rooms to provide employees who are parents with information on infant, child, and adolescent development, parenting skills, and school, family, and community partnerships; establish child care services for preschool children; offer afterschool, vacation, summer, and other special programs for school-aged children; provide "substitute parents" or alternative child care for children with minor illnesses; award grants to schools and community agencies for family and community involvement programs; and conduct other activities to benefit employees, their children, and the local school systems and communities.

Establish advisory committees so that education leaders hear from parents and the community on partnerships and other educational issues. Each state should have an advisory committee for the state superintendent on school, family, and community partnerships with representatives of key stakeholders across the state. This group should provide diverse views on state level topics that will assist parents and educators; suggest ways to explain or clarify state requirements and reports on state education policies and tests; and provide input to ways that state leaders can strengthen family and community involvement in all districts and schools.

Each district should establish a district advisory council with parent or ATP representatives from all schools to provide the superintendent and other leaders with ideas on important topics that families need to understand and ways to strengthen partnership programs in all schools.

Establish a Web site, library, or dissemination center for research on promising practices of school, family, and community partnerships. States and districts may collect and disseminate information on partnerships on their Web sites, in family resource centers, via mobile units, or in other convenient locations. In different ways, district and state leaders can use new technologies to collect and share results of research on partnerships; effective approaches for organizing partnership programs; teachers' practices for involving parents in conferences, homework, extracurricular, and other activities; tools to evaluate the quality and progress of partnership programs; forms and technologies for communicating with parents; information on child and adolescent development and parenting strategies; and other information and materials. District leaders will tailor these messages for their own families and communities and disseminate best practices across schools. State leaders can provide information that will be understandable and useful statewide.

Support requirements for preparing new teachers and administrators to conduct excellent partnership programs. State leaders, in particular, should support or press for legislation for state certification that requires preservice and advanced education that prepares teachers and administrators to conduct effective programs and practices of school, family, and community partnerships. This goes beyond statements that new teachers and administrators should communicate with families. It includes requirements with clear evidence that educators are prepared to develop and support *programs* of family and community involvement with plans and practices aligned with school improvement goals. District leaders should reinforce the importance of this knowledge, experience, and positive attitude toward family and community involvement when they hire new teachers and administrators (Epstein, 2001).

Support research and evaluation on the quality and effects of programs and practices of school, family, and community partnerships. District and state leaders may collect data to learn whether and how well their own work and their schools' programs of partnerships progress over time. Some evaluations will be relatively simple, such as taking inventory of present practices to identify starting points in program development and collecting evidence and artifacts on practices that are conducted. Other evaluations may be more complex, such as gathering and analyzing families' suggestions for partnerships, reactions to practices, and long-term results of particular practices for student achievement and behavior. District and state leaders also may work with university researchers or other external evaluators to conduct formal studies of the results of partnerships (see Chapter 9 on evaluations).

In sum, district and state leaders have important responsibilities for developing and continually improving their own knowledge and activities of school, family, and community partnerships. They also must take active steps to facilitate the knowledge and skills of schools' Action Teams for Partnerships so that every elementary, middle, and high school is able to develop its own program of partnership.

State leaders for partnerships may collaborate with colleagues across departments, work with regional staff development offices, or connect with university partners and others to develop and implement a long-term plan for communicating with and assisting district leaders across the state with their work on partnerships at the district level and in all schools.

District leaders for partnerships must plan and implement activities not only to strengthen the districts' commitment to communicate and partner with families but also—and mainly—to help all elementary, middle, and high schools establish and sustain well-functioning Action Teams for Partnerships. This includes helping all ATPs plan, implement, evaluate, and continually improve the quality of their programs of partnerships.

District and state leaders will be assisted to fulfill these responsibilities by all chapters in this *Handbook.* Additional information and examples of district and state leaders' practices are online at www.partnershipschools.org in the section Success Stories, in all collections of *Promising Partnership Practices*, and in the summaries of award-winning programs.

References

Epstein, J. L. (2001). Strategies for action in practice, policy, and research. In *School, family, and community partnerships: Preparing educators and improving schools* (Chap. 7). Boulder, CO: Westview Press.

Epstein, J. L. (2007). Research meets policy and practice: How are school districts addressing NCLB requirements for parental involvement? In A. R. Sadovnik, J. O'Day, G. Bohrnstedt, & K. Borman (Eds.), *No Child Left Behind and the reduction of the achievement gap: Sociological perspectives on federal educational policy* (pp. 267–279). New York: Routledge.

Epstein, J. L., Galindo, C., Sheldon, S. B., & Williams, K. J. (2007, April). *Effects of district leadership on the quality of school programs of family and community involvement.* Paper presented at the annual meeting of American Educational Research Association, Chicago.

National Network of Partnership Schools. (2007). Annual *UPDATE* surveys. Baltimore: Johns Hopkins University, Center on School, Family, and Community Partnerships.

Sanders, M. G. (2005). *Building school-community partnerships: Collaborating for student success.* Thousand Oaks, CA: Corwin Press.

Lead and Succeed: An Inventory of District Leadership & Facilitation Strategies for Partnerships

Natalie Rodriguez Jansorn and Joyce L. Epstein

District leaders who are specialists in partnership program development must guide all schools in conducting and sustaining excellent research-based partnership programs. To reach this goal, district facilitators must write and implement a Leadership Action Plan for Partnerships to (1) establish an office on partnerships and (2) directly assist schools to develop goal-oriented programs of school, family, and community partnerships.

This inventory is organized around six leadership strategies: *create awareness, align program and policy, guide learning and program development, share knowledge, celebrate milestones,* and *document progress and evaluate outcomes.* The inventory outlines 50 activities that district facilitators may select to conduct a districtwide program of school, family, and community partnerships. The strategies and activities in the inventory are based on the results of research on districts' partnership program development and examples shared by district leaders with NNPS for many years.

District facilitators are *not* expected to implement all of the activities listed. They should, however, consider which ones to include in their plans to increase the effectiveness and sustainability of district-level and school-based programs of family and community involvement.

Directions:

Check (✓) all activities that presently are conducted in your district.

Star (✶) the activities that you want to initiate in the future, as you develop your district's program.

At the end of each section, add other activities that you presently conduct or plan to conduct that are not listed.

Use this information to write your district's Leadership Action Plan for Partnerships (pp. 264–266 and CD).

<u>Strategy</u>: Create awareness. Actively promote the partnership program to all key stakeholders, including teachers, administrators, families, and community groups.

- ❒ Convene a one-on-one meeting with the district superintendent to discuss the goals for the partnership program.
- ❒ Conduct presentations about the district's goals for its partnership program to the school board, parent advisory council, and/or other key leadership groups.
- ❒ Conduct awareness sessions for school principals on the partnership program, including the assistance that will be provided to all schools' Action Teams for Partnerships (ATPs).
- ❒ Accompany school principals and/or key district level stakeholders to conferences related to program initiatives (e.g., NNPS Leadership Development Conference in Baltimore).
- ❒ Identify schools to participate in the district's partnership initiative.
- ❒ Announce the district's program on the school district Web site.
- ❒ Disseminate a press release announcing the launch of the district's partnership initiative.
- ❒ Conduct presentations in schools for School Improvement Teams, PTAs, faculties, and/or others to inform them of the district's program.
- ❒ Meet individually with each school principal at the start of the school year to clarify the work of the district facilitator(s) and how the principals will support the program in their schools.
- ❒ Distribute information on the district's partnership program and, if appropriate, its affiliation with the National Network of Partnership Schools (NNPS) at Johns Hopkins University.

OTHER DISTRICT ACTIVITIES TO CREATE AWARENESS

❒ ______________________________

❒ ______________________________

<u>Strategy</u>: Align program and policy. With support from district leadership, integrate the partnership program with district policies, requirements, and procedures.

- ❒ Ensure that the district policy on partnerships refers to district level leadership activities and to direct assistance to help all schools develop their partnership programs with goal-oriented action plans.
- ❒ Write a district Leadership Action Plan for Partnerships that includes district level actions and direct assistance to schools—use this inventory as a resource.
- ❒ Identify a budget to implement the district partnership program.
- ❒ Obtain approval and support from the superintendent for schools to establish Action Teams for Partnerships and to link their action plans for partnerships to goals in their school improvement plans.
- ❒ Arrange a formal announcement from the district leadership that the various schools' School Improvement Plans and the Leadership Action Plan for Partnerships will be integrated.
- ❒ Develop or review district policies so that work and progress on family and community involvement is one component of the evaluations of principals and teachers.
- ❒ Assist schools to identify a school-based budget to implement partnership programs.

OTHER DISTRICT ACTIVITIES TO ALIGN PROGRAM AND POLICY

❒ ______________________________

❒ ______________________________

Strategy: Guide learning and program development. Organize and conduct professional development activities to assist schools in developing their partnership programs.

- ❒ Assist schools with preliminary steps to begin the program (e.g., identify the members of the Action Team for Partnerships, arrange team-training workshops).
- ❒ Conduct a training workshop for all participating schools that includes support to schools on how to link the Leadership Action Plan for Partnerships with each school's School Improvement Plan.
- ❒ Meet with ATP leaders and team members at least monthly at each participating school.
- ❒ Organize a clear process for the district facilitator to provide feedback and support for each school's program.
- ❒ Convene regularly scheduled cluster meetings for schools' ATP chairs or co-chairs to share experiences and learn about specific program topics.
- ❒ Develop and implement professional development workshops and presentations for all teachers and school staff on partnerships.
- ❒ Conduct workshops for parents on ways to partner with the school to increase student success.
- ❒ Conduct a refresher workshop to help schools continue developing their partnership programs from year to year.
- ❒ Award small grants to schools as incentives to build their partnership programs using research-based approaches.

OTHER DISTRICT ACTIVITIES TO GUIDE LEARNING AND PROGRAM DEVELOPMENT

- ❒ ______________________________
- ❒ ______________________________

Strategy: Share knowledge. Foster ongoing communication throughout the district to build knowledge about programs of school, family, and community partnerships.

- ❒ Share progress on the district's partnership program efforts with the superintendent, school board, principals, and others in leadership positions.
- ❒ Facilitate a midyear meeting for schools to share best practices and solutions to challenges.
- ❒ Disseminate a weekly or monthly fax that shares important information, upcoming events, and specific school highlights connected with the district's partnership program.
- ❒ Disseminate an e-newsletter that shares information, events, and highlights.
- ❒ Write a regularly featured column on partnership programs for the district newsletter.
- ❒ Facilitate regularly scheduled meetings with other district departments working on family involvement issues (e.g., special education, ESOL/bilingual education, Title I).
- ❒ Moderate a bulletin board on the district Web site that enables schools to post information, events, and questions for others about partnerships.
- ❒ Assist schools to share information about their partnership activities through the local news media throughout the school year.

OTHER DISTRICT ACTIVITIES TO SHARE KNOWLEDGE

- ❒ ______________________________
- ❒ ______________________________

Strategy: Celebrate milestones. Recognize school and district successes in partnership programs and practices, and disseminate the successes widely.

- ☐ Host an end-of-year celebration for all schools' Action Teams for Partnerships.
- ☐ Edit and distribute a collection of promising partnership practices from each school.
- ☐ Send thank-you letters to schools for submitting promising partnership practices to the district collection.
- ☐ Send letters to principals thanking them for their support for partnerships.
- ☐ Write an annual progress report on the district's partnership program to share with key stakeholders.
- ☐ Organize a recognition program to celebrate schools for achieving milestones such as implementing their first partnership activity, increasing attendance at activities, etc.
- ☐ Create a video of selected partnership activities to share with the school board, principals, community groups, district parent advisory council, and others.
- ☐ Assist schools to recognize and thank partnership leaders in their schools.

OTHER DISTRICT ACTIVITIES TO CELEBRATE MILESTONES

- ☐ ______________________________
- ☐ ______________________________

Strategy: Document progress and evaluate outcomes. Collect information to document activities and to assess progress in meeting district program goals, and assist each ATP to document and evaluate progress in implementing their action plans for partnerships.

- ☐ Provide schools with a recordkeeping system to document and save records of the work of the Action Teams for Partnerships.
- ☐ Collect schools' action plans for partnerships each year and use them to check schools' progress regularly.
- ☐ Establish a quarterly or monthly recordkeeping system for the district facilitator(s) to document visits to schools and technical assistance that is provided or requested.
- ☐ Use the *Summary of School Visits* (*Handbook* CD) for each visit to schools.
- ☐ Evaluate the district facilitator(s) for partnerships annually on established indicators.
- ☐ Encourage schools to complete the annual *School UPDATE* survey (required to maintain NNPS membership) to assess the quality of their partnership programs.
- ☐ Collect and review all schools' *UPDATE* surveys.
- ☐ Complete the annual *District UPDATE* survey (required to maintain NNPS membership) to assess the quality of the district's partnership program.
- ☐ Assist schools to use the evaluation tools including the Annual Evaluation of Activities (pp. 330–341 and *Handbook* CD) and the Annual Review of Team Processes (p. 112 and CD) to continually improve their partnership programs.

OTHER DISTRICT ACTIVITIES TO DOCUMENT PROGRESS AND EVALUATE OUTCOMES

- ☐ ______________________________
- ☐ ______________________________

DISTRICT LEADERSHIP ROLES

FOR SCHOOL, FAMILY, AND COMMUNITY PARTNERSHIPS

Conduct some or all of the following to strengthen district partnership programs:

1. **WRITE A POLICY** that identifies district goals for partnerships, applies the six types of involvement, and recognizes the need for schools to take a team approach in developing partnership programs. Specify the district's commitments to assist schools in implementing the policy. Review and revise the policy periodically, with parent input.
2. **ASSIGN A LEADER FOR PARTNERSHIPS** to oversee the district's work on family and community involvement and to guide all schools' with their work on partnerships. In large districts, the leader will require a staff of facilitators for partnerships. (One facilitator can assist up to 30 schools in developing their partnership programs.)
3. **WRITE A LEADERSHIP ACTION PLAN FOR PARTNERSHIPS** that lists and schedules district leadership activities and direct assistance to schools.
4. **IDENTIFY A BUDGET WITH ADEQUATE FUNDS** for staff salaries and program costs. This may include funds for workshops for schools' Action Teams for Partnerships, small grants for school projects, strategies for sharing best practices, and other activities.
5. **GUIDE EACH SCHOOL TO FORM AN ACTION TEAM FOR PARTNERSHIPS (ATP)** consisting of teachers, parents, administrators, and others who will plan, implement, and evaluate the school's partnership program. The ATP, a committee of the School Council or School Improvement Team, bases plans for partnerships on school improvement goals.
6. **PROVIDE INSERVICE EDUCATION** for teachers, parents, and administrators, and conduct training workshops for schools' action teams for partnerships. Each ATP will write an annual One-Year Action Plan for Partnerships to involve all families in their children's education, linked to school improvement goals.
7. **CONDUCT AN END-OF-YEAR CELEBRATION WORKSHOP** for action teams to share best practices, discuss progress, solve problems, and plan ahead. District leaders also should recognize excellent programs and practices.
8. **DEVELOP OR SELECT TOOLS AND PRODUCTS** that schools may use or adapt to improve their partnership programs.
9. **ESTABLISH A DISTRICT WEB SITE, LIBRARY, NEWSLETTER COLUMN,** and/or other communications to disseminate materials, research, resources, and other information that will help schools' action teams improve their partnership programs. Share information on partnerships with the public and media.
10. **WORK WITH BUSINESSES AND OTHER COMMUNITY GROUPS AND ORGANIZATIONS** on partnerships to improve the curriculum and programs for students and to assist families.
11. **SUPPORT RESEARCH AND EVALUATION** to learn which practices help schools produce specific results for students, parents, teachers, the school, and the community. Organize an accountability system to document and monitor all schools' progress on partnerships.
12. **CONDUCT OTHER DISTRICT LEADERSHIP ACTIVITIES** to build strong and permanent programs of partnership at the district level and in all schools.

DISTRICT LEADERSHIP CHECKLIST

Steps in Developing Excellent Programs of School, Family, and Community Partnerships

This list helps district leaders take basic steps to establish a program of school, family, and community partnerships at the district level and in all schools.

CHECK ☑ WHEN YOU HAVE COMPLETED THE FOLLOWING:

- ☐ **Develop or periodically review a district policy on school, family, and community partnerships.**
- ☐ **Identify the district goals for school improvement and student success that would benefit from family and community involvement.**
- ☐ **Write an annual district Leadership Action Plan for Partnerships that identifies strategies, activities, timelines, and persons responsible for accomplishing specific family and community involvement activities.**
- ☐ **Secure a budget to implement the planned partnership activities.**
- ☐ **Enlist schools to participate in the district's partnership initiative. Create a local network with ties to the National Network of Partnership Schools (NNPS) at Johns Hopkins University.**
- ☐ **Conduct staff development for district colleagues and initial team-training workshops for schools' Action Teams for Partnerships.**
- ☐ **Facilitate the work of each school's Action Team for Partnerships on a regular schedule to help school-based programs succeed.**
- ☐ **Establish procedures and select tools to evaluate the quality and results of the district and schools' partnership programs.**
- ☐ **Celebrate end-of-year successes and help schools share best practices.**
- ☐ **Convene periodic meetings with leaders from other district departments who work on various aspects of family and community involvement to share ideas and to discuss new directions.**
- ☐ **Disseminate information about the district's work and schools' progress on partnerships to the media, educators throughout the district, and families.**
- ☐ **Outline strategies for sustaining the district's partnership program in the event of changes in leadership.**

SAMPLE: DISTRICT LEADERSHIP ACTION PLAN FOR SCHOOL, FAMILY, AND COMMUNITY PARTNERSHIPS

GOAL 1. Promote a comprehensive definition of school, family, and community partnerships.

Leadership and facilitation strategies: Create awareness.
Align policy and program.

Target Audience: All school principals, teachers, other groups

SAMPLE ACTIVITIES

1. Send a letter on the district's policy, goals, and services on partnerships from the superintendent to all school principals.
2. Call attention to partnerships at each monthly district meeting of all principals.
3. Call attention to partnerships at each monthly school meeting with teachers.
4. Conduct periodic information sessions for school principals and district colleagues on approaches and progress on partnerships.

GOAL 2. Train school-based teams to develop and maintain goal-oriented partnership programs.

Leadership and facilitation strategies: Guide learning and program development.
Document progress and evaluate outcomes.

Target Audience: All elementary, middle, and high schools

SAMPLE ACTIVITIES

1. Provide an initial One-Day Team-Training Workshop for all schools' Action Teams for Partnerships (ATPs).
2. Award and monitor seed grants to schools' ATPs to support activities for specific school goals (e.g., family involvement with students on reading).
3. Provide on-site professional development and on-call technical assistance to advance the skills of all schools' ATPs in developing and evaluating their partnership programs.

GOAL 3. Serve as a resource and link for partnerships

Leadership and facilitation strategies: Share knowledge.
Celebrate milestones.

Target Audience: All schools in the district and other family and community groups and audiences

SAMPLE ACTIVITIES

1. Establish a Web site and resource library for information on partnerships to share with all schools.
2. Establish a database or knowledge bank to catalogue all family involvement activities in schools' Action Plans for Partnerships.
3. Conduct an end-of-year celebration and create Web files to share best practices among schools.
4. Contribute to district newsletter columns on plans and progress on partnerships.

For each goal, use one page of the Leadership Action Plan for Partnerships.

What Do Facilitators Do?

District level facilitators help schools set a course, stay on course, reach their goals, share ideas with each other, and continue their plans and programs of partnerships. They conduct some or all of the following activities.

- Help each school establish an Action Team for Partnerships (ATP).
- Provide training to ATPs to help them understand the framework of the six types of involvement and how to apply the framework to reach specific school improvement goals, such as improving attendance, achievement, behavior, and a school climate of partnership.
- Help ATPs use the framework to write One-Year Action Plans for Partnerships.
- Help schools' ATPs focus on meeting specific challenges to engage all families and to increase the success of their practices of partnership.
- Help schools' ATPs assess the results of their practices of partnership in activity-specific and annual evaluations.
- Meet with or contact ATP leaders and team members at least once a month.
- Conduct quarterly cluster meetings for small groups of ATP chairs or co-chairs to share best practices and to discuss problems and solutions.
- Meet with principals at the start of the school year to clarify the work of the facilitator and to discuss how the principal will support the work of the ATP.
- Conduct an end-of-year celebration with all schools' ATPs to share best practices, discuss and solve challenges, and continue planning.
- Conduct other activities that assist ATPs with their work, such as presentations to teachers, families, school improvement teams, or others.

Facilitators also conduct meetings and presentations with others in the district.

They may:

- Meet with district administrators to discuss their expectations for the program and for facilitators and to clarify how they will encourage principals to support the work of their schools' ATPs.
- Make presentations to groups of principals, administrators, the school board, other district leaders, parents, or other groups interested in improving partnerships.

Facilitators are essential for helping all schools in a district improve their partnership programs, reach all families, and continue to build knowledge and skills over time.

FACILITATORS' TASKS AT THE START OF THE SCHOOL YEAR

At each school:

- Schedule a meeting with each principal and the chair or co-chairs of the Action Team for Partnerships (ATP) to discuss the school's One-Year Action Plan for Partnerships, goals for family and community involvement, and how the facilitator can best assist the school.
- If invited to do so, present information on the district's program of school, family, and community partnerships at Back-to-School Nights and at other school meetings of the faculty, parent organization, school council, or other groups. Or, attend these meetings to support the chair or co-chairs of the ATP.

With the chair or co-chairs of each Action Team for Partnerships:

- Set a date for the first meeting of the full team.
- Check that the ATP replaced team members who left the school.
- Collect lists of contact information for members of the ATP and team and committee leaders, (pp. 107–108 and CD) and give copies to all ATP members.
- Review and discuss activities in the One-Year Action Plan for Partnerships, and check which activities are scheduled in the next two months.
- Discuss the responsibilities of team members and others to ensure that the planned activities will be well implemented and on schedule. Provide direct assistance as needed.
- Commend the ATP members for their service to the school.

In the district office:

- Meet with the director of school, family, and community partnerships or your immediate supervisor to discuss the year's partnership plans.
- If possible, attend and participate in the superintendent's meetings of principals, community and parent groups, or other groups.
- Contribute to the district newsletter with a column on school, family, and community partnerships. Include short reports of district level activities on partnerships and the work of schools' ATPs.
- If you are in the field visiting schools' ATPs, provide your supervisor (or staff) with your schedule so that you can be located.
- Provide a short, monthly report of activities and progress to your supervisor.
- Conduct other district leadership activities on school, family, and community partnerships (see What Do Facilitators Do?, p. 255 and CD).

States Lead and Succeed: An Inventory for Leadership on Partnerships

Joyce L. Epstein

State leaders for partnerships are working (1) to improve state level policies and actions and (2) to encourage and guide districts and schools in developing effective programs of family and community involvement. To reach these goals, state leaders must write and implement an annual Leadership Action Plan for Partnerships.

This inventory is organized around six leadership strategies: *create awareness, align program and policy, guide learning and program development, share knowledge, celebrate milestones,* and *document progress and evaluate outcomes.* The inventory outlines over 40 activities that state leaders may select for statewide initiatives on school, family, and community partnerships. The activities in this inventory are based on analyses of data from state leaders in NNPS over many years.[1, 2]

State leaders are *not* expected to implement all of the activities listed. They should, however, consider which ones to include or adapt in their plans and how to increase the quality of partnership programs at the state, district, and school levels.

Directions:

Check (✓) all activities that your office or colleagues in other departments conduct now.

Star (✶) the activities that you want to initiate in the future, as you develop your state's leadership on partnerships.

Add other activities that you conduct now or plan to conduct that are not listed in each section.

Use this information to write your office's Leadership Action Plan for Partnerships (pp. 264–266 and CD).

1. With input from state and organization leaders at the October 2007 Leadership Development Conference, Baltimore.
2. Also see pp. 248–251 and CD in Jansorn, N., & Epstein, J. L. (2008), *Lead and Succeed: An Inventory of District Leadership and Facilitation Strategies for Partnerships.* Baltimore: National Network of Partnership Schools.

Strategy: Create awareness. Actively promote the state's partnership program to all key stakeholders, including administrators, teachers, families, and community groups.

- ❒ Identify a state leadership core of colleagues who work on partnerships across departments. Convene periodic meetings of this interdepartmental group to discuss their various activities and the state's partnership agenda.
- ❒ Convene periodic one-on-one meeting with the state superintendent (designee or supervisor) to discuss goals for the state's partnership programs, initiatives, and progress.
- ❒ Conduct presentations to promote the state's partnership program for the state board of education, councils, committees, conferences, and other key leadership groups.
- ❒ Conduct awareness sessions for district superintendents and district leaders for partnerships, specifying the assistance that the state will provide to districts and schools.
- ❒ Post information on the state's Web site about the state's policies, recommendations, leaders, and actions for partnerships.
- ❒ Identify districts and schools that will participate in the state's partnership initiative.
- ❒ Attend professional development conferences with state colleagues and/or selected district leaders to gain knowledge and skills on partnership program development.
- ❒ Convene and build collaborative projects with business, industry, and community groups.
- ❒ Disseminate press releases, periodically, on the state's accomplishments on partnerships.

OTHER STATE ACTIVITIES TO CREATE AWARENESS

- ❒ ____________________
- ❒ ____________________

Strategy: Align program and policy. With support from state leaders, integrate the partnership program with other state policies, requirements, and procedures.

- ❒ Review, develop, or update state's policy on school, family, and community partnerships.
- ❒ Identify a budget and other resources to implement the state partnership program.
- ❒ Obtain approval and support from the state superintendent to inform and encourage districts and schools to strengthen research-based programs of family and community involvement linked to state goals for school improvement.
- ❒ Obtain approval for districts and schools to include plans for partnerships as official sections of or appendices to their annual School Improvement Plans.
- ❒ Develop a broad three- to five-year plan of state goals for partnerships and for how your office will scale up outreach on partnerships to include more districts and their schools over time.
- ❒ Write an annual state Leadership Action Plan for Partnerships with a detailed schedule of state level actions and activities to encourage districts and schools on partnerships. Include goals, strategies, activities, timelines, people responsible, budgets, and other resources.
- ❒ Establish a state advisory council or advisory group on state policies and practices for increasing and improving meaningful family and community involvement for student success.
- ❒ Develop strategies for the continuity of plans and actions in the event of changes in leaders.
- ❒ Work with colleges and universities to develop teaching and administrative courses or modules so that all educators are prepared to conduct effective programs of family and community involvement.

OTHER STATE LEVEL ACTIVITIES TO ALIGN PROGRAM AND POLICY

- ❒ ____________________
- ❒ ____________________

Strategy: Guide learning and program development. Organize, conduct, or support professional development activities to assist state colleagues and districts and schools in the state to develop and strengthen their partnership programs.

- ❒ Conduct or support periodic two-day training workshops for district leaders for partnerships who are ready to guide their schools in developing comprehensive partnership programs.
- ❒ With district leaders, conduct or support periodic one-day workshops for schools' Action Teams for Partnerships on developing effective programs linked to school goals for student success.
- ❒ Convene regularly scheduled meetings for district (or regional) leaders for partnerships to share ideas and experiences and to update knowledge on partnership topics.
- ❒ Develop and implement professional development workshops for teachers and school staff on partnerships. These may be conducted online, in district offices, or in other locations.
- ❒ Develop information and training opportunities for parents and for business and community leaders. These may be made available online, in district offices, or in other locations.
- ❒ Conduct annual state or regional conferences with workshops to help district leaders for partnerships and school teams share best practices and continue to increase knowledge and skills on partnerships.
- ❒ Develop or identify and test useful tools, products, or materials to guide districts and schools in developing their partnership programs.
- ❒ Award small grants to districts and schools as incentives to build their partnership programs using research-based approaches.

OTHER STATE ACTIVITIES TO GUIDE LEARNING AND PROGRAM DEVELOPMENT

- ❒ ______________________________
- ❒ ______________________________

Strategy: Share knowledge. Foster ongoing communications throughout the state department of education, with state partners, and with district leaders to increase knowledge about programs of school, family, and community partnerships.

- ❒ Facilitate regularly scheduled meetings with state colleagues across departments working on family involvement issues (e.g., special education, ESOL/bilingual education, Title I) to share work and progress.
- ❒ Coordinate SEA actions on federal (Title I) requirements for parental involvement, and guide districts to meet requirements for involvement in Section 1118 and other parts of the law.
- ❒ Disseminate a monthly e-mail, fax, or periodic newsletter to state colleagues and to district leaders for partnerships with important information, upcoming events, and highlights of work across the state on partnerships.
- ❒ Guide districts across the state to share information about district level and school-based partnership activities throughout the school year.
- ❒ Develop and maintain an informative Web site on the state's program and actions on school, family, and community partnerships.
- ❒ Write a regular column on partnership programs for the state's education newsletter.
- ❒ Work with business and industry to create flexible leave policies so that parents can volunteer and/or attend conferences with teachers at their children's schools.

OTHER STATE ACTIVITIES TO SHARE KNOWLEDGE

- ❒ ______________________________
- ❒ ______________________________

Strategy: Celebrate milestones. Recognize state, district, and school successes in partnership programs and practices, and disseminate information on the successes.

- ❒ Write an annual progress report on the state's partnership program to share with the superintendent, state board, and key stakeholders.
- ❒ Organize a recognition program to celebrate excellence in districts and schools on partnerships linked to school improvement goals. Spotlight these programs at the annual state conference on partnerships or at other meetings.
- ❒ Encourage district leaders to collect and disseminate best practices across their own schools.
- ❒ Collect, edit, and disseminate (in print or online) promising partnership practices from the districts and schools in the state.
- ❒ Create videos or CDs of especially successful partnership activities in districts and schools across the state to highlight on the state's Web site section on partnerships.
- ❒ Guide districts and schools to recognize and thank those who assist them in strengthening their partnership programs.
- ❒ Hold an appreciation breakfast or event for state partners who assist your office in implementing activities in the state's annual plan for partnerships.

OTHER STATE ACTIVITIES TO CELEBRATE MILESTONES

❒ ____

❒ ____

Strategy: Document progress and evaluate outcomes. Collect information to document your office's activities and progress in meeting state goals for partnerships. Guide districts and schools to document and evaluate progress in their partnership plans and programs.

- ❒ Establish procedures and identify tools (including those in this *Handbook)* to evaluate the quality and results of the state's work on partnerships and the programs in districts and schools.
- ❒ Collect district policies and annual district leadership plans for partnerships. Check these for compliance with federal and state requirements for district leadership and research-based approaches on partnerships.
- ❒ Use evaluation tools to improve and sustain plans for partnerships from year to year.
- ❒ Guide districts to establish viable recordkeeping systems to document their work and their schools' work on partnerships.
- ❒ Conduct or sponsor periodic surveys of district, school, and parent leaders on the quality of their partnership programs, needed improvements, and services needed from your office.
- ❒ Support research and evaluation to learn which structures, processes, and practices help districts improve leadership on partnerships and which practices enable schools to reach all families in ways that support student success.
- ❒ Complete the annual *State UPDATE* survey (required to maintain NNPS membership) to assess the quality of the state's work on partnerships and ways to improve.
- ❒ Guide districts and schools to complete the annual *UPDATE* survey (required to maintain NNPS membership) to assess the quality of their partnership programs and ways to improve.

OTHER STATE ACTIVITIES TO DOCUMENT PROGRESS AND EVALUATE OUTCOMES

❒ ____

❒ ____

STATE LEADERSHIP ROLES

FOR SCHOOL, FAMILY, AND COMMUNITY PARTNERSHIPS

Conduct some or all of the following to strengthen state partnership programs:

1. **WRITE A POLICY** that identifies state goals for school, family, and community partnerships, including all six types of involvement. Specify enactments to assist districts and schools to understand and implement the policy. Periodically review the policy with input from educators, families, and the public.
2. **IDENTIFY A DEPARTMENT AND DIRECTOR** for school, family, and community partnerships, with adequate staff and resources. This office will develop plans, take actions, and coordinate work on family and community involvement. The director for partnerships also will identify and periodically convene a leadership team of colleagues across departments to share their work on family and community involvement and to discuss next steps and new directions.
3. **WRITE A LEADERSHIP ACTION PLAN FOR PARTNERSHIPS** that lists and schedules actions to promote, increase, and support knowledge and skills for conducting effective partnerships at the state level and in districts and schools across the state.
4. **IDENTIFY A BUDGET WITH ADEQUATE FUNDS** for staff salaries and program costs. This may include funds for professional development, small grants for districts or schools, conferences to share best practices, evaluations, state advisory committee on partnerships, and other leadership activities.
5. **PROVIDE INSERVICE EDUCATION AND ANNUAL TRAINING WORKSHOPS** for district leaders across the state who are ready to build capacity on partnership program development. Workshops on partnerships also may be offered to schools' Action Teams for Partnerships and/or other educators or parents.
6. **CONDUCT END-OF-YEAR WORKSHOPS OR ANNUAL CONFERENCES** to celebrate and recognize excellence and to encourage statewide or regional exchanges of best practices and to discuss solutions to challenges of school, family, and community partnerships.
7. **DEVELOP OR SELECT TOOLS AND PRODUCTS** that districts and schools can use or adapt to improve their partnership programs. Help district leaders learn of available resources for improving district level and school-based partnership programs.
8. **ESTABLISH A WEB SITE, LIBRARY, NEWSLETTER, AND/OR OTHER COMMUNICATIONS** to disseminate effective practices, ideas, materials, research, and other information that will help districts and schools improve their partnership programs. Share information on partnerships with the public and the media.
9. **SUPPORT RESEARCH AND EVALUATION** to learn which practices contribute to specific results for students, parents, teachers, schools, and communities. This includes an accountability system to monitor progress in district leadership and school program development.
10. **WORK WITH STATE COLLEGES AND UNIVERSITIES** to set requirements for teaching and administrative credentials to prepare teachers and administrators to understand and conduct comprehensive programs of school, family, and community partnerships.
11. **WORK WITH BUSINESS AND INDUSTRY** to establish flexible leave policies so parents can attend conferences at their children's schools. Increase business-school partnerships and volunteer programs.
12. **CONDUCT OTHER STATE LEADERSHIP ACTIVITIES** to build strong and permanent programs at the state level and in all districts and school.

STATE LEADERSHIP CHECKLIST

Steps in Developing Excellent Programs of School, Family, and Community Partnerships

This list assumes that an office for partnerships has been identified and that a director or coordinator is ready to take basic, initial steps to advance programs of school, family, and community partnerships at the state level and with districts and their schools.

CHECK ☑ WHEN YOU HAVE COMPLETED THE FOLLOWING:

- ☐ **Develop or periodically review the state policy on school, family, and community partnerships.**
- ☐ **Write an annual state Leadership Action Plan for Partnerships that identifies strategies, time lines, and persons responsible for accomplishing specific family and community involvement activities. Focus on key state goals for expanding and improving partnership programs in districts and schools across the state.**
- ☐ **Secure a budget for staff salaries and for the planned partnership program activities.**
- ☐ **Identify and periodically convene meetings of interdepartmental leaders who are working on various aspects of family and community involvement to share their views and activities.**
- ☐ **Conduct professional development on partnerships with state colleagues, district leaders, and/or schools' Action Teams for Partnerships.**
- ☐ **Facilitate the work of districts and schools with a regular schedule of professional development workshops, conferences, or other activities to continually improve program quality.**
- ☐ **Establish procedures and select tools to periodically evaluate the quality and results of the state's partnership program and the quality and results of partnership programs in districts and schools.**
- ☐ **Celebrate successes at the end of each year, and help districts and schools share their best practices.**
- ☐ **Disseminate information about the state's work and districts' and schools' progress on partnerships to the media, state educators, and families.**
- ☐ **If the state joins the National Network of Partnership Schools (NNPS), report that connection to major policy and decision making groups in the state department of education, other state agencies, the business community, and districts and schools statewide.**
- ☐ **Outline strategies for program continuity in the event of changes in leadership.**
- ☐ **Develop and implement customized activities to advance research-based programs of school, family, and community partnerships throughout the state.**

SAMPLE: STATE LEADERSHIP ACTION PLAN FOR SCHOOL, FAMILY, AND COMMUNITY PARTNERSHIPS

GOAL 1. Promote a comprehensive definition of school, family, and community partnerships.

Target Audience: District, school, and community leaders

SAMPLE ACTIVITIES

1. Send letter on partnerships from the state superintendent to all district superintendents.
2. Review and update the state board's policy on partnerships.
3. Conduct a policy forum on partnerships with statewide representation.
4. Develop and distribute model policies for local boards of education.
5. Join and sustain membership in the National Network of Partnership Schools.

GOAL 2. Train district leaders to guide schools in developing effective partnership programs with all families

Target Audience: Urban districts and their schools; "Ready districts" and their schools.

SAMPLE ACTIVITIES

1. Provide training workshops for district leaders for partnerships.
2. Provide seed grants to the selected districts for their work with schools.
3. Conduct on-site technical assistance for the districts and assist district leaders with team training for their schools.
4. Provide information to the districts and schools on the state's resource library on partnerships and how to use it.
5. Collaborate with other organizations in the state to increase district leaders' knowledge and skills in working with schools on partnerships.

GOAL 3. Serve as a resource and link for partnerships

Target Audience: Other state agencies and organizations

SAMPLE ACTIVITIES

1. Establish and maintain a Web site with information on partnership program development and helpful resources.
2. Establish a database for tracking the dissemination of information.
3. Link with other organizations for training, presentations, and conferences.
4. Serve as a resource on partnerships for state department of education committees and other state agencies.
5. Publish a semiannual newsletter on partnerships to distribute statewide.

The authors thank the leadership team at the Connecticut State Department of Education for sharing their goals for state leadership on partnerships. These or other goals and activities should be outlined in detail in the Leadership Action Plan for Partnerships (pp. 264–266 and CD) or equivalent template.

DISTRICT LEADERSHIP ACTION PLAN FOR PARTNERSHIPS

Duplicate Pages for Additional Activities

DISTRICT:	LEADER FOR PARTNERSHIPS:	SCHOOL YEAR:
GOAL: **CONDUCT DISTRICT LEVEL LEADERSHIP ACTIVITIES on school, family, and community partnerships.**		BUDGET FOR THIS GOAL:

LEADERSHIP & FACILITATION STRATEGIES: CHECK THE STRATEGIES THAT ARE ADDRESSED BY THE PLANNED ACTIVITIES.

- ☐ **Create Awareness**
- ☐ **Align Program and Policy**
- ☐ **Guide Learning and Program Development**
- ☐ **Share Knowledge**
- ☐ **Celebrate Milestones**
- ☐ **Document Progress and Evaluate Outcomes**

ACTIVITIES	EXPECTED RESULTS	TIMELINE/ DATES	PERSON(S) RESPONSIBLE	COSTS SOURCES OF FUNDS AND RESOURCES	EVALUATION TOOLS

The planned activities will help this district fulfill

- ☐ **DISTRICT Policies**
- ☐ **Federal Requirements (Title I) (list)** __________
- ☐ **STATE Policies**
- ☐ **Other Policies, Recommendations (list)** __________

DISTRICT LEADERSHIP ACTION PLAN FOR PARTNERSHIPS

Duplicate Pages for Additional Activities

DISTRICT:	LEADER FOR PARTNERSHIPS:	SCHOOL YEAR:
GOAL: **<u>FACILITATE SCHOOLS</u> in developing comprehensive, school-based, goal-oriented programs of school, family, and community partnerships.**		BUDGET FOR THIS GOAL:

LEADERSHIP & FACILITATION STRATEGIES: CHECK THE STRATEGIES THAT ARE ADDRESSED BY THE PLANNED ACTIVITIES.

☐ **Create Awareness** ☐ **Align Program and Policy** ☐ **Guide Learning and Program Development**

☐ **Share Knowledge** ☐ **Celebrate Milestones** ☐ **Document Progress and Evaluate Outcomes**

ACTIVITIES	EXPECTED RESULTS	TIMELINE/ DATES	PERSON(S) RESPONSIBLE	COSTS SOURCES OF FUNDS AND RESOURCES	EVALUATION TOOLS

The planned activities will help this district fulfill

☐ **DISTRICT Policies** ☐ **Federal Requirements (Title I) (list)** ______________________

☐ **STATE Policies** ☐ **Other Policies, Recommendations (list)** ______________________

LEADERSHIP ACTION PLAN FOR PARTNERSHIPS
Template for State Departments of Education

Duplicate Pages for Each Goal and for Additional Activities

DISTRICT:	LEADER(s) FOR PARTNERSHIPS:	SCHOOL YEAR:
GOAL:		BUDGET FOR THIS GOAL:

LEADERSHIP & FACILITATION STRATEGIES: CHECK THE STRATEGIES THAT ARE ADDRESSED BY THE PLANNED ACTIVITIES.

☐ **Create Awareness** ☐ **Align Program and Policy** ☐ **Guide Learning and Program Development**

☐ **Share Knowledge** ☐ **Celebrate Milestones** ☐ **Document Progress and Evaluate Outcomes**

ACTIVITIES	EXPECTED RESULTS	TIMELINE/ DATES	PERSON(S) RESPONSIBLE	COSTS SOURCES OF FUNDS AND RESOURCES	EVALUATION TOOLS

NOTES:

Leadership and Facilitation Strategies for District and State Leaders of Partnerships

Research and fieldwork indicate that successful leaders conduct activities to organize strong partnership programs at the district and state levels *and* to facilitate the work of schools' Action Teams for Partnerships. Their efforts reflect six leadership strategies, briefly described below and detailed in the "lead and succeed" inventories in this chapter.

Create awareness. Actively promote district or state partnership programs to all key stakeholders, including teachers, administrators, families, businesses, and community groups.

Align program and policy. With support from district or state leaders, integrate the partnership plans and practices with official policies, requirements, and procedures.

Guide learning and program development. Organize, conduct, and support professional development workshops, conferences, and materials to assist district or state colleagues and schools strengthen their partnership programs.

Share knowledge. Foster ongoing communication throughout the district or state to increase knowledge about effective programs of school, family, and community partnerships and to share best practices.

Celebrate milestones. Recognize progress and excellence on partnerships at the school, district, and state levels.

Document progress and evaluate outcomes. Collect information to monitor and record activities and assess progress toward goals set in annual Leadership Action Plans for Partnerships. Help all districts and schools evaluate their practices and results of partnerships.

Sample Pledges, Compacts, or Contracts

Pledges, compacts, or contracts are symbolic agreements that formally recognize that students, families, teachers, and administrators must work together to help students succeed each year in school. The form, content, and wording of pledges must be appropriate for the elementary, middle, and high school levels. The items should reflect the developmental stages of the students, the organizational characteristics of the schools, and the situations of families.

Pledges, compacts, or contracts should include parallel forms for parents, students, teachers, and administrators. By signing parallel pledges, all signers become aware of their common goals, shared responsibilities, and personal commitments.

It helps to do the following:

- Use the term *pledge* instead of *compact* or *contract* to recognize the voluntary, good-faith nature of these commitments.
- Keep the list of commitments short and clear, including 5 to 10 items.
- Include a short cover letter signed by the principal that explains to students, families, and teachers that pledges are *part of* a comprehensive program of school, family, and community partnerships.
- Provide partners with copies of pledges they have signed.
- Implement school practices that enable parents, students, teachers, and administrators to fulfill the commitments in the pledges. For example, if parents are asked to communicate with the school, then the school must provide parents with clear information and easy avenues for contacting teachers, counselors, or administrators. If parents are asked to volunteer, then the school must establish an effective program to recruit, welcome, and train volunteers.
- Include an "open" item that students and families can insert to tailor the pledge to their own situations, interests, and needs. For example: Add one more pledge for partnerships that tells something you will do this year.
- Discuss the content of pledges annually with students, families, teachers, and others; obtain input, and revise as needed.
- Develop a full program of partnerships including the six types of involvement. Pledges are one of many Type 2–Communicating activities that strengthen school, family, and community connections.

The sample pledges in this section may be tailored to match your school's policies and goals for students and for partnerships. Topics for parallel pledges include student effort; behavior; attendance; communications from school-to-home and home-to-school; parent-teacher conferences; volunteers; homework; study habits; appropriate dress; and specific school improvement goals.

SCHOOL-FAMILY-COMMUNITY PARTNERSHIPS

PARENT PLEDGE

✓ I will help my child to do his or her best in school. I will encourage my child to work hard and cooperate with teachers and other students.

✓ I will send my child to school on time each day with a positive attitude about school. If my child is absent due to illness, I will see that the missed work is made up.

✓ I will read notices from the school and communicate with teachers or others about questions that I have about school programs or my child's progress. I will participate in parent-teacher-student conferences and other school events.

✓ I will check to see that my child completes homework that is assigned. I will encourage my child to discuss homework, classwork, report card grades, and academic goals with me.

✓ I will volunteer at school *or* at home to conduct activities that assist my child, the teacher, the class, the school, or the community. I will encourage my child to contribute her or his talents and time to home, school, and community.

SIGNATURE ______________________ **DATE** ____________________

Parent or Guardian

SCHOOL-FAMILY-COMMUNITY PARTNERSHIPS

STUDENT PLEDGE

✓ I will do my best in school. I will work hard and cooperate with my teachers and other students.

✓ I will attend school on time each day with a positive attitude about school. If I am absent due to illness, I will make up the classwork and homework that I missed.

✓ I will take notices home from school promptly and will deliver notes from home to my teacher. I will participate in parent-teacher-student conferences and inform my family about school activities and events.

✓ I will complete my homework assignments. I will discuss homework with my family to share what I am learning in class. I will discuss my report card grades and academic goals with my family.

✓ I will welcome volunteers to my school and work with parents or others who assist me, my classmates, my teacher, and my school. I will contribute my talents and time to my family, school, and community.

SIGNATURE ______________________ DATE ____________________

Student

SCHOOL-FAMILY-COMMUNITY PARTNERSHIPS

TEACHER PLEDGE

✓ I will help all of my students do their best in school. I will encourage each student to work hard, develop his or her talents, meet high expectations, and cooperate with teachers and students.

✓ I will come to school each day with a positive attitude about my students and their families and with well-prepared classroom lessons to assist student learning. I will help students and families understand and fulfill the school's attendance policies.

✓ I will communicate clearly and frequently so that all families understand school programs and their children's progress. I will enable families to contact me with questions about their children. I will conduct at least one parent-teacher-student conference with each family.

✓ I will use interactive homework that enables students to discuss and demonstrate skills at home that we are learning in class. I will guide families to monitor their children's homework and to discuss report card grades and academic goals with their children.

✓ I will arrange ways for parents and other volunteers to use their time and talents to assist my students at school, in my class, or at home. I will vary schedules to encourage families to attend events, assemblies, and celebrations at school.

SIGNATURE ______________________ DATE ____________________

Teacher

SCHOOL-FAMILY-COMMUNITY PARTNERSHIPS

ADMINISTRATOR PLEDGE

✓ I will encourage all students to do their best in school. I will encourage each student to work hard, develop his or her talents, meet high expectations, and cooperate with teachers, the school staff, and other students.

✓ I will come to school each day with a positive attitude about the faculty, students, and their families and communities. I also will help the faculty, families, and students understand, contribute to, and follow the school's attendance and other policies.

✓ I will communicate clearly and frequently so that all families understand the school's programs and their children's progress. I will encourage families to contact teachers and administrators with questions and ideas about their children and school programs. I also will support and assist teachers to conduct at least one parent-teacher-student conference with each family each year.

✓ I will assist teachers, families, and students to understand and discuss homework policies, report card grades, academic goals, and other activities that encourage family involvement in student learning.

✓ I will arrange ways for parents or other volunteers to use their time and talents to assist students and the school. I also will encourage families to attend events, assemblies, and celebrations at school.

✓ I will help establish a team of teachers, parents, and administrators to strengthen and sustain a comprehensive program of school, family, and community partnerships at this school.

SIGNATURE ______________________ **DATE** ____________________

Administrator

STANDARDS FOR EXCELLENT PARTNERSHIP PROGRAMS

- **Teamwork**
- **Leadership**
- **Plans for Action**
- **Implementation and Facilitation**
- **Evaluation**
- **Funding**
- **Support**
- **Network Connections**

Research shows that these essential elements contribute to high-quality partnership programs that improve from one year to the next. Each section of this *Handbook* helps schools, districts, state departments of education, and organizations meet these standards for excellent partnerships.

References to research on these elements are at www.partnershipschools.org in Research and Evaluation. Also see Success Stories for these elements in practice.

8

Implement Teachers Involve Parents in Schoolwork (TIPS)

This chapter presents background information and guidelines for two research-based approaches for increasing family involvement in students' education. These practical programs were designed, developed, tested, and evaluated to help educators systematically, productively, and more equitably involve families at home and in school to improve student learning.

TIPS Interactive Homework

Teachers Involve Parents in Schoolwork (TIPS) interactive homework enables teachers to design and use homework assignments to connect school and home on curriculum-related activities. TIPS activities guide students to share their work and ideas with a family partner. The assignments improve parents' understanding of what their children are learning and promote positive conversations about schoolwork at home. If well implemented, TIPS improves students' homework completion, subject-matter skills, and readiness for classwork.

In this chapter, the purposes of homework are outlined. Then, the goals and components of TIPS interactive homework in language arts, math, and science are discussed. Sample assignments are given for the elementary, middle, and high school grades. Steps for implementing TIPS interactive homework are explained.

The information in this chapter is supported by teacher manuals for the elementary and middle grades and a CD with over 600 prototype interactive homework assignments in math, science, and language arts (Epstein, Salinas, & Van Voorhis, 2001; Epstein & Van Voorhis, 2000; Van Voorhis & Epstein, 2002). A video, *How to Make Homework Meaningful by Involving Parents* (Association of Supervision and Curriculum Development, 2001), presents and supports the TIPS process. These resources may help district leaders for partnerships work with colleagues and specialists in curriculum and instruction to assist schools in developing a TIPS Interactive Homework program in one or more subjects. ATPs also may develop TIPS in one or more subjects for their own schools. For more information, visit www.partnershipschools.org and follow the links to TIPS Interactive Homework.

TIPS Volunteers in Social Studies and Art

Teachers Involve Parents in Schoolwork (TIPS) *Volunteers in Social Studies and Art* creates a corps of volunteers who discuss famous art prints with students in their social studies classes in the middle grades. The presentations integrate art and history, increase students' knowledge and appreciation of art, and ensure that volunteers assist teachers and students in productive ways in making interdisciplinary connections for student learning.

In this chapter, the rationale for and components of TIPS Volunteers in Social Studies and Art are explained along with steps for implementing this process. A sample presentation for da Vinci's *Mona Lisa* is included.

The information in this chapter is supported by a teacher/leader's manual, prototype lessons, workshops, and other resources that are listed as references. For additional information visit www.partnershipschools.org and follow the links to TIPS Social Studies and Art.

How to Implement Teachers Involve Parents in Schoolwork (TIPS) Processes

Interactive Homework and Volunteers in Social Studies and Art

Joyce L. Epstein and Frances L. Van Voorhis

There are two TIPS processes—one that increases family involvement *at home* on interactive homework assignments and one that increases involvement *at school with family members* as volunteers.

1. TIPS Interactive Homework

If enough studies show the same result, you begin to believe it. That is how it is with school, family, and community partnerships. Research is accumulating that shows that certain parent involvement practices improve student achievement, attitudes, homework, report card grades, and aspirations. Surveys of parents indicate that most families want to talk with, monitor, encourage, and guide their children as students, but many say they need more information from the schools about how to help their children at home.

Studies also demonstrate that when teachers guide parental involvement and interactions with students, more parents become involved in ways that benefit their children. For example, when teachers frequently use practices to involve families in reading, students gain more in reading than do similar students whose teachers do not involve families (Sheldon & Epstein, 2005). Similarly, students whose families are guided to be involved in math, science, and language arts with interactive homework improve homework completion, report card grades, and/or achievement test scores over time (Epstein, Simon, & Salinas, 1997; Epstein & Van Voorhis, 2001; Van Voorhis, 2001, 2003, 2004, 2008, under review). These and other studies suggest that there are important connections between parental involvement in particular subjects and student success in those subjects.

The findings also confirm the important roles teachers play in helping families become involved in schoolwork at home. When parents are assisted by the schools and teachers to become involved in specific subjects with their children at home, they become more aware of their children's education and interact with their children more. When students see that their parents and teachers are in contact, they are more likely to talk with someone at home about schoolwork and school decisions.

Students also need guidance about how to keep their families aware of and involved in the work they do in school. Over time, if TIPS activities are used on a regular schedule, students learn that their teachers want their families to know about what they are learning. The students also see that they can conduct conversations that help their parents participate in positive ways on homework.

Family Involvement at Home

Of all the types of family involvement in children's schooling, the one that parents most want to know about is how to help their own children at home. This request is at the top of parents' wish lists because they want to do what they can to help their children succeed in school. Yet, this type of involvement is the one that schools have the most difficulty organizing. It requires every teacher at every grade level to communicate with all families about how to interact with their children on learning activities at home.

All teachers can provide basic communications about their homework policies and, about what students will learn in each unit of work, and they can provide guidelines on monitoring and discussing schoolwork, homework, and students' questions and progress. There are some major misunderstandings about what it means for parents to "help with homework." To clarify, *all* homework is the *students'* homework; it is never work that parents do. In addition, parents should not be made to think that they are supposed to "teach" school subjects to their children. It is neither realistic nor possible for every parent to teach every subject at every grade level to children at all levels of ability. Rather, parents can be guided to help their children by motivating, encouraging, interacting, appreciating, and celebrating the children's work and ideas. There also are some strategies that guide students and their parents in productive interactions about the skills that students are learning in class.

To address the need to help parents create realistic and positive connections with their children on homework, researchers worked with teachers to design, implement, and test the process called *Teachers Involve Parents in Schoolwork (TIPS) interactive homework.* With TIPS, any teacher can help all families stay informed and involved in their children's learning activities at home. Designed to be used once a week on a regular schedule, TIPS interactive assignments require *students* to talk to someone at home about something interesting that they are learning in class.

TIPS helps solve some important problems with homework:

- TIPS enables all families to become involved, not just those who already know how to discuss math, science, or other subjects.
- TIPS makes homework the student's responsibility and does not ask parents to teach subjects or skills that they are not prepared to teach.
- TIPS asks students to share and enjoy their work, ideas, and progress with their families.
- TIPS allows families to comment and request other information from teachers in a section for home-to-school communication.

With TIPS, homework becomes a three-way partnership involving students, families, and teachers at the elementary, middle, or high school level. Families immediately recognize and appreciate the efforts of teachers to keep them informed and involved. The TIPS activities keep school on the agenda at home so that children know that their families believe schoolwork is important and worth talking about.

Teachers' Roles in Designing Homework

Designing homework is the teachers' responsibility, but many teachers report that they feel unprepared to design effective homework activities. Well-designed homework assignments should meet specific purposes to help teachers advance students' skills in specific subjects. Epstein identified ten broad purposes (or 10 Ps) of homework: *practice, preparation, participation, personal development, parent-teacher communications, parent-child connections, peer interactions, policy, public relations,* and *punishment* (Epstein, 2001; Epstein & Van Voorhis, 2001). All are valid purposes except punishment.

The purposes of homework serve instructional, communicative, and political functions (Van Voorhis, 2004). Each purpose yields different results for student learning and development, for parent information and involvement, and for teaching and administrative practice. The TIPS interactive homework process fulfills several purposes. Each assignment is designed to extend student learning time, provide students with opportunities to *practice* skills and *participate* actively in learning, help students *prepare* for the next day's lessons, increase *parent-teacher communications* about the curriculum, and improve *parent-child connections* on learning activities at home.

Overcoming Obstacles

Jump Hurdle 1: Homework Should NOT Always Be Done Alone

Some teachers believe that all homework should be completed in a quiet place, away from the family or other people. Its purpose is to allow students to practice what was taught in class, to study for a quiz, or to complete other work *on their own.* Although *some* homework is for these purposes, *other* homework should fulfill different goals. TIPS homework—assigned once a week or twice a month in math, science, or language arts—is designed to (a) keep teachers communicating with all families about the curriculum in selected subjects and (b) keep students and their families talking about schoolwork at home. More than quarterly report cards, lists of required skills, or occasional explanations for parents, TIPS brings school home on a regular schedule of homework that requires children to talk with their parents and other family partners.

Jump Hurdle 2: Just ANY Homework Won't Do

Some homework can be boring, requiring students' time but not much thinking. TIPS activities are designed to be challenging and engaging—homework that students will want to explain and share with their families. TIPS includes higher-level thinking skills and interactions with family members that make students think, write, gather information, collect suggestions, explain, demonstrate, draw, sketch or construct things, and conduct other interactive activities with parents and other family members at home.

Some students do not like or want to do *any* homework, though they will do their assignments if teachers make homework an important part of classwork and learning. Studies indicate that compared to "regular homework," more students

TEN PURPOSES OF HOMEWORK

Category	Purpose	Description
INSTRUCTIONAL PURPOSES	PRACTICE	Give each student an opportunity to demonstrate mastery of skills taught in class; review and strengthen skills; increase speed and confidence; maintain skills
	PREPARATION	Ensure readiness for the next class; complete activities and assignments that are not finished in class; gather ideas, suggestions, or materials for a new assignment
	PARTICIPATION	Increase each student's individual involvement in applying specific skills and knowledge and in enjoying learning
	PERSONAL DEVELOPMENT	Build each student's responsibility, perseverance, time management, self-confidence, and feelings of accomplishment; develop and recognize students' diverse talents and skills that may not be taught in class
COMMUNICATIVE PURPOSES	PARENT-CHILD CONNECTIONS	Establish communications between parent and child on the importance of schoolwork; encourage conversations on applying school skills to real-life situations; enable parent or family partner to engage in positive conversations about each student's ideas and assignments
	PARENT-TEACHER COMMUNICATIONS	Enable teachers to inform families and involve them in their children's curricular activities; keep families aware of topics that are taught in class, how their children are progressing, and how to support their children's work and progress at home
	PEER INTERACTIONS	Encourage students to work together on assignments or projects to motivate and learn from each other
POLITICAL PURPOSES	POLICY	Fulfill directives from administrators at the district or school levels for a prescribed amount of homework per day or week; increase attention to better designs of homework that tap into and build diverse skills
	PUBLIC RELATIONS	Demonstrate to the general public that a school has rigorous standards for student work in school and at home; establish a base for productive business and community partnerships for student learning
	~~PUNISHMENT~~	Correct problems in student conduct or productivity (not a valid or defensible purpose)

Sources: Epstein, 2001; Epstein & Van Voorhis, 2001; Van Voorhis, 2004.

complete TIPS, because it is interesting, attractive on a page, and makes students the leaders of the interactions at home.

What Are TIPS Interactive Homework Activities?

TIPS prototype activities are homework assignments that teachers can use or adapt to match their own curriculum and specific learning objectives for students. There are TIPS prototype activities in math for all elementary grades, science activities at the elementary level, activities in language arts and science for all middle grades, and math activities for the middle level. The examples can be adapted through a professional development process to all subjects and all school levels.

TIPS LANGUAGE ARTS provides a format for students to share skills in writing, reading, thinking, grammar, and related language arts activities. Students do the work—reading and writing, but students and parents enjoy thinking together, discussing, sharing, and exchanging ideas. Family members may listen to children read aloud what they have written, help students edit their writing or think about words, react to students' writing, and provide ideas, memories, their own experiences, and other interactions. TIPS Language Arts homework should be assigned on a regular schedule (once a week or twice a month) to keep families aware of and involved in students' work and progress in language arts.

Goals for TIPS Language Arts

- Encourage teachers to design homework that builds students' skills in reading, writing, speaking, and listening through communications with family partners.
- Guide students to conduct, discuss, and enjoy language arts activities at home.
- Enable parents to stay informed about their children's language arts work and progress.
- Encourage parents to communicate with teachers about their observations and questions concerning their children's homework and progress in language arts.

TIPS Format—Language Arts

1. **Letter to Parent, Guardian, or Family Partner** explains the purpose of the activity. The student writes in the due date and signs the letter.
2. **Objectives** explain the learning goal of the activity if this is not clear from the title and letter.
3. **Materials** are listed if more than paper and pen are needed. In writing activities, pre-writing gives the student space to plan a letter, essay, or story by outlining, brainstorming, listing, designing language nets and webs, or performing other planning activities.
4. **Interactions** guide students to interview someone for ideas or memories, read work aloud for reactions, edit their work based on responses, practice a

speech, take turns with others in giving ideas, conduct a survey, or carry out other interactions.

5. **Home-to-School Communication** invites a family partner to share comments and observations with the language arts teacher about whether the child understood the homework, whether they both enjoyed the activity, and whether the parent gained information about the student's work in language arts.

6. **Parent Signature** is requested on each activity.

TIPS MATH provides a format for students to share what they are learning about a specific math skill. The TIPS Math format allows students to show parents exactly how they learned a skill in class. Then, students complete other math activities and obtain reactions from parents. TIPS Math emphasizes the mastery of basic and advanced math skills. The activities may include related math games, extensions of skills, and finding examples of specific math skills in real life. TIPS Math homework should be assigned once a week to keep students and families talking about math at home on a regular schedule.

Goals for TIPS Math

- Illustrate clearly how the teacher taught the skill in class.
- Allow students to demonstrate, discuss, and celebrate their mastery of new math skills.
- Enable parents to stay informed about their children's math work.
- Encourage parents to communicate with teachers about their observations and questions concerning their children's homework and progress in math.

TIPS Format—Math

1. **Look This Over** shows an example of a skill that was taught in class and guides the student to explain the skill to a parent or family partner. The answer to this example is given at the top of the page.

2. **Now Try This** presents another example for the student to demonstrate how to do the particular skill, with the answer on the back of the page.

3. **Practice and More Practice** are regular homework problems for the student to master the skill. The teacher may change, simplify, or increase the number and difficulty of problems to meet the special needs of students.

4. **Let's Find Out or In the Real World** helps the student and family partner discover and discuss how the math skill is used at home or in common situations. Games or other interactions may be included to reinforce the math skill.

5. **Home-to-School Communication** invites the family partner to record an observation, comment, or question for the math teacher about the skill the student demonstrated.

6. **Parent Signature** is requested on each activity.

TIPS SCIENCE provides a format for students to conduct and discuss hands-on "home lab" or data collection activities related to the science topics they study in class. Some TIPS Science activities require students to discuss topics, gather reactions, or collect data from family members on issues of health and student development. The hands-on science activities help students and their families see that science topics are enjoyable, enriching, and part of everyday life.

In science, it is important that TIPS activities require only inexpensive or no-cost materials that are readily available at home. Special equipment, if it is needed, must be provided by the school to all students. TIPS Science activities include a brief letter to parents explaining the topic. Then, the activities outline objectives, materials, space for lab reports or data charts, challenges, discussion questions, conclusions, and home-to-school communications. TIPS Science homework should be assigned on a regular schedule (once a week or twice a month) to keep students and families discovering and talking about science at home.

Goals for TIPS Science

- Encourage teachers to introduce science topics in class and follow up with discussions or demonstrations after the TIPS interactive homework assignments are completed.
- Guide students to conduct and discuss science activities at home.
- Enable parents to stay informed about their children's science work and progress.
- Encourage parents to communicate with teachers about their observations and questions concerning their science homework and progress.

TIPS Format—Science

1. **Letter to Parent, Guardian, or Family Partner** briefly explains the topic and specific science skills involved in the activity. The student writes in the due date and signs the letter.
2. **Objectives** explain the learning goal(s) of the activity.
3. **Materials** are common, inexpensive, and available at home or easily obtained. If they are not, the school must provide the materials.
4. **Procedure** guides the students, step by step. Each assignment includes hands-on actions that require the student to think and act like a scientist. The teacher may change, simplify, or increase the difficulty of activities to meet the special needs of students.
5. **Lab Report** or **Data Chart** gives space for the student to report findings.
6. **Conclusions** guide the student to discuss results and real-world applications of science with family partners.
7. **Home-to-School Communication** invites the family partner to share comments and observations with science teachers about whether the child understood the homework, whether they both enjoyed the activity, and whether the family partner gained information about the student's work in science.
8. **Parent Signature** is requested on each activity.

Some TIPS prototype assignments may be useful and usable just as they are. But, because homework must match the teachers' own learning objectives and local curriculum, teachers must check to align assignments with the topics they teach. Assignments may be used or adapted, or new activities must be designed, with the TIPS examples as a guide. Teachers who see TIPS activities usually say, "I can do that!" It is, indeed, possible for every teacher in every grade level and every subject to design interactive homework for students to conduct with their families.

TIPS is not a canned program. Teachers should not distribute "someone else's homework" to their own students without a careful review process. See the section, below, on developing a TIPS program before adopting TIPS in schools and classrooms.

Goals for TIPS Interactive Homework

- Build students' confidence by requiring them to show their work, share ideas, gather reactions, interview parents, or conduct other interactions with a family partner.
- Link schoolwork with real-life situations.
- Help parents understand more about what their children are learning in school.
- Encourage parents and children to talk regularly about schoolwork and progress. Enable students to lead positive and productive conversations about their work.
- Enable parents and teachers to frequently communicate about children's work, progress, and problems.

Why Does the TIPS Process Work?

- Can be used with any text or curriculum
- Helps teachers organize homework into manageable, focused segments
- Emphasizes connections between school and home
- Involves the child as an active learner and guides students to share and demonstrate their skills to show parents what they are learning
- Offers opportunities to link homework to the real-world experiences of children and families
- Provides families with the information they ask for on how to help at home each year
- Emphasizes mastery of basic and advanced skills.

How Do You Develop and Implement TIPS Homework?

Teachers, administrators, district leaders for partnerships, or district leaders for curriculum and instruction may develop a TIPS program. There are seven basic steps:

1. Select the subject(s) for TIPS interactive homework.

Teachers and curriculum leaders should decide the subject(s) and grade level(s) for which the TIPS process will be used. A separate team of educators should be identified to organize, design, and guide the implementation of each TIPS subject at each grade level.

2. Select one skill for each week for TIPS assignments.

The team of teachers for each TIPS subject and grade level should consider the sequence of skills that are taught in each unit that they teach throughout the school year. Teachers should identify one skill or learning objective each week that would lend itself to enjoyable and useful student-parent interactions. These will be the topics for TIPS interactive homework assignments.

3. Select, adapt, or develop TIPS activities to match the curriculum.

Teachers should work together during summer vacation months to examine the existing TIPS manuals and prototype activities. Teachers must decide which of the available TIPS assignments will be useful to them for the skills they teach, which can be adapted to fit their curriculum, or what new interactive homework assignments must be written to match their learning objectives.

A point system may be added to new and existing TIPS assignments to help teachers mark and grade the homework. Each component of students' work should be assigned appropriate points, with all sections adding to 100 points for easy marking.

Two sections of TIPS assignments—the letter to parents and home-to-school communications—may be translated into the major languages families speak at home. Other sections for students' work should be in English or treated, linguistically, the same as other non–TIPS homework assignments.

4. Orient students and families to the TIPS interactive homework process.

Teachers must explain the TIPS process and purposes to students and to their parents or other family partners. This may be done in a letter home, in discussions with students in class, in presentations at parent meetings, or in other ways. Special attention is needed to inform and involve parents with limited reading proficiency or who speak languages other than English at home. Guidance is needed for students so they will involve family partners effectively, regardless of family culture or educational background.

5. Assign TIPS on a regular, family-friendly schedule.

Teachers assign TIPS activities to students weekly or every other week. Teachers give students several days or a weekend to complete each assignment to allow time for students to work with a family partner. Students follow directions in each assignment to share their skills and activities with their parents or another family partner.

6. Evaluate student work and respond to family questions.

Teachers grade TIPS activities just as they would any other homework assignment. Teachers also respond to the family feedback in the home-to-school communication section to encourage open channels of communication about students' needs and progress.

7. Revise and improve activities as needed.

Teachers should note any problems with particular sections of assignments throughout the year and revise activities or develop new activities as needed.

Research on TIPS indicates that a parent is the most common family partner. In an orientation session, teachers should acknowledge that students may interact with a parent, aunt, grandparent, older sibling, neighbor, tutor, or other relative or family friend. Because teachers typically give students more than one day to complete TIPS activities, most students will find a family partner with whom to interact. If, however, there is no family partner for a particular assignment, the student still must complete the homework independently, skipping the interactions. TIPS homework is not a novelty or option; it is assigned work that is the student's responsibility to complete.

The Importance of Teacher Collaboration in the TIPS Process

One way to develop TIPS in a particular subject is for a school or district to provide salaries for teams of teachers from each grade level to work together during the summer or vacation period. Support is needed for each teacher for from two to four weeks to develop, edit, and produce the TIPS homework that may be used by many other teachers throughout the school year.

TIPS homework must be enjoyable as well as challenging for students. This requires teachers to think carefully about the design of homework and about how to build in students' communications with parents or other family members. It helps for two or more teachers to work together discussing, writing, and editing the homework assignments. It also helps if this work is guided by a curriculum supervisor, department chair, assistant principal, master or lead teacher, school-family coordinator, or other individual who understands good curricular designs and the purposes of TIPS interactive homework.

TIPS homework designs may be shared with other teachers who follow the same curriculum objectives. The assignments selected or adapted from the TIPS CD or designed for the local curriculum should be saved in a computer file that can be shared with and adapted by other teachers in the school district that are teaching the same skills. Support for a few teachers to write and organize interactive homework during the summer, then, yields materials that can be used or adapted by many teachers for many years. The TIPS process is very cost effective.

How Do All Partners Participate in TIPS Homework?

Teachers, students, parents, and administrators all have responsibilities for the success of TIPS:

- **Teachers** design the homework assignments or select activities from existing TIPS assignments that match their classwork, orient parents to the process, explain TIPS and family involvement to students, conduct follow-up activities in class, and maintain homework records.
- **Students** complete the TIPS assignments and involve their parents or other family partners as directed in the activities.
- **Parents or family partners** learn about the TIPS process, set aside time each week to discuss TIPS homework activities with their children, and complete the home-to-school communications.

- **Principals** help teachers orient parents to the program and support and recognize teachers, students, and families who use TIPS well.

To introduce parents to TIPS, teachers may send letters, explain the TIPS process at parent-teacher conferences and meetings, and/or include an article in the school newsletter. Teachers may conduct classroom or grade level meetings to show parents examples of the TIPS activities and to discuss how parents should proceed when their children bring TIPS activities home. After the first TIPS assignment, teachers should call any parent whose student did not complete TIPS as intended to discuss the TIPS process with the parent and to encourage full participation.

Students must be oriented to the program and reminded about the importance of involving a family partner *each time* TIPS assignments are made. Teachers must reinforce that they want the student to talk with someone at home about the work and that they believe it is important for families to be aware of what children are learning in school.

How Do Teachers Evaluate TIPS Homework?

There are two main goals for TIPS:

1. To encourage students to complete their homework well and to improve attitudes, behaviors, and achievements
2. To create good information and interactions at home between students and their families about schoolwork

TIPS interactive homework comes with two built-in evaluations. First, students are expected to complete TIPS assignments just as they do any homework. Teachers grade, return, and discuss TIPS just as they do other homework. Second, every TIPS activity includes a section called "Home-to-School Communication" for parents to give observations and reactions to their children's work. This section asks parents to check whether their child understood the homework and was able to discuss it, whether the assignment was enjoyable for the parent and student at home, and whether the activity informed the parent about schoolwork in a particular subject. Teachers monitor parents' reactions and respond to questions with phone calls, notes, or e-mail messages.

When educators use TIPS, they must evaluate whether and how the process helps them reach their goals for homework completion and for school and family connections. Follow-up activities may be needed to learn whether students and parents need more information, explanations, or guidance to ensure that TIPS promotes positive interactions about schoolwork at home. Teachers may obtain information through discussions with students, informal interviews, phone calls, class or grade level meetings with parents, and formal surveys. Researchers have conducted formal evaluations of the effects of TIPS on parent involvement and student learning (Balli, Demo, & Wedman, 1998; Epstein, Simon, & Salinas, 1997; Epstein & Van Voorhis, 2001; Van Voorhis, 2003, under review). Surveys for parents and students on their reactions to and experiences with TIPS are available at www.partnershipschools.org in the section Publications and Products in a packet of TIPS Surveys.

How Do Parents, Students, and Teachers React to TIPS Homework?

One school using TIPS reported a parent's reaction: "When I see that yellow paper, I know that is important homework for my son to complete with me."

Interviews and surveys of parents, students, and teachers in the middle grades revealed overwhelmingly positive reactions. Parents said they get to talk about things with their children that they would otherwise not discuss. For example, when students worked on TIPS Language Arts, parents wrote,

- I can tell from Jenneaka relating the story to me that she really enjoyed reading it.
- Anthony is improving every day. I believe his report card will be better.
- This blue paper is a learning experience for me.
- Very interesting assignment. I enjoyed this and it brought back good memories.

When students worked on TIPS Science, parents wrote,

- We are still working on neatness.
- Althea's thought process was more mature than what I knew.
- I think she could have done a better job with the consequences.
- This opened up an easier way of communicating.

When students worked on TIPS Math in the elementary and middle grades, parents wrote,

- I like them—I can play like I don't get it, and then she explains it to me.
- I like the green sheets because sometimes I learned along with my child.
- I enjoyed doing the [math activities] with my child. The sheets were very self-explanatory and easy to follow.
- They were very good. (Teachers) should consider doing TIPS in other grades and in English and spelling.

Students said that they like TIPS because they do not have to copy the homework from the board, because it is not boring, and because they learn something from or about their parents or families that they did not know before. Most teachers reported that more children complete TIPS than other homework.

Sample TIPS Interactive Homework Activities

Four sample TIPS activities are on the pages that follow.

- TIPS activities are limited to two sides of one page. This keeps copy costs down and requires teachers to focus their attention on the quality of questions rather than on quantity.
- TIPS activities are clear and attractive. Computer graphics should be added, where relevant.

- TIPS activities should be reproduced on light-colored paper to help students and families identify and enjoy the activities. For example, a math teacher assigning TIPS weekly may choose to copy each assignment on blue paper. Then, students and families will look for the "blue homework" each week.

Other sample TIPS activities, templates, and information are at www.partnershipschools.org in the TIPS section.

Subject	Grade Level	Title	Topic
TIPS Math	Elementary	Fractional Parts	Identifying fractions
TIPS Math	Middle grades	I Mean It	Finding averages
TIPS Language Arts	Middle grades	Hairy Tales	Improving writing skills
TIPS Science	Middle grades	On Your Mark, Get Set, Go!	Understanding viscosity

TIPS MATH-ELEMENTARY GRADES

Name ______________________________ **Date** __________

Fractional Parts

Dear Parent/Family Partner,

Let me show you what we learned in math. I hope you enjoy this activity with me.
This assignment is due ______________.

Sincerely,

____

Student's signature

I. LOOK THIS OVER: Explain this to your family partner.
Who is your family partner? ____________________

Sample: What part of the shape is shaded?

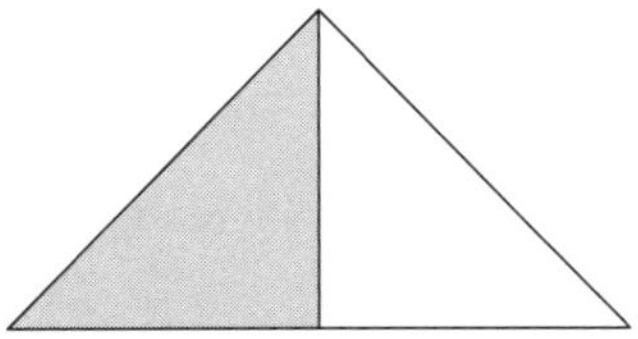

Count the parts: **2 parts**

How many are shaded? **1 part**

1 part out of 2 parts = $\frac{1}{2}$ **part out of parts**

Answer: $\frac{1}{2}$ **of the shape is shaded.**

II. NOW, TRY THIS: Show your family partner how you do this example.

Example: What part of the shape is shaded?

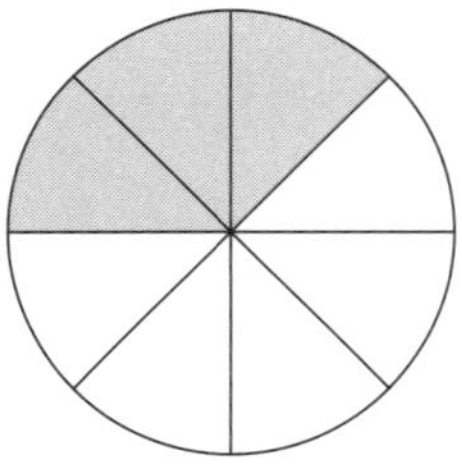

Count the parts :

How many are shaded?

Answer: ______________________________

If you need some help, ask your family partner to go over the example with you.
When you understand the work, explain what you did.

III. PRACTICE SECTION: Complete these examples on your own. Show your work.
Explain one example to your family partner.

What part of each shape is shaded?

1.

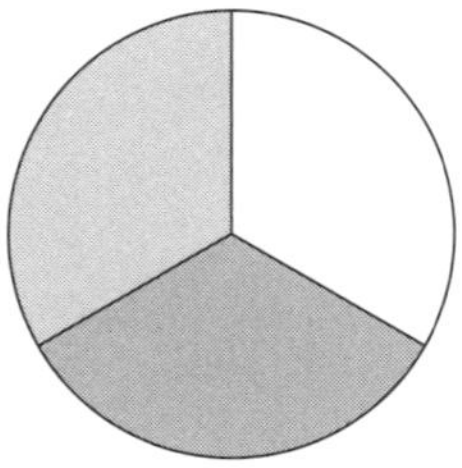

Answer: ______________________

2.

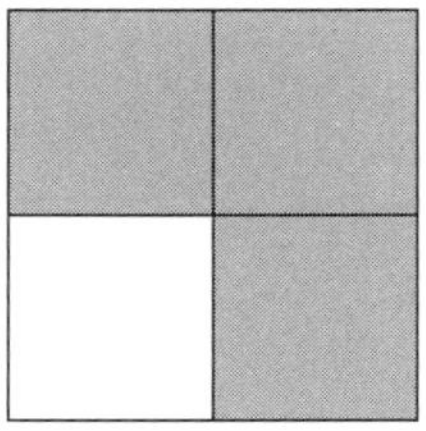

Answer: ______________________

MORE PRACTICE

What part of each shape is shaded?

3.

Answer: ____________________

4.

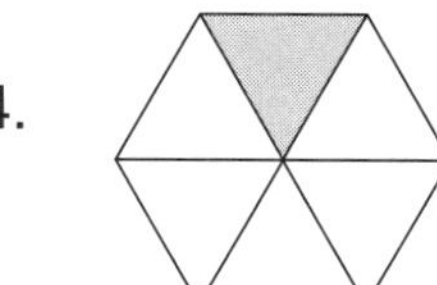

Answer: ____________________

5.

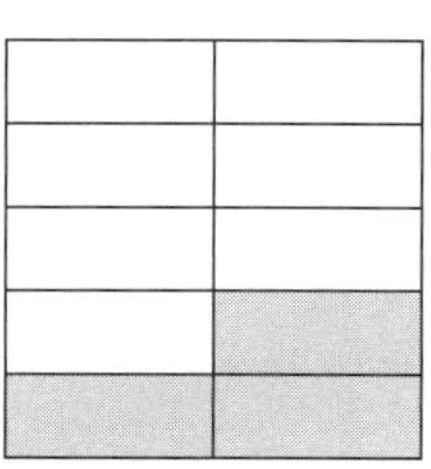

Answer: ____________________

6. (Create a shape of your own.)

Answer: ____________________

Discussion: 1)With a family partner, look over the examples you finished and **tell what fractional parts are <u>NOT</u> SHADED.**

2) Ask a family partner: **When do you use fractions at home?**

____

ANSWER TO NOW TRY THIS

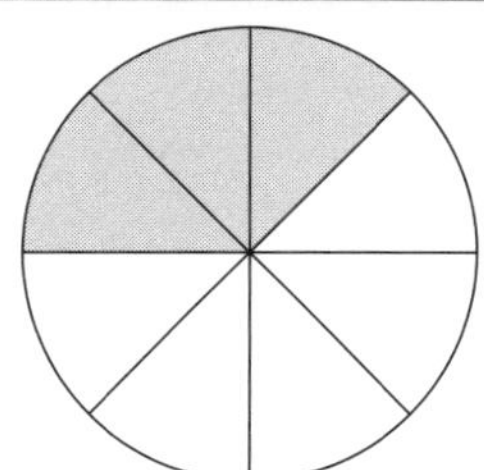

Count the parts: **8 parts**

How many are shaded? **3 parts**

3 part out of 8 parts = $\frac{3}{8}$ **part out of parts**

Answer: $\frac{3}{8}$ **of the shape is shaded.**

IV. HOME-TO-SCHOOL COMMUNICATION:

Dear Parent/Family Partner,

Please share your reactions to your child's work on this activity.

____ **O.K.** My child seems to understand this skill

____ **Please Check.** My child needed some help on this, but seems to understand.

____ **Please Help.** My child still needs instruction on this skill.

____ **Please Note.** (Other comments) ______________________________

____

Parent's signature: ______________________________________

Epstein, J. L., Salinas, K. C., & Van Voorhis, F. L. (2001). *Teachers Involve Parents in Schoolwork (TIPS) Interactive Homework for the Elementary Grades* (Rev ed.). Baltimore: Johns Hopkins University, Center on School, Family, and Community Partnerships.

TIPS MATH-MIDDLE GRADES

Name: ______________________________ **Date:** ______________________________

I MEAN IT!

Dear Parent/Family Partner,
In math we are learning how to find the average of a set of numbers.
I hope you enjoy this activity with me. This assignment is due ______________________.

Sincerely,

____
Student's signature

LOOK THIS OVER **Explain this example to your family partner.**

Remember: To find the average (or **mean**) for a set of data:

(1) add all of the data,
(2) divide by the number of pieces of data (items), and
(3) round to the nearest whole number if necessary.

Data: 4, 9, 5, 6, 11
Add: 4 + 9 + 5 + 6 + 11 = 35
5 pieces of data
Divide the sum by the number of items: 35 ÷ **5** = 7
The average (or mean) is 7.

NOW TRY THIS **Show your family partner how you do this example.**

Data: 7, 13, 23, 3, 17, 9, 12
Add:

Divide the sum by the number of items:
The average (**Mean**) is ______.

PRACTICE SECTION **Gather information with a family partner and find the averages on your own. Show your work. Then, explain one example to your family partner.**

1. List the ages of all of your family members and find the mean age.

Data:
Add:
Divide by Number of Items:
Average (**Mean**) = Is your age close to the mean? __________

2. Find the mean shoe size for your family (round all half sizes up).

Data:
Add:
Divide by Number of Items:
Average (**Mean**) = Is your own shoe size close to the mean? ___

IN THE REAL WORLD

People use averages or **means** to report survey results.
Poll four of your family members or friends. Try to include at least one family partner.
ASK: How many hours each day do you work?
How many hours each day do you sleep? Fill in this chart:

Names of people you surveyed	Number of hours at work or at school each day	Number of hours of sleep each day
	AVERAGE =	AVERAGE =

Find the average (mean) amount of time the people you selected spend on each activity.

WORK SPACE

Explain your results to a family partner. **Discuss with your family partner:** Would I find the same means if I surveyed only friends my own age? Why or why not?

____

____

ANSWER TO NOW TRY THIS

Add = 7 + 13 + 23 + 3 + 17 + 9 + 12 = **84**
Divide the sum by the number of items: 84 ÷ 7 = **12**
Average (**Mean**) = **12**

HOME-TO-SCHOOL COMMUNICATION

Dear Parent/Family Partner,

Please share your reactions to your child's work on this activity.

Write YES or NO for each statement.

________ 1. My child understood the homework and was able to complete it.
________ 2. My child and I enjoyed the activity.
________ 3. This assignment helped me know what my child is learning in math.

Other comments: ____

Parent's Signature: ____

Epstein, J. L., Salinas, K. C., & Van Voorhis, F. L. (2001). *Teachers Involve Parents in Schoolwork (TIPS) Interactive Homework for the Elementary Grades* (Rev ed.). Baltimore: Johns Hopkins University, Center on School, Family, and Community Partnerships.

LANGUAGE ARTS-MIDDLE GRADES

Name: ______________________________ **Date:** ______________________

HAIRY TALES FROM THE PAST

Dear Parent/ Family Partner,
We are writing clear explanations. In this assignment, I will collect good information from you. I hope you enjoy this activity with me. This assignment is due ________________.

Sincerely,

____
Student's Signature

PROCEDURE

1. **Family Interview. Who are you interviewing?** ______________________________
   Ask:

   a. In what decade were you born? (1960s, 1970s, etc.) ______________________

   b. When you were my age, what hairstyles were popular . . .

      for boys? ______________________________

      ____

      for girls? ______________________________

      ____

   c. What hairstyle did you wear at my age? ______________________________

   d. Did your parents agree with your choice of hairstyle? ______________________

      Why or why not? ______________________________

   e. Which of today's hairstyles do you like most, and why? ______________________

      ____

   f. Which of today's hairstyles do you dislike most, and why? ______________________

      ____

   Ask your family partner for a photograph with a hairstyle from the past. OR, draw a favorite hairstyle he or she wore at your age.

2. Now, write an explanatory paragraph based on the answers to your interview. You may write about hairstyles of the past or compare past and present hairstyles.

THINGS TO REMEMBER

1. **Give your paragraph a title.**
2. **If you compare or contrast things, tell how they are alike and how they are different.**
3. **Indent the first sentence of the paragraph.**
4. **Be sure all of your sentences relate to your main idea.**
5. **Use descriptive words to make your writing interesting.**

Title: ____

____

____

____

____

____

____

____

____

____

____

____

3. **Read your paragraph aloud to your family partner.** Fix any sentences that are unclear.

4. **Select another topic to compare past and present**—e.g., styles of clothes, types of music, ways to have fun, rules at home, or a topic that you are curious about when your family partner was your age. Which topic did you choose?

   ____

   Write **3 questions (Q)** on this topic and **interview** your family partner for the **answers (A)**.

   1. Q: ____

   A: ____

   2. Q: ____

   A: ____

   3. Q: ____

   A: ____

   Bring these to class for further discussion and writing.

HOME-TO-SCHOOL COMMUNICATION

Dear Parent/Family Partner,
Please share your reactions to your child's work on this activity.

Write YES or NO for each statement.

_________ 1. My child understood the homework and was able to discuss it.

_________ 2. My child and I enjoyed the activity.

_________ 3. This assignment helped me know what my child is learning in language arts.

Other comments: ____

Signature: ____

Epstein, J. L., Salinas, K. C., & Van Voorhis, F. L. (2001). *Teachers Involve Parents in Schoolwork (TIPS) Interactive Homework for the Elementary Grades* (Rev ed.). Baltimore: Johns Hopkins University, Center on School, Family, and Community Partnerships.

TIPS SCIENCE-MIDDLE GRADES

Name: ______________________________ **Date:**______________________

ON YOUR MARK, GET SET, GO!

Dear Parent/Family Partner,

In science we are studying the phases of matter. This activity focuses on liquids to help build skills in observingand recording data, and drawing conclusions. I hope you enjoy this activity with me. This activity is due ____________________.

Sincerely,

____
Student's Signature

OBJECTIVE To understand **viscosity—**a liquid's resistance to **flow**.

MATERIALS ONE TEASPOON of **4 liquids** that have different thicknesses—such as ketchup, mustard, water, syrup, honey, milk, or others that your family partner will allow you to use; a baking pan; teaspoon; a clock or watch that shows the seconds or someone to count seconds.

PROCEDURE

1. Explain the following to a family partner to share what we are learning in class:
Who is working with you? ______________________________

   Some liquids are thicker and **more viscous** than others. They **flow slowly**.
   Some liquids are thin and **less viscous** than others. They **flow quickly**.

2. With your family partner decide: **Which 4 liquids will you test?**

   a. ______________________ c. ______________________

   b. ______________________ d. ______________________

3. Tilt the pan and prop it up against something like a phone book or against another pan so that it is at an angle (between 45 degrees and 60 degrees). At about what angle is your pan tilted?

   ____

   Make sure the pan remains tilted at the same angle throughout the experiment.
   Identify a "starting line" at the top of the pan and a "finish line" at the bottom.
   One of you will put each liquid in the pan The other will serve as the timer.
   You can switch roles to check each other to get an accurate observation.
   When you are ready with all of the materials, follow these directions.

   a. Place one teaspoon of liquid at the "starting line" at the top of your pan.
   b. Time the seconds it takes for the liquid to reach the "finish line" at the bottom of the pan.
   c. Record the information in the Data Chart.
   d. Continue to test each teaspoon of liquid in turn. Make sure that you start each liquid at the same level at the top of the pan, but at least one inch away from the previous liquid.

DATA CHART

LIQUID	SECONDS TO "FINISH" LINE	OBSERVATION HOW VISCOUS IS IT?
______	______	______
______	______	______
______	______	______
______	______	______

CONCLUSIONS

1. **Which liquid finished:**

   first (fastest) ______

   midway ______

   last (slowest) ______

2. Which liquid has **high viscosity?** ______

3. Which liquid has **low viscosity?** ______

4. Why was it important that your pan remained at the same angle for all tests?

______

FAMILY SURVEY. ASK: Can you think of any foods or other products that use **viscosity (how fast or slow the flow)** as part of the advertising to get you to buy it?

Family partner's idea ______

My idea ______

Why is high viscosity (slow flow) a good feature (or a bad feature) of a product you use?

______

Why is low viscosity (quick flow) a good feature (or a bad feature) of a product you use?

______

HOME-TO-SCHOOL COMMUNICATION

Dear Parent/Family Partner:
Please share your reactions to your child's work on this activity.

Write YES or NO for each statement.

______ 1. My child understood the homework and was able to discuss it.

______ 2. My child and I enjoyed the activity.

______ 3. This assignment helped me know what my child is learning in science.

Other comments: ______

Signature: ______

Epstein, J. L., Salinas, K. C., & Van Voorhis, F. L. (2001). *Teachers Involve Parents in Schoolwork (TIPS) Interactive Homework for the Elementary Grades* (Rev ed.). Baltimore: Johns Hopkins University, Center on School, Family, and Community Partnerships.

2. TIPS Volunteers in Social Studies and Art

Family Involvement at School

A second TIPS process—Teachers Involve Parents in Schoolwork (TIPS) Volunteers in Social Studies and Art—addresses the problem of organizing productive volunteers. The process establishes a teacher-volunteer partnership to enrich the social studies curriculum for all students.

The TIPS Volunteers in Social Studies and Art process integrates art with social studies in the middle grades. The process brings volunteers (parents, other family members, or members of the community) to the school on a regular schedule to introduce artists and art work to students in their social studies classes. When students study American history, for example, they see and learn about American artists; world history is linked to the work of artists from around the world; government and citizen participation is linked to artwork on themes of government and citizenship.

How Does TIPS Volunteers in Social Studies and Art Work?

Volunteers introduce a new art print to students each month from October to May. Over three middle grades (e.g., 6–8 or 7–9) students are introduced to the work of at least 24 artists with different styles, media, and topics who lived at different times and places in history.

Presentations by parents or other volunteers on each art print require only 20 minutes of class time each month. Each presentation includes information on the artist's life, style and technique, the specific artwork, connections to social studies, and topics for class discussion, writing, and artwork. Discussions include anecdotes and interesting information about the artist and artwork that should interest middle grades students. Time is allotted in each presentation for students' reactions, likes and dislikes, thoughts, and questions about the art and artists. Research for the presentations may be conducted by parents who cannot volunteer at school but who want to contribute time and ideas to improve school programs.

Why Implement TIPS Volunteers in Social Studies and Art?

TIPS Volunteers in Social Studies and Art is designed to increase connections of art with history, geography, and issues of importance in society. The TIPS process helps solve three common problems in the middle grades: the need for integrated or interdisciplinary curricula, the need for more productive parent volunteers, and the need for students to learn something about art as an important part of cultural literacy.

Designed for the middle grades, the process is adaptable to other grade levels, other social studies units, and other subjects (e.g., art or music may be linked to English or literature, foreign language classes, or other subjects).

Prototype presentations in American History (14 artists), World Cultures (14 artists), and Government and Citizen Participation (12 artists) are available, along with a manual that outlines how to organize, implement, and evaluate TIPS Volunteers in Social Studies and Art. The prototype presentations were designed by parents and other volunteers in partnership with teachers and researchers, tested by middle grades teachers, and evaluated by researchers (Epstein & Dauber, 1995). The manual includes prototype worksheets for students to use on field trips to art museums, sample quizzes to assess students' knowledge and reactions to the program, and questionnaires for teachers and volunteers about the program.

How Do You Implement TIPS Volunteers in Social Studies and Art?

The implementation process follows 10 clear steps.

1. Select a teacher-coordinator or teacher co-coordinators. This may be the chair of the social studies department, a team leader, or a social studies teacher who is committed to implementing an interdisciplinary program and who supports family and community volunteers. The teacher may be a member of the Action Team for Partnerships or a designated leader for this program.
2. Select a parent-coordinator or parent co-coordinators. This person will coordinate the schedules of the parents or other volunteers and help train the volunteers. The assistant or parent co-coordinator will assume leadership for the volunteers in the next school year. The parent may be a member of the Action Team for Partnerships or a designated leader for this program.
3. Order the prints that fit the social studies curriculum at each grade level. Prints, dry mounted and laminated, may be ordered at a reasonable price from Shorewood Fine Art Reproductions/New York Graphics Society. Mailing address: Art Beats, 130 Scott Road, Waterbury, CT 06705. A catalogue of art prints, an art reference guide, and an art biographies guide can be ordered. These references will enable teachers and volunteers to select the prints for the school's social studies units. Telephone: (800) 677–6947. Fax: (203) 757–5526. Download order form at www.nygs.com.

   Shorewood's and other art reproduction collections also are online at www.liebermans.net. Click on Publishers We Carry and Shorewood Fine Arts for the museum collection.

   Order enough prints for monthly rotations among participating teachers. For example, a school with up to eight social studies teachers per grade level who teach different units in Grades 6, 7, and 8, will need at least 8 prints per grade level to rotate over eight months of the school year, for a total of 24 art prints. (Schools with more than eight social studies teachers per grade level will need more prints or more copies of the prints for the grade level units for monthly rotations.) If the prints are dry mounted and laminated, they will last for several years, making this a thrifty investment in art appreciation.
4. Select the art prints to be presented and discussed each month by the volunteers for each grade level.

5. Recruit volunteers to make classroom presentations once a month from October to May. (Year-round schools must adjust the schedule to fit their needs.)
6. Train the volunteers so they are comfortable about making presentations to students in their assigned social studies class(es). The manual for TIPS Volunteers in Social Studies and Art describes, in detail, how to conduct the orientation session for volunteers in about an hour. The manual and prototype presentations are available at www.partnershipschools.org in the TIPS section, under Resources.
7. Schedule monthly presentations at times that are mutually convenient for the volunteers and the teachers. Volunteers will meet with the same class or classes each month.
8. Check in. Parent coordinators will check in with volunteers after the first visit and periodically through the year to see that the program is working as planned.
9. Evaluate results. Teachers will evaluate the program to determine if students gain knowledge of the artists and artwork and develop an understanding and appreciation of art. Sample end-of-unit tests for students are included in the manual.
10. Make necessary improvements in implementing the program, training volunteers, monitoring results, replacing prints as needed, and continue the program. These steps run smoothly as the parent-coordinators and teacher-coordinators become familiar with their roles and as the volunteers and teachers work together.

Sample TIPS Social Studies and Art Presentation

This section illustrates a sample TIPS Social Studies and Art presentation on the painting *Mona Lisa* by Leonardo da Vinci in the World Cultures series. All prototype presentations include information on the artist's life, style of painting, and characteristics or stories of the painting. Also included are suggestions for tying the print to social studies lessons, other prints, and other school subjects. Finally, all prototypes present ideas for art experiences and writing across the curriculum that teachers may use to supplement the volunteers' presentations.

ARTIST: Leonardo da Vinci (1452–1519)

PAINTING: Mona Lisa, also called La Giaconda

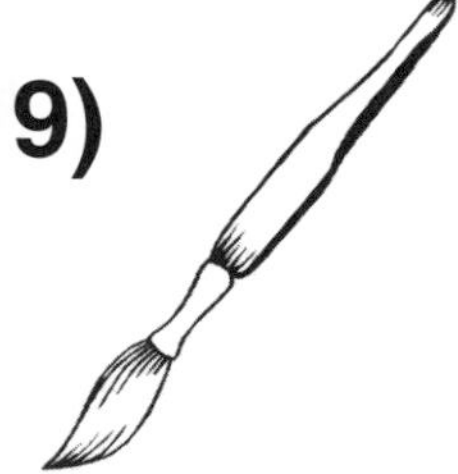

PERSONAL

Leonardo da Vinci was born in 1452. He was Leonardo from Vinci—the city where he was born—or, in Italian, Leonardo da Vinci.

He received art training in Florence—a city in Italy famous for art. For 17 years, he worked at the Court of Milan.

Da Vinci was talented in many ways. The King of France once said, "No man knows more than Da Vinci." Although primarily a painter, he was also a scientist, musician, inventor, engineer, mathematician, architect, and writer.

Today, we call a person who has many abilities a "Renaissance man or woman." Da Vinci lived during the Renaissance, an age of genius, new ideas, new ways of thinking, and exploration. With his many talents, he really was a Renaissance man.

STYLE

Leonardo da Vinci believed that in order to paint objects or people, an artist had to understand their structure—how they are formed or put together. He was able to study things and understand them clearly. He figured out and drew diagrams to explain how birds fly several centuries before slow motion cameras showed the same ideas.

Da Vinci believed that an artist could show emotions in portraits. He did this with a technique called *sfumato* (sfū -mă -tō , meaning *smoke*) in which he painted a color that turned slowly from light to dark tones to give off a kind of misty glow or smoky mystery. He tried to paint portraits that showed emotions, not just a blank stare.

IN THIS PAINTING

The *Mona Lisa* is the most famous portrait in the world. In the *Mona Lisa*, Da Vinci painted an elegant woman gazing at you with a strangely calm yet haunting look. The mysterious quality of the portrait is achieved by the use of the technique of *sfumato*. You can see a three-dimensional quality that comes from the soft background that makes the horizon look very far away.

Da Vinci was so interested in perfect form that he painted some other woman's hands to go with the face of the *Mona Lisa.*

Notice the use of portrait and landscape together in the picture. This combination was one of Da Vinci's artistic inventions.

The smile of the *Mona Lisa* seems to glow from within. Is the smile in her mouth or in her eyes? Cover her mouth. Do you think her eyes are smiling?

Not long ago, some art historians proposed a new theory about the *Mona Lisa.* They believe that the *Mona Lisa* was really based on a self-portrait of Da Vinci. They looked under the paint with a type of x-ray machine and discovered lines and drawings *under* the picture you see. A computer researcher compared a self-portrait by Da Vinci with the painting and found that the eyes, hair, cheeks, nose, and famous smile were very similar. These lines and drawings supported the art historians' theory. Others insist she is Monna Lisa Gherardini del Giocando, the wife of an Italian nobleman.

The painting is so popular that officials of the Louvre Museum in Paris say that people even write letters and send New Year's greetings to "Madame Mona Lisa." About three million people visit the museum to see the Mona Lisa every year.

Some say that the Mona Lisa looks at you wherever you are standing. Test this in class with people who are in different parts of the room. Some people say, "She's very plain." Others say, "She has an interesting face." What do you think?

TYING THIS PRINT TO SOCIAL STUDIES UNITS

Columbus and other explorers were conducting their adventures around the world at the same time that Leonardo da Vinci was painting and inventing things in Italy. *Perspective painting* was invented, which allowed artists to control their view of the world much as explorers controlled their travels across oceans. It was an Age of Exploration in life and in art.

During the time Da Vinci painted, Italy was a collection of city-states, not a unified nation. A city-state was a small, self-contained political area—something like a big city or small country today. People pledged their allegiances and worked and paid taxes to the city-state in which they lived. Da Vinci's name shows the strong connections between the people and where they lived, as he was from Vinci.

In Da Vinci's time, educated people needed to learn how to read Latin and to understand and appreciate art and literature. Artists and their work became an important part of everyday life during the Renaissance.

A new class called the "middle class" was developing in addition to the classes of nobles and peasants. Members of the middle class began to earn enough money to purchase art. The increasing amounts of money available for purchasing art created more opportunities for artists.

Geography: Locate Italy and the cities of Milan and Florence.

TYING THIS PRINT TO OTHER SCHOOL SUBJECTS

Math: Da Vinci borrowed and used the shape of the pyramid from his knowledge of math to give strength to his paintings. Ask the students where they "see" a pyramid form in the picture (e.g., the shape of the head and shoulders of Mona Lisa).

Advertising: The Mona Lisa has been used as a trademark for Spanish olive oil, Italian hair pins, a restaurant in Berlin, Germany, called The Smile, computer companies, and many other businesses.

TYING THIS PRINT TO OTHER PRINTS

Compare the *Mona Lisa* with other portraits—for example, Gainsborough's *Blue Boy.* What does Da Vinci do differently from later artists? How do the different pictures make the viewer feel? Which print conveys deeper emotion? Which print do you like more and why?

WHERE YOU CAN SEE ORIGINAL WORK BY DA VINCI

The National Gallery of Art in Washington, D.C., has a portrait called *Ginevra de Benci,* which is the only original painting by Da Vinci in a U.S. museum. It was purchased for five million dollars in 1967.

The *Mona Lisa* is in the Louvre in Paris, but many galleries in the United States have copies of it.

Check local museums and galleries for original art or reproductions by Leonardo da Vinci.

Art Experiences

1. Choose one color crayon or pencil and draw a square. Use the crayon to fill the square with color going very slowly from light to dark. Start at the bottom of the square with very, very light color and gradually get darker and darker as you reach the top of the square. Does the color "glow"? This is called *sfumato* (sfū -mă -tō, meaning *smoke*).

2. Da Vinci liked to sketch almost anything he saw in order to learn from his drawings. He sketched buildings, animals, hands, trees, rocks, inventions, and even knots of rope to learn about shape, line, light, and shadow. His notebooks, filled with sketches, became famous. (Students may be able to locate the notebooks or books about them in a public library.) Pick a common object in school, at home, or outside to sketch. Try to sketch the same object 3 or 4 times to see what you learn about its form by drawing it from different angles.

3. Draw a portrait of yourself or another person that shows emotion.

Writing

Across the Curriculum

1. The *Mona Lisa* is probably the world's best-known and most famous portrait. It may be the most famous painting in the world. Why do you think people like this painting? What does the painting "say" to you?

2. You may see the *Mona Lisa* today. For example, some commercials for modern products have used the *Mona Lisa* in their advertisements. Why would a company do this (e.g., to connect the product with a "masterpiece," to connect the product with the world's definition of "beautiful" or "mysterious")? What product would you link with the *Mona Lisa* and why? Draw your advertisement to show how you would use the *Mona Lisa* to sell a product.

3. Write a paragraph that tells how a portrait that is drawn or painted is different from a photograph.

4. Write a paragraph explaining why you think art is important in your education. Can someone be "educated" without understanding and having an appreciation for art?

How Do You Get Started With TIPS Interactive Homework or TIPS Volunteers?

Professional development tools and materials are available to help district leaders, principals, and teachers understand and implement the TIPS processes. Manuals for interactive homework, prototype homework assignments on a CD for the elementary and middle grades, PowerPoint presentations, and workshop materials for developing a TIPS interactive homework program are disseminated by Johns Hopkins University's Center on School, Family, and Community Partnerships. For details and order forms see www.partnershipschools.org and the TIPS section.

A videotape produced by the Association for Supervision and Curriculum Development (ASCD), *How to Make Homework More Meaningful by Involving Parents,* features the TIPS interactive homework process in a middle grades school. See how the teachers developed the program and how TIPS works in the classroom and with students at home. Visit the ASCD Web site: www.ascd.org. Click on Videos and find the "How to . . . " Series, Tape 10, or search by the title of the video.

Manuals and packets of up to 40 prototype presentations for TIPS Social Studies and Art Volunteers for units on American History, World Cultures, and Government and Citizen Participation may be ordered at www.partnershipschools.org in the TIPS section.

References

Association of Supervision and Curriculum Development. (2001). *How to make homework more meaningful* [Video, How To: Tape 10]. Alexandria, VA: Author.

Balli, S. J., Demo, D. H., & Wedman, J. F. (1998). Family involvement with children's homework: An intervention in the middle grades. *Family Relations, 47,* 149–157.

Epstein, J. L. (2001). *School, family, and community partnerships: Preparing educators and improving schools.* Boulder, CO: Westview Press.

Epstein, J. L., & Dauber, S. L. (1995). Effects on students of an interdisciplinary program linking social studies, art, and family volunteers in the middle grades. *Journal of Early Adolescence, 15,*114–144.

Epstein, J. L., Salinas, K. C., & Van Voorhis, F. L. (2001). *Manuals for Teachers Involve Parents in Schoolwork (TIPS)* (Elementary grades math and science; middle grades language arts, science, and math, grades 6–8; and prototype interactive homework assignments). Baltimore: Johns Hopkins University, Center on School, Family, and Community Partnerships.

Epstein, J. L., Simon, B. S., & Salinas, K.C. (1997, September). Effects of Teachers Involve Parents in Schoolwork (TIPS) language arts interactive homework in the middle grades. *Phi Delta Kappa Research Bulletin, 18,* 1–4.

Epstein, J. L., & Van Voorhis, F. E. (2000). *Teachers Involve Parents in Schoolwork (TIPS) interactive homework workshop training materials.* Baltimore: Johns Hopkins University, Center on School, Family, and Community Partnerships.

Epstein, J. L., & Van Voorhis, F. L. (2001). More than minutes: Teachers' roles in designing homework. *Educational Psychologist, 36*(3), 181–193.

Sheldon, S. B., & Epstein, J. L. (2005). School programs of family and community involvement to support children's reading and literacy development across the grades. In J. Flood & P. Anders (Eds.), *Literacy development of students in urban schools: Research and policy* (pp. 107–138). Newark, DE: International Reading Association.

Van Voorhis, F. L. (2001). Interactive science homework: An experiment in home and school connections. *NASSP Bulletin, 85*(627), 20–32.

Van Voorhis, F. L. (2003). Interactive homework in middle school: Effects on family involvement and students' science achievement. *Journal of Educational Research, 96*(9), 323–339.

Van Voorhis, F. L. (2004). Reflecting on the homework ritual: Assignments and designs. *Theory Into Practice, 43,* 205–212.

Van Voorhis, F. L. (2008, April). *War or peace? A longitudinal study of family involvement in language arts homework in the middle grades.* Paper presented at the Annual Meeting of the American Educational Research Association, New York City.

Van Voorhis, F. L. (Under review). Adding families to the homework equation: A longitudinal study of family involvement and math achievement. Manuscript submitted for publication.

Van Voorhis, F. L., & Epstein, J. L. (2002). *Teachers involve parents in schoolwork: interactive homework CD.* Baltimore: Johns Hopkins University, Center on School, Family, and Community Partnerships. Includes over 500 prototype assignments in math (grades K-5 and middle grades review) and language arts and science (grades 6–8).

9

Evaluate Your Partnership Program

Educators know they *should* evaluate their programs and practices. They *want* to improve their programs every year. Many struggle, however, with *how* to feasibly evaluate programs of school, family, and community partnerships. As one district leader for partnerships explained, "Evaluation is our greatest challenge." Often this is because impossible questions are asked, untested measures are used, budgets for evaluation are low, and time for assessments is short.

As in the past, most districts and schools still evaluate family and community involvement activities by counting the *number* of parents attending events, business partners, volunteer hours, home visits, phone calls to and from parents, and making other tallies. These counts can be useful, but more pointed measures are needed to monitor the underlying structures and processes of program development.

This chapter provides clear guidelines and tools that any school, district, state, or organization can use to begin to assess the quality and progress of work on partnerships. An introductory article discusses how to think about evaluating a partnership program so that the questions posed match the goals that have been set for family and community involvement. In the article, we discuss the kinds of assessments that may be made, the questions that may be addressed in simple to complex evaluations, how to schedule evaluative activities throughout the school year, how district leaders can help schools evaluate their programs, and how to report results to various audiences. Educators will learn the important differences between evaluating the quality of program *implementation* and evaluating program *results.*

The chapter also includes two basic tools for school-based Action Teams for Partnerships (ATPs) to evaluate the quality of the design and implementation of their partnership programs. These tools are designed to address the goals that are set in schools' One-Year Action Plans for Partnerships (see Chapters 4 and 5). Other built-in planning and evaluation tools are listed in the introductory article, along with tools from other sources that can help schools, districts, states, and organizations evaluate the quality of key program components and to monitor progress over time.

Measure of School, Family, and Community Partnerships

This inventory helps an ATP assess how strongly and extensively the school focuses on various activities and approaches for the six types of involvement. The measure includes activities that show the school is working to meet key challenges to involve all families. Used annually, the *Measure of School, Family, and Community Partnerships* promotes insights and ideas about which practices to continue, improve, or add to the next One-Year Action Plan for Partnerships.

Annual Evaluation of Activities

Form G–Goals or Form T–Types

This form should be completed after each activity in the One-Year Action Plan for Partnerships is implemented. By the end of the year, the collection of ratings will help the ATP reflect on the quality, strengths, and outreach of each activity and on how to improve it if it is repeated in the next school year.

Evaluate Programs of Partnership: Critical Considerations

Joyce L. Epstein and Steven B. Sheldon

Educators are familiar with the saying, "What gets measured gets done." That is true for programs of school, family, and community partnerships, too. In order to keep improving family and community involvement, it is imperative to keep evaluating the quality of program plans, activities, and results.

Evaluations of family and community involvement include assessments of the quality and progress of the following:

1. Program development (e.g., teamwork, plans, collegial and district support for partnerships, links of plans to school goals for student success)
2. Outreach to families and the community (e.g., strategies to invite, communicate, and include all families and various community partners)
3. Results for parents (e.g., responses to communications, input, patterns of involvement by major racial, ethnic, and socioeconomic groups)
4. Results for schools (e.g., welcoming climate, safety of the school, family-friendly atmosphere, attitudes and participation in partnerships of teachers, principals)
5. Results for students (e.g., academic and nonacademic outcomes, social development, postsecondary education and career plans)
6. Improvements on all of the above from year to year and in extended longitudinal patterns

Each of these evaluation topics requires different methods and measures—some simple and some complex.

Many studies confirm that family involvement is important for student success. Research conducted with hundreds of schools and scores of districts indicates that when schools implement well-planned programs and practices, all families can be productively engaged in their children's education regardless of their racial, ethnic, socioeconomic, educational, and linguistic backgrounds (see Chapter 1). The research supports decisions by schools and districts to establish and sustain effective partnership programs. Although most educators cannot and need not duplicate complex and costly research studies, every school and district can and should evaluate the quality of its work and progress on family and community partnerships.

Research on partnership programs addresses questions such as, "What works? How do we know?" Educators may ask other pertinent evaluation questions, such as, "How well is *our* program of family and community involvement working *here*—for *our* students, parents, teachers, and schools?" Specifically, local evaluations of partnership programs may explore these questions:

- Which involvement activities are well planned and well implemented and engage parents in ways that promote student success?
- How many—and which—families feel welcomed and appreciated by the school?
- How many—and which—parents feel comfortable talking with teachers and sharing ideas with the school?

- Are more parents (indeed, all parents) involved in some ways every year?
- Which structures, processes, and practices of family and community involvement need to improve?

Evaluations focused on these and related questions should increase an understanding of how well partnership program goals and plans are implemented, of program accomplishments, and of needed next steps for developing a strong and sustainable program. These questions can be addressed in feasible and thrifty evaluations. The research-based tools and guidelines in this *Handbook* will help.

Tools for Program Evaluations

Assess school-based programs. At the school level, the annual One-Year Action Plan for Partnerships written by the Action Team for Partnerships (ATP) is the basis for useful evaluations. This tool outlines the goals of a partnership program and the specific activities that will be implemented to help reach the stated goals. Specific questions can be asked to assess the quality of a school's partnership program. At the very least, school teams and district leaders for partnerships need to know the answers to these questions:

- Is the ATP well organized and functioning efficiently?
- Does the One-Year Action Plan for Partnerships include activities that ensure a welcoming school climate? Are activities scheduled throughout the school year?
- Which families, at what grade levels and with which demographics, are involved in activities that support student success in academic subjects and in other nonacademic attitudes and behaviors?
- What results of the implemented activities are observed and documented?
- In the next school year, what should the ATP and others at the school do to improve specific practices and outreach to all parents (especially those who are not typically involved)?

Assess district and state programs. Similar questions must be asked about the quality and progress of leadership on partnerships at the district and state levels. A Leadership Action Plan for Partnerships is the basis for useful evaluations in districts and states. (See district and state level planning templates in Chapter 7.) Annual written plans should reflect a district's or state's official partnership policies, recommendations, and mission statements. District leaders identify clear goals for family and community involvement, write an annual Leadership Action Plan for Partnerships with actions for district level leadership, and assist all schools to develop their own school-based partnership programs and practices. Using tools in this and other chapters of the *Handbook*, leaders should be able to continually improve their own and their schools' partnership programs.

Evaluate the Quality of Implementation

Measure implementation first. There are logical steps for useful program evaluations. It is necessary, for example, to know that a program is "there" and at what level of quality *before* measuring its results. Thus, evaluations of family and community involvement must begin with measures of the quality of program *implementation.* There must be some measure of how well a program is being implemented (e.g., whether structures, processes, plans, and practices are in evidence) before asking questions about program results.

Measure quality over time. A moving picture is more informative than a snapshot. Although it is important to learn from immediate assessments, trend data on program quality over time are more informative than one-time measures. By writing annual plans for partnerships and by completing and collecting annual evaluations, educators and parents will better understand whether and how well a program is implemented and improved from year to year.

Include all partners in evaluations. The concept of "partnership" applies to all aspects of programs of family and community involvement, including evaluations. That is, all partners must participate in assessing program plans, actions, and results. This can be done in feasible ways by an ATP that includes educator, family, and community representatives and by participants in specific activities. However, members of the ATP should not be the only ones evaluating a partnership program. Periodically, all members of the school community should participate in program evaluations.

Parents and community members who are members of schools' ATPs will be involved in team meetings that are conducted to evaluate program quality. Other parents serve on school improvement teams, as PTA or PTO officers, and on other committees. They, too, should be involved in reviewing partnership program plans and actions.

Parents and community members who attend specific events (e.g., workshops, meetings, Family Nights) or who lead or participate in involvement actions (e.g., volunteers) should assess the organization and quality of the activities they experience.

All parents, not just those in leadership roles, should be invited, periodically, to evaluate school and district plans and practices of family and community involvement. Some schools and districts conduct annual surveys of parents to obtain opinions and ideas for district and school policies, programs, children's experiences, and parental involvement policies and activities. Because annual surveys require data collection, processing, and analyses, these activities may be conducted every two or three years, for budgetary reasons. Some use less costly strategies such as focus groups, forums, and interviews with diverse parents and community members to gather ideas for school improvement and for new directions for family and community involvement.

Each evaluation technique has pros and cons in terms of costs, time, participants included and excluded, kinds of data collected, and expertise needed to interpret the data. Schools and districts must decide which evaluations will be conducted to address questions of interest with the resources that are available.

Built-In Evaluations of Program Quality

There are "built-in" evaluations in this *Handbook* for district leaders and school teams to plan their programs and to assess the quality of program development, outreach to all families, and progress on these measures over time. The built-in evaluations begin with *Starting Points: An Inventory of Present Practices of School, Family, and Community Partnerships* (pp. 174–177). This information helps an ATP systematically catalogue the many partnership practices that are already being implemented but that might not have been visible to everyone.

Starting Points contributes to decisions about which practices should be sustained or improved in an initial One-Year Action Plan for Partnerships. Subsequent evaluations will, then, focus only on the activities that are planned and implemented, not on unrelated practices. Table 9.1 outlines tools in this *Handbook* and reasons to use them.

TABLE 9.1 "Built-In" Evaluation Tools in This *Handbook*

Use These Measures	*For These Purposes*	*How to Use*
Starting Points: An Inventory of Present Practices of School, Family, and Community Partnerships pp. 174–177 and CD	Help an ATP become familiar with the six types of involvement and take stock of family and community involvement activities that are presently conducted at the school. Show that the school is not starting from zero and already is working with the framework of six types of involvement. Enable an ATP to see how it can improve the school's partnership program with goal-linked activities and at different grade levels.	Use *Starting Points* as one of the first steps in planning a school's partnership program. Members of the ATP should complete the inventory together, as a group, to have the broadest knowledge of the practices occurring at the school.
Measure of School, Family, and Community Partnerships pp. 324–329 and CD	Help an ATP become familiar with and assess how well activities for all six types of involvement are working for the school as a whole. Provide a metric on which the implementation of each partnership activities might be rated.	Use the *Measure* to examine whether activities are rare or frequent and prevalent at all grade levels and in all classrooms to engage all families in many different ways. Use the *Measure* annually before the ATP writes the next One-Year Action Plan for Partnerships. Or, use it periodically to track progress in creating a welcoming school environment and full partnership program.
Annual Evaluation of Activities pp. 330–341 and CD	Help an ATP reflect on and rate the quality and outreach of each partnership practice after it is implemented. The comments and ratings accumulate over the year.	Use the collection of ratings and reflections on all implemented activities prior to writing the next One-Year Action Plan to determine which activities should be repeated, removed, added, or improved.
Annual Review of Team Processes p. 112 and CD	Help an ATP examine how well it organizes its work, leadership, meetings, and interactions. Help it identify where improvements in teamwork are needed.	Complete the *Review* annually, midyear, to make adjustments and improvements in how the ATP works as a whole team and in committees.
Lead and Succeed: An Inventory of District Leadership & Facilitation Strategies for Partnerships pp. 248–251 and CD	Help district and state leaders for partnerships take stock of how they are working on partnerships to *create awareness, align program and policy, guide learning and program development, share knowledge, celebrate milestones,* and *document progress and evaluate outcomes.*	Use these inventories annually to monitor progress and to improve leadership on partnerships.
States Lead and Succeed: An Inventory of Leadership on Partnerships pp. 257–260 and CD	Help district and state leaders for partnerships identify leadership activities that will facilitate the work of all schools in developing effective partnership programs with all students' families.	

Simple to Complex Evaluations

In addition to the built-in evaluations in this *Handbook,* districts and schools may conduct other assessments of their partnership programs. Table 9.2 outlines several ways to monitor programs and practices of school, family, and community partnerships, ranging from simple inexpensive strategies to more complex and costly studies. Of course, any evaluation that is conducted—simple or complex—should address clearly stated questions about the quality of a program or its results.

Simple evaluations can provide useful information. Sign-in sheets are appropriate for collecting evidence of whether an activity was well attended. Short exit evaluations that enable parents who attended a workshop to report whether the information was of value and to give ideas for improving future workshops are appropriate for collecting evidence about how well a workshop was designed and implemented. By monitoring activities in these simple ways, schools and districts can learn if more and different parents attend activities during the school year and if more attend when family supports such as child care, dinner, transportation, incentives, and other features are provided.

Simple assessments cannot, however, tell if the parents who attended a workshop or meeting altered their actions at home or if their children benefited. Questions about results require systematic contacts with parents after the events. These, too, may be simple or complex. A simple follow-up evaluation can be conducted with spot-check or random-sample phone calls or interviews with parents who attended a workshop or who received guidelines for involvement at home. Simple evaluations, generally, cannot provide causal evidence about the effect of a program or practice on parents or students. More and different resources are needed for complex pre- and post-workshop studies or comparisons of results for parents who did or did not attend specific workshops or receive information.

When districts and schools are reviewed for *compliance* with federal regulations for parental involvement (e.g., Title I), federal and state monitors usually ask for evidence that program components are being addressed. The monitor may be looking for simple assessments such as those represented by the acronym *SANE* for Sign-in sheets, Agendas, Notes, and Evaluations (an example used for Title I program reviews by the Maryland State Department of Education). Compliance may be approved with evidence of actions by a school board (e.g., passing a policy), district leaders (newsletters, Web site information), and school teams (written plans and documents showing that activities were implemented). The planning and evaluation forms in this *Handbook* provide ample evidence for federal and state monitors that goal-linked activities to inform and involve families were scheduled and conducted in ways that support student achievement success in school. In combination with examples of invitations, flyers, newsletters, Web site postings, sign-in sheets, exit evaluations, and other surveys and feedback forms, ATPs have many ways to show how their partnership programs are developing and improving.

Evaluating Results of Partnerships

Combined Effects. An ATP's One-Year Action Plan for Partnerships (Form G, see pp. 181–184) is based on goals in a school improvement plan. The planned activities for parent and community involvement are expected to contribute to the same goals that teachers, counselors, and administrators are working on with students. This approach to partnerships recognizes that, together, educators, parents, and

TABLE 9.2 Evaluating Partnership Programs and Practices

Purpose of Evaluation[1] (from Simple to Complex)	***NNPS and Site-Specific Tools***
• Assess the status of present partnership practices. Identify current activities and needed additions.	• *Starting Points* Inventory (pp. 174–177)
• Document and save partnership policies, plans, and other records.	• Folders and computer files (local decisions)
• Account for number who attend events/meetings.	• Sign-in sheets (local designs)
• Account for number who obtain information from events/meetings.	• Dissemination and distribution of activities (local designs)
• Evaluate reactions to activities and events (exit ratings).	• Workshop evaluation forms (pp. 191–192 or local designs)
• Gather input from parents in two-way communications	• Tear-offs in newsletters, exchanges on Web sites, e-lists, suggestion boxes, phone surveys (local designs)
• Evaluate the quality of each event as it is implemented.	• *Annual Evaluation of Activities* (pp. 330–341)
• Collect ratings, opinions, and ideas about the quality of programs and activities for the next year's One-Year Action Plan.	• Annual surveys of teachers, parents, and students in elementary, middle, and high schools (NNPS Web site) • Site-specific customer-satisfaction surveys, focus groups
• Celebrate and share successes, collect and disseminate excellent activities.	• *Promising Partnership Practices* (NNPS Web site) • District and state collections of best practices (local designs)
• Assess frequency of partnership practices; monitor progress in meeting key challenges for the six types of involvement.	• *Measure of School, Family, and Community Partnerships* (pp. 324–329)
• Measure specific components of partnership program implementation and chart progress over time.	• Annual *UPDATE* survey (NNPS Web site)
• Review and reflect on partnership program goals, activities, and progress to make decisions on the next One-Year Action Plan.	• Site-specific retreats or equivalent meetings • *Annual Review of Team Processes* (p. 112)
• Assess effects of family and community involvement on student outcomes (e.g., attendance, behavior, achievement in reading or other subjects, homework completion, credits earned, graduation rates, or other indicators of success in school).	• Studies of effects of partnerships on students or other partners with adequate samples, appropriate measures, and advanced statistical methods of analysis (NNPS Web site and local designs)
• Assess quality, progress, and/or equity of input and outcome indicators.	• Third party, external contracts with research and evaluation experts to study program qualities and results (local school, district, or state decisions)

1. These assessments were conducted by and with schools, districts, and states in the National Network of Partnership Schools (NNPS) to evaluate the quality and progress of their programs and the results of activities for family and community involvement.

community partners can boost students' attainment of important goals more than any one group can do alone. In assessing school improvement, then, progress in meeting specific goals may be attributed to the combined efforts of *all* partners, and failure reflects the need for *all* partners to review and improve their collaborations to support students' learning and development.

After it is clear that a program is "there," educators and their evaluation partners may assess the results of a partnership program. School ATPs will, first, focus on whether they have attained or are making progress toward the goals listed on the pages of the One-Year Action Plan for Partnerships. For example, one page of a plan may focus on involving families and the community to help students improve their reading or literacy skills. The goal may be stated as follows: "Improve students' reading achievement scores 10 percent over last year in Grades 3, 4, and 5." In this case, family and community involvement is one part of the school's complete focus on helping students improve in reading. If test scores increase, it will be due to teachers' work with students *and* to family and community involvement in reading.

Another page of the plan may have the goal, "Increase average daily attendance incrementally to 96 percent." The plan will include scheduled activities that involve parents and the community in helping more students attend school every day on time. The ATP will use the official rates of average daily attendance, chronic absence, on time arrival, class cutting, and related indicators to gauge the results of work by teachers, administrators, *and* family and community involvement. If attendance improves, it is interpreted as the result of the school's comprehensive focus on attendance, including partnerships.

Independent Results of Partnerships. Some schools, districts, and states want to extend their evaluations of partnership programs to isolate the *independent effects* of family and community involvement on students, parents, teachers, and the school. The question is as follows: Does parental involvement contribute measurably to specific goals (e.g., improve reading scores), *over and above* the work that teachers do with students? Similar questions may be framed to study the *value added* by family and community involvement to the attainment of specific goals for student academic, behavioral, or attitudinal success.

Studies of the independent results of partnerships require more sophisticated measures and research methods than evaluations of partnership program quality, outreach, or the combined results of components in comprehensive school improvement. Effects studies require well-specified research models, adequate samples, and appropriate longitudinal measures of inputs and outcomes.

For example, a research model may specify paths of influence as shown in Figure 9.1. This model requires measures of student, family, and school background factors (e.g., parents' education, language at home, socioeconomic status of students), district leaders' programs and actions, school-based implementations of partnership practices, parents' responses of involvement, and targeted student outcomes. Analyses could, then, explore questions such as:

- After accounting for background factors, does district leadership on partnerships affect the quality of implementation of schools' partnership programs? Outreach to families?
- Which paths in the model affect the number of parents who become involved?
- Does involvement in goal-linked activities boost students' skills or scores on theoretically linked outcomes (e.g., reading) over and above the students' scores on these measures in the prior school year?

Researchers have conducted studies examining some or all of these paths. (See references throughout Chapter 1 and see the Research and Evaluation section and List of Publications on the Web site www.partnershipschools.org.) Most schools and districts need assistance from their research and evaluation offices or from outside consultants to conduct effects studies.

FIGURE 9.1 Effects Model for Research on School, Family, and Community Partnerships

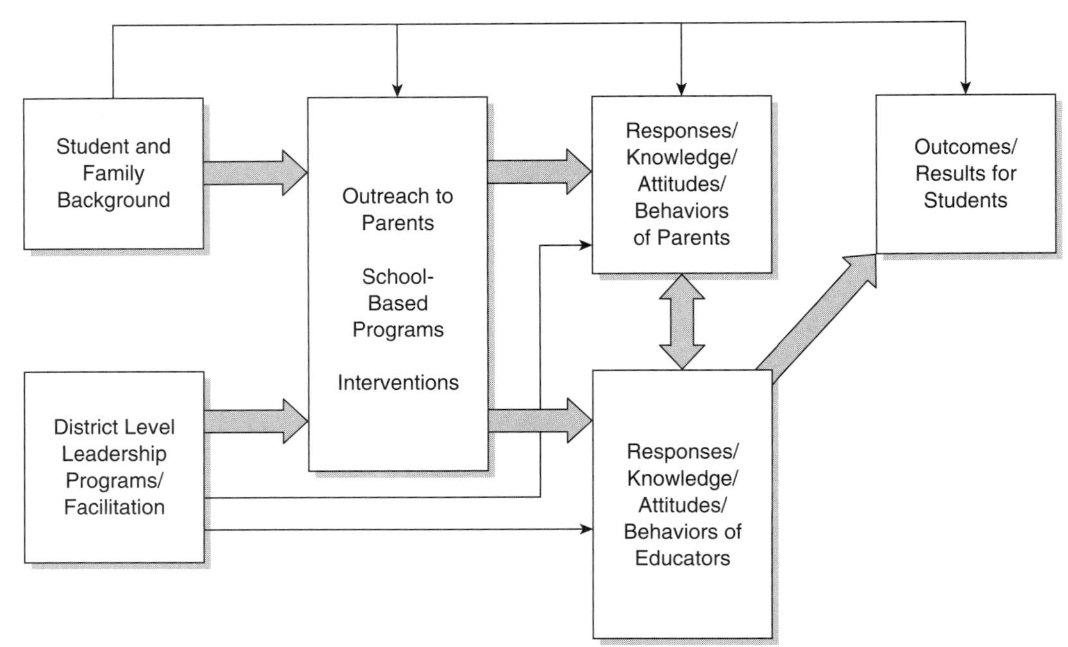

*Assume longitudinal paths that link these variables over time in multiyear measures.

A research model also may be translated into a theory-of-change (TOC) diagram. A theory of change describes the various steps of a program, how they are interconnected, and how they are expected to produce a long-term goal. The paths illustrate the expected connections between program activities, intervening steps and outcomes, and how interim outcomes contribute to desired long-term program results.

In Figure 9.1, for example, evaluators may operationalize "Outreach to Parents" by writing a One-Year Action Plan for Partnerships that schedules activities to involve families and the community in students' education. The entries in the written plan reflect TOC expectations that the selected activities will (a) improve parents' knowledge, attitudes, beliefs, and behaviors that support students' success in school and (b) improve educators' knowledge of families and willingness to collaborate with parents. If the activities for the six types of involvement are linked to goals and well implemented, the assumption is that more families and community partners will become involved with students in productive ways. In time, the TOC should produce measurable results on theoretically linked student outcomes of attendance, behavior, achievement, or other indicators of success in school. Developing a TOC diagram and rationale may be especially helpful at the beginning of an evaluation process to identify how planned actions are expected to affect the interim and long-term outcomes that will be evaluated.

Using Research Results as the Base for Other Evaluations

School and district leaders, increasingly, are seeking *research-based approaches* to improve school programs and practices, including family and community involvement. When research-based programs are implemented, educators can draw from the research studies that underlie the approaches and proceed with thoughtful and realistic on-site evaluations.

For example, in a study of TIPS interactive science homework, Van Voorhis (2003) statistically controlled students' prior science abilities, parents' education, and the amount of homework completed, and showed that students in TIPS classes had more parental involvement in science, higher grades, and more positive attitudes about science and homework than similar students in control classes, in which TIPS interactive homework was not used.

In that study, the researcher organized comparison groups and collected background data, implementation indicators, and multiple outcome measures, including students' science achievement test scores and short surveys from hundreds of parents and students. Now, districts and schools can use the research as the basis for decisions about whether to implement TIPS without having to conduct the same, complex study over and again.

Still, each district or school must evaluate and monitor how well any intervention works for *its* teachers, students, and families. TIPS, for example, includes built-in evaluations for teachers to monitor students' homework completion, accuracy, and responses from parents. Teachers also will monitor "regular" indicators, such as students' classwork, report cards, class test results, and achievement test scores to learn whether TIPS contributes to student success along with the teachers' lessons.

Make Time–Take Time to Evaluate

School teams and district leaders should schedule ATP meetings to complete evaluations at strategic points throughout the school year. Studies show that when ATPs take time to evaluate their programs, schools are more likely to improve the overall quality of their partnership program (Sheldon, 2007; Sheldon & Van Voorhis, 2004).

Similarly, research reveals that district leaders who evaluate their own and their schools' work on partnerships reported fewer obstacles to developing their programs, more collegial support, and higher-quality partnership programs over all (Epstein, 2007; Epstein, Galindo, Sheldon, & Williams, 2007; Sanders, 2008). The results indicate that when district leaders and school teams take their work on school, family, and community partnerships seriously enough to conduct evaluations, they are more likely to use the results to improve their plans and activities for the next school year.

Using the built-in tools and guidelines in this *Handbook,* ATPs and district leaders should schedule useful assessments throughout the year. The following schedule will ensure that schools' partnership programs are evaluated and that information is generated to help improve the next year's plans.

At the Start of a Program. ATPs must think about what will be evaluated when they plan their programs, not as an afterthought. The One-Year Action Plan for

Partnership requires ATPs to specify goals for partnerships and how progress will be measured on each page. By planning to evaluate the quality and progress of their programs and practices systematically, ATPs should be able to use the results of the assessments to improve their programs from year to year.

At Each ATP Meeting. ATPs should take 10 minutes at each monthly meeting to debrief and reflect on the quality of activities that were conducted in the past month. They can use the *Annual Evaluation of Activities* to discuss the strengths and weaknesses of each activity and use locally designed documents (e.g., sign-in sheets, exit evaluations) to inform the discussion.

At One ATP Meeting at the End of the Year. Schools should schedule one full ATP meeting toward the end of the school year to review the cumulative record of activities using the *Annual Evaluation of Activities.* This discussion will help ATPs decide which activities should be continued, removed, improved, or added in the next One-Year Action Plan for Partnerships. At the same or another full team meeting, ATPs can complete a *School UPDATE,* available from the National Network of Partnership Schools (NNPS) at Johns Hopkins University (see below). *UPDATE* includes scales and items on essential elements for partnership program development and will help ATPs strengthen the next Action Plan for Partnerships.

At One ATP Meeting on a Regular Schedule. Periodically (every year or every other year), ATPs should each assess their school's progress in meeting challenges to reach all families using the *Measure of School, Family, and Community Partnerships.* The responses indicate whether activities for the six types of involvement are prevalent at the school for families of students at all grade levels and inform discussions of whether more outreach is needed to involve particular groups of families.

At One ATP Meeting Midyear. ATPs should use the checklist, *Annual Review of Team Processes,* to discuss the quality of teamwork and how to work better together and with others at the school.

Well-organized ATPs take time to plan what they will evaluate and to conduct these basic evaluations to assess how their work is progressing and to improve their partnership plans and practices from one year to the next. It is important to make time to take time to evaluate the quality of these programs.

District Collections of School Evaluations

District leaders for partnerships not only guide schools to conduct the basic evaluations but also should collect schools' One-Year Action Plans for Partnerships and formal program evaluations (e.g., their *Annual Evaluations of Activities*). At one level, this information enables district leaders to assist each ATP in obtaining resources, implementing activities, and improving programs every year. District leaders can use these records to create simple charts that document schools' progress throughout the district. The information can, then, be summarized to report progress on family and community involvement to the superintendent or other administrators, school boards, and the public.

Other Measures

In addition to the tools in this *Handbook,* researchers at the Center on School, Family, and Community Partnerships at Johns Hopkins University make other measures available for simple and complex evaluations.

UPDATE Surveys of Partnership Program Development. Leaders for partnerships in schools, districts, and states can assess the development and progress of their partnership programs with an annual survey entitled *UPDATE,* developed by the NNPS at Johns Hopkins University. There are *UPDATE* surveys for schools, districts, states, and organizations with scales and items on essential elements that have been found to contribute to the quality of partnership programs. These include measures of *leadership, teamwork, written plans, implementation, funding, collegial support, evaluation,* and *networking.* By discussing and completing *UPDATE,* schools' Action Teams for Partnerships and education leaders at all policy levels can monitor progress and gain ideas for improving their next One-Year Action Plans for Partnerships. The most recent *UPDATEs* can be downloaded from the Web site of the NNPS at www.partnershipschools.org. Follow the links to NNPS Model, the policy level of interest, evaluation, and *UPDATE.*

Partnership Surveys of Parents, Teachers, and Students. Questionnaires for individual parents, teachers, and students in the elementary and middle grades and in high schools may be obtained from the Center on School, Family, and Community Partnerships at Johns Hopkins University. The surveys explore the perspectives, attitudes, experiences, interests, and suggestions of key partners in students' education. Table 9.3 shows the questionnaires and reliability reports that are available on the Web site, www.partnershipschools.org. Follow the links to Publications and Products and Surveys and Summaries. Many districts and schools want to conduct surveys, but must recognize that questionnaires require resources for printing, mailing, attention to return rates, and data processing. The survey packets include suggestions for simple summaries and descriptive reports. Other questions call for expertise in statistical analysis.

School Level Outcomes. Researchers at the Center on School, Family, and Community Partnerships at Johns Hopkins University developed another set of questionnaires called *Focus on Results* to study whether family and community involvement activities contributed to school level outcomes of student attendance, behavior, reading achievement, and math achievement. Pre- and post-indicators are available for individual schools to explore the nature of their goal-linked practices of partnerships and for district leaders to use across all schools for general and preliminary effects studies. Among the scales embedded in each of these surveys is a list of goal-oriented family and community involvement practices that a school might implement to improve specific student outcomes. For example, the *Focus on Reading Results* questionnaires could be used with an adequate sample of schools to learn if activities that involve parents and the community with children on reading are associated with changes in school level reading test scores from one year to the next. Similarly, *Focus on Behavior Results* questionnaires explore whether activities with parents and the community help reduce schools' disciplinary actions. For information about these questionnaires, visit the Web site, www.partnershipschools.org, and follow the links to Publications and Products and Surveys and Summaries, then Focus on Results and the outcome of interest.

TABLE 9.3 Surveys on School, Family, and Community Partnerships

Which Survey Should You Use?

Survey Title and Author	*Date*	*School Level*	*Measures*	*Features*
Parent Survey of Family and Community Involvement in the Elementary and Middle Grades Sheldon, S. B. & Epstein, J. L.	2007	Elementary and middle grades	**Parents' reports** of • School outreach to involve families • Attitude about the school • Present family involvement • Parents' responsibilities and skills (role construction and efficacy) • Social networks (with other parents and other adults) • Topics of conversation with other parents • Family demographics • Parents' comments	Information and Guidelines • Notes on administering the survey • Scales and reliabilities • CD included with electronic copies Spanish translation (electronic) on request
Student Survey of Family and Community Involvement in the Elementary and Middle Grades Sheldon, S. B., & Epstein, J. L.	2007	Elementary and middle grades	**Students' reports** of • Self confidence about school • Sense of belonging in school • Views of parental involvement • Present family involvement • School and home connections • Parents' social networks • Student success in school • Personal demographics • Students' comments	Information and Guidelines • Notes on administering the survey • Scales and reliabilities • CD included with electronic copies
School and Family Partnerships: Surveys and Summaries, Questionnaires for Parents Epstein, J. L., & Salinas, K. C.	1993	Elementary and middle grades	**Parents' reports** of • Attitudes about the school • Present family involvement • Present and desired school outreach to involve families • Requests for workshop topics, information on school subjects, and community services • Time students spend on homework • Perceptions of student abilities and success in school • Family demographics • Parents' comments	Information and Guidelines • Notes on administering the survey • Scales and reliabilities • Suggestions for summarizing data for cooperating schools Spanish (paper copy), on request
School and Family Partnerships: Surveys and Summaries, Questionnaires for Teachers Epstein, J. L., & Salinas, K. C.	1993	Elementary and middle grades	**Teachers' reports** of • Importance of family involvement • Present practices of involvement by the teacher and by the school • Estimates of family engagement • Teaching experience • Personal demographics • Teachers' comments.	Information and Guidelines • Notes on administering the survey • Scales and reliabilities • Suggestions for summarizing data for cooperating schools

Survey Title and Author	Date	School Level	Measures	Features
High School and Family Partnerships: Surveys and Summaries, Questionnaires for Parents Epstein, J. L., Connors-Tadros, L. J., & Salinas, K. C.	1993	High school and Grade 9	**Parents' reports** of • Attitudes about the school • Present family involvement • Present and desired school outreach to involve families • Requests for workshop topics and community services • Time students spend on homework • Perceptions of student abilities and success in school • Family demographics • Parents' comments	Information and Guidelines • Notes on administering the survey • Scales and reliabilities Suggestions for summarizing data for cooperating schools
High School and Family Partnerships: Surveys and Summaries, Questionnaires for Teachers Epstein, J. L., Connors-Tadros, L. J., & Salinas, K. C.	1993	High school and Grade 9	**Teachers' reports** of • Attitudes about the school • Importance of family involvement • Present practices of involvement by the teacher and by the school • Estimates of parents' involvement and responsibilities • Community problems • Teaching experience • Personal and school demographics • Teachers' comments	Information and Guidelines • Notes on administering the survey • Scales and reliabilities Suggestions for summarizing data for cooperating schools
High School and Family Partnerships: Surveys and Summaries, Questionnaires for Students Epstein, J. L., Connors-Tadros, L. J., & Salinas, K. C.	1993	High school and Grade 9	**Students' reports** of • Attitudes about the school • Transition to high school • Present family involvement • Present and desired school outreach to involve families • Willingness to conduct and participate in family involvement activities • Family decision making on teen behaviors • Time on homework • Success in school • Activities in community • Personal demographics • Students' comments	Information and Guidelines • Notes on administering the survey • Scales and reliabilities Suggestions for summarizing data for cooperating schools

Creating Questionnaires

In addition to using the surveys with tested scales and measures described above, school, district, and state leaders may create their own surveys to obtain input and reactions to programs of family and community involvement. Schools often create short surveys for exit evaluations of parent workshops, Family Nights, and other events. Some schools survey parents each year to identify volunteers' interests, talents, and time available to assist school administrators, teachers, and students. Some districts conduct annual surveys for parents' reactions to family and community involvement and other aspects of school climate and students' academic programs.

There are guidelines for developing simple and clear questionnaires that enable parents, teachers, or others to assess aspects of family and community involvement:

- Determine what you want to know.
- Tailor the questionnaire to focus clearly on a particular topic or practice.
- If multiple choice answers are offered, make each response category clear and unique.

  Limit "yes or no" answers. Yes/no answers will tell whether respondents like or dislike something (but not how much) and whether they have ever or never done something (but not how often). "No" is a clear response, but "yes" may refer to 1 to 100 occasions or more.

- If open-ended answers are requested, include sufficient space for written responses.
- Keep surveys anonymous.
- Keep surveys short.
- Make surveys easy to read. For parents' questionnaires, keep the vocabulary at a fourth grade reading level, and provide translations as needed.
- If possible, have surveys completed on site (e.g., in a teachers' meeting, at a parent workshop) to increase the response rate.
- Give enough time to complete the questionnaires.
- Explain how you will use the information.
- Provide a summary of results.

Reporting Evaluations

Evaluations of partnership activities should be reported to the audiences for whom the assessments were conducted. Some evaluations are for limited audiences. For example, the results of the *Review of Team Processes* is for the ATP to help improve its own effectiveness. The results may also be shared with and helpful to a district leader for partnerships who will be facilitating teamwork of all schools' ATPs.

Other evaluations may be shared with many audiences. For example, all families should receive information about a school's One-Year Action Plan for Partnerships so that they learn about, have input to, and participate in a school's program for family and community involvement. Because all families are participants, they also should receive a summary of the ATP's evaluations of program progress at the end of the school year. This may include a short, but informative, summary of activities conducted from the *Annual Evaluation of Activities,* a summary of progress made on the *Measure of School, Family, and Community Partnerships,* or other summaries of activities conducted, participation rates, and assessments. Information for all families and the community may be provided via school newsletters, Web sites, e-mail lists, and other technologies. School and local media (newspapers, radio, and cable TV, including foreign language outlets) can publicize activities and events, feature best practices, and report annual progress.

Detailed reports should be presented to the school council or school improvement team, PTA or PTO, district school board, and other interested groups. By sharing plans and the results of evaluations of partnerships, all parents and the public will learn that partnership programs are ongoing, inclusive, and always improving.

Reports should be clearly written, objective, and used to increase knowledge and spark discussions about a program. The reports should cover basic information about the program, why the evaluation was conducted, major questions, results, implications of the findings, recommendations, and next steps (Sanders & Sheldon, 2009).

Evaluate to Improve, Not to Pass Judgment

Evaluations are not conducted to label a program "good" or "bad." Useful evaluations help district leaders and schools' ATPs clarify program goals, identify strengths and weaknesses, and plan improvements. Educators know that they *should* evaluate their policies, plans, programs, and practices to understand whether they are involving all families, including those who, typically, have not been engaged in their children's education. The built-in tools in this *Handbook,* locally designed assessments, and other instruments should help districts and schools conduct evaluations that will strengthen their programs and involve more families in productive ways every year. It is very clear that time spent evaluating is time well spent.

References

Epstein, J. L. (2007). Research meets policy and practice: How are school districts addressing NCLB requirements for parental involvement? In A. R. Sadovnik, J. O' Day, G. Bohrnstedt, & K. Borman (Eds.), *No Child Left Behind and the reduction of the achievement gap: Sociological perspectives on federal educational policy* (pp. 267–279). New York: Routledge.

Epstein, J. L., Galindo, C., Sheldon, S. B., & Williams, K. J. (2007, April). *Effects of district leadership on the quality of school programs of family and community involvement.* Paper presented at the annual meeting of the American Educational Research Association, Chicago.

Sanders, M. (2008). Using diverse data to develop and sustain school, family, and community partnerships: A district case study. *Education Management, Administration, and Leadership, 36.*

Sanders, M. G, & Sheldon, S. B. (2009). *A principal's guide to school, family, and community partnerships.* Thousand Oaks, CA: Corwin Press.

Sheldon, S. B. (2007). Getting families involved with NCLB: Factors affecting schools' enactment of federal policy. In A. R. Sadovnik, J. O' Day, G. Bohrnstedt, & K. Borman (Eds.), *No Child Left Behind and the reduction of the achievement gap: Sociological perspectives on federal educational policy* (pp. 281–294). New York: Routledge.

Sheldon, S. B., & Van Voorhis, F. L. (2004). Partnership programs in U.S. schools: Their development and relationship to family involvement outcomes. *School Effectiveness and School Improvement, 15,* 125–148.

Van Voorhis, F. L. (2003). Interactive homework in middle school: Effects on family involvement and science achievement. *Journal of Educational Research, 96,* 323–338.

Measure of School, Family, and Community Partnerships

Karen Clark Salinas, Joyce L. Epstein, & Mavis G. Sanders, Johns Hopkins University, Deborah Davis & Inge Aldersbaes, Northwest Regional Educational Laboratory

This instrument helps assess whether your school is involving parents, community members, and students in meaningful ways. The measure is based on the framework of six types of involvement and focuses on how well activities are meeting challenges to involve more – or all – families in their children's education.

At this time, your school may conduct all, some, or none of the activities or approaches listed. Not every activity is appropriate at every grade level. Not every activity should be conducted often – some may be implemented once or twice each year. In a goal-oriented partnership program, activities will be selected and outlined in detail in your One-Year Action Plan for Partnerships to help reach specific school improvement goals.

Your school may implement other activities for each type of involvement. These should be added on the blank lines and rated to account for the major partnership practices that your school conducts.

Directions: Use the scoring rubric below to rate your school on the six types of involvement. As you review each item, circle the response that comes closest to describing how the activity is implemented at your school.

Scoring Rubric:

1 – Never: Strategy does not happen at our school.

2 – Rarely: Conducted in one or two classes or with a few families.
Not emphasized in this school's partnership program.

3 – Sometimes: Conducted in a few classes or with some families.
Receives minimal emphasis in this school's partnership program across the grades. Quality of Implementation needs to improve.

4 – Often: Conducted in many, but not all, classes, or with many, but not all, families. Given substantial emphasis in this school's partnership program across the grades. Quality of implementation is high; only minor changes are needed.

5 – Frequently: Occurs in most or all classes and grade levels, with most or all families. An important part of this school's partnership program. Quality of implementation is excellent.

The *Measure* is designed to be discussed and completed annually or every other year by an Action Team for Partnerships (ATP) to assess program progress. The results not only indicate the scope and quality of involvement activities, but also suggest new directions and needed improvements for the next One-Year Action Plan for Partnerships.

I. PARENTING: Help all families understand child and adolescent development and establish home environments to support children as students. Help schools understand families' backgrounds, cultures, and goals for students.

	Rating				
Our School:	**Never**	**Rarely**	**Sometimes**	**Often**	**Frequently**
1. Conducts workshops or provides information for parents on child or adolescent development.	1	2	3	4	5
2. Provides information to all families who want or who need it, not just to the few who can attend workshops or meetings at the school building.	1	2	3	4	5
3. Produces information for families that is clear, usable, and linked to children's success in school.	1	2	3	4	5
4. Asks families for information about children's goals, strengths, and talents.	1	2	3	4	5
5. Sponsors home visiting programs or neighborhood meetings to help families understand schools and to help schools understand families.	1	2	3	4	5
6. Provides families with age-appropriate information on developing home conditions or environments that support learning.	1	2	3	4	5
7. Respects the different cultures represented in our student population.	1	2	3	4	5
Other Type 1-Parenting activities: ______________________________	1	2	3	4	5
______________________________	1	2	3	4	5

II. **COMMUNICATING:** Conduct effective forms of school-to-home and home-to-school communications about school programs and children's progress.

Our School:	**Rating**				
	Never	**Rarely**	**Sometimes**	**Often**	**Frequently**
1. Reviews the readability, clarity, form, and frequency of all memos, notices, and other print and non-print communications.	1	2	3	4	5
2. Develops communications with parents who do not speak or read English well, or need large type.	1	2	3	4	5
3. Provides written communication in the language of the parents and provides translators as needed.	1	2	3	4	5
4. Has clear two-way channels for communications from home to school and from school to home.	1	2	3	4	5
5. Conducts a formal conference with every parent at least once a year.	1	2	3	4	5
6. Conducts an annual survey for families to share information and concerns about student needs, reactions to school programs, and satisfaction with their involvement in school and at home.	1	2	3	4	5
7. Conducts an orientation for new parents.	1	2	3	4	5
8. Sends home folders of student work weekly or monthly for parent review and comment.	1	2	3	4	5
9. Provides clear information about the curriculum, state tests, school and student results, and report cards.	1	2	3	4	5
10. Contacts families of students having academic or behavior problems.	1	2	3	4	5
11. Teachers, counselors, and administrators use e-mail and the school website to communicate with parents, including information on Internet safety	1	2	3	4	5
12. Trains teachers, staff, and principals on the value and utility of family involvement and ways to build positive ties between school and home.	1	2	3	4	5
13. Builds policies that encourage all teachers to communicate frequently with parents about the curriculum, expectations for homework, and how parents can help.	1	2	3	4	5
14. Produces a regular school newsletter with up-to-date information about the school, special events, organizations, meetings, and parenting tips.	1	2	3	4	5
Other Type 2-Communicating activities: ______________________	1	2	3	4	5
______________________________	1	2	3	4	5

III. VOLUNTEERING: Recruit and organize parents to support the school and students.

Our School:	Rating				
	Never	Rarely	Sometimes	Often	Frequently
1. Conducts annual surveys to identify interests, talents, and availability of parent volunteers to match their skills and talents with school and classroom needs.	1	2	3	4	5
2. Provides a parent or family room for volunteers and family members to meet and work, and to access resources about parenting, tutoring, and related topics	1	2	3	4	5
3. Creates flexible volunteering opportunities and schedules, enabling employed parents to participate.	1	2	3	4	5
4. Schedules special events at different times of the day and evening so that all families can attend as audiences.	1	2	3	4	5
5. Reduces barriers to parent participation by providing transportation and child care, and by addressing the needs of English language learners.	1	2	3	4	5
6. Trains volunteers so they use their time productively.	1	2	3	4	5
7. Recognizes volunteers for their time and efforts.	1	2	3	4	5
8. Encourages families and the community to be involved with the school in various ways (e.g., assist in classrooms, monitor halls, lead talks or activities, serve as audiences)	1	2	3	4	5
Other Type 3-Volunteering activities: ______________________	1	2	3	4	5
______________________	1	2	3	4	5

IV. LEARNING AT HOME: Provide information to families on how to help students with homework, other curriculum-related activities, course decisions, and future plans.

Our School:	Rating				
	Never	Rarely	Sometimes	Often	Frequently
1. Provides information to families on how to monitor and discuss schoolwork at home.	1	2	3	4	5
2. Provides information to families on required skills in major subjects.	1	2	3	4	5
3. Provides specific information to parents on how to assist students with skills that they need to improve.	1	2	3	4	5
4. Asks parents to focus on reading, listen to children read, or read aloud with their child.	1	2	3	4	5
5. Assists families in helping students set academic goals and select courses and programs.	1	2	3	4	5
6. Provides information and ideas for families to talk with students about college, careers, postsecondary plans.	1	2	3	4	5
7. Schedules regular interactive homework that requires students to demonstrate and discuss what they are learning with a family member.	1	2	3	4	5
Other Type 4-Learning at Home activities: ______________________	1	2	3	4	5
______________________	1	2	3	4	5

V. **DECISION MAKING:** Include parents in school decisions and develop parent leaders and representatives.

Our School:	Rating				
	Never	Rarely	Sometimes	Often	Frequently
1. Has an active PTA, PTO, or other parent organization.	1	2	3	4	5
2. Includes parent representatives on the school's council, improvement team, or other committees.	1	2	3	4	5
3. Has parents represented on district-level advisory council and committees.	1	2	3	4	5
4. Involves parents in organized, ongoing, and timely ways in planning and improving school programs.	1	2	3	4	5
5. Involves parents in reviewing school and district curricula.	1	2	3	4	5
6. Recruits parent leaders for committees from all racial, ethnic, socioeconomic, and other groups in the school.	1	2	3	4	5
7. Develops formal social networks to link all families with their parent representatives.	1	2	3	4	5
8. Includes students (with parents) in decision-making groups.	1	2	3	4	5
9. Deals with conflict openly and respectfully.	1	2	3	4	5
10. Guides parent representatives to contact parents who are less involved for their ideas.	1	2	3	4	5
11. Develops the school's plan and program of family and community involvement with input from educators, parents, and others.	1	2	3	4	5
Other Type 5-Decision Making activities: ____________	1	2	3	4	5
____________	1	2	3	4	5

VI. **COLLABORATING WITH THE COMMUNITY:** Coordinate resources and services from the community for families, students, and the school, and provide services to the community.

Our School:	Rating				
	Never	Rarely	Sometimes	Often	Frequently
1. Provides a resource directory for parents and students on community agencies, services, and programs.	1	2	3	4	5
2. Involves families in locating and using community resources.	1	2	3	4	5
3. Works with local businesses, industries, libraries, parks, museums, and other organizations on programs to enhance student skills and learning.	1	2	3	4	5
4. Provides "one-stop shop" at the school for family services through partnerships of school, counseling, health, recreation, job training and other agencies.	1	2	3	4	5
5. Offers afterschool programs for students with support from community businesses, agencies, and volunteers.	1	2	3	4	5
6. Solves turf problems of responsibilities, funds, staff, and locations for collaborative activities to occur.	1	2	3	4	5
Other Type 6-Collaborating With the Community activities: ____________	1	2	3	4	5
____________	1	2	3	4	5

REFLECTIONS

Review the ratings of activities for all six types of involvement. Discuss the following questions and consider ways to improve the school's program of family and community involvement in the next One-Year Action Plan for Partnerships.

A. What major factors contributed to the success of your school's family and community involvement efforts this year?

B. What major factors limited the success of your school's family and community involvement efforts this year?

C. What are your school's major goals for improving its program of school, family, and community partnerships in the next year or two?

School Name ______________________ School Year ______________________

ANNUAL EVALUATION OF ACTIVITIES

Form G–Goals

School, Family, and Community Partnerships to Reach School Goals

This annual report helps an Action Team for Partnerships (ATP) evaluate its progress in developing its comprehensive program of school, family, and community partnerships. The first page helps an ATP discuss and rate the quality of the school's partnership program overall. The other pages ask the ATP to consider how well *each* activity was implemented and how to improve activities in the next school year for specific school improvement goals.

Each activity in the school's *One-Year Action Plan for Partnerships—Form G* should be assessed at an ATP meeting after it is implemented. At the end of the year, the completed *Annual Evaluation of Activities* should assist the ATP in deciding which activities to continue, omit, or improve in plan for the next school year.

COMPLETE THIS PAGE AT THE END OF THE SCHOOL YEAR.
Complete all other pages as the activities are implemented throughout the year.

OVERALL PROGRAM EVALUATION

1. What has changed most in the past year as a result of the school's work on family and community involvement?

____

2. Overall, how does the ATP rate the quality of the school's program of school, family, and community partnerships? This school's partnership program is:

_____ **WEAK/JUST STARTING: Not well developed; needs a great deal of work**
_____ **FAIR: Implemented, but needs improvement and expansion**
_____ **GOOD: Well developed, focused on school improvement goals, covers all six types of involvement, and addresses the needs of *most* families at *most* grade levels**
_____ **EXCELLENT: Well developed and well implemented, focused on school improvement goals, covers all six types of involvement, and addresses the needs of *all* families at *all* grade levels**

3. ACTION TEAM FOR PARTNERSHIP (ATP). List the members of this year's ATP. Put a star (*) next to those completing their terms or leaving the school who will be replaced by new members.

	ATP Members This School Year	Position (teacher, parent, administrator, etc.)	Role on Action Team (chair, co-chair, committee member, etc.)	*Need to Replace?
1.				
2.				
3.				
4.				
5.				
6.				
7.				
8.				

If there are more than eight members on the ATP, continue this list on another page.

Goal 1–ACADEMIC: **Which curricular goal for improving student learning and achievement was listed in the One-Year Action Plan for Partnerships?**

____

PROGRESS IN REACHING ACADEMIC GOAL 1

Use *Excellent* ***(E)****, Good* ***(G)****, Fair* ***(F)****, or Poor* ***(P)*** to rate each **partnership activity** that is implemented to help reach **Academic Goal 1**. As a team, discuss the next steps that should be taken to maintain and improve each activity in the next school year. Use additional pages if more than three family and community involvement activities were conducted to reach Academic Goal 1.

Partnership Activity	Action Team Planning How well was the activity planned?	Support How helpful were ATP members and others at the school?	Implementation How well was the activity implemented? Did it reach the target audience?	Results How well did the activity contribute to desired result(s) for Goal 1?
1. ______________	☐	☐	☐	☐

Will this involvement activity be conducted in the next school year? **YES** or **NO**

If **NO**, why not? ______________________________

If **YES**, what should be done to improve this activity? ______________________________

Partnership Activity	Action Team Planning	Support	Implementation	Results
2. ______________	☐	☐	☐	☐

Will this involvement activity be continued in the next school year? **YES** or **NO**

If **NO**, why not? ______________________________

If **YES**, what should be done to improve this activity? ______________________________

Partnership Activity	Action Team Planning	Support	Implementation	Results
3. ______________	☐	☐	☐	☐

Will this involvement activity be continued in the next school year? **YES** or **NO**

If **NO**, why not? ______________________________

If **YES**, what should be done to improve this activity? ______________________________

END-OF-YEAR REVIEW OF GOAL 1:

Did family and community involvement contribute to results for Goal 1 this year? **YES or NO**

Will Goal 1 be continued in the new One-Year Action Plan for Partnerships—Form G for the next school year? **YES or NO**

Goal 2–ACADEMIC: **Which curricular goal for improving student learning and achievement was listed in the One-Year Action Plan for Partnerships?**

____

PROGRESS IN REACHING ACADEMIC GOAL 2

Use *Excellent* ***(E)****, Good* ***(G)****, Fair* ***(F)****, or Poor* ***(P)*** to rate each **partnership activity** that is implemented to help reach **Academic Goal 2**. As a team, discuss the next steps that should be taken to maintain and improve each activity in the next school year. Use additional pages if more than three family and community involvement activities were conducted to reach Academic Goal 2.

Partnership Activity	**Action Team Planning** How well was the activity planned?	**Support** How helpful were ATP members and others at the school?	**Implementation** How well was the activity implemented? Did it reach the target audience?	**Results** How well did the activity contribute to desired result(s) for Goal 2?
1. ______________	☐	☐	☐	☐

Will this involvement activity be continued in the next school year? **YES** or **NO**

If **NO**, why not? ______________________________

If **YES**, what should be done to improve this activity? ______________________________

Partnership Activity	**Action Team Planning**	**Support**	**Implementation**	**Results**
2. ______________	☐	☐	☐	☐

Will this involvement activity be continued in the next school year? **YES** or **NO**

If **NO**, why not? ______________________________

If **YES**, what should be done to improve this activity? ______________________________

Partnership Activity	**Action Team Planning**	**Support**	**Implementation**	**Results**
3. ______________	☐	☐	☐	☐

Will this involvement activity be continued in the next school year? **YES** or **NO**

If **NO**, why not? ______________________________

If **YES**, what should be done to improve this activity? ______________________________

END-OF-YEAR REVIEW OF GOAL 2:

Did family and community involvement contribute to results for Goal 2 this year? **YES or NO**

Will Goal 2 be continued in the new One-Year Action Plan for Partnerships—Form G for the next school year? **YES or NO**

Goal 3–BEHAVIORAL: **Which goal for improving student behavior, attitudes, or other outcome was listed in the One-Year Action Plan for Partnerships?**

___

PROGRESS IN REACHING BEHAVIORAL GOAL 3

Use *Excellent* ***(E)****, Good* ***(G)****, Fair* ***(F)****, or Poor* ***(P)*** to rate each **partnership activity** that is implemented to help reach **Behavioral Goal 3**. As a team, discuss the next steps that should be taken to maintain and improve each activity in the next school year. Use additional pages if more than three family and community involvement activities were conducted to reach Behavioral Goal 3.

Partnership Activity	Action Team Planning How well was the activity planned?	Support How helpful were ATP members and others at the school?	Implementation How well was the activity implemented? Did it reach the target audience?	Results How well did the activity contribute to desired result(s) for Goal 3?
1. ______	☐	☐	☐	☐

Will this involvement activity be continued in the next school year? **YES** or **NO**

If **NO**, why not? ______

If **YES**, what should be done to improve this activity? ______

Partnership Activity	Action Team Planning	Support	Implementation	Results
2. ______	☐	☐	☐	☐

Will this involvement activity be continued in the next school year? **YES** or **NO**

If **NO**, why not? ______

If **YES**, what should be done to improve this activity? ______

Partnership Activity	Action Team Planning	Support	Implementation	Results
3. ______	☐	☐	☐	☐

Will this involvement activity be continued in the next school year? **YES** or **NO**

If **NO**, why not? ______

If **YES**, what should be done to improve this activity? ______

END-OF-YEAR REVIEW OF GOAL 3:

Did family and community involvement contribute to results for GOAL 3 this year? **YES or NO**

Will Goal 3 be continued in the new One-Year Action Plan for Partnerships—Form G for the next school year? **YES or NO**

Goal 4–CLIMATE OF PARTNERSHIPS (Required Goal): *Strengthen the six types of family and community involvement*

PROGRESS IN REACHING GOAL 4–A WELCOMING PARTNERSHIP CLIMATE

Use *Excellent* ***(E)****, Good* ***(G)****, Fair* ***(F)****, or Poor* ***(P)*** to rate each **partnership activity** that is implemented to help reach **GOAL 4—A Welcoming Climate**. As a team, discuss the next steps that should be taken to maintain and improve each activity in the next school year. Use additional pages if more than three family and community involvement activities were conducted to reach Goal 4.

Partnership Activity	Action Team Planning How well was the activity planned?	Support How helpful were ATP members and others at the school?	Implementation How well was the activity implemented? Did it reach the target audience?	Results How well did the activity contribute to desired result(s) for Goal 4?
1. ______	☐	☐	☐	☐

Will this involvement activity be continued in the next school year? **YES** or **NO**

If **NO**, why not? ______

If **YES**, what should be done to improve this activity? ______

Partnership Activity	Action Team Planning	Support	Implementation	Results
2. ______	☐	☐	☐	☐

Will this involvement activity be continued in the next school year? **YES** or **NO**

If **NO**, why not? ______

If **YES**, what should be done to improve this activity? ______

Partnership Activity	Action Team Planning	Support	Implementation	Results
3. ______	☐	☐	☐	☐

Will this involvement activity be continued in the next school year? **YES** or **NO**

If **NO**, why not? ______

If **YES**, what should be done to improve this activity? ______

END-OF-YEAR REVIEW OF GOAL 4:

Did family and community involvement contribute to results for Goal 4 this year? **YES or NO**

Will Goal 4 be continued in the new One-Year Action Plan for Partnerships—Form G for the next school year? **YES or NO**

School Name ______________________ School Year ______________________

ANNUAL EVALUATION OF ACTIVITIES

Form T–Types

School, Family, and Community Partnerships to Reach School Goals

This annual report helps an Action Team for Partnerships (ATP) evaluate its progress in developing its comprehensive program of school, family, and community partnerships. The first page helps an ATP discuss and rate the quality of the school's partnership program overall. The other pages ask the ATP to consider how well *each* activity was implemented and how to improve activities in the next school year for the six types of involvement.

Each activity in the school's *One-Year Action Plan for Partnerships—Form T* should be assessed at an ATP meeting after it is implemented. At the end of the year, the completed *Annual Evaluation of Activities* should assist the ATP in deciding which activities to continue, omit, or improve in plan for the next school year.

COMPLETE THIS PAGE AT THE END OF THE SCHOOL YEAR.
Complete all other pages as the activities are implemented throughout the year.

OVERALL PROGRAM EVALUATION

1. What has changed most in the past year as a result of the school's work on family and community involvement?

____

2. Overall, how does the ATP rate the quality of the school's program of school, family, and community partnerships? This school's partnership program is:

_____ **WEAK/JUST STARTING: Not well developed; needs a great deal of work**
_____ **FAIR: Implemented, but needs improvement and expansion**
_____ **GOOD: Well developed, focused on school improvement goals, covers all six types of involvement, and addresses the needs of *most* families at *most* grade levels**
_____ **EXCELLENT: Well developed and well implemented, focused on school improvement goals, covers all six types of involvement, and addresses the needs of *all* families at *all* grade levels**

3. ACTION TEAM FOR PARTNERSHIP (ATP). List the members of this year's ATP. Put a star (*) next to those completing their terms or leaving the school who will be replaced by new members.

	ATP Members This School Year	Position (teacher, parent, administrator, etc.)	Role on Action Team (chair, co-chair, committee member, etc.)	*Need to Replace?
1.				
2.				
3.				
4.				
5.				
6.				
7.				
8.				

If there are more than eight members on the ATP, continue this list on another page.

PROGRESS ON TYPE 1–PARENTING

Review <u>each</u> Type 1–Parenting activity in the One-Year Action Plan for Partnerships—Form T after it is implemented.

Use *Excellent **(E)**, Good **(G)**, Fair **(F)**, or Poor **(P)*** to rate each **partnership activity** that is implemented to strengthen **Type 1–Parenting**. As a team, discuss the next steps that should be taken to maintain and improve each activity in the next school year. Use additional pages if more than three family and community involvement activities were conducted to strengthen Type 1–Parenting.

Partnership Activity	Action Team Planning How well was the activity planned?	Support How helpful were ATP members and others at the school?	Implementation How well was the activity implemented? Did it reach the target audience?	Results How well did the activity contribute to desired result(s) listed for Type 1?
1. ______________________ ______________________	☐	☐	☐	☐

Will this involvement activity be continued in the next school year? **YES** or **NO**

If **NO**, why not? ______________________

If **YES**, what should be done to improve this activity? ______________________

Partnership Activity	Action Team Planning	Support	Implementation	Results
2. ______________________ ______________________	☐	☐	☐	☐

Will this involvement activity be continued in the next school year? **YES** or **NO**

If **NO**, why not? ______________________

If **YES**, what should be done to improve this activity? ______________________

Partnership Activity	Action Team Planning	Support	Implementation	Results
3. ______________________ ______________________	☐	☐	☐	☐

Will this involvement activity be continued in the next school year? **YES** or **NO**

If **NO**, why not? ______________________

If **YES**, what should be done to improve this activity? ______________________

<u>END-OF-YEAR REVIEW OF TYPE 1:</u>

Did family and community involvement contribute to desired results listed for Type 1 in the One-Year Action Plan for Partnerships? YES or NO

Which Type 1–Parenting activities should be added next year? ______________________

PROGRESS ON TYPE 2–COMMUNICATING

Review <u>each</u> Type 2–Communicating activity listed in the One-Year Action Plan for Partnerships—Form T after it is implemented.

Use *Excellent **(E)**, Good **(G)**, Fair **(F)**, or Poor **(P)*** to rate each **partnership activity** that is implemented to strengthen **Type 2–Communicating**. As a team, discuss the next steps that should be taken to maintain and improve each activity in the next school year. Use additional pages if more than three family and community involvement activities were conducted to strengthen Type 2–Communicating.

Partnership Activity	Action Team Planning How well was the activity planned?	Support How helpful were ATP members and others at the school?	Implementation How well was the activity implemented? Did it reach the target audience?	Results How well did the activity contribute to desired result(s) listed for Type 2?
1. ________	☐	☐	☐	☐

Will this involvement activity be conducted in the next school year? **YES** or **NO**

If **NO**, why not? ________

If **YES**, what should be done to improve this activity? ________

Partnership Activity	Action Team Planning	Support	Implementation	Results
2. ________	☐	☐	☐	☐

Will this involvement activity be continued in the next school year? **YES** or **NO**

If **NO**, why not? ________

If **YES**, what should be done to improve this activity? ________

Partnership Activity	Action Team Planning	Support	Implementation	Results
3. ________	☐	☐	☐	☐

Will this involvement activity be continued in the next school year? **YES** or **NO**

If **NO**, why not? ________

If **YES**, what should be done to improve this activity? ________

<u>END-OF-YEAR REVIEW OF TYPE 2:</u>

Did family and community involvement contribute to desired results listed for Type 2 in the One-Year Action Plan for Partnerships? YES or NO

Which Type 2–Communicticting activities should be added next year? ________

PROGRESS ON TYPE 3–VOLUNTEERING

Review <u>each</u> Type 3–Volunteering activity in the One-Year Action Plan for Partnerships—Form T after it is implemented.

Use *Excellent **(E)**, Good **(G)**, Fair **(F)**, or Poor **(P)*** to rate each **partnership activity** that is implemented to strengthen **Type 3–Volunteering**. As a team, discuss the next steps that should be taken to maintain and improve each activity in the next school year. Use additional pages if more than three family and community involvement activities were conducted to strengthen Type 3–Volunteering.

Partnership Activity	Action Team Planning How well was the activity planned?	Support How helpful were ATP members and others at the school?	Implementation How well was the activity implemented? Did it reach the target audience?	Results How well did the activity contribute to desired result(s) listed for Type 3?
1. ______________________ ______________________	☐	☐	☐	☐

Will this involvement activity be conducted in the next school year? **YES** or **NO**

If **NO**, why not? ______________________

If **YES**, what should be done to improve this activity? ______________________

Partnership Activity	Action Team Planning	Support	Implementation	Results
2. ______________________ ______________________	☐	☐	☐	☐

Will this involvement activity be continued in the next school year? **YES** or **NO**

If **NO**, why not? ______________________

If **YES**, what should be done to improve this activity? ______________________

Partnership Activity	Action Team Planning	Support	Implementation	Results
3. ______________________ ______________________	☐	☐	☐	☐

Will this involvement activity be continued in the next school year? **YES** or **NO**

If **NO**, why not? ______________________

If **YES**, what should be done to improve this activity? ______________________

<u>END-OF-YEAR REVIEW OF TYPE 3:</u>

Did family and community involvement contribute to desired results listed for Type 3 in the One-Year Action Plan for Partnerships? YES or NO

Which Type 3–Volunteering activities should be added next year? ______________________

PROGRESS ON TYPE 4–LEARNING AT HOME

Review <u>each</u> Type 4–Learning at Home activity in the One-Year Action Plan for Partnerships—Form T after it is implemented.

Use *Excellent* ***(E)****, Good* ***(G)****, Fair* ***(F)****, or Poor* ***(P)*** to rate each **partnership activity** that is implemented to strengthen **Type 4–Learning at Home**. As a team, discuss the next steps that should be taken to maintain and improve each activity in the next school year. Use additional pages if more than three family and community involvement activities were conducted to strengthen Type 4–Learning at Home.

Partnership Activity	Action Team Planning How well was the activity planned?	Support How helpful were ATP members and others at the school?	Implementation How well was the activity implemented? Did it reach the target audience?	Results How well did the activity contribute to desired result(s) listed for Type 4?
1. ____________	☐	☐	☐	☐

Will this involvement activity be continued in the next school year? **YES** or **NO**

If **NO**, why not? ____________

If **YES**, what should be done to improve this activity? ____________

Partnership Activity	Action Team Planning	Support	Implementation	Results
2. ____________	☐	☐	☐	☐

Will this involvement activity be continued in the next school year? **YES** or **NO**

If **NO**, why not? ____________

If **YES**, what should be done to improve this activity? ____________

Partnership Activity	Action Team Planning	Support	Implementation	Results
3. ____________	☐	☐	☐	☐

Will this involvement activity be continued in the next school year? **YES** or **NO**

If **NO**, why not? ____________

If **YES**, what should be done to improve this activity? ____________

<u>END-OF-YEAR REVIEW OF TYPE 4:</u>

Did family and community involvement contribute to desired results listed for Type 4 in the One-Year Action Plan for Partnerships? YES or NO

Which Type 4–Learning at Home activities should be added next year? ____________

PROGRESS ON TYPE 5–DECISION MAKING

Review each Type 5–Decision Making activity in the One-Year Action Plan for Partnerships—Form T after it is implemented.

Use *Excellent* ***(E)****, Good* ***(G)****, Fair* ***(F)****, or Poor* ***(P)*** to rate each **partnership activity** that is implemented to strengthen **Type 5-Decision Making**. As a team, discuss the next steps that should be taken to maintain and improve each activity in the next school year. Use additional pages if more than three family and community involvement activities were conducted to strengthen Type 5-Decision Making.

Partnership Activity	Action Team Planning How well was the activity planned?	Support How helpful were ATP members and others at the school?	Implementation How well was the activity implemented? Did it reach the target audience?	Results How well did the activity contribute to desired result(s) listed for Type 5?
1. ______________ ______________	☐	☐	☐	☐

Will this involvement activity be continued in the next school year? **YES** or **NO**

If **NO**, why not? ______________

If **YES**, what should be done to improve this activity? ______________

Partnership Activity	Action Team Planning	Support	Implementation	Results
2. ______________ ______________	☐	☐	☐	☐

Will this involvement activity be continued in the next school year? **YES** or **NO**

If **NO**, why not? ______________

If **YES**, what should be done to improve this activity? ______________

Partnership Activity	Action Team Planning	Support	Implementation	Results
3. ______________ ______________	☐	☐	☐	☐

Will this involvement activity be continued in the next school year? **YES** or **NO**

If **NO**, why not? ______________

If **YES**, what should be done to improve this activity? ______________

END-OF-YEAR REVIEW OF TYPE 5:

Did family and community involvement contribute to desired results listed for Type 5 in the One-Year Action Plan for Partnerships? YES or NO

Which Type 5–Decision Making activities should be added next year? ______________

PROGRESS ON TYPE 6–COLLABORATING WITH THE COMMUNITY

Review each Type 6–Collaborating With the Community activity in the One-Year Action Plan for Partnerships—Form T after it is implemented.

Use *Excellent* ***(E)****, Good* ***(G)****, Fair* ***(F)****, or Poor* ***(P)*** to rate each **partnership activity** that is implemented to strengthen **Type 6–Collaborating With the Community**. As a team, discuss the next steps that should be taken to maintain and improve each activity in the next school year. Use additional pages if more than three family and community involvement activities were conducted to strengthen Type 6–Collaborating With the Community

Partnership Activity	Action Team Planning How well was the activity planned?	Support How helpful were ATP members and others at the school?	Implementation How well was the activity implemented? Did it reach the target audience?	Results How well did the activity contribute to desired result(s) listed for Type 6?
1. ____________	☐	☐	☐	☐

Will this involvement activity be conducted in the next school year? **YES** or **NO**

If **NO**, why not? ____________

If **YES**, what should be done to improve this activity? ____________

Partnership Activity	Action Team Planning	Support	Implementation	Results
2. ____________	☐	☐	☐	☐

Will this involvement activity be continued in the next school year? **YES** or **NO**

If **NO**, why not? ____________

If **YES**, what should be done to improve this activity? ____________

Partnership Activity	Action Team Planning	Support	Implementation	Results
3. ____________	☐	☐	☐	☐

Will this involvement activity be continued in the next school year? **YES** or **NO**

If **NO**, why not? ____________

If **YES**, what should be done to improve this activity? ____________

END-OF-YEAR REVIEW OF TYPE 6:

Did family and community involvement contribute to desired results listed for Type 6 in the One-Year Action Plan for Partnerships? YES or NO

Which Type 6–Collaborating With the Community activities should be added next year? ____________

10

Network With Others for Best Results on Partnerships

You may use this *Handbook,* independently, to develop a comprehensive program of school, family, and community partnerships. Or, your school, district, or state may join the National Network of Partnership Schools (NNPS) at Johns Hopkins University.

This chapter includes two resources that will help you and your colleagues decide whether to link with researchers and with leaders in other schools, districts, and states across the country working to improve programs of family and community involvement to increase students' success.

National Network of Partnership Schools at Johns Hopkins University

The flyer reproduced here reviews the mission, benefits, services, requirements, and how to join the NNPS. Benefits include leadership development conferences, newsletters to guide progress in program development, annual collections of best practices, annual evaluations of program progress, annual awards for excellent programs, and ongoing professional development through phone, e-mail, and Web site connections with the researchers at Johns Hopkins University.

NNPS Web Site
www.partnershipschools.org

This dynamic Web site serves the members of the NNPS and others developing programs of school, family, and community partnerships. The Web site includes summaries of new research; program guidelines for elementary, middle, and high schools and for state and district leaders; professional development resources; and avenues for exchanging best practices with others who are working on developing and improving partnership programs.

National Network of Partnership Schools

at Johns Hopkins University

Joyce L. Epstein, Director

Educators and families agree that school, family, and community partnerships are essential for children's success in school.

Based on more than three decades of research and the work of many educators, parents, students, and others, we know that it is possible for all elementary, middle, and high schools to develop and sustain strong programs of partnerships that help students succeed.

Districts and states can establish policies and take leadership to help all schools develop excellent programs of partnerships.

As a member of the National Network of Partnership Schools (NNPS), you will be guided, supported, and recognized in your efforts to maintain goal-oriented school, family, and community connections.

What is the National Network of Partnership Schools?

Established at Johns Hopkins University in 1996, the National Network of Partnership Schools (NNPS) assists schools, districts, states, and organizations that are committed to developing strong programs of school, family, and community partnerships. Each Partnership School strengthens its program with an Action Team for Partnerships, a framework of six types of involvement to engage parents in different ways, and a written action plan for goal-oriented family and community involvement linked to the school improvement plan. District, state, and other leaders assist schools to develop, evaluate, and continually improve their partnership programs.

Why Become a Member of the National Network?

- ★ **Comprehensive handbook to guide partnership program development**
- ★ **Certificate of membership**
- ★ **Invitations to attend leadership and development conferences**
- ★ ***Type 2,* NNPS Newsletter**
- ★ **Annual collection, *Promising Partnership Practices***
- ★ **Colorful posters of six "keys" to successful partnerships**
- ★ **Technical assistance by phone, e-mail, and website**
- ★ **Opportunities to participate in research and evaluation projects**
- ★ **Other benefits and experiences**

Members benefit from the experience of the NNPS staff and by sharing ideas with other schools, districts, and states working to increase and improve partnerships. In every issue of the NNPS newsletter, at workshops, and on the NNPS website, members share creative solutions for improving family and community involvement.

Who May Join the National Network of Partnership Schools?

Membership is open to all schools, districts, states, and organizations that agree to the requirements listed on the following page.

Membership Requirements

Developing good connections of home, school, and community is an on-going process that takes time, organization, and effort.

NNPS offers a research-based framework, tools, and strategies that enable all schools, districts, and states to organize school, family, and community partnerships to improve schools, strengthen families, and increase student success.

Organization and university partners are welcome to join NNPS to assist schools and districts in their regions.

To join NNPS, there is a $200 processing fee for schools; $300 for districts, states, and organizations.

Annual renewal fees are waived for all members that return the annual UPDATE survey.

Members work with NNPS to improve connections with students, families, and communities. Schools, districts, and states must meet a few requirements.

At the SCHOOL LEVEL, each Partnership School will:

- ✓ Create an Action Team for Partnerships.
- ✓ Use the framework of six types of involvement to plan and implement a goal-oriented program of partnerships linked to school improvement plans.
- ✓ Allocate an annual budget for the work and activities of the school's Action Team for Partnerships.
- ✓ Allocate time for an initial One-Day Team-Training Workshop and at least one hour per month for the Action Team Partnerships to meet to plan and evaluate activities.

At the DISTRICT LEVEL, each Partnership District will:

- ✓ Assign the equivalent of one full-time facilitator to assist 15 to 30 schools to create their Action Teams for Partnerships. Part-time coordinators may work in districts with fewer than 15 schools.
- ✓ Allocate an annual budget for the district facilitator's salary and activities to develop, strengthen, and maintain partnership programs in all schools.
- ✓ Assist each participating school to fulfill the requirements listed above for the school level.

At the STATE LEVEL, each Partnership State will:

- ✓ Create or identify an Office or Department for School, Family, and Community Partnerships.
- ✓ Assign the equivalent of one full-time coordinator and adequate staff to conduct state-wide leadership activities or school, family, and community partnerships.
- ✓ Allocate an annual budget for the work of this office and for the activities to support districts and schools to develop excellent partnership programs.
- ✓ Assist districts and schools to fulfill the membership requirements listed above.

ALL MEMBERS will:

- ✓ Complete an annual UPDATE survey to report progress and to renew membership in NNPS.

If your school, district, state, or organization is ready to develop strong programs of school, family, and community partnerships for student success, you are invited to join the National Network of Partnership Schools (NNPS).

For more information and membership forms visit www.partnershipschools.org and the section Join NNPS.

Or contact us at NNPS, Johns Hopkins University, 3003 N. Charles Street, Suite 200, Baltimore, MD 21218

E-mail: nnps@csos.jhu.edu Tel: 410-516-2318 Fax: 410-516-8890

Visit us at www.partnershipschools.org

www.partnershipschools.org

No Child Left Behind | **Military Child Initiative** | **Meet the Staff**

NNPS MODEL For Schools, Districts, States, & Organizations

Learn the components of research-based programs of school, family, and community partnerships in schools, districts, states, and organizations. See the School Model for the framework of six types of involvement, Action Team for Partnerships, and other features of school-based successful programs of family and community involvement.

Success Stories

Explore over 600 activities from annual collections of *Promising Partnership Practices* submitted by school, district, state, and organization members of NNPS. Also, meet the winners of NNPS Partnership Awards and read about their excellent programs.

Research & Evaluation

Read summaries of past studies and new research agenda on the nature and effects of family and community involvement. See a list of over 60 publications by Center researchers that provide the research base for NNPS's tools and guidelines for partnership program development.

Professional Development

Plan to attend an NNPS Leadership Development Conference, District Leadership Institute, or schedule other Professional Development Workshops to strengthen leadership and improve the quality of partnership programs and results.

Publications & Products

Order NNPS books, tools, surveys, and other resources to strengthen knowledge, skills, and programs of family and community involvement. Read archived editions of *Type 2*, review the PowerPoint CDs to conduct workshops, and shop for NNPS incentives (posters, mugs, T-shirts, pens) to motivate teams and colleagues.

TIPS Teachers Involve Parents in Schoolwork

Learn how TIPS Interactive Homework in math, science, and language arts promotes connections of school and home for student success. Download examples of TIPS activities and see resources available. Also, learn how to organize volunteers in the middle grades with TIPS Social Studies and Art Volunteers.

JOIN NNPS

Download a membership form for your school, district, state or organization or request an invitation-packet. Join others across the country who are using the NNPS framework and research-based approaches to improve policies and practices of partnerships.

Center on School, Family, and Community Partnerships | **CSOS** | **Johns Hopkins University**

Index

The Corwin Press logo—a raven striding across an open book—represents the union of courage and learning. Corwin Press is committed to improving education for all learners by publishing books and other professional development resources for those serving the field of PreK–12 education. By providing practical, hands-on materials, Corwin Press continues to carry out the promise of its motto: **"Helping Educators Do Their Work Better."**